One should see the world, and see himself as a scale with an equal balance of good and evil. When he does one good deed, the scale is tipped to the good — he and the world are saved. When he does one evil deed, the scale is tipped to the bad — he and the world are destroyed.

— Maimonides

ميزان

balance

bob freeland

Pp

Prose Press

www.prosepress.biz

Published by Prose Press
75 Red Maple Drive,
Pawleys Island, South Carolina 29585

proseNcons@live.com
www.Prosepress.biz

ISBN: 978-0-9851889-3-1

Comments: Contact Bob Freeland
balancethebook@yahoo.com

Cover Design : Bob Freeland

ACKNOWLEDGMENTS

My deepest gratitude and respect are offered to the men and women who answered the call to duty and wore the uniform. I am humbled by your service.

America thanks you.

Foreword

This is a work of fiction. The events described are imaginary, and the characters are fictitious and not intended to represent specific living persons. Characterizations of public figures are meant as parody. Even when settings are referred to by their true names, the incidents portrayed as taking place are entirely fictitious — the reader should not infer that the events ever happened. Many of the organizations and some of the programs are of course real. For example, CEXC exists; the 5th Brigade Combat Team, REDDI and the Judas program do not. While based on actual organizations affiliated with the Department of Defense, all of the people associated with them in this book are fictional.

My extensive use of acronyms will likely give some readers heartburn. Nevertheless, I chose to leave them in to keep the action real. Acronyms are not exclusive to the military. Many civilian bureaucracies create smart sounding ones meant to instill fear in their competition and adoration from the consuming public. Conversely, the military uses acronyms for quick, unambiguous communication critical to a soldier's survival during combat when stress levels are amped up. I believe their omission would be more disturbing to those who were in Iraq than their inclusion. To aid the non-veteran, I decided the least cumbersome way to decode the alphabet soup, was to include a glossary and parenthetical references.

Allow me to get one obvious caveat out of the way — I ain't no grammarian. I apologize to the authentic writers out there in the literary circles and to the reader, but I was a marginal student in high school and even more pathetic in college. I hope the speed bumps do not detract too much from the story and you are able to negotiate the many mistakes along the way. Please contact me at **balancethebook@yahoo.com**, to let me know about errors you find. In addition, I welcome your comments, be they positive or negative. If the book survives long enough for a reprint, I will incorporate your suggestions.

I joined a writer's group to help me overcome my substandard education and to learn some of the 'dos' and 'don'ts' about telling a story. It is a good crowd and includes some of the genuine writers I mentioned earlier. Unfortunately, their vast experience did not rub off too well on me so I voted myself off the island. Before I dropped out, I discovered you first must know the rules of sentence structure and grammar before you can violate them. That's a tough one. I did not learn enough to know if I violated the rules. In fact, if I happened to get some of the rules right it was by accident, and I apologize for the inconsistency. I hope that they helped me rise from absurdly sophomoric writing to several notches below ho-hum mediocre.

One person in particular challenged me — not about grammar but the story's theme. Following my first submission to the group, the person approached with a stern expression and asked me this question: "What makes your book about the *Afghanistan War* any different from the others that line the shelves at the book store?" I looked down at the prototype for the book cover I had in my hand and the copy this person also held — the one that reads 'a novel about the *Iraq War*.' Well, um, actually the book is about the — I stopped. Ignoring the fact the wrong war had been pegged, the question still caused me some anxiety. The more I thought about the nub of the query the less anxious I was because it was inherently flawed. More than one million U.S. military and civilians deployed to Iraq, consequently there are more than a million unique stories from the war. The question should have been *is your story worth telling*. Now that is one I cannot answer. You must decide.

In addition to the caveat mentioned earlier, please heed the warning on the back cover. This book contains raw, graphic violence and possibly disturbing concepts; however, in my mind, none of it is gratuitous. If my use of gutter language bothers you or the brutality seems too real, do not read the book. I relate the violence and use expletives not to poke the reader in the eye, but because that is the way it was. I have many shortcomings. At the top of the list is crudeness, followed closely by political incorrectness. On the other side of the list, I rank honesty uppermost — hence, the warning.

Now for a pet peeve of mine — writers who champion some agenda with slyly worded messages buried within the text. There are no obscure or subliminal messages in this book. There is a point, but not hidden, as I am soon going to tell you what it is. Before I reveal the book's objective, a little background is in order.

In March 2003, my son boarded a plane in Georgia for the invasion of Iraq. It is one of the few occasions in my adult life I can remember getting misty eyed. The first was when I received my draft notice and the last on some bleak road in Afghanistan. The day my son marched off to war, I was pissed — at myself for not taking his place, at the President for sending him, at the Muslim jihadists for causing the need. I am sure I am not alone in those thoughts. Every parent who sent a son or daughter off to any war must have gone through the same gamut of emotions. I know my father did when my brother headed off to Vietnam and again as my other brother sailed into an uncertain future for the first Gulf War. My grandfather did when my dad went off to help defeat Hitler, as I am sure my great grandfather did when my granddad boarded a troop ship bound for Europe in 1917.

If one only considers casualty numbers, the Iraq War is a blip in our history, ranking just above the Philippine-American War (1899-1902) and below the Mexican-American war (1846-1848). By the numbers, the Iraq War pales in comparison to the Civil War, World War I, World War II, Korea and Vietnam. Between the first American deaths, two days after the invasion began, and the last to die by a roadside bomb on November 14, 2011, about 4,500 U.S. service members died in Iraq and 32,000 were wounded.

I see beyond the statistics. To me they translate into agonizing heartbreak a thousand times over. Too many fathers, mothers, wives, children, brothers, sisters and grandparents received the dreaded visit from a person dressed in a uniform — we regret to inform you that your son-daughter-husband-wife-father-mother died, or was wounded, in Iraq. Numbers do not console the grief stricken. I was one of the lucky fathers. My son returned a little older, somewhat wiser, but most important intact. To those other parents and spouses whom luck failed, I offer my heartfelt condolences.

Did we win or lose? Does it matter? I am not a big picture type so I will leave those questions for the learned ones. I do know that many in the media, political pundits, both right and left, and particularly Hollywood, have, and will continue to focus on the atrocities. War by its very nature invites atrocities. The media, however, need balance in their treatment of perceived misdeeds.

I am getting closer to the message.

In late November 2004, I landed in Iraq. I took several breaks after first stepping onto the desert but remained in country pretty much through July 2008. I served in various positions in Baghdad and Mosul. However, this book is set in southern Iraq and exploits two of the eighteen months I spent with the 82nd Airborne Division. Remarkable young men and women, those devils in baggy pants — I will always have a soft spot in my heart for the heroes who served with the 82nd, as well as their predecessors from the Virginia Army National Guard. I thank them for putting up with a clueless old man and keeping me from hurting myself and becoming a statistic.

In theater, I fell under the broad umbrella of the Joint IED Defeat Organization and worked in the counter IED program as a fifth wheel on a special weapons exploitation team. During many discussions I had with the soldiers while cramped inside a Humvee, sitting around a mess table or straddling MRE boxes at some lonely outpost, we talked about only three or four topics. Upcoming R&Rs — do you remember that guy who got blown up — you won't believe my next tattoo — Dude, I'm buying a kick-ass Harley when I get back to the world, etc. I am sure we also discussed women but I sometimes experience memory lapses. Many of these chats evolved into spirited exchanges about war crimes allegedly committed by some in the military.

Those talks were the genesis for this book. When I returned home from Iraq in 2008, I started writing. As it were, a short time later an opportunity arose for me to go to Afghanistan; this time embedded with an assortment of units, and as luck would have it one from the 82nd Airborne. I put my writing away and forgot about it until I returned stateside in 2010. Afghanistan was an eye-opener. I was motivated to write again.

Our military fought a ruthless enemy in Iraq and continues to fight another enemy in Afghanistan, cut from the same cloth. Perhaps ruthless is too mild. America's enemies are savages. They give no quarter. Yet we, as a nation, berate our young warriors when in the fog of war a 'civilian' dies in the crossfire, or a prisoner's Qur'an is confiscated, or another is subjected to having a photo taken of him in the nude surrounded by security dogs.

After the fall of Saddam Hussein's regular military not one American service member survived captivity in Iraq — none. All executed, many tortured horrendously before they died. The enemy beheads an American — that's war. An American snaps a photo — that's a war crime.

The objectives of this book are simple — show what the war was like, how it felt, the fear, and the pain — give the reader a peek behind the curtain. Meeting that goal is the difficult part. Words cannot do the subject justice, or at least not the way I string them together. That said, as you read the story keep an open mind and park any preconceived notions concerning the atrocities you heard about. Let the facts percolate up from the efforts of those charged with that awesome responsibility, not forced down your throats by those only charged with increasing their network's market share, or the politician playing to his base for re-election.

"Military justice is to justice what military music is to music." Some attribute this quote to Groucho Marx, others to George Clemenceau. Whether the comic said it, or *le Tigre* of Versailles, I do not adhere to the specious analogy. The military has the expertise to flesh out the facts. Furthermore, the officers and enlisted personnel selected for an inquiry had a front seat to the war, if not in body then in spirit. They have skin in the game. The military is the arbiter of the facts, not Chris Matthews, Brian Williams, Katie Couric, Bill Maher, Michael Moore, or the nice young/old, Republican/Democrat who has promised swift justice. They have skin in a different game.

You must appreciate whom our warriors fight. If you do, my hope is that when the media pounces on the next young soldier or Marine who made a mistake, you will empathize with that nineteen-year old, thousands of miles away from family and scared beyond stupid. Feel something for the kid who squeezed the trigger at the wrong moment, threw a grenade at what to him looked like a threat, or lobbed a mortar round into the wrong house. Do not sympathize with an enemy who would slit your throat just because you follow a different religion, or enjoy the freedom to vote, women's rights, pulled pork barbeque, or an occasional stiff drink — an enemy who will kill you because you were born in the United States of America, the great Satan. Believe it, folks. It is our reality. Let me put it another way by hijacking Pogo's environmental message and relate it to America's penchant for self-flagellation and its refusal to face the collision of religions, cultures and ideologies set before it. "We have met the enemy...and he is us."

Whew, sorry about that but without an editor to rein me in, I write weird stuff. Lacking an editor caused another problem — lack of editing. I set out to spin a yarn in a single book, but alas, it was not to be. Consider this volume as the beginning and early middle of the story. The end will come in the sequel. Judas Rising will be in print by the end of 2013.

Finally, the price of the book, like the acronyms, may also cause some heartburn. This novel is self-published and carries certain inescapable expenses. All profits will be donated to a Veterans organization and the children of three service members who were killed in action on a bleak road in Afghanistan. I know that does not put money back in your pocket, but I hope it eases some of your pain.

Setting for the story

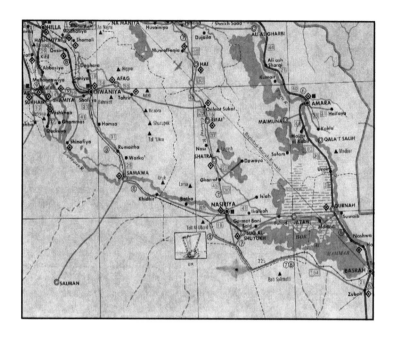

The fictional combat outpost 6 is located 16 km south of Diwaniyah and 28 km southwest of Afak (also known as Afag).

Forward Operating Base Adder/Talil airfield is located 18 km west of Nasiriya (also known as Nasariyah), and 30 km northwest of Suq ash Shuyukh.

ن‌ازیم

Balance

Part One

"It is not the critic who counts; not the man who points out how the strong man stumbles, or where the doer of deeds could have done them better. The credit belongs to the man who is actually in the arena, whose face is marred by dust and sweat and blood; who strives valiantly; who errs, who comes short again and again, because there is no effort without error and shortcoming; but who does actually strive to do the deeds; who knows great enthusiasms, the great devotions; who spends himself in a worthy cause; who at the best knows in the end the triumph of high achievement, and who at the worst, if he fails, at least fails while daring greatly, so that his place shall never be with those cold and timid souls who neither know victory nor defeat."

— *Theodore Roosevelt, April 23, 1910*

Chapter 1
Birds, bugs, bullets and bombs

Suq ash Shuyukh, a Shi'ite village 400 km southeast of Baghdad, Iraq, March 3, 2008

There are crimes and there are sins. One can be punished by man — the other can only be forgiven by God. Two combatants had entered the walled arena. Both were slaves. One to his God — the other only to a cause. There was no crowd to judge them. God was absent.

"No, no…can't be." The untested soldier stumbled away from the open door, his mouth frozen in a silent scream. Legs buckled — he fell. His rifle broke free from its sling and careened forward. Racked with spasms, dry heaves worked their way through the bowels and stomach into his throat. The retches came fast, he was about to black out. He gulped air between gags. An irrepressible explosion emptied all he had ever consumed in his life.

Minutes passed, more gasps. Oxygen slowly nurtured his blood cells — some rule restored. He forced his eyes open and wiped vomit from his chin. He picked up the rifle and stood, bracing his back against the doorway.

Had he actually seen it, or were his senses playing a cruel trick on him?

He did not want to do what he did next, but he was a duty-bound American, a volunteer, a soldier and eighteen years old — a man. This was war, a dirty war. Deal with the horror. It was expected — choice was never an option. Safety off, he moved the rifle's selector to the three-round burst mode. He looked again into the dim room.

Before his eyes could adjust to the darkness, he glanced over his shoulder to his brothers in arms. "Here, over here," he whispered.

They did not hear.

He again whispered, "Here."

Still they did not hear.

1

He waved at the squad.

They did not see.

His voice grew bolder, "Sarge."

The platoon sergeant raised a fist and halted the patrol. Squinting in the failing light, he turned toward the voice. When he saw the young paratrooper across the alley he smiled.

The private was not alone. Self-confidence returned. He turned from the sergeant and faced the darkening shadows inside the room. What he thought he had seen could not have been real. Pupils swelled; the terror swept back in. He lost it….It was not an illusion. It was…

"Sarge!" he screamed. "Oh, sweet Jesus! Sarge! God, oh God — I found him!"

*****

The late evening sun bled red through the bullet riddled ancient door and walls. Inside the arena, fading spindly rays slow danced across the dirt floor revealing the dead. Two dead — yet one still breathed. The breather sat cross-legged in a black-crimson puddle. Soaked in the ooze and his own sweat and piss, he rocked back and forth. Held tight against his chest — the prize.

He laid the proof of his own survival on his crotch and stopped rocking. Then he looked up at the shape framed in the doorway.

Backlit by the western sun, the soldier yelled at him.

He did not understand the shouts. He did not understand the living anymore. That world was gone.

He turned from the screaming poser to the other puzzle, the trophy moistening his lap. He lifted the severed head close to his face and scoured it for remnants of the core. Dead eyes spoke to him through a milky film. *You are a sinner.*

He dropped the head to the dirt, where for a moment it wobbled before coming to rest facing hell.

He picked up the rifle.

He knew it was empty.

He pointed it at the screamer standing in the sun.

Nine months earlier

The Plantation, a gated community, Pawleys Island, South Carolina, June 3, 2007

Begin.

Gabe was here, or a part of him. Distracted for the fortieth time in as many minutes, he forced himself to look down again. Pointless. His concentration was lost for the forty-first time. He looked up and scanned his world. Phil's house across the street caught his eye. He gave into this newest distraction and tried to focus on the suburban prison he hated, but a four-day binge bested him. Slouched in the porch chair, he rubbed the growth on his chin. Soon bored with that, he ran fingers through his hair — hair tossed and turned from an edgy half sleep snuck in sometime during the past ninety-six hours. Days lived in the same clothes gave him an odor that reeked of sweat — sweat that reeked of despair.

Sleep was his enemy now, or so he thought. He battled it by drinking his fourth cup of coffee and lighting his twelfth cigarette from a fresh pack, his seventeenth smoke since the sun rose less than an hour before. Three empty packs lay crushed on the brick floor, nicotine caked so thick on his fingers they smelled yellow. Eighty-two degrees and humid, yet he shivered like a wet puppy taking its first bath.

Again, he looked at the blank piece of paper on his lap. *Make the damn list.* Minutes ticked away — tens of minutes.

Overwhelmed by the white space between the blue lines, he dropped the sheet and escaped into the suburban backdrop — a mosaic of grass, azaleas, trees, bricks, shingles, siding, asphalt. A neighbor he did not know, being dragged by a tethered dog. A sprinkler slinging water on the lawn and the road — but mostly on the road. A passing car splashing water on the drooling dog and its master — the frothing pet owner cursing the driver and flipping the bird — Fido breaking the leash, running wild like a canine banshee snapping at the manmade rain.

More minutes ticked away — tens of minutes.

An intense pain drilled into his frontal lobe and everything behind

3

it. "Damn!"

He dug deep into his temples with clawed hands fighting against the migraine. Before he was able to vanquish the enemy, another attacked. *Never quit, never surrender, adapt, overcome, defeat — you've been in worse places.*

He covered his mouth to block the fresh onslaught. Gurgling noises snaked their way through the intestines into his belly. Frantic, he manufactured caffeine-laced saliva until he could brew no more, regurgitated other mysterious substances from the depths and then swallowed repeatedly. The sputum blended well with his stomach enzymes. The newest attack was blunted.

His former foe reemerged — a demolition derby run amuck. He beat his fists against his head until the internal pounding gave way. A veneer of calm surfaced.

He finished the tepid coffee. Then he looked at the garage. *Looks bad — worse than bad.*

He clutched the pen in one trembling hand, the blank challenge in the other. *Be decisive — no action is worse than a failed one. Begin. Do it.* He did.

1.- *Paint the dormers.*

2.-*Clean the gutters.*

3-*Wash the….*

A Carolina wren came into view as it made a beeline for the porch. Throughout the dips and rises of her glide slope, she let loose a litany of low, scratchy chirps. Once she landed on a porch fan, her frenzied, hoarse song grew louder. A male wren joined her, and together they performed a bizarre dance, hopping from one fan blade to the next. They tried each of the five blades before moving to the second fan above him. Frozen in the chair, he watched. After several minutes of voyeuristic invasion of the birds' mating ritual, he lit another cigarette.

Alerted to the interloper's presence by the rising smoke, the male cocked his head down toward him. Pupils alternately dilating and then constricting, it checked him out from his bare feet to his shaggy hair. A quick chirp, then it looked back toward its intended mate, then Gabe, back to the female, four, five, six, seven, eight times, before it returned to the other fan. Almost immediately, the female followed. She swooped in next to him, ruffled her feathers and then ruffled his, relentlessly pecking at his tail. The male fled to the rocking chair, followed by the porch rail, finally settling on top of the far column.

Gabe put down the pen. He believed he understood the male's

dilemma. He also thought he recognized these particular wrens. Years before, when he was building the house, a mating pair had nested in the unfinished master bedroom. The framing crew laughed when he told them to stop construction until the hatchlings had fledged. Dan, the carpenters' boss, offered to dispose of the birds so the construction could continue. None of that for Gabe. He was firm. More than money was at stake. For three weeks, he endured the carpenters' snickers and jeers as they sat idle on their butts drawing full pay. The decision cost him big, thousands. In his mind, however, the result was worth the price. He told the crew, "I don't want my grandkids to remember me as the baby bird killer of Pawleys Island."

Gabe's reward — five, chirping, baby wrens. He drank from his other reward, a K-Mart 'blue light special' coffee mug complete with hearts, Xs and Os, and the hand painted inscription, 'bestest grandpa in the whole wide world.' The children had pooled their allowances to pay tribute to their hero. It was a big deal to them. Judging from their excitement, one would have thought it was an Olympian gold medal instead of a five-dollar piece of ceramic. He thought it was better than gold, greater than any award or trophy he had received in his adult life.

That was when the grandchildren were at the neat age when 'Pops' was their champion, their buddy. The day was more than a thousand yesterdays ago — a different lifetime, a different reality. Time moves in only one direction. Actions are also linear. Neither can be reversed. Both axioms change a man. Gabe, although not a deep-thinker, realized that both truisms combined forces and changed him. He fired up post-sunrise-cigarette nineteen and thought of the nineteen jihadists who had set in motion a string of events that rocked his world.

He studied the burning cigarette, then the birds. Speaking aloud to his winged audience, he said, "Back to the list."

3. ....siding

4.- Clean the ....

Gabe heard the echoes of shoe heels move from the bedroom, a stop at the hallway powder room, soon followed by a flush and the sound of running water. The steps moved across the foyer, down another hall, past the butler pantry, into the kitchen, and after a brief stop, more steps toward the breakfast room. *Morning coffee*, he thought.

Then he heard the coldness of hard plastic against harder stone chased by softer sounds reverberating off the wood floors. The pace quickened on the return trip — breakfast room, kitchen, hall, butler pantry, u-turn to the dining room, through the pocket door, back to the hallway, foyer, stop at the entry table, jangling sound of keys, and then....

Gabe straightened his posture, flicked the cigarette over the porch to the azalea bushes, flattened and slicked his hair down with a fair measure of spit and managed a weak smile just as the front door opened.

Nicole stepped down onto the porch. Before she made it to the edge, she smelled him. She stopped, took off her sunglasses and stared at him. "I don't remember you coming to bed last night. In fact, I don't recall you getting out of bed either. Rough night?"

Gabe cleared his throat ready to answer.

She held up her hand. "Don't! Are you going to accomplish anything today?"

I'm screwed. He readied for a tongue-lashing over something important in her world that he must have bungled. "Nicole, you look great in that outfit. New?"

How did I ever get so lucky to meet her and then win her heart and womanhood? More than three decades of marriage and she still resembled the striking young girl he had pursued all over the college campus. A flood of blonde hair, a complexion that never needed make-up, and an athlete's body with perfectly sculpted muscles that clung to her runway model-like frame. Clear mind, motivated, purpose driven — she took life by the balls and squeezed hard.

On the other hand, there was Gabe — a disaster trapped in a rollicking, misguided downhill slide, on the wrong side of middle age, rolls of flesh that no longer qualified as baby fat, blood pressure through the ceiling, cholesterol even higher, borderline diabetic — borderline insane.

"You bought this for me over two years ago during one of your *visits*. Nice try. Now back to my original question. Gabriel Montgomery Quinn, are you going to finish anything, or just let another day be sucked into that black hole you call your 'tomorrow's a better day' philosophy. Is that your genius plan?"

She's pissed — used my full name. Gotta get past it and deal with the reality standing in front of me in a dress. Don't bring the dress up again. I must've done something dumb last night. I can't remember anything after 'how was your day at work, Nicole?' Say something, but what? Choose your words wisely — she's cunning — could be a post-menopausal trap.

6

Unfortunately, the words dribbled out.

"Ah, let's see… I've started a list of projects to do around the house— "

Nicole grabbed the paper from him and glanced over it. She lobbed a preparatory laugh before unleashing the main barrage. "You're kidding. This is the list. You started that list two weeks ago, or so you told me. Not a damn thing has happened yet. Home for six weeks and this is what you have to show for it — almost four complete sentences. I'm impressed, Gabriel. Really, I am. You know how many days you've been sober in those six weeks? Don't answer — I can count them with two fingers, Bucko!"

She stuck a hand in his face, and with her fingers, formed a zero. "Damn you! Do you even remember last night, Gabriel? Do you?"

She balled up the paper and threw it at him. He ducked.

"Of course I do." He looked down at the bricks, and then returned his hangdog stare to Phil's house. "Um, did I, did I…do something last night?"

It was not the brightest response he could have made. *Can't retract that one. Roll with it.* He broke away from the serenity of Phil's yard to face marital justice — his second mistake in as many seconds.

"You don't remember, do you?"

He stared at the judge.

"That's what I thought," she said. "I'm late for work and I have a lot on my plate. I don't have time to bring you up to speed on your life last night or your life for the last six weeks."

She shot him a look that was devoid of everything except contempt. "Get over whatever it is you need to get over, put it behind you and move on."

Gabe swallowed hard. Then, almost in a whisper, said, "I love you, babe."

Nicole recoiled. She turned away from him and bounded down the steps to the driveway.

Before she reached the car, Gabe resurrected the smile that had worked so well earlier and called out to her, "Nicole, what do you want tonight? Steak, shrimp, or both?"

She stopped midstride, wheeled around on her four-inch heels, jaw in her chin, mouth wide, and eyes aflame. Her voice, just low enough for the neighbors not to hear, nevertheless hit him like a tidal wave. "I told you days ago we are going to the Petersons' for an 'Island' party tonight. I guess that one didn't register either.

7

Maybe you should include that on your 'to do' list, along with stay sober, and don't make an ass of yourself tonight. I actually live in this neighborhood and would like to continue some sort of a cordial relationship with *my* neighbors. Understood?"

Gabe managed a weak "fine." *Who are the Petersons, have I met them, where do they live, should I give a damn.* He kept those questions to himself, deciding that sometime before the party she would lead him to the answers.

Nicole swapped the question mark with an exclamation point to her final 'understood' by squealing the tires as she raced down the driveway onto the street. The effect was not lost on him. In the present, he was relieved the morning combat was behind him. In the context of his relationship with Nicole, he chalked the disaster up as inevitable marital bullshit served in bite-size portions, common, he was sure, with every couple. He returned to a slouched posture and lit the twentieth cigarette of the morning.

"Well birds, I don't think I'll be getting the blue light special 'bestest husband in the whole wide world' coffee mug anytime soon."

He flattened the balled paper on the settee's glass top and picked up the pen.

4. ... *garage* —

He saw a palmetto bug leave the darkness and safety of the garage for the Mecca of the sun-warmed concrete driveway. Bad timing for the hapless bug, because not only had he seen it, the quarry had caught the alert eyes of the wrens. They swooped in from the high ground and ambushed the clueless insect.

Trapped, no possibility for escape, it froze and awaited the inevitable...*three clicks out from Camp Shield* — we're gonna make it. Damn it's hot, so damn hot. Must be a hundred-thirty degrees outside, one-forty in here. Crotch soaked, armpits can't put out anymore sweat, all caked up, shirt turned chalky white...need to piss — nothin' to give. It doesn't help wearin' all this armor. Will it stop anything? Too tight, way too tight in the death seat. Can't move, can't breathe, no place to go. Can't get over the bench seat, too much gear — never make it. At least I'm not the trunk monkey on this run.

Can't use my rifle, no shooting ports. I'm suffocating inside this tomb. Good, we're moving faster now...two clicks out. We'll make it. No sweat — no more to give.

Mad Dog 4 — Mad Dog 1, there's an accident on the other side of the bridge. Too late to divert — traffic blocked our side — two lanes now four — can't go around...keep our six clear. Spacing brothers.

Don't let any hajjis get in between our vehicles. Smells like ambush. Everyone stays put, make like porcupines — guns out — watch the rooftops —

Tooomff, tooomff…thud, thud.

Hail in June? No way, that ain't hail. Ah shit, we're taking fire, taking fire. *Kick it man, fucking kick it. Get us the hell out of here!* Can't move, stuck in traffic. Guns up, find the source, suppressing fire. Shoot something, anything. No targets.

Thud, thud, pop, pop.

Why is that hajji shouting at me?

Pop, pop, pop, thud, thud, craaack.

Damn, the armor's compromised. *Let's go man, get us moving!* Move your head, keep moving your head. Don't give 'em a target. Side to side, duck, raise, twist turn, twist some more. I'm turning flips here. I really need to piss. I gotta shit….

Mad Dog 1, make a damn hole! Let's go!

Who's shouting, damnit?

Stay tight people, keep your positions…they're shooting from the rooftops at our four and eight — it's AK fire.

Don't tell me they're at my four or eight. Tell me left or right, damnit.

Return fire — keep their heads down.

Get their heads down. Their heads, what about my head? They want to kill me! They don't know me —

Our armor will hold —

Who's talking now?

Armor ain't holding, dude.

Who said that?

Lay suppressing fire on the rooftops.

Rooftops? I can't see my damn pecker, and you're talking rooftops! Wait, there's a hajji family right next to me. Maybe they can see your fucking rooftops. Why are they crawling to the other side of their car? Okay, okay, I get it. Put some real estate between a bunch of Yankee mercenaries and your precious Muslim asses. Smart little brown people, real smart. Guess what hajji, your shit stinks, too.

Those faces, their faces — scared. Damn, they're scared. Who cares, *I'm shittin' my pants here.* Who's shouting? It's me. Quit shouting hero, get control. I can't see. I'm in a tunnel — fog in the tunnel. There ain't any damn tunnels in Baghdad. Not today, not today, it can't be my time. *Kid, stay in the car. Don't get out of the car. Stay where you are, kid. Don't do it. You'll never make it. Don't do —*

9

Didn't you hear me, boy? I knew you'd be hit. Two, maybe three steps — what a waste. Rounds blew your spine out. You really didn't need a back did you, kid. Must've hurt. Better you than me, loser.

A red Toyota has broken through our six coming on your three.

Who said that? Who's talking now? Will somebody take control of this goat fuck?

We can't get our guns on it. It's yours, brother.

Whose is it? Mine? Where, where, damnit? All right, tell me it's at my four, my eight, left, right, I don't care. Just tell me where — and who the hell is talking? Why has the shooting stopped? Did he say a Toyota? That's a Toyota. Red? It's red. Did he say a red Toyota? Someone said a red Toyota. It is! It is! It's a red — what's he shouting? *Allahu Akhbar?* What in hell does that mean? I don't speak hajji. Speak English, asshole. You hate me! Well what'd I ever do to you? *Fuck you too, hajji! Fuck you! Fuck you!*

What's in his back seat? Oh, shit! Artillery rounds and plastic jugs filled with…with…what? What's he holding? That's a, that's a, oh Jesus, that's a detonator in his hand. Think. It's comin' fast, real fast. Can't shoot him, no time to get out. Where do I want it to hit me? Front, back, where? Protect the spine, head, vitals. Fetal position. Yeah, that's it. Tuck in the legs, arms, lower the head…back to the blast. More armor there. Love you, Nicole. Here goes.

No blast. Why didn't it blow? Maybe it did and I'm — you gotta look, dumbass. He's fumbling around on the floorboard. Thank you Jesus, he dropped the detonator. He found it. It's over. Now we blow. Nicole I'm…

Tat-tat-tat-tat-tat…tat-tat-tat-tat…thump…thump…thump….

Bullets, bullets, more bullets. They're blowin' out his window. Good, good, good. Rain steel on his head. What head? Where's his — there it is…it's all over the car. Red, grey, white, yellow, bone, tendon, meat, skin — I love this shit — exploding — he's explodin', not me! I'm gonna live, I'M GOING TO LIVE! I'm gonna make it, Nicole. I'm gonna live to make love to you again, babe.

He's twitching. Left, right, forward, backwards, more rounds ripping him. *More, more, hit him more, hit him again, you SON OF A BITCH! Hit him. Hit him hard!* Windshield's blown out. *Side windows, hit the side windows.* More rounds, yeah baby, more, tear his ass up. Move like a marionette you damn hajji. Do that palsied death dance. Love it. He's going down. Heads mush. Blood spraying. More. Make sure. Now he's gone. Yeah, he's tits up. All right, he's doing the death rattle.

Phew, that was close. Thank you, God, I owe you one.

Monty, you all right?

Don't call me Monty, Dog Shit I'm fine. I'm checking... checking, checking...check...oh shit, check me! Check me! Check me! Dog Shit, is that my blood... yours? I can't....

Pop...pop...pop...pop...crack...thud...thud.

Taking fire again. *It ain't over brother...Mad Dog 1, Mad Dog 1, make a fucking hole. Blow through it. Let's go...we're taking more hits. Go over them fucking hajjis, go through 'em, I don't give a shit, just get us out of here!*

Dog Shit, I think I'm hit...I'm spittin' — I'm spittin' blood.... Saliva streamed from his mouth. Gabe cleared his throat and spat a glob of phlegm over the porch rail. Then he wiped sweat beads from his throbbing forehead, and with a shaking hand, raised the empty mug to sip imaginary coffee. As he did, he noticed that some of the stringy mucous had not cleared the porch. At least three inches of the goo defiantly hung from the rail — flapping in the breeze, taunting him and his inept aim. *Never was a sharpshooter.*

Like a robot, he stood and walked mechanically forward. He grasped the rail for balance, then leaned closer until he was at eye level with his brackish green creation. Furrowed wrinkles scored his brow, mouth locked in a frown, as if he did not believe the mess came from him, he studied it from several angles. Ready to swipe the cocktail and rub it on his shirt, he stopped. Out of the corner of his eye, he glimpsed a sacrilege in progress — the wrens ripping apart the bug's carcass.

"Fucking hajjis!"

Without thinking, he flung the Xs and Os coffee mug at the birds. He threw like a girl. The mug missed the wrens by yards, but not the pickup's windshield. The initial sound of impact was followed by 'craaaack,' a second 'craaaack,' then tinkling sounds as hundreds of porcelain pieces showered the driveway. *Never was a sharpshooter.*

Disgusted with his miss, he shuffled back until he was blocked by the chair. He fell into it.

The wrens, seemingly unfazed by his outburst, gave credence to the expression birdbrain, by perching on the column nearest him. Then it began — non-stop, shrill screeching.

Ignoring their boos, he steadied his hands enough to light the twenty-first cigarette, inhaled deeply several times, then laid it on the ashtray.

The birds, already forgiven and almost forgotten by him, cocked their heads toward Gabe and shut-up, ready for another show.

"Get estimate for a new windshield, cook steak and shrimp. Scratch that. Petersons' house. Island party. Find a ridiculous Hawaiian shirt for the evening *fete*. Damn, which island did she mean? Hawaii, Caribbean or Pawleys?"

He lit cigarette number twenty-two, oblivious to the one burning in the ashtray. He looked at his watch and decided that 9:00 a.m. in South Carolina was 5:00 p.m. in Baghdad. Remembering better times with brother cops, he spoke aloud, "choir practice," a slang expression popularized by Joseph Wambaugh.

He placed number twenty-two beside its twin, pushed up from the chair and went inside — straight to the library liquor cabinet, one of six strategically positioned around the house, but the closest one this morning. He poured rum to within a quarter inch of the highball's rim, added a dash of Coke for color, drank some, then replenished it with more rum. Calmed, he cruised back to the porch and sat in the Kennedy rocker. Drink held high toward the birds, he winked and then downed half of the drink. "Sorry, brothers."

"Chirp…chirp," the wrens replied. No second act this morning.

He fired up number twenty-three.

Chapter 2
Redemption or disgrace is but a fork in the road

Pawleys Island, SC, June 3, 0930 hours

It took Gabe a few seconds to realize the ringing was not inside his head. He stubbed out the cigarette, downed his drink and stepped inside in time to intercept the call before it rolled over to the answering machine. "Hello?"

"Monty!" the caller shouted, "how is my white brother?"

The voice on the other end of the line sounded familiar. Unsure, but knowing that not too many people were aware of his rarely used middle name, and fewer still, dumb enough to use it, Gabe said, "Dog Shit?"

"Of course, man."

Unique and bold in his own right, his quirky name was enough to suck the air out of a room full of Puritans and enlightened alike. According to Dog Shit, his father had a drunk's warped sense of humor. Jacoby Kieyoomia had survived the horrors of Guadalcanal and Tarawa as a wind talker only to become a cliché on the Navajo Indian Reservation near Kayenta, Arizona. His second child was ominously born just before the witching hour on October 31, 1948. Jacoby learned of his son's birth when he was piss-ass wasted at a nearby bar. Upon hearing the news that he had another boy, he bought a round for every white and red man in the lounge. Then he stumbled outside, tripped over his battered cowboy boots and fell headlong into a pile of poop. Smeared in crap, reeking with the smell of firewater, he stood and wiped the excrement off his face onto his trousers. Surrounded by his equally inebriated and amused barroom friends, he joined in their laughter. At first, they cheered the brave warrior of the Pacific. Then it turned — the celebration went from laughs and handshakes to a demand that he give his son an appropriate name. Jacoby played along. In jest, he said, "I name boy, Łééchąą'í chaunt, a name to be feared and respected by all that walk under sun and moon."

Bad is remembered more often than the good, so what began as a proud father's intoxicated joke, stuck. Word spread quickly throughout the reservation — fear the newest Kieyoomia boy, Dog Shit. Jacoby was prescient. His son hardened as a child dealing with endless jibes about his name; taunts that always led to fisticuffs. As a teen, the 173rd Airborne 'Thundering Herd' forged him into a man, cured him of meaningless pugilistic encounters, and trained him to kill with extreme efficiency. During the battles of Katum, Hill 875 near Dak To, the central highlands of Pleiku, and later, Tuy Hoa during Tet '68, 'Charlie Cong' learned to fear and respect the scary young paratrooper.

Gabe's father, also a veteran of the same global contest, but of the European theater and later the Korean War, was a teetotaler and slightly more introspective than Jacoby. Though not a particularly religious man, his father paid homage to his Judeo-Christian roots by giving his third born the name, Gabriel — acceptable and easily truncated to 'Gabe' — most religious undertones obscured. Maybe it was because his dad was cold, hungry, homesick, scared or pissed while fighting in the 'forgotten' war when Gabe entered the world, but for whatever the reason, in a mordant twist, he wrote his wife and told her to add Montgomery to the newborn's moniker. Monty — the WW II British general despised by his father and most GIs of the era. His mother, always the peacekeeper, assured Gabe his middle name was actually a tribute to her matinee heartthrob, Montgomery Clift. He did not know whom to believe or which was worse — Dad and his hated Brit, or Mom and her closet homosexual. He wished his dad could have hated someone with a normal name, or his mom had idolized anyone outside of Tinsel Town.

"When'd you get back, Monty?"

Gabe squelched his 'what's in a name' thoughts and smiled at the phone as if it were the actual person thousands of miles away. "Someone reminded me this morning that it has been about six weeks. It must be kismet, Dog Shit. I was just thinking about that day on the bridge and the 'Order of the Crappy Pants' award you presented me afterwards. I framed it and hung it with reverence above my toilet after a brief ceremony — poignant reminder of shitty times. How long have you been home?"

14

"I've been stateside just shy of two years. I left Baghdad in June '05 — had to get back to my honey and my money. Hell man, you should remember, you scrounged the booze for my send off."

"I remember the booze, but not much else." Gabe chuckled. "I bought it for your going away party? Wow, Dog Shit, I am a nice person. So how are your honey and your money?"

"Between the IRS and my soon-to-be ex — the money's gone. Before I left Iraq, she found religion, my bank account and a young stud. The bitch even managed to blow what I set aside for taxes. Hell of a homecoming."

After what seemed to Gabe to be a pained silence, Dog Shit continued, "Hey, good riddance. It was time to trade up. Besides, the tax lady was a looker and a nice hobby for a while, but that's another story best told over a few beers at choir practice. I met my new honey, Jenny, on the internet after I went back to the reservation. You know me — the connoisseur of bravo-sierra. She bought it and things have developed nicely. She's a keeper."

Gabe asked in a deadpan voice, "Did you find her on the 'Anastasia' or the 'Russian Mail Order Brides' website?"

"Ha-ha-ha, too funny, white man. You're so funny, always the comedian. You ought to take it on the road. How are the wife and grandkids? Three of them, right?"

Gabe struggled to match faces with names. Nevertheless, he performed the mental imaging and finger-count at nosebleed, mind-shattering speed. In less than eight seconds, he answered, "Last count three — all doing fine. I hope the daughter takes a breather — having trouble keepin' up with all of the daddies. Since my son returned from Iraq, his bride has been squeezing him to perform. Her clock's ringin' a loud ding-dong, ding-dong. Unless my son's shooting blanks, they'll probably have their first one next year. Nicole's fine, just fine. In addition to lamenting your lost fortunes, screwing the IRS and what's her name, what've you been up to, Dog Shit?"

"Careful there, Monty. You can slight my money and the IRS all you want, but my lady friend is off limits." He dropped his fun-loving tone. "What I'm doing is the reason I called. But first, let me ask what've you been doing since you got home?"

Gabe looked out the window for a long time before he answered. "You mean besides watching the grass grow and going out of my fucking mind?"

"That's what I thought. I did the same thing for a long time, too damn long." Dog Shit dropped the gloom and reverted to his jovial tone. "I'm ready to get back in the saddle, brother. You wanna go chase some more dragons and get back in the game?"

The game. "You mean…Iraq?"

"Spot on. What other game is there?"

"Ready? Of course, I'm ready, but I think Nicole might do a 'Bobbitt' on me if I go again. She talked divorce during my last tour. I could end up like you — resorting to the mail order bride websites, only lacking the private parts and funds to close the deal."

Gabe swallowed his drink, then grinned. "What the hell — tell me a story."

"I've been picked up on a new contract, same company, but a different gig — handled separately from the CPATT clowns. Monty, it's a nice set-up, not some bullshit white man's treaty. REDDI, the Roadside Explosive Device Defeat Initiative, is a pure Department of Defense mission with no Justice or State Department involvement. I just finished orientation in Reston and I'm on my way to the redeployment center at Ft. Bliss to get equipped and pick up my assignment. It will — "

"Dog Shit, I think I saw a recruitment email for the project when I was in Mosul. If that's what you're talking about, no way I'm qualified. From what I remember, they're looking to recruit a cross between J. Edgar Hoover, Sherlock Holmes and Jesus Christ. I have an aversion to wearing women's underwear, not too keen on our friends across the pond, and when on water, I sink even if I'm wearing a life preserver and sober."

"Monty, you're always the same — totally unaware of your hidden talents." His hoots blasted through the phone line. "You gotta trust me on this one. I just finished the orientation and out of the initial class of twenty-three, twenty were empty suits. You'd be a perfect fit, you know, the empty suit. Hey, even a red man can make funny."

"Yeah, Dog Shit, I'm rolling all over the floor thinking the only good injun's a dead injun."

"There you go again, you damn bigot!" Dog Shit laughed. "Didn't I teach you anything about political correctness? Anyhow, you know the scam. Beltway bandits dream up a proposal, lace it with flowery expectations, throw in a few important sounding acronyms to capture the military mindset, make the proposal so specific that the bid process becomes a sole source, find the right general to stroke, promise him a revolving door job upon retirement, and sell it. The company execs are masters of the process. Hell, three quarters of the VPs are retired generals. They sold the military what could end up being a bill of goods, but it should be a nice ride. All kidding aside, the concept is solid — just a matter of getting the bureaucrats out of the way and making it a viable mission. I heard you had a rough go of it up in Mosul, but the best part about this job — no bang-bang. You'd work from a desk inside the military's think-tank in a pure intelligence billet."

"It'd mean me giving up yard work, scraping, painting, cooking, laundry and all." Gabe balanced the positives against the negatives for two seconds before he said, "Okay, who do I call?'

"I knew that'd be your answer. I already laid the groundwork for you. Russ Bensen, the company's recruiter, is expecting your call. Nice guy, you probably remember him. He came to Baghdad about the time I ended mission. They stuck him in an admin slot working out of the AA building. Four months into it, his bride started playing wife and crying all that 'I can't live without you' shit. He did what I should've done — ended mission and saved his marriage. The company, in a rare stroke of genius, was good to him. They kept him on the payroll until this contract was approved and gave him the recruiting job to raid the other companies' talent pools to steal mission rats for this gig."

Gabe tried to dredge up a mental picture of Bensen, but failed. "Don't know him. Unless ordered, I steered clear of the AA building — too many damn suits. Maybe we just missed each other when I left for Mosul."

Back in his deadpan mode, Gabe said, "You still believe my gift of booze was an act of kindness and goodwill for your going away party? Really? Dog Shit, I got out of Baghdad a day before you recovered from your hangover. Hell, I bought the liquor for me since I knew it would be dry in Mosul. Your needs never entered into my thought process. Some low-life barracks rat bastard filched from my spirits survival kit for your bon voyage gala. I know that hurts, but you should be used to pain by now — ex-wife, ex-fortune and all."

"That does hurt, Monty. Watch your Yahoo account. I'll forward the job announcement and Bensen's contact info in a few minutes. Say hello to Nicole for me and tell her if she ever gets tired of your sorry ass, there's an injun out there who can shake her world in unimaginable, red man ways. See you in the desert, brother."

Gabe returned the phone to its cradle. He pushed up from the chair, and with a noticeable bounce in his step, headed to the bar and poured a fresh Bacardi — this time, no coke. He grinned as he mimicked Nicole's quick stride during her earlier escape from her lost cause. He even threw in an exaggerated swish of his hips as he bounded toward the front door on his way to the porch to retrieve his 'to do' list.

Breathing the humid air, he coughed. He coughed several more times before he lit another cigarette. Vigor renewed, and a clearness of mind and purpose not displayed since his return from Iraq, Gabe blurted, "Hire a painter and a divorce attorney. Strike that — call Bensen."

Back ramrod straight and his chest thrown out, he aimed a salute at the flag flying in Phil's yard. Ignorant of the irony, he quoted the 2003 banner for the only Republican president that he had not voted for since Nixon, "Mission accomplished!"

Pawleys Island, June 3, 1057 hours

Dog Shit and Gabe lived some good, some bad, some real ugly times together. His Indian brother was not a fair weather friend, like others in his life, but a solid one — kinship born of and sealed with blood. When the especially bad, 'someone's about to die,' shit hit the fan, he wanted a dozen more just like him covering his back. As promised, the email was blinking at the bottom of the screen.

Gabe opened his account and the message popped up. Now in his 'just the facts ma'am' serious mode, he clicked on the PDF file and for the next couple of hours, read the sixty-eight page contract proposal. He highlighted several sections in yellow. *This is definitely my ride back.*

Thoroughly versed in the contract language and astute enough to ignore the window dressing, he focused on the essence of the job. He got it. He was ready to make the call.

The first thing he did when he opened the file was to print the contact information for Bensen. Now, it was gone. He looked under papers, bills and cruise ship brochures scattered across the desktop. After a frenzied search, he remembered he had stuck it in his front pocket. He squinted as he read the paper, dialed the 703 area code and the other numbers, then waited. Seven rings later, his ticket back to war spoke.

"Russ here."

"Mr. Russ Bensen?"

"Yes. Who am I speaking to?"

"Sir, my name is Gabe Quinn. A friend told me about the REDDI mission and gave me your contact information. I'm calling to — "

"Gabe, I need to put you on hold for a second. Things are pretty hectic around here."

Thirty-eight seconds into the bumper music, Bensen was back on the line. "Sorry for the delay. Okay, Gabe Quinn — got it. Yes, Dog Shit told me that you might be calling. Good man, but he really needs to do something about his name. I understand you served with him on the Civilian Police Assistance Training Team contract. By the way, our company is very proud of it — an outstanding program. I am sure that it will elevate the Iraqi police to our standards within short order. Great success story for Iraq and America. Don't you agree, Gabe?"

Either he's thinking of another program, or he drank the Kool-Aid.

Russ cleared his throat, waiting for a response that was not coming. "Okay, uh…that's not why you called. Moving on, have you read the mission document?"

"Yes, sir."

"So you have the bug and are raring to go back. Let me go over some of the high points with you. This is a new program, so new Dog Shit is part of the first team heading over to see how this is going to unfold. He'll have an assignment in the next couple of weeks, just as soon as we find him a unit. The concept for this program originated during a bar conversation between General Brewster and the Bosnia CIVPOL director in 1999. They kicked around the idea of hiring a group of former law enforcement officers with gang related, organized crime and narcotics investigation backgrounds, to team with the military to get a handle on the Bosnia corruption."

Gabe realized that this call was not to set up an interview but was the interview. He decided that he had better engage. "In Iraq, I met quite a few former CIVPOL guys who worked that mission. The universal opinion was that it was a snafu from the get-go because it was a 'blue-berry' mission."

"Yes, they hit the nail on the head with their assessment. The same problems have surfaced in the UN civilian police mission in Haiti. Forget all of that, Gabe, and allow me to get through my elevator presentation and bring you up to date. The idea sat for a few years until someone remembered the proposal, dusted it off, and tweaked it a little to make it specific to the roadside bomb problem in Iraq. Without getting into the details of who, what, when, etcetera, REDDI was born and we've been awarded the initial contract. In a nutshell, we're sending about seventy former law enforcement officers to Iraq as embeds with Army and Marine line units. Their job is to analyze the IED cells as criminal organizations, identify the players, and think outside of the box to give the military another set of eyes on a problem that is taking far too many American lives. Elevator speech concluded. Gabe, give me a Readers Digest version of your time in Iraq."

"I arrived in November '04 and was assigned to Baghdad Police College, initially as a police instructor. Then I — "

"I was there from July '05 through October '05. Personal problems forced me to return home early. What was your time frame?"

"I left Baghdad in July '05 for Mosul," Gabe said, "so I think we just missed each other. I was part of an eight-man team sent north to reopen the academy after the insurgents overran it. The 3rd Infantry Division's secured the facility, then we rebuilt and reopened within a month. I stayed until January '06 and then moved to Diamondback. I was an advisor to the Iraqi police in the Nineveh province. Our team worked primarily out of One West in Mosul, but we moved around quite a bit to Quarrayah, Q-West, Al Karama and Tal Afar."

"I'm trying to remember a dude who worked in that area around the same time. He was a psych-evac sometime early '06. Matt, Matthew, Martin, no it was Marty something — "

Gabe hoped to close the door quickly on this new thread in the conversation, so he completed the sentence for Bensen. "Marty Brenton was my partner on the Judas project."

"Holy shit!" Bensen shrieked. "Judas! You were a part of the Judas project?"

The interview had taken a wrong turn down a one-way street, so Gabe returned to the safety of short replies, "Yes."

After an extended quiet that seemed to Gabe like minutes, Bensen finally said, "Uh…Gabe…what exactly was your role in Judas?"

"Well, sir, I worked with General Hassan Matthiq — "

"Sorry to interrupt you, Gabe. I'll tell you what, let's not talk about that for now. Judas is dead and buried. It may end up being a black eye for the company and the military. Did you know that Matthiq is dead?"

Bensen's tone had changed, almost sympathetic. Gabe, however, was irked. *I can salvage this interview, but screw it. I'm tired of all of these half-stepping whiners bitchin' about how to fight a war.* "I was with him. Sir, I don't know what you've heard about the program but I was following what I thought were legal orders from the palace. General Matthiq was a motivated, courageous man, and if the country survives, he'll be remembered as a national hero. Iraq needs a few heroes. The program exposed a shit load of bad apples, saved

American lives — "

Bensen interrupted, "Gabe, please call me Russ. Enough about Judas. Allow me to tell you the good part about the job — unbelievable salary, bountiful fringe benefits package, and — "

"I don't really care what it pays. If I can clear the screening process, how soon can I be back in Iraq?"

"Straight to the point," Bensen said. "My kind of man. Just a few more questions, Gabe and we'll be finished. What is your clearance?"

"Top secret. Years ago I had an SCI — excuse me, Sensitive Compartmentalized Information."

Gabe glanced at his wall collection of 'been there, done that' photos and other memorabilia. Almost hidden by an Iraqi flag, was a picture of him — looking emaciated, younger and sad faced as he stared at something off camera. Propped against his thigh was an AK 47 — in his hand a Bible. He leaned against a battle damaged Land Rover camouflaged so well it almost disappeared into the jungle that surrounded it. Standing by his side and dwarfing him, was a ragged group of Africans from the Bakongo tribe. Outfitted in a fusion of military and indigenous garb, armed with machetes and a smorgasbord of Russian, Chicom and Czechoslovakian automatic weapons, they looked in the same direction as Gabe. The guns had been purchased by the United States with black money run through several of the alphabet agencies before landing in a U.S. Agency for International Development front. Finally, the laundered funds were doled over to America's friend, Mobutu Sese Seko — Zaire's corrupt dictator.

All except Gabe smiled for the camera. Not shown in the picture was the reason for his dour look and their glee — a pile of bodies. Taken at some long forgotten border crossing near a refugee camp, team members made their mark on the photo as a tribute to him. Shortly after the picture was snapped, all, aside from Gabe, met the same end as their enemies missed by the camera lens that day.

"During the eighties," Gabe said, "I was attached to an embassy in West Africa. I didn't keep up with the paperwork after the Angola thing, so I lost the SCI part of the clearance."

"So...you worked for the CIA?"

"Not for — with."

"What does that mean?"

Again, Russ waited for a response that would never come. "OK, I understand. A top secret is fine. Currently, that's all we require. As the program develops you may need a higher clearance. Can you pass a polygraph?'

"If the wrong questions are asked — not a problem."

"I won't ask if you have a sense of humor. Last item, do you have any military experience?"

"Yes, but nothing relevant."

"Please explain."

"I was drafted out of college in '71." Always the cop, Gabe fished for personal information, nothing important, just habit. "Russ, having not met you in person, I'm guessing from your voice and word choices that you had not yet been born."

"Born in '79, Gabe."

"Fort Campbell for basic, Polk for advanced training, then Fort Benning for jump school. While at airborne training, I discovered that I had an inherent disqualifying birth defect — fear of heights. I received orders for the 199th Replacement Company, Long Binh, Republic of Vietnam. My older brother was flying helicopters in Vietnam at the time, and because of the one-son rule, kept my 19-year-old butt out of the jungle. The Army decided it needed my no-talent ass in Korea to keep the communist hordes at bay. Bottom line, the only action I saw was in the bars and brothels of Uijongbu and Tongduchon. What can I say, young, dumb, and not yet twenty-one. It was all good though. Thanks to the G.I. Bill, I was able to finish college."

"You're familiar with the military structure — that's all that's important. Gabe, if I can get your updated resume today, I can walk it through the halls and get it approved, probably by the end of the week. I should be able to get a reporting package to you by early next week. Can you be packed and ready for the company orientation in Reston, let's say… in two weeks?"

Feeling like he was already home in the desert, Gabe breathed a sigh of relief. "That works for me. Russ, if there is a need for any phone calls, don't call my house. Use my cell phone instead."

"Not a problem on this end. Let me turn the tables on you with a little police inquiry — you're married and haven't discussed this with your wife."

"Roger, but it won't be an issue. Just waiting for the right moment. Is that it?"

"That's it, interview over. Gabe, do me a favor. When you submit your resume, leave out the part about the Judas project. I don't need that information to get you approved."

"Understood, and Russ, thanks. You're a lifesaver."

"You have that one backwards, Gabe. Thank you. I'll see you in about two weeks — first round's on me."

Gabe ended the call and glanced up at decades of memories covering one wall. Countless ghosts from third world countries stared back. *Too many — this time will be different.*

He pushed away from the desk and stepped to the bookshelf below the wall of shame. Scanning the volumes, he stopped when he saw the black, worn, dog-eared book. He plucked it from the stack and flipped through the pages. *Screw it. Don't mean a damn thing.*

He dropped the Bible in the trashcan on his way to the bar.

Chapter 3
Surf, sex, and drugs, but no rock n' roll

Qadisiyah Province, Iraq, June 3, 2007, 0455 GMT +4

Soon... soon they will be here. Less than an hour before the sunrise. Soon. His information was always correct, his preparations complete. He relaxed. Alone in the desert, except for the occasional bark of a distant dog guarding one of the ubiquitous Bedouin encampments, he lost himself in the serenity of the early morning dark. The wasteland's air, cooler since the sun disappeared behind the hills ten hours earlier, floated across him. The breeze rustled the *dishdasha* against his chest and legs, much like his wife's soft touch just before the children awakened.

Ali Sabah stroked the hardened, dead skin that ran from his forehead, across the left eye to his cheek. Then he moved his fingers to his upper lip and brushed his thick mustache straight down until it covered his mouth. He could not conceal the disfigurement, the ugly reminder fixed forever on his face. He had learned to revere it — his Northern Star that now guided his destiny. His wife never tasted his briny whiskers, never touched the scar. He missed her, God how he missed her. *Allah, why did you let the Amerikees take her life...my life?*

He and his father had traveled this desert many times. They had walked for hours, moving their few sheep from one *wadi* to the next. He enjoyed the long talks with him about the future — a future that would include marriage to his cousin. He hoped to produce many sons for *Allah.*

Work was not difficult — it came natural to him. Being the oldest son, he knew his role within the family and the tribe. Eventually he would take his father's place as the head of the family, just as his father replaced his father, and his grandfather had replaced his father, and so on through time, probably to the days when Abraham traveled these sands.

Their ways were simple — predictable and unchanging over the millennia. They were a proud family, well respected in the village. Wanting for little, since Allah had provided all for their meager needs, they were able to help the rest of their clan during the downturns set before them.

Life took an eventful turn after his *tahira*, or purification, at the age of seven. His circumcision was a momentous occasion. Manhood was upon him and he would enjoy full participation in the Islamic rituals. The newfound joy was short lived because his father decided that Ali Sabah and his younger brother needed a modern education that could lead to a better life. Despite their childish protests, he sent them north to live with a great uncle with the understanding that his sons would be educated in the ways of the world.

The uncle was a man of means and equanimity. Immersed in this benevolent atmosphere, Ali Sabah drank heartily from the learning well, eventually graduating from the university with a chemical engineering degree and an understanding of the infidel's spoken language. His brother, who mastered English even beyond his significant grasp, chose a different path. Their paths crossed again — not as blood brothers, but as brother *mujahedeen*.

After graduation, Ali Sabah took a job in Baghdad. Although *Shi'ite*, therefore not allowed in Saddam's Ba'ath party, the government needed his skills to develop chemicals for military use. His supervisors were pleased with his work, but he yearned to return to the simple village life of his youth. Every night he explored the sky above Baghdad for the star that had guided his father and him across the featureless desert. The brilliance of the ground lights blanketing a prosperous Baghdad made his search difficult.

One evening he hit upon the star. Not quite a whim, more of a sub-conscious understanding of his karma, Ali Sabah boarded a bus and went home.

He searched the skies for his star. The tranquility of the moment was broken as he saw a light rushing to the north. Frowning, the thoughts of his golden youth destroyed by this 20th century invention, he studied a jet as it moved through the night's clear sky. Soon he saw another winged warrior join the first and entwine, as if in the midst of lovemaking, eight kilometers above him. He knew from his studies of the Americans, the dance performed under the offended eyes of *Allah* was a refueling operation. *Amerikees, they have so much, yet they are so weak. Weak in spirit, mind, resolve and body — lower than the foul dogs baying at a dead moon.*

As the lights disappeared beyond the curvature of the earth, he tried to recapture the pleasant memories of his youth. It was impossible, stolen by the winged lovers. He drifted through the turbulent times that followed him after he left Baghdad.

Marriage to Houdah had been *Allah's* reward to him for coming home. In the first year of his marriage, he had a son and named him to honor the prophet. Mohamed was all that he dreamed about. His powerful young body grew straight and strong. As soon as he could walk, Ali Sabah began to reveal the secrets of *Allah* to him. Someday, together they would enjoy long walks in the desert, just as it had been with his father. Moreover, someday Mohamed would replace him in the long proud lineage of the family.

Through marriage, his land holdings doubled, as did his family — two daughters — not the male heirs he had hoped for, but beautiful children nonetheless. He increased the herd, dug a well close to the Euphrates, and added a room to their house.

Thanks to the generosity of *Allah* and Ali Sabah's knowledge of the way things worked in a corrupt society, he acquired a German pump and a French generator. The pump brought the life-blood into their piece of the desert. With good water, date production doubled, the bee hives flourished, honey flowed, the sheep reproduced, as did the goats. Finally, able to sell goods in the market, his family partook in the new prosperity of Iraq. He gained status within the tribe. His thoughts had turned to finding a second wife, producing more sons, and increasing his standing in the village. Someday, *insha Allah*, he would be the village's sheikh.

Conscripted by Saddam's army, his father went to Kuwait to free their brothers and reclaim the land that rightfully belonged to Iraq. He had wanted to join him, but his father insisted that he remain and take care of the family. At great expense, his father bribed the right official and exempted Ali Sabah from service.

After the initial glory of the liberation of Kuwait the war turned, it turned badly. The infidels came. During the retreat north, an American bomb killed his father. Nothing was left of him, nothing to bury. He died on the same highway that Ali Sabah was now studying. *Soon.*

Further missteps made by Saddam had caused much pain for Iraq — Ali Sabah's village suffered more than most. The American embargo completed the destruction — there was nothing to be purchased or bartered. He could not find replacement parts for the pump or the generator. The few parts that his cousin fabricated soon failed. The pump died, then the generator. Even if the machinery was made pristine, the diesel it needed to drink could not be purchased. No longer did they have an abundance of water. The date palms withered, the honeybees and sheep perished. There was nothing to take to market.

The embargo caused a shortage of the simple vaccine he needed to protect his children from polio. Mohamed was first. His son survived, but now his limbs were useless, ravaged by the effects of this virus. He shuffled about with fabricated crutches for short distances, but was constantly fatigued and pained by the exertion. Mohamed would produce no sons. Mohamed would never walk again with his father in the desert night. Mohamed would not replace him as the leader of the family.

He knew American spies had introduced the virus into the Iraqi reservoirs, just as they had slaughtered millions of Africans with the HIV virus they created in Washington, D.C. His oldest daughter escaped the disease. The youngest did not. He sent his surviving daughter north to a cousin's village. The decision was just — after all, she was a daughter, not capable of advancing his dreams or the family legacy. Houdah died — possibly from heartache, but more likely from the waste borne of famine and contaminated water. *Mohamed crippled, Houdah dead, daughter dead, village dead, dream dead. Amerikees, damn Amerikees!*

Ali Sabah heard them before he saw them. At first, it was a low rumble far off in the distance disturbing the quiet night air. The rumble became a pulsating throb with a beat similar to the hum of the long dead generator. The rumble became a roar that shook the ground. He sat up, not frightened, but in quiet disbelief as he watched a snake-like string of lights extending beyond the horizon.

The snake moved closer. His patience was rewarded. *Lah ilaha ill Allah,* praise be to *Allah.* He readied his Kalashnikov beside him, but knew that he would not need it. Tonight he would use the new weapon. He removed a Nokia cell phone from underneath the *dishdasha.* Squinting at the approaching headlights four or five kilometers south, he turned away to scan the highway west and north. *Empty.*

Again, he looked at the serpent. Holding the Nokia angled toward the moonlight, he entered the five digits he had memorized. *Soon.*

*****

27

Staff Sergeant Reeves, the lead truck commander, had been in the Army for just over four years. His wife, Amber, and his children, a two-year-old daughter and a four-month-old son he had yet to hold, had moved to Myrtle Beach for the length of his deployment. He planned to be a career soldier and give them the life he never had. The Army had been good to him, giving him a job after the coal mine closed in his West Virginia hometown. He had just re-enlisted two weeks ago. Consumed with thoughts about the Dodge 1500 4X4 Hemi pickup truck he planned to buy with the re-up bonus, he knew that his wife had other plans for the money. Her dream also had wheels — a Fleetwood doublewide, three bedroom, two bath, elite plush combo living-dining room, complete with a leatherette sofa, love seat, recliner, simulated granite kitchen countertops and a one year g-u-a-r-a-n-t-e-e-d, bullet proof warranty.

The winner of the competing dreams would be decided in twenty-eight days and a wake-up when he stepped off the freedom bird. He knew Amber was much too hot for his country ass, but nonetheless, he was sure she loved him. He thought about the homecoming sex often. He thought about his kids almost as much, but saved those private feelings for his quality time when alone in his bed and not on a patrol. The open desert was meant for thoughts about manly things like pickup trucks.

Private Ramirez, the gunner operating the turret's fifty-caliber, was an eighteen-year old, tattooed gang banger from southern Cali. He did not contemplate his future much. Life flowed over, under, around and through him — pushed in a direction instead of choosing one. His only goal in life was sleep, more sleep and an occasional blunt to help him sleep. Ramirez was the only E-2 private in his platoon and held the unique distinction for pissing hot twice before graduating basic training. Along the way, he garnered several counseling statements from Reeves; not for weed, but for falling asleep on duty. Finding marijuana in Iraq had proven to be like the Knights Templar's search for the Holy Grail. Yet, as impossible as scoring was in Iraq, Reeves had popped him several times with a wiz-quiz.

The driver, barely able to shave and sporting bleached hair a little longer than military grooming standards permitted, was from Daytona Beach. Specialist Tuttle's claim to fame was winning a local surfing event in the eighteen and under-class the year he enlisted — exactly sixteen months prior to this patrol. He dreamed about two things — surfing and sex. His notions about love were perverted by the abundant porno collection his fellow warriors had supplied, all in violation of General Order Number One. Unlike Reeves, Tuttle would not re-up. A year in hell without a surfboard and a fine piece of ass had been enough punishment. He had managed to squirrel a few dollars away during the deployment. The extra $150 a month combat pay would make for one hell of a 'kegger' when he was back on the beach. He planned to travel up, down and around the east and gulf coasts in search of the perfect wave and the perfect lay — not chasing any more of those teasing 'butter-heads' that had slinked their way into the Army.

Awake for twenty-two plus hours, not knowing when or where he would be able to find a bed, Reeves grabbed a Red Bull from the cooler. He chugged the drink and then worked a chunk of ice around his neck, finally dropping it under his body armor to cool his chest. As the point Humvee commander for a 250-truck super-cell convoy, his responsibility was huge — not only to his crew, but also to the hundreds of civilian truck drivers and soldiers pulling convoy security. It was an awesome duty for a twenty-two year old.

Reeves sipped a second Red Bull, enjoying the sudden rush of the energy boost. Alternately scanning the dark terrain passing by at fifty miles per hour, and his vehicle's blue icon crawling across the screen of the Blue Force Tracker (BFT), he hoped for another routine mission. He did not need the BFT to find his location on main supply route (MSR) Tampa. He had been up and down the highway hundreds of times over the past twelve months. Yet he found some comfort looking at the numerous, friendly blue icons in the convoy. *Safety in numbers.*

He enjoyed some relief from the only airflow through the open gun turret. He nudged Ramirez's legs dangling from the bolster seat harness above him and shouted in the intercom, "Ramirez, wake the heck up."

Shaking the sleep from his head, Ramirez said, "Awake Sarge, awake. Sarge, do we have any Red Bull left?"

"On the way, Ramirez. Keep your eyes open. We're too damn short to screw the pooch now." Reeves knew Ramirez needed a gentle boot up the ass every once in awhile. *Keep him motivated, in the game.* "Tuttle, how you doin'?"

Tuttle, in addition to keeping the truck moving in a straight line, had been continuously scanning the road from the left to the right shoulder, and toggling the aftermarket 'go-lights' mounted on the front bumper and hood. Maintaining his search for anything out of place, he said, "Doing fine, Sarge."

The convoy's ranking officer positioned further back in the pack, hailed combat outpost 4 (COP) on the Sheriff's net. "COP 4…Grizzly 6…radio check."

After some crackling, a voice responded, "Grizzly 6…roger. BFT shows you ten clicks from check point 4-alpha…confirm."

"COP 4, roger. We are a super cell with 250 vics (vehicles) and 285 paxs (persons). Approachin' CP (checkpoint) two-alpha-sierra, nine clicks north of CP 4-alpha…destination BIAP (Baghdad international airport). Requesting SITREP (situation report)."

"Roger… 250 vehicles, 285 passengers. No IEDs reported in the last twelve hours. Small arms fire (SAF) reported earlier near CP twelve-bravo. Rock throwing incident at CP fourteen-bravo. Current weather conditions are MEDEVAC amber, deteriorating to red before daybreak in vicinity of CP 10-bravo as dust storm moves in from the northeast. Recommend you redirect to Scania in expectation of deteriorating conditions."

"COP 4, Grizzly 6, roger. Scania it is. Tango-mike."

"Grizzly 6, roger. Keep the piss bottles in the vehicles…stay safe…COP 4 out."

"Hot damn!" Reeves shouted. "Did you guys hear that? We're forty clicks out from Scania. When we get there, Tuttle, pull PM (preventive maintenance) and top it off. Ramirez, secure the fifty in the cab, chain the doors. I'll find some racks in the transient tent. We'll meet up at the DFAC (dining facility). Everyone gets a hot and a cot. Seriously, people, no fucking around — forget about internet, TV, writing letters. Everyone gets some shuteye. Damn, life's good. Ramirez, put some tunes on your IPOD and pipe it through the internal."

"Roger, Sarge."

Reeves shouted one more command, "Tuttle, bump it up another five, and Ramirez, none of that 'gangsta' crap, I want country music. Put on some Travis — "

*****

The passive infrared device (PIR) was adapted from its normal use on a garage door opener, but acted much the same way. A cheap cell phone was taped to the power source, a motorcycle battery. Thin electrical wires went from the battery to blasting caps in the rear of four canisters, each about the size of a coffee can. Packed inside were three kilos of high explosives, twelve kilos in all. The canisters, faced with concave copper plates, weighing about two pounds, were canted to afford a better spread. The four canisters, battery, cell phone and PIR were encased in an expanding foam spray, similar to the kind that can be purchased at any home improvement store. The entire package was mounted on a two-inch piece of dimensional lumber, less than a foot wide, and about three feet long. Camouflaged with a mixture of grey, brown and tan paint, and then dusted with sand and dead plant material indigenous to the surrounding terrain, only the lens of the PIR was visible from a distance of a few meters to a trained eye — a highly trained eye.

Armed earlier by a five-digit code, the re-programmed dual tone multiple frequency decoder board inside the cell phone had already served its purpose by waking up the sleeping PIR. Sensing the heat signature of the Humvee's engine block as it entered its narrow angle view, the PIR transmitted an electrical impulse to the blasting cap. Upon receipt of the impulse, the blasting cap detonated the high explosives inside the canisters. Following the laws of physics, the explosives directed most of the force forward. The copper plates inverted their shape and formed slugs. Because of copper's pliability, there was little spalling as the metal blasted outward. The copper and the plasma fireball, intrinsic to the explosion, burst out at a speed of between 1.75 and 2.0 miles per second.

The liquid metal breached the right side of Ramirez's turret and Reeves' armored door. The compromised armor was instantly hit with a firestorm that engulfed the interior of the cab. No metal, plastic, Kevlar, bone, or flesh could survive the intense sun created within the confines of the Humvee or the speed of copper ripping through all matter in its path. The damage was complete in a nano-second.

In that nano-second, Sergeant Reeves left — a sultry blonde goddess, a son who would never know his dad, a daughter who would soon forget she had one, a mother, a father, two surviving paternal grandparents, a maternal grandmother, one brother, two sisters, two uncles, four aunts, twelve cousins — and dreams of a Dodge 1500 4X4 Hemi pickup truck.

In a nano-second, Private Ramirez left — a girlfriend, who never told him she was pregnant, a mother, step-father, another step-father, biological father, three sisters, four step-sisters, one brother, two step-brothers, a bunch of *tios*, *tias* and 'cuzzins', possibly some grandparents across the border — he never knew for sure — and no real dream — just a desire to see the next moment.

31

In a nano-second, Specialist Tuttle, virginity intact, left — a mom, dad, no brothers or sisters, four grandparents, two uncles, two aunts, three surfboards and dreams of breaking the hearts of 'tens' across the southeast.

*****

The brilliance of the explosion registered on Ali Sabah's ocular nerves four seconds before the sound found his ear canal. The shockwave rushed in with the roar and sent a pulse through his brain that surpassed the pleasures of an orgasm, completely overwhelming his senses. He looked to the heavens, then to the hell played out in front of him.

The Americans would eventually leave just as the sun would rise shortly. Being a simple man and never asking for much, at morning *fajr* he would ask *Allah* for one great thing. He would ask that the Americans stay longer, so he could send more of them to hell.

Satisfied with his work, he picked up his Kalashnikov and walked toward the car, faintly visible as the golden red aura of the sun peeked above the distant dunes. He opened the door and placed the rifle in the passenger seat. He quickly removed his *dishdasha* and exchanged his soiled undershirt for the clean one folded on the passenger seat.

He opened the rear door to the blue and white GMC Jimmy, paid for by the Americans, reached inside and grabbed a freshly pressed blue shirt. He took a final look at the scene on the highway, then buttoned the shirt. He pulled the right sleeve down tight against his wrist and buttoned the cuff, careful to cover the tattoo on his forearm — three green dots and a crescent moon. He rearranged the police badge on the breast pocket and checked the shoulder epaulets to make sure they looked proper. Then he holstered the Glock 17 on his belt. Looking at his reflection on the car's side window, he performed a final once-over. Satisfied his uniform was correct — he got in, made sure the headlights were not in the auto position, and started the ignition.

The SUV crawled east on the same washed-out animal path that he had negotiated twelve hours earlier. When he was positive that he was no longer visible from the highway, he stopped and lit his first cigarette since sunset the prior evening. Casually, he removed the microphone from the center console and contacted the Al Oamzah police station.

"Lieutenant Bassam, Captain Ali Sabah. There has been an

explosion on the expressway two kilometers south of ad Diwaniyah. Send officers immediately. That is all."

He dropped the radio handset on the passenger seat and removed the cell phone from his pocket. He pressed one and seven. Within seconds, the speed-dialed number connected. *"Asalaam aleekum,* Kaseem."

"Aleekum asalaam, Ghazi Codar el Ahmar," Kaseem answered. "Did it work, Ghazi?"

"Yes." Unperturbed by the name shift, Ali Sabah smiled. "Prepare more bombs."

Chapter 4
Tim, James, Bob, ₹udas and a dildo

Pawleys Island, South Carolina, June 3, 1717 hours

Shave, shower, and maybe trim the hair. Okay where did Nicole hide my trusty scissors? God, how can she use so much stuff? My sink has a razor, toothbrush, toothpaste, and a comb.

What in hell else does a person need? Let's see what her ten-foot vanity holds. Looks like a damn pharmacy. If it can't be packed in a Ziploc, it ain't important.

What's here? Cotton balls, Q-tips, hair clips, bows, ribbons — what twenty or thirty? She does have a lot of hair. Confess body spray, hair remover wax kit, Suave finishing hair spray, perfume, more perfume, Curel ultra healing — I didn't know she was ailing. I think I'm getting close. Natural Glow clarity moisturizer, Body Dew Sensuous bath oil, Artistry clarifying oil control toner, Frizz-Ease style wind down — I guess she needs that for when — wait nobody needs that. Thermasilk heat activated condition mist, Frizz-Ease daily moisturizing leave-in fortifying spray. I just saw a Frizz-Ease something. Olay clarifying and cleansing daily scrub, Aveeno daily moisturizing lotion, Passion Jewels moisturizing lotion, gel cuticle remover.

I forgot what I was looking for. Oh yeah, scissors. Think, think. She wouldn't put my scissors in plain view and I don't have time to recon the other eight feet. Try the drawers. Okay, I'm getting warmer.

Hair dryer, curling iron, nail-trim kit, batteries…batteries. Who needs batteries in a bathroom? What's that? California Exotics. What the…? I guess I've been replaced by a dildo. Screw it — I don't need a trim.

A little hot water and a fresh razor. No shaving cream. Oh well, use the hand soap. Aaah, a fresh blade against the face, one of life's few pleasures. Ranks right up there with an undisturbed morning constitution and double ply quilted, scented and ultra soft toilet paper. Wait, a good drunk makes that list. Blacking out is better. Can't remember a thing and there's the reward — a hangover. Makes me feel alive. Then it clears. Always a downside. However, there's always another drink. Maybe there's a God after all. What do you see in the mirror? An older me. Any wiser? Shit no.

ご Who put that on the mirror? Who's here? Who's here damnit? Did I do that? It's gone. Here and now, stay here and now. Forget war. Forget Iraq. Fuck Iraq. Fuck war.

Clean up, shower, put on a happy face, be nice, fake it. Good plan, but how do I tell Nicole that I'm leaving again and why? Maybe don't tell her. Yeah, just leave. Send a post card. Why not? It's free mail from war zone.

Why are you going back? Do you have a death wish? You were scared twenty four-seven from the moment you landed. Hell, you were scared before you landed. You're a chicken shit, candy-ass, pussy. A weenie, always have been, always will be. I hate confrontation. And violence, that thing where I can get hurt. Who am I kidding?

Ah, but it feels so good afterwards. No drug better. Hell, I've tried them all. Right up there with Timothy Leary. Nothing compares. Besides, I'm bulletproof. Look at the twisted metal dangling on your necklace. I'm invincible. That round landed at my feet and didn't kill me.

Ouch, nicked the old neck. Must remember, a fresh blade is sharper than a dull one. It'll stop bleeding when I'm in the shower. I'll start out with steaming hot water and follow it with cold. That'll stop it. The pain does feel good, though. At least I know I'm alive for the moment.

What's important? Food, sleep, staying alive. I guess that about covers it. Sex? God, it used to be. The days of monkey sex are gone forever. Now just hallway sex. Trade passionate 'fuck you' looks when we pass each other. Another bodily function — like trimming toenails or maybe pissing. Love? Just a word I gotta use to keep confrontation at bay. Don't let 'em in. Nothing good will come from it.

Damn, another nick.

Did I really kill him? I guess I did. Can't remember his face. Would it be better if I could see his face? Naw, that's movie shit. Maybe I didn't kill him. Yeah I did. Two to the chest — one to the head. Only hits count. Hey, don't beat yourself up. He deserved to die. Did he? Sure, he got off easy. All I did was take his life. What'd he take from me?

Thank God, I don't believe in God. Think about it, I'm thanking God that I don't believe in God. Don't think, my head will just start hurting again.

Two to the chest, one to the head. What about the others? Others?

35

Maybe, maybe not. Can't remember. Did I do them, too? So what. Who the hell cares. Don't mean a damn thing.

Judas.

What? Stop that man. Wait a damn minute — Judas was a good program. I was one of the good guys. I wore the white hat. Those hajjis wore man dresses. Well screw 'em all. They're just hajjis.

On to one of life's greater joys. I paid good money to the plumber for the deluxe eight-nozzle body spray. Rebel and use it. Nicole will get mad — those pesky water spots on the glass and all. Hey, I put in the garden tub for her. I never use the damn thing. Yeah, I'm the rebel.

Damn that feels so good. A little hotter, scalding. No combat shower today. I'm gonna enjoy this. In fact, I think I'll use Nicole's bath scrunchie, or whatever it's called. Not just face, armpits and crotch today. Shampoo? Why not.

Judas.

Could've been two to the floor and one to the ceiling. Sure, that's it. I didn't kill him. Maybe...maybe he did it himself...or maybe it was someone else. That's the way it was. Forget about it. It wasn't me after all. Someone else zapped his ass. Probably they wasted the others, too. So, there were others. I do remember. Funny how the old brain plays tricks like that. I'm clean, in more ways than one. No guilt here — pure as the driven snow. Maybe cliché, but if the shoe fits —

Pumice stone. Good idea. Clear some of the dead skin from the feet. Man, they're bad. I thought dying came from the inside and here it is on my feet.

Okay, she won't like it. We'll argue. Not really, what's to argue? I'm going. My mind's made up. The answer's in the desert. Not here. Takes two to tango, babe. What'll it cost? Think about that. Our marriage? Love? I can't even remember what that word means. Now closer to like. No, not even that...maybe fond. That's a good word. I'm fond of you, Nicole. It does have a nice ring to it. Much better than like, but still a little strong. Recognize maybe? I recognize you. I recognize the kids, grandkids and you. Keep the peace. Just find the right moment and get it out. *Que sera, sera.*

I can pitch the money. Should've asked what the mission pays. Naw, not important. She knows we don't need the money.

How about the truth? Nicole, I'm fond of you, I recognize you, I like you, and because of that I need to leave. I don't want you to see me for what I am. It'll drag you down to my level. You don't want to go there. Don't come into my world. I didn't want to be here. I don't know how I got here. I don't know how to get out. It's not a nice place.

Damn Judas. It's beyond evil. It's what's in the closet, what's under your bed, what your daddy wanted to protect you from. Evil. More than that, if there's more than that. Don't rot with me, but remember me. Please remember me. Don't join me. No return. You are at zero. You are zero. The balance is gone.

Calm down, get a grip. This is easy, don't make it difficult. Tonight, get her a little tipsy at the party and then take her to a club afterwards. Few more drinks, a little dancing. That could work. Then hit her with it. Good plan. Just a few more minutes in the shower and I can whip the world.

Oh, God, that was good. There I go again with that God shit. Gabe, the rebel. I like that, a rebel without a God, a conscience, or a cause. Watch out James Dean, I'm two up on you. Well don't invite an argument, rebel. Use a towel and clean the water spots. Smart. Note to self — self, you're a friggin' genius. In fact, use some deodorant. What does she have? Secret. That works for me. Babe, I've got a secret. Splurge man, I know there's some smell good somewhere in this bathroom. In the drawer, look in the drawer, dumbass. Aha, my scissors. Too late.

Old Spice. Yeah, she likes that. A little splash on the face and neck? Sure. How about the chest? Why not. Crotch? Now I'm pushin' it. Fuck it, I'm the man, I'm the rebel.

What to wear, what to wear? Party, casual, fun. These cargo shorts work. How about the Bob Marley tee? Perfect. Top it off with a Hawaiian shirt with pineapples and palm trees and I'll look faaa-buuul-ous. Where are my damn Jesus cruisers? Got 'em. Okay, I'm ready.

Now for a little current news so if I'm cornered tonight I can make some small talk with Nicole's neighbors.

Fox News? Commercial.

CNN? Okay CNN, enlighten me. Wolf Blitzer, tell me the news. What's selling your sponsors' products today?

"Just reported, three American soldiers died earlier this morning in Iraq when their vehicle hit a roadside bomb near Diwaniyah south of Baghdad. That brings U.S. casualties to thirteen this month. Since hostilities started in March 2003, three thousand two hundred and seventy three American military have died. In other news, Atlanta Falcons quarterback Michael Vick has been indicted — "

Damnit.

Click.

Chapter 5
Seven dead puppies and a bitch saloon

Pawleys Island, June 4, 1657 hours

Gabe heard the final sputter as the car engine died. He downed the drink and shoved a dozen breath mints inside his mouth, then crunched them into finer chunks. He worked the pieces around before swallowing, then smelled his shirt, hands and arms for any telltale odors. He stood just as the side entry door slammed shut.

"You home?" Nicole yelled.

"Upstairs."

The familiar clacking noises of her heels echoed up the open balcony as she moved across the floor. The sound stopped at the bottom of the stairs.

"I'm taking a quick shower." Nicole shouted. "I'll be dressed and ready in ten minutes. You ready?"

Ten minutes means I've got at least thirty to sober up. "I'm dressed and ready to limbo."

"I don't think it's that kind of a party."

He waited a minute to make sure she was fully involved in dolling herself up, then crept down the stairs. Four steps before he reached the bottom landing a tread creaked —

"What happened to my shower?" she squealed from the master bath. "It looks like a hurricane struck? Did you use the body spray?"

Damn, she doesn't miss a thing. Maybe she didn't hear me.

Forty-five minutes later, he caught a glimpse of her through an open window as she rushed through the rooms in search of something — probably him. While passing the family room bar, she paused, sniffed the air and smiled.

The Old Spice worked.

Then she took in a bigger whiff and frowned.

Not enough cologne in the world to mask the smell of rum — get ready to pay the piper. He ducked lower in the chair until he was well below the windowsill.

"Gabriel Montgomery." The sound of her steps edged closer to the front door, "Where are you?"

Busted, he sat up straight and mumbled, "Front porch." *Need a diversion — think quickly — anything.* "Do you want me to start the car?"

Not quite a bark, closer to a frosty low growl, she said, "Gabriel, the Petersons live just a few houses down the street. I think we can walk. At least I can."

They're almost next-door neighbors. Jesus, I should've known that — way to go, rebel. "Of course, I just thought…you know, I thought maybe you're wearing heels or something and — Yeah, OK, you're right. Walking is a great idea."

The front door's brass lever moved. He braced. The door swung inward.

She glided onto the front porch like Giselle, only looking much better than the conflicted, doomed lover of the Rhineland had. Nicole's blonde mane flowed behind her, soft luminous skin, highlighted with a minimalist approach to make-up, and wearing a silk floral sundress that accentuated her well-proportioned feminine magnetism — her appearance would speak to every male she encountered — she looked stunning.

Gabe, on the other hand, was no Albrecht. He looked the peasant part for sure, but unlike the ballet's hero, his was not an act. No matter what ruse he conjured, there was no fooling her — she knew him too well. Nevertheless, he felt a momentary fever between his thighs — an ode to better days. Ambivalence settled in, the fervor was lost. *Will the passion ever return? Do I care? Fifty ways to leave your lover, and I've come up with fifty-one.*

She took one look at him and laughed. "You look ridiculous!"

I've got a chance. Turn it on and throttle the volume. "It's an Islands party. I thought I did good."

"Oh yeah, you did great, honey." Still chuckling, she said, "You look like your mother dressed you. Lose the Gonzo sunglasses. Those things went out of style before we even met."

He jumped up from the patio chair and feigned a slap to his face. Then, he did his best impression of John Travolta dancing across a disco floor. Not well though — he looked more like a wounded animal flopping around the porch.

"Ooooh, baby!" he said, "you're such a tease. I love the foreplay." He moved to her and grabbed her hand. "Let's go move to the reggae beat, mon. Do the mamba, la rumba, and *salsa el noche con bailando la tango, chica bonita* — or whatever one does at an Islands theme party."

He let go of her hand, pushed the sunglasses to the end of his nose and looked over the frame. "But I'm keeping the shades, babe."

He thought he saw a slight smile at the corner of her mouth, but it could have been the bad lighting or his alcohol-tainted imagination. She turned away from him and took the four steps to the driveway as if in a race. She led — he followed, only stumbling twice.

The Peterson's circular and side driveways, as well as both sides of the street stretching more than fifty yards, resembled an exclusive import dealership. The valet had parked more than forty cars, and except for one, none of them American made. The automobile inventory included Jaguars, Mercedes, BMWs, Lexus, Porsches, Audis, Infinitis, Volvos, even a Ferrari. The sole patriot was an identity challenged soul, evidently trying to recapture his youth with a babe magnet — a new red Corvette. Gabe's concept of mid-life crisis was all the bad shit that happens between birth and death.

Parked alone, and farther down the street away from the party, was an aging Ford minivan — complete with a 'Jesus Saves' bumper sticker, out of state tag, broken windshield, coat hanger for an antenna, Bondo body filler and duct tape holding everything else together. Mounted on the right front wheel — a donut spare tire. *Must be the hired help.*

The Peterson's sprawling mini-mansion nestling among transplanted palms, native live oaks and wax myrtles, sat on four acres of professionally manicured abundance. Although the homeowners' association prohibited swimming pools on golf course lots, the Peterson estate had a whopper. It had helped that Mr. Peterson was the chair of the association. The argument he needed a pool to fit his executive image was a bit shallow, but threatening to expose key board members' closet skeletons and bury the HOA in a mountain of lawsuits, carried the day. After the board approved his variance request, he went first class. Aside from the Olympic size, other amenities included a hot tub, waterfall, swim up bar, travertine decking, stone and stucco pool house with inlaid, hand painted Mexican tiles on the walls, a gazebo built of tabeuia imported from Argentina, and nearer to the house, another bar with spiral columns supporting the pergola's beam and lattice roof.

Nicole stopped short of the driveway, turned around and waited until Gabe caught up. She arched an eyebrow and looked at him with a stern countenance that could wilt an Egyptian mummy. "Be good."

Then, she left him in the dust and charged forward toward several women bunched up underneath the entry portico.

Dressed, coiffed and manicured to perfection, the aging women looked as if they were attending a cotillion debutante ball instead of a senior citizens cocktail party. *It ain't working, girls. Botox, Silicon implants, facelifts, tummy tucks, imported French underwear, fitted Italian designer dresses, can't hide the obvious. Nothing wrong in trying, though.*

Preoccupied with her friends, Nicole had unwittingly given Gabe his opening. He stepped off the cobblestone driveway onto the lush mowed carpet of St. Augustine grass. His uncanny powers of deductive reasoning produced the desired result — a side entrance to the pool and patio. He crossed over the yard to a flagstone path that directed foot traffic to an open wrought iron gate. As he got closer to the back yard he heard music — not Jah B, Bob Marley, Black Uhuru, or even Don Ho from the other islands, but Frank Sinatra crooning 'New York, New York.' He wondered if he had misunderstood Nicole. Then he smiled to himself. *What the hell, New York's an island. Break out the ganji and party on, mon!*

He followed the curving trail, bounded by lush plantings, until a vista appeared. He stopped and scanned the crowd of seventy to eighty strangers scattered around the patio and yard. He detected a pattern to the seeming less random gatherings. The crowd, ranging in age from fiftyish to sixtyish and none dressed for any island he had visited, were clustered in defined groups.

Sheltered by umbrellas and sitting on color coordinated pillowed loungers — nine former trophy wives. Strategically positioned at the far edge of the pool for all to see and admire, they seemed to enjoy their mimosas and reprieve from their inattentive mates. As each newcomer emerged from the screen porch onto the shaded lanai, the trophies looked up and acknowledged the fresh gossip fodder with waves, blown kisses or winks. It was clear from their chatter and body language they were deciding which new guest met their lofty standards.

In the cheap seats, near the pool pump house, were the party police — no trophies in their group, ex or otherwise. Not quite as animated as the trophy collection — a little older, plumper and not bedecked in the latest fashions purchased from Macy's online or at the new Dillards — they also scrutinized each caller. They, however, did not contrive smiles, a twinkling in the eyes, or blown kisses — more a collective disinterested frown — boredom, resentment, or

41

possibly disgust. No mimosas at their table — they nursed diet sodas or iced tea.

Along the periphery of the pool were more tables with umbrellas and coordinated table decorations, but not the posh cushioned loungers. For the most part, these tables were available, at least until the crowd hovering around the pergola thinned.

He had not quite pegged this group yet. All male, more sixtyish than fiftyish, impeccably dressed in slacks, hundred-dollar golf shirts, two hundred-dollar loafers — *sans* socks — gold chains, Rolexes, and even some with diamond studs drilled through their ear lobes that glinted in the late afternoon sun. They looked in the same direction concentrating on something. A few laughed, while others carried on sidebar discussions. Most, however, were spellbound, busy in some activity Gabe could not see. *Yep, retired executives, attorneys, business owners and probably some brokers and financial investment gurus thrown in the mix.*

Looking between the gaps in the executive crunch, he saw a beacon of hope — the bar. Tending it was a very attractive young girl who did not look a day over twenty years old, if that. *That explains their gripping fascination — a titillating, tempestuous diversion from their former trophies.* Now he understood why the neglected women seemed to wince each time they glanced in the direction of their husbands. *The Viagra crowd will stroke their egos at the expense of the young lass, only to end up with their reality later. Whoopee! The wives will get a little thrill later tonight, and all will be forgiven — until the next party and the women meet again. Then the gossip will fly. Hey hubby, you want to keep stroking that libido thing, just keep the dollars flowing for the Botox, golf and tennis lessons — and don't forget, you old limp coots, to fork over some extra dinero so we can tip the country club's towel boy Raul, oh, what a chiseled hunk — Ouu-la-la!*

He needed to refuel. However, he was reluctant to maneuver through the crowd of unknowns. Suffering in silence behind his mirrored sunglasses, waiting for the right opportunity, a timely rescue materialized. Several of the trophies approached the bar carrying empty cups. Good cover. Their conspicuous ploy worked. He overheard the trophies tell their aging studs they were virile, charming, and among the plantation's best movers and shakers — but also married. Seeing his opening, he moved fast before the second wave of newcomers found the bar.

As he neared the bar, the young girl disappeared. *Please come back, don't close! I need you. God, I hope she's just restocking essentials.*

Wading through the crowd of hyper-excited, testosterone driven men, he overheard one say, "She could be mine for a Ben Franklin." Another responded, "You wouldn't know what to do with her, Fred. I'll pony up a Franklin if you give my gal a bounce. It'll take the pressure off me for awhile and then my wife will appreciate I'm really a good thing."

Finally arriving at his destination, Gabe was relieved to see that she had not closed the bar. As he suspected, she stood with a handful of plastic cups and napkins.

"Miss."

The cute, honey blonde half turned toward him. Although the weather was mild, she had loosened the top three buttons of her blouse, exposing a large patch of tanned cleavage. With a perfunctory smile fixed on her face, she said, "Can I help ya — " Her blue-green flecked eyes laughed before she did. The forced smile turned genuine. "Ya look funny, mistah."

"Jeez, it's a conspiracy." He looked at the nametag pinned to her tuxedo style blouse. Then he saw a medallion that was vaguely familiar. "Miss Amber Reeves, I'll have you know that my mother insisted I wear knickers, suspenders and a bow tie. I protested vehemently and dressed myself."

Not quite in a deep southern Dixie accent, but more of a hill-country twang, she said, "You talks funny too, suh. What's up with those birth control glasses? They looks like they from one of those old movies my granddaddy used to watch on his black and white TV set."

"Young lady, I will have you know that James Dean, the Rebel, the man, the legend, wore shades like these the day he drove his sports car into oblivion and cinematic history." Putting on an air of hurt, he said, "Take it back, or this conversation and our relationship as bartender and charming bar patron, is over."

"Well, suh, we don't have a relationship. You not trying to pick me up, are ya, suh?"

Gabe blushed. "Miss, I…I did not mean to give you that impression. I apologize. I would never — "

"Mistah, slow down. Don't get your panties all in a wad. I know ya ain't flirtin' with me. I was juz playin' with ya. I may be from the sticks, but I'm pretty good at figurin' people out. Ya ain't no playa, suh. Too bad. Now what kin I get ya?"

Boy, this young woman doesn't need my help. "Simple tastes for a harmless old man. I will take a Bacardi and coke. Please make it a double, but no fruit."

With what might be viewed by others as a suggestive smile, she said, "Double Bacardi and coke, no lime. Suh, I think I can handle that order. I'm here to serve and please. If we're to continue this mastah-servant relationship, it would help if I knew ya name."

He held out his hand and lightly shook hers. "Name's Gabe. Pleased to meet you, Miss Amber Reeves. Nicole, my wife, is somewhere inside the house catching up with her friends. You should meet her shortly when she discovers that I'm MIA. When you do, please make her drink strong."

"Well, mistah Gabe, maybe ya is a playa. Liquor's quicker, right?"

Comfort level spiraling south again, Gabe said, "Um…let's shift gears, Miss Amber. I have not met the hosts. Can you tell me their names and give me a hint about how they look? Great party they're throwing. I'd like to thank them."

"Ya really don't belong here, do ya? Ya look like a fish out of water, as they say."

Amber pointed at the women lounging on the plush pillows near the far end of the pool and said, "Missus Sarah is sittin' over yonder, the one wearing the floral scarf. Bonar, well ya'll know him when ya see him. He has a way of makin' sure everyone's aware of his entrance. Yes, suh, he's kind of, well not kind of — ya'll know him when ya see him."

Gabe noted that Sarah Peterson was at the center of the trophy collection and Bonar was definitely a player. "Thanks for the heads up. So I don't belong here. Perceptive, Miss Amber. Please explain that to Nicole when you meet her. It'll save me some grief later. Young lady, I don't think you belong here either. This kind of a gathering of wolves can be dangerous."

Amber frowned, and waited a long time before she answered. Almost in a whisper, she said, "I needs tha money." Then, as if a switch had been flicked, she beamed and continued, "What Bonar has promised me fo tonight is more than I make in three nights at the Masters Gentleman's club. And if I'm good tonight, I think he'll pay more. He promised me that — "

She covered her mouth as if she had let out a trusted secret. After a few seconds, she touched Gabe's arm and winked at him. "You should come by and see my act. All the men ya age really like it."

Bowled over by her bluntness, yet in spite of his embarrassment, he forged ahead into dangerous territory. "I'm sure they do enjoy your act, but I'll pass. I already have a lady in my — Miss Amber, it looks like you may have a man in your life. The necklace you're wearing, I was trying to place it. Then I remembered it is a Saint Michael's medallion, patron saint of paratroopers. You must have a soldier out there somewhere."

She held the pendant close to her face and studied it briefly. "So that's what it is." She let go, allowing it to settle between her breasts. "Yeah, I have a soldja out there. The only thing he gave me waz stretch marks and this dang piece of metal that ain't worth nothin'. Oh yeah, and a monthly allotment check, while he's out playin' in tha desert over there. Ya wouldn't know how much make-up I use to cova them damn stretch marks. Don't get me wrong, I finally got ma washboard flat belly back and ma legs — well they fine, at least tha's what I been told."

Wow, feel sorry for that soldier. This girl's advertising with a neon sign to every Jody out there — you pay, we play. Jody, the generic name assigned to the scourge and fear of every deployed soldier. Jody stays at home, drives the soldier's car, uses his razor, sleeps in his bed and screws his girl.

"I assume that the tan line on your finger is from a wedding ring. Did you marry that soldier?"

Amber stared at the aging rebel for several moments. "Well, mistah Gabe, I don't really know if that's any ya business." She broke off her intense stare and looked down at the bar's surface, plucked a swizzle from a plastic container and stuck it between her teeth. After several chews, she threw it in a garbage can. Then she looked up at him. "Yeah, we's married, but not fa long. What he wants in life and what I want are two different thangs. His idea of the good life is a pickup truck and me pregnant. Sure, he got me out of West Virginia all right, but then takes off to play army while I have to play momma." She threw out her arms, and nodded. "I want this and he sure ain't gonna get it for me. He's a damn hillbilly hick. I'm better than that."

Happy she could not see his eyes, Gabe said, "Well I hope you get what you want. Here's what I want. I want — "

"Mistah Gabe…I thinks I knows what ya want, but what I can give ya may not be what ya hope for. Besides, I'm spoken for tonight."

I hope soldier Reeves can find a cheap divorce lawyer. He's not going to get the homecoming he's been dreaming about. "Miss Amber, what I want….Listen, I tend to go overboard sometimes with the rum. If it looks like I'm heading to the netherworld can you slow me down?"

"Sure. Like I always say, I'm here to please. Ya look like ya may be fun when ya go overboard. Where's this netha world anyways? Is it like Disney World?"

"Don't worry Miss Amber, you'll find it someday. You've made a good start."

Flashing a smile at him, she giggled. "I can't wait. That netha world must be a good place." Pointing to a patio table close to the party police, she said, "Ya see that old man who's sitting by hisself over yonder? The one smoking a cigarette?"

Gabe nodded.

"That be Clemson. Ya needs to join him. He talks funny like ya'll do. He dresses funny, too. A loner. Sho' nuff, everybody will come by and see him sometime, but they'll all leave. I'll tell ya what, ya put a handsome tip in ma jar and when ya'll ready for a fresh one, I'll bring 'em to ya."

"Well thank you for the good advice. I will join him. Is twenty enough to keep us fueled for awhile?"

"Why thank ya, suh."

"My pleasure, Miss Amber. Best to arrive bearing gifts. What's Clemson drinking?"

"Scotch neat. Ya might as well carry two. I think he may stay ahead of ya."

While Amber was busy preparing the drinks, Gabe thought about the earlier, overheard conversation. *A Ben Franklin. No, not more than a Ulysses Grant. Hell, more like an Andrew Jackson. Amber, a trophy in training. Careful girl, trophies have a way of tarnishing and gathering dust.*

Deftly balancing three drinks in his hands, Gabe negotiated the growing crowd and approached the table. Clemson's glazed eyes, trapped in a suntanned, leathery and craggy, pockmarked face, followed Gabe's approach with mild curiosity.

Gabe did not think Clemson was dressed funny. In fact, his shirt, shorts and sandals looked like they were purchased at the same store where Gabe found his. Arriving with a smile, he said, "Sir, I have been told by a very knowledgeable sage that you do not like people, but do enjoy a good Scotch. May I join you?"

"Why sure, son, pull up a chair. Your sage is dead-on about the Scotch, but wrong about the other. Hell, I find most people to be very entertaining. Why, look at you. I'm already entertained. The two of us might be mistaken as pool boys by this crowd. We should put out a tip

46

jar." He stood and extended his hand to Gabe. "I'm Clemson Huntley. Pleased to meet you, sir."

He set the drinks on the table, then shook hands. "Gabe Quinn. Nicole's husband."

"So you're the mystery man in her life. Don't see much of you around here, except the few times you've been on the porch. Didn't you just return from Iraq?"

"Last month." Gabe sat next to him and said, "I'm glad you know Nicole. I was hoping she was meeting the neighbors and settling in. Great neighborhood. I especially the like the security of a guarded gate."

"It's an exceptional neighborhood, especially after you learn all of its dirty little secrets. Don't know if the gate is supposed to keep the nuts out or us in. But that's not what you want to hear, just back from over there." Clemson gulped down one of the two Scotches Gabe brought then lit another cigarette. "My bride, gets along great with Nicole. They compare grandkids. How does the Plantation compare to Iraq?"

"I lived in a gated neighborhood there also." Gabe grinned and continued, "No themed parties with Mimosas, though."

"Good to be home, I bet. How is the war going, Gabe? We winning?"

"Listening to the news here, it's like, well, sort of like what war. Our military's dealing with everything thrown at them. You gotta love those kids, they're America's best, the cream of society — givers not the takers. Each day, they get up and kick *hajji's* ass. Never complain, they just do it. Someone said it better than I ever could. Clemson, you ever heard of Emma Sky?"

"Can't say that I have. Who is she, Gabe?"

"I didn't have a clue about her either, until I read an article in the Stars and Stripes. She's a British academic who followed General Odierno around Iraq. Odd pairing, him a career soldier, her, a staunch pacifist. When a journalist asked her what she thought about our soldiers and Marines, she said America doesn't deserve them. I'm not keen on Brits, and definitely not peace freaks, but she's absolutely right. But in this country, it seems like nobody gives a damn — the war's just a distraction, something that pops up on the news every once in awhile. Not their problem, doesn't affect them, merely an inconvenience. No weapons of mass destruction, no Iraqis in those planes on nine-eleven, Bush's war, not theirs. Ah, screw it, what's the point. Clemson, tell me the advantages of Scotch over Bacardi. I'm in the market for a new kind of high."

Four similarly dressed Viagra candidates approached their refuge just as Clemson finished the second Scotch and Gabe drained his first.

"Clemson, I see you found my bar," the leader of the pack said. "Who's your friend?"

"Bonar, as long as your bar stays stocked, I'm freeloading. Meet fellow pool boy and soon to be Scotch drinker, Gabe Quinn. Gabe, meet the host, Bonar Peterson."

Gabe stood and shook hands with Bonar. "Mr. Peterson, pleased to meet you, sir. You have a beautiful piece of paradise here and a wonderful party. Thanks for the invite."

"Yes, it is paradise and a wonderful party," he said. "I invested wisely and made bold decisions at the right times. I decided it was time to spread the joy around when the market rewards my genius. But I don't recall inviting you — wait a minute. Quinn…you must be Nicole's husband."

"My apologies," Gabe said. "I should've come by before the party and introduced myself."

"Think nothing of it. Allow me to introduce these other fine gentlemen. This wily looking character is Fred Durst, formerly of Bear Stearns. Watch him closely — you blink, that's an invitation for him to get inside your wallet. The educated looking one is John Varner, my scoundrel attorney. Sorry for the redundancy. Finally, George Miklos. I'm not quite sure what he does, other than carry a four handicap, the bastard. Together, we are the foursome from hell on the links."

Shaking hands with each, Gabe said, "Gentlemen, nice to meet you. One day I hope to try a round of golf. Is the Plantation's course challenging?"

"For my three partners here," George said, "a putt-putt course is a challenge. My toughest challenge is containing my laughter."

"You're so full of it," Bonar said. He glared at George before he sat next to Clemson. "Gabe, to answer your question, the course is in great shape, especially after I had the groundskeeper fired. He used the wrong fertilizer on the fairways and failed to cut the greens in the proper direction. The idiot didn't understand bent grass must be mowed at a very exacting angle to the ocean. My God, the man is a damn simpleton. I hope he's enjoying his work with the wetbacks and eating the homeless shelter's cuisine."

"Bonar," Fred said, "speaking of cuisine, what are you doing about the country club's chef? Last night my lobster was tough, the mushy asparagus was wrapped in some terrible prosciutto, and the salad…let me tell you about — "

"Fred," Bonar interrupted. "On top of it, my friend. Not for public consumption yet, but I'm recruiting the chef from Wachesaw Plantation. We're trying to get his salary request down to reality. He believes he's some kind of a gastronomy artiste, not just a short order cook dressed in a poplin chef's hat and coat. More changes are coming. The wait staff…well, what can I say — a little long in the tooth. We need some young, vibrant, sexy girls at the club. The piece I have behind the bar tonight, Amber something…I brought her on for a try-out."

Fred ogled Amber and said, "You did good, first rate, Bonar. In fact, I wouldn't mind giving her a try-out and do things to her that a seasoned — "

"No, no, no, Fred," Bonar said. "I hired her. Young, hungry, poor and given the proper motivation, willing. Her audition is mine. Leave it alone, old boy."

Silent during the exchange, Clemson stared at his empty cup. Gabe tapped his leg and whispered, "You ready for another?"

"Bring three. I feel unclean for some reason."

As soon as Gabe stood, several of the ex-trophies quickly moved in to take their places next to their men. Gabe doubted their interest had anything to do with them, but more to do with Clemson. His grizzled exterior was a repellant to some, but to others, just a crust to be picked at, scraped, chiseled and pierced to get to the fruit within. Gabe recalled a few things Nicole told him about his new friend. Clemson held an abundance of the drug of the partiers' choice — money. The trophies, certainly as shallow as their mates, and obvious in their attempt to form an alliance to separate Clemson from some of that drug, rushed in. Everyone knew he was the alcoholic millionaire of the Plantation.

Clemson, unquestionably an alcoholic, but a functioning one, was still on his game. Gabe had little doubt the man knew the scent of wolves and their pack mentality. Yet he paused, thinking he should hang around a little longer to make sure Clemson could deal with the threat — *never leave a buddy behind.*

Clemson pushed his chair further away from the table and allowed them free access to their men — also to fix an invisible barrier to shield him from their pitiless coldness. To add a little more insulation, he lit a cigarette, purposely sending the smoke clouds in their direction.

Clemson can handle these pups. Confident his friend was secure and safe, Gabe was happy to escape but not looking forward to another possibly embarrassing encounter with Amber. He gave in to the rum calling. *Keep it simple. Soldier-boy Reeves is not the first one screwed over by a slut.*

She was bent down behind the bar restocking supplies again. He leaned across the bar and said, "Amber, I need two more Scotches and two Bacardis."

"No fruit, suh. See, I remembered." She looked up at him. "I met ya wife and as requested, I made her drink a double. She seems like a nice lady and I think she'll give ya a very nice time later."

"Yeah, Nicole is a very nice person. Her only flaw is me. Miss Amber, the netherworld is calling out to me and I have accepted its invitation. Disregard my prior request."

"Like I said, I am here to pleez ya. More rum and cokes on the way, suh."

Amber stood with a fresh bottle of Bacardi in one hand, a canned Coke in the other. She poured two cups almost to the rim with the rum, and then splashed the tops with the soft drink. After handing him one drink, she placed a napkin under the other and set it near the edge of the bar. As if waiting for his approval, she stared at him with an expectant smile at the corner of her mouth.

He downed one of the rums.

"Strong enough?" Amber asked.

"Perfect." He dropped another twenty in the tip jar. Turning away from the bar, Gabe surveyed his surroundings, searching for a familiar face. He saw Nicole talking with several of the women sitting in the cheap seats. Once eye contact was made, she smiled. *Thank you Amber, the plan is gelling.*

"Amber," he said, "one more request. Freshen my drink and give Nicole a double of whatever she's having."

Nicole paused by each table on her way to meet Gabe. She was obviously enjoying the effects of her drink. As she made her way, she winked.

She has plans for this evening. Maybe a delay in the worn and tested 'I am running off again' speech would be wise. A little 'birthday sex' could be in the offing. Even I need to scratch that itch occasionally. Damn, I'm a dog. But then again, all is fair in love and war. No, not my style — mission creep. "Nicole, I take it you're having fun?"

She giggled in a style peculiar to her after she had a few drinks.

Dabbling in French, inadvertently elongating words and adding emphasis to the wrong syllables, she said, "*C'est magnifique!* Have you seen the inside of the Peterson's palace? It's reeaallly neeaat! They have an actual Dali hanging in the dining room."

With a puzzled look, Gabe said, "Dali?"

"You know, Salvador Dali. Bonar took the time to explain his art to me. Did you know Dali — "

"Nope, haven't met him, but if he's at the party I'm sure I will." Gabe held up a fresh Mojito and said, "Have another. I was thinking that after the party...maybe the two of us, and my new friend Clemson and his wife...well, maybe we could head over to the Islander for a couple of drinks and some music. What do you think?"

She winked, and in her southern accented attempt at annihilating the French language, said, "*Fantastique! Certainement!*"

Piss poor prior planning promotes piss poor results. Ah, but proper planning produces the preferred result. Maybe that's not the saying, but it works. "Great. Enjoy yourself, and party on! Another hour or so, we head out, okay?"

"*Je vous comprenez, mon chef!* Tonight your wish is my command. Roger dodger and all that military stuff." Still giggling, she said, "And if you find Dali, invite him."

Got her! This could go well. Returning to his table, he saw that Clemson looked pensive, as if cornered, about to be served up as the main course in a feeding frenzy. Three people firing concurrent salvos at him, they had him bracketed. *Give the man some space, people. Jeez, he's my pool buddy.* Just within earshot, he caught part of Bonar's pitch.

"Clemson, I promise you this is better than an investment. It's golden. In the bag, my friend. We're almost through the details for the long-term lease and with your initial investment of a quarter million...well, let me tell you — "

"Gabe, where've you been with my drink?" Clemson's expression was one of relief, bordering on salvation. "I thought you had run off to Iraq again."

Bonar's head snapped toward Gabe. "You were in Iraq?"

He smells fresh meat. Gabe's alarm bells sounded and the sensors not yet dulled by the rum activated. "Yes."

Sizing him up like he was prey, Bonar said, "I hear a lot of money's being made in Iraq. Are you one of those mercenaries making the big bucks?"

"Mercenary? No. More like a voyeur, but not in the popular

51

sense, though. Big bucks? Not really, but enough."

Bonar eyed him for several seconds before he pounced. "Hmm…I was just discussing a proposal…an investment I should say, with Clemson. It is only available to a few — "

"Mr. Peterson, I appreciate you considering me in your scheme. Sorry, wrong word. Investment opportunity."

Gabe saw a crack in Bonar's polished façade. *What the hell, I don't even like this guy. Over the years, I've dealt with human waste and met plenty of his type*

"My idea of an investment is a good set of work boots, jeans and a solid pickup truck. I'm lost if it gets beyond simple and tangible. I'm more of a touch, smell, taste, and see type guy. Nicole's my investment manager. She handles all of the finances and does quite well. We don't need much and she makes sure we have that and a little bit more. But, thanks for your consideration."

Stung, Bonar punched back. With an air of superiority, he said, "Well I can certainly understand that. Investments beyond boots, pants and a truck do carry a measure of risk."

One punch was not enough. As if the word disgusted him, Bonar said, "*Iraq*! I support our troops. They're fine men and women, but I certainly don't support Bush's war — Cheney getting rich from the Halliburton contracts, Abu Ghraib, no end in sight. What a mistake."

Happy to be in the presence of one so gifted, Bonar's entourage looked at him with adulation as if he were the second coming, some kind of a magnanimous, astute, erudite champion.

"Bonar — " Gabe checked himself. *There it is again. Let it go. Rum makes me stupid. Support the troops but not the war, the new mantra for the post Vietnam guilt over the shameful treatment dished out to our returning warriors. It should be a bumper sticker. Probably is. You don't think our adversaries study history. They know all too well that the will of the American public is vapid, constantly changing directions, committed to a cause only if it lasts no longer than a sit-com.*

The enemy knows one Jane Fonda is worth ten brigades in the field. Fonda, silent for a generation, has been replaced by the other Hollywood elites, the politicos, and your Jody-ass. Yes, and all of your Jody buddies, Bonar. You deserve the Ambers of this world — two peas in a pod. Aid and comfort to the enemy…aid and comfort. While you put it to the wives and girlfriends of the ones you support with your phony smile, they make the sacrifices. Sure, throw it out anytime the war comes up. See, I support you guys, just keep it clean, and, oh yeah, thanks for your women.

War's not antiseptic. People get hurt, people die. War is foul, dirty, bloody. It's a gut wrenching, gut-checking affair, but necessary. How can you separate the troops from the war? You can't. They don't ask for your support. In fact, stay the hell out of it, don't judge, let them do their job. Do you think they decide which war is the good war? No. There is the enemy — kill him. It's like separating cops from the crimes they try to stop. I support you officer, but must you do your job? Do I need to remind you, Bonar, their job keeps your unappreciative ass safe?

Abu Ghraib, are you kidding? See through my eyes if you want to know what real abuse looks like. See through the eyes of any soldier who deals with the aftermath of clearing a torture room. Do you know that a drill has many uses? Do you know what can be done with a simple tablespoon? How about a wood chipper? Piece of wire? Screwdriver? Straight pin?

I can't believe I'm listening to this four flusher whose only service is to himself and his libido. The uninitiated, the takers in our society. You don't get a vote until you play in my sand box, Bonar. You don't support the troops — they're just a convenient cocktail party conversation piece. Leave 'em alone, stay the hell out of the way. They could care less about your support. They do care about the war. They eat, sleep, and breathe war twenty-four hours every day, not only when they are downrange, but also when they return to a place that will never be home again. You never return home. War is a one-way ticket.

How about this for a bumper sticker — be polite, be professional, but have a plan to kill every son of a bitch you meet because they may want to kill you. Add Jody to that sticker and we'll have a winnah. Try supporting that, all of you friggin' Bonars of America.

Gabe, not realizing the conversation had shifted gears three times since Bonar espoused his stale, pious diatribe, looked at him and said, "That's nice."

Midstream in another conversation with Fred, Bonar turned to Gabe with a puzzled expression. "Huh?"

Gabe ignored him. Thoroughly involved in his trip to the netherworld, he retreated from the table and the boorish conversation. Moving his chair closer to the patio's edge, he lit a cigarette, ignorant of, or not caring about, the obvious disapproval by all at the table — except, of course, Clemson. Clemson was well along in his trip, too. There was no talking between him and Gabe — more a clairvoyant

53

understanding of the words not spoken and the journey's final destination.

Several drinks later, Gabe was forcibly reengaged into the aimless bantering. Coming out of his self-imposed silence and cerebral voyage to better places, he noticed that several more revelers had joined the conversation. Nicole was not one of them. He would have hated her to be sucked in to this vacuum. *Stay with the Mojitos, babe. They have a purpose.*

Bonar, still leading the congregation, looked at Clemson and said, "What do you think of golden boy Michael Vick and his current predicament?"

Before Clemson could formulate a response, one of the trophies, shook her head and contorted her face in feigned, or real, disgust — hard to tell with all of the Botox that had been pumped into her shiny little forehead — and said, "He is disgusting. How any person could do that to a dog is beyond comprehension. He should rot in prison."

Several other women nodded agreement. One said, "You go, girl."

Clemson remained silent, as if hoping to be entertained by the upcoming discussion.

Bonar turned toward Gabe and asked, "What do you think?"

For the first time during the discussion, all were silent, waiting to see if the pool boy wanted to dance with the master. They would need to wait because Gabe, more than a little touched by the rum, failed to take a position. In fact, he was unaware that a position was needed. "Who is Michael Vick?"

Fred Durst smirked. "You don't follow sports?"

Sports? I guess that's a safe subject for a party — can't get in trouble with that one — Nicole will be pleased. But I don't know a thing about the who, what, when or the where trivia concerning current sports heroes. I haven't been interested in sports since my school days. This is what's important in America? Sports? What the hell, I'll play. "Sure. I caught some of the World Series last year on the Armed Forces Network. I'm sorry, but I can't tell you who won or even who played."

Bonar jumped in for his piece of the thrashing. "World Series? We're talking football. You know the American version, not that wimpy-ass European 'futbol' soccer crap. Michael Vick — quarterback — Atlanta Falcons. Gabe, a quarterback is an offensive position, sort of the maestro on the field. Atlanta Falcons, an NFL team hailing from…you guessed it…Atlanta, Georgia. Ring a bell?"

Gabe took another quick pull on his drink, but still not knowing whom they were talking about, attempted a fake. "Sure the Atlanta Falcons, I knew that. Good team and Victor's a pretty good quarterback."

Bonar laughed and said, "Victor? The name's Vick and I think the past tense is more appropriate. You really don't know who he is? Where in hell have you been living, under a rock? Vick has been indicted for dog fighting and killing eight pit bulls."

Feeling a fire in his belly, the alcohol level well beyond legal for driving, much less coherent thought, Gabe boarded the train leaving the station. "I like cats — they eat rats. I don't have much use for dogs."

Sarah Peterson moved her sunglasses to the top of her head and looked sternly at him. "My precious Pierre is more than just a dog. He sleeps with me, eats from my table and goes to the hairdresser with me. Why, we do everything together! He is like my child. What Vick did to those poor animals was like killing his own children. Despicable, scandalous! My God, a dog is man's best friend and certainly a woman's."

The train picked up speed and was approaching a curve at way, way, way too much speed. A wall up ahead there somewhere. The rebel stoked the firebox. "Maybe some man's best friend, but not mine. A pack of dogs can clean a corpse in less than an hour. I mean clean — everything — stripped right down to the marrow. I've never seen a cat do that. But one cat can keep three tents clear of rats for a year."

Bonar, apparently enjoying some great entertainment for his guests, kept pushing. "Let me get this straight. You believe Vick did mankind a favor?"

Train, train, train's a comin' — choo-choo-choo, here it comes, can't stop it now — a train wreck in the making. The rum had done its job — the demons had been unleashed — he had crossed netherworld's threshold.

Oblivious to the contemptuous looks directed his way, Gabe spoke. "We had dogs in my camp. Unauthorized. Violation of General Order Number one. No pets allowed. Cats were overlooked. They had a purpose — killing rats. Dogs are nothin' but, flea-ridden, disease carryin' mongrels. Shit, there's a thousand ways to die in Iraq, but a dog bite? Give me a fucking break. I'd sooner take a bullet to the brain pan."

After pausing to drain his drink, Gabe continued, "We had

a couple of female contractors in our camp. No real purpose for them, more like someone's furniture. Forty of us guys and these two airheads. Three shower stalls for the whole lot of us. Of course, the ladies had to have a private shower. That left the rest of us to compete for the other two stalls. You know how dirty you can get in the desert? A shower once a week is a fucking luxury. Well these gals take in this bitch about to whelp. It did. Oh yeah, seven pups. And where do these geniuses hide the bitch and its litter? In one of our shower stalls, leaving forty of us competing for one stall while the two ladies enjoy their private stall, and the dogs pissing and crapping all over the other. Someone dropped a dime, so in comes the Army medical officer saying, 'this is in direct violation of General Order Number one. Unsanitary. The dogs go. Not to the perimeter; they'll return. Kill them. You created the problem. Take care of it.'"

Gabe lit another cigarette, inhaled and then studied the red cherry burning at its tip. Exhaling the blue grey smoke towards the sky, he looked at Bonar and grinned. "We got sufficiently juiced at choir practice sittin' around the fire pit we built between the T walls... excuse me, blast walls. We took care of it. We fucked up on the first pup. One guy grabbed it around its haunches, wound it up above his head like a sling and flung it against the wall. Splat! Wrong plan, very messy, plus it kind of squirmed around for a few minutes. Of course the bitch started going crazy on us yelping, jumping, snapping and all. Have another drink, boys. We did the bitch next. K-bar to the throat. Again not a good plan. It kind of walked and flopped around letting out soundless barks spurting blood everywhere including our fire pit. Have another drink, boys."

Gabe stopped and looked at his empty cup. "Where's my fucking drink?" He reached across and grabbed Clemson's half-full Scotch from his hand, drank it and threw the plastic cup onto the patio.

"We got smart. The cleanest and quickest way to do the deed was to hold the pup in your hands, belly down, while another slowly drove the K-bar through the back of its neck. You know, high up between the shoulder blades. Keep drivin' until you hear a little pop. I don't know shit about dog anatomy but there was a lot less blood, no real squirming, quieter and a hell of a lot easier to clean up. All done in five minutes. The timing was perfect for me. We had a competition going on about the best name for our fire pit. It was staring up at me from the ground. Seven dead puppies and a bitch saloon. Naw, cats are better than dogs. They eat rats."

The train hit the wall.

Gabe's audience was in shock. Baring a variety of disgusted, angered expressions, they pushed away from the table. Some shook their heads. Others looked nauseous. All stood and backed away.

Standing above him, looking triumphant, Bonar smiled. "Gabe, you need to leave now. Clemson, you can stay." Then he turned his attention to Amber and was gone.

As the host left, Nicole approached. She walked the way some people do when they hit their limit — exaggerated, careful toe to heel steps.

"Gabe. What happened? What'd you do this time?"

Still roaming the netherworld, Gabe looked at her but did not see.

Clemson threw a lifeline. "Gabe did nothing. We were just talking about pets. Nicole, Gabe mentioned earlier about going over to the Islander for some fun. You ready?"

"Leeet's dooo it," she squealed. "I wanna try one of those fruity things with an umbrella stuck in it."

"Nicole, you round up my wife and we'll head over."

Clemson placed his hand on Gabe's shoulder and said, "Gabe... Gabe...let's go, son. Time for us pool boys to swim in another pool. This one's closed."

Chapter 6
The astronaut

Nirvana Motel, Room 1214, Myrtle Beach, SC, June 5, 0430 hours—only thing missing was the red light

He didn't know — he had no reason to even suspect. But she had used him as much as he did her. She lifted his cupped hand from her breast. Then she peeled the top sheet from her side of the bed, completely exposing her body to the ocean breeze drifting through the curtains. Sore, she lingered on the stained fitted sheet long enough to make sure he was still asleep. Satisfied he was, she slipped from the bed and tiptoed toward the open balcony.

The faint song of seagulls rose above the sounds of waves lapping against the sand. As she crossed the door's threshold, a surprised gull squawked before taking off in a panicked flight. She froze. Hearing a slight stir behind her, she waited. He tossed some, but did not wake. She inched the slider across its sea-salt pitted track until only a slight gap remained.

A gust raced up the wall from twelve stories below and blew her hair back. Just as suddenly, another flurry hit her broadside and whipped her raven tresses across her face. She brushed the hair from her eyes and stepped closer to the edge until her navel touched the balcony railing's cold metal. She did not shiver — she still had a fever between her legs that warmed her. Standing naked before the fading moon, she savored her soreness. It had been a night she would replay repeatedly until the memory dulled, and finally was forgotten.

Sounds of his labored breathing snuck through the sliding door's gap. She studied his nude body. He showed the signs of age. Probably in his late forties, sparse hair sprinkled with grey where the Grecian formula had washed thin, muscle tone gone, flabby, the way of a former athlete growing old — he was married. The ring was missing, but she knew. She liked it that way. It was one of her rules — no entanglements, anonymous, uncomplicated. Just sex.

He had told her his name, but probably not his real one. Fair, even expected. She rarely used her real name, and then only for official documents. Most men leered at her when she said it — Miracle. The name was cute in her youth, but as she reached puberty, she decided to shorten it to Mira. She could do nothing about her last name.

She smiled as she thought about their lovemaking. He had wanted to toast their anticipated union. She declined, preferring sobriety and clear thinking — another rule in her life. She would choose the time to surrender control and only on her terms. When she did, she relished her captivity and the freedom it brought.

He knew he would have her, but did not rush. He led her down the path. She knew he would. That is why she chose him. She had learned in her twenty-three years that older men were more appreciative than her contemporaries were. Thankful, more than that — reverent. She had experienced boys but found them to be inadequate. They did not give her the punishment, the absolution she wanted. It was all about their needs. Their concept of sexual arousal was a few drinks, boasts about their prowess, a mauling of her breasts as if they were not a part of her. And the only foreplay; fellatio. Never any consideration for her needs. Only theirs. Wham-bam, thanks, you whore! Damn, that was good for me. I'm finished with you so get dressed and get out, bitch. Tossed like trash.

Not anymore, those days were long gone. Now her lovers slowly awakened her passion, exploring the shadows, the nooks, the mysteries, before entering her secret garden. She enjoyed their touch, the adventure, the building, the explosion. Older men needed to prove something, not to her, but to themselves. In her mind, they were just a tool to fix a need. She rewarded them with intimacy so visceral her primordial beast broke free and consumed them. When her beast was unleashed, they could do what they wanted with her. They owned her. She was theirs to be exploited — a pleasure to be dominated. She could handle rough. She enjoyed being conquered.

Her thoughts mixed with the pounding waves. *Is there more than just pounding, more than bumps and grinds? The next lover, yes, the next time, we will talk. Nothing important, just spoken intercourse to ease the guilt that will sneak in later. Next time maybe. But now he must go.*

Enjoying the freedom of her nakedness, she searched the watery desert below. There was nothing there — only a link to another desert six thousand miles distant. She must also go. It was her time. Yet the steady drone of the waves captivated her. The constant murmur took her home.

Her adoptive, barren mother, had named her. Victoria thought the discarded infant was a miracle. She said Mira's real mother had abandoned her in a dumpster during the coldest winter to hit west Texas in half a century. Mira survived for two days in the bin, nearly frozen, hungry and soiled along with the other trash. A motorist had stopped to relieve himself and heard her cries. The story made the local news. Victoria heard about the miracle child and convinced her husband that she was the baby they needed.

Mira never said his name. Not even dad or daddy was allowed, only father or sir. Prodded by Victoria, father spoke to Jesus and sought his guidance. Father, a Southern Baptist preacher, often spoke to Jesus. They had a connection. Jesus told father that Miracle was a blessed creature who should be saved and exposed to the glory of father's secrets. The preacher, his Victoria and Miracle were family.

Victoria doted on her miracle baby. Numb to all else, her world had become the miracle. Sure, she faithfully muddled through the mundane chores of being a preacher's wife, like keeping the house ready for the unannounced parishioners' visits. She was dutiful to her husband's calling and the endless prayer meetings, Wednesday meetings, visitations, youth ministry, choir practices, Sunday sermons, funerals, weddings, baptisms, hospital visits, church bazaars. She did it all; all with her Miracle in tow. Victoria did not have the same calling as her husband, but she suffered through it nonetheless, because that is what a preacher's wife did. She wanted more for her baby. Victoria could not escape her prison of a life, but she would through Miracle. She vowed to give her daughter the knowledge and education that would guarantee Miracle could avoid a similar fate.

Father took little interest in Miracle, other than to remind her that she was a sinner, a vagrant to this world, saved by him and the great sacrifice of Jesus. He left her earthly nurturing to Victoria — until her ninth birthday.

As the moon died and the burgeoning colors of the living sun appeared, a tear slipped onto Mira's cheek. She barely heard the sound of the door sliding. Another tear broke free.

Fingers gently stroked the nape of her neck.

Mira recoiled, almost falling over the railing. She spun around, her flailing arms lashing out. "Don't touch me!" she screamed. "No more, please, no more. Please, father, no more."

"You crazy whore, I'm not your daddy!"

She stared at the reflection in the mirror. Animated by the flickering, near-dead fluorescent light, the damage to her body seemed to move. Fresh bruises pulsed on her breast and arms, blood trickled from her swollen lip. The beating was bad, but not as bad as others had been. She deserved, needed, planned, and hoped for it — the true climax she sought. His role was defined just as hers was.

Father's right. I am a sinner, a vagrant in this life. Father is the absolver, as are the other men. He gave me absolution. They give me absolution now. I am penitent, Jesus. Forgive me.

She was in control again and ready to return to her other life.

Staring at the crumpled dress thrown underneath the bathroom sink during the peak of the passion, she smiled. She looked good in red. The color set off her shoulder length jet-black hair that in sunlight sometimes shimmered blue. It also accented her ghostly grey-blue eyes that drew men in. The low cut neckline made her rarely sun-touched, flawless white skin and breasts, radiate like a beacon to her candidates. The tightness of the short dress hinted at the toned, flat abdomen beneath the silk — perfection reaped from countless push-ups, sit-ups and crunches. The high heels forced her ankles and calves to an unnatural angle that helped define her strong body, shaped and muscled by daily five-mile runs.

Before each escapade, she replaced the cross with a necklace and added blue topaz earrings. The other piece of jewelry she removed — identification tags. A simple piece of rolled stainless steel stamped with her surname, given name, social security number, blood type, and religion. A piece of metal that defines her life. Loving, Miracle, 265-45-3…, A negative, Protestant.

Lieutenant Loving, US Army, had escaped west Texas soon after her high school graduation. Victoria had made sure Mira received the public domain's education along with more intense home schooling. Mira embraced the words, the numbers, the ideas, and the theories. There were few options for a vagrant from a small west Texas town, but with a perfect score on the SAT, math tutors and her mother's help, Mira was one of several hundred who walked through West Point's gate in 2002.

She enjoyed the regimen and cadence of the academy, but mostly the constant control over her. She discovered that there was more in life than church, obedience and submission to the 'sir'. She was not bridled with thoughts of a future like those of her high school friends — marriage, children, brick rancher with a minivan parked in the garage. Father had closed that door, killing her womb before it had a chance to form properly. The Army gave her a sense of being, a place where she was no longer a vagrant in this world. The Army was her 'sir' now. At least most of the time, until she needed to visit the other 'sir'.

West Point had been a challenge. Many of the barriers had been lowered by former female cadets, but not all. She was still viewed as an oddity, a threat, and by some as a potential conquest. Their attitudes drove her, shaped her, led her, but never defeated her. She had rules formed in her earlier years to block out the 'sir,' and to keep herself in control when necessary. She was in control most of the time.

Prior to graduation, she returned to Texas, but only for the funeral. Victoria was taken by Jesus in 2003. Mira wept from a distance, never allowing the 'sir' to know she was there. Providence, divine coincidence, or Jesus sent a message to her —the Columbia space shuttle tearing across that cold February sky at the very moment her mother was returned to the earth. Victoria was now safe in the presence of the real father. As the Columbia remains littered the Texas landscape, she was hit with an epiphany of sorts. Mira decided that she would use the Army to keep her far away from the animal. She would never step on west Texas dirt again. Her future was over the horizon, under a different sky with a better view of the stars. Mira wanted to get closer to her mother and to her own salvation.

It was time to return to Ft. Bragg. There was much busy work to do at the 82nd Airborne Division, 5th Brigade Combat Team's headquarters. In less than three weeks, the brigade would be in Iraq — her first deployment. She would campaign hard to make Colonel Erickson take notice of her. If she stood out and kept her other life under the radar, chances would be greatly enhanced that he would approve her package for selection to the NASA training program. She was not a warrior, but fifteen months in another desert was a small price to pay for a ride to the heavens.

Lieutenant Miracle Loving stuffed the red dress in her purse and dropped the key on the dresser as she headed off to war.

Chapter 7
Mission. What mission?

Pawleys Island, June 7, 1015 hours

The vibration roused him. Then the steady beep-beep-beep pissed him off.

"What the fuck," Gabe said. "All right, already. I'm awake, damnit!"

Confused and suffocating in an azure sea, he beat against the blue only to become more tangled. He relaxed for a moment to collect his thoughts. It didn't help. The fight was back on with a renewed vigor. Finally, he grabbed a handful, ripped and tore until he unraveled the tarp. Wheezing from the fight, he scooted back against the bed's sidewall and reached down for the pack of Marlboros in his cargo shorts. The shorts were gone, he only wore polka dot boxers. Then he saw them hanging from the edge of the pickup's tailgate next to his cell phone.

Where in hell am I? What happened? Clarity seeped in. Panic returned. He needed to calm down. He snatched the shorts from the tailgate and fumbled through all five pockets before he found a crumpled pack of cigarettes. He found a book of matches with the logo for the Islander Bar stuck in his wallet. Squinting against the sun, it dawned on him where he was — home, in his truck, parked in the driveway. The where of the riddle had been solved, but not what happened.

He crawled to the rear of the truck bed, rolled the tarp into a blue mass and sat on it. Digging through the pack, he found a single, intact cigarette. *Home alone, one smoke to my name, hung-over. Fantastic.*

The rest of the story slowly unfolded. The prior evening had gone well enough, he thought, but then again he could only remember the high points — like Nicole throwing a drink in his face after he said he was returning to Iraq. Then she yelled something about him not caring about her, or the grandchildren.

"Yeah, they're great kids. What are their names again?" He messed up a few more times after that.

As the fog lifted and memories sharpened, he turned pensive. *Maybe it didn't go all that well.* He shook the gloom off and smiled.

She'll forgive me, she always does. Then more painful tidbits emerged from the fog.

"Sure," she said, "you go, you're not here anyway. You love that desert so damn much. Well, screw you! I may not be here if you return, but I'll pray for you."

It should have ended there on a high note, but it had not been that kind of a night. "Nicole, don't pray for me, you'll jinx me."

Massaging his aching jaw stimulated the other gaffes to percolate through the forced temperance filter. "I love you, Sabirra." Why he said that was not clear. Maybe it was something Nicole said, a look she gave him, or just the effects of alcohol. Whatever the reason, it had sparked a forgotten memory of the young woman.

Nicole slapped him hard across his face and screamed, "You bastard! Who's Sabirra?"

That must be when we took it outside the bar. "It's not what you think, babe. She's just an Iraqi girl I — "

Gabe rubbed his stinging groin. He should have seen it coming, but Nicole's kick had caught him completely unaware. He was no saint, not even a defrocked monk, but he also was not a Lothario. Through decades of marriage, he had been tempted, but he never took the gigantic leap into infidelity. Sabirra meant a lot to him, but not as a lover. She was a police officer whom he had collaborated with years earlier in Iraq. Saying her name at the worst possible time was a major blunder, but an innocent one nonetheless.

The vibrations came again, breaking his concentration.

Shit, who in hell is calling me in the middle of a hangover. Where'd I put the cell? Then he remembered. He reached across the truck bed and caught the phone just before it danced off the edge of the tailgate. *Must be her — ready to kiss and make-up.*

"Nicole?"

"Um, no…it is not. Mr. Gabriel Quinn?"

"Who's asking?"

"Mr. Quinn, my name is Clyde Concet. I head the company's human resources division. Russ Bensen instructed me to contact you at this number. Something about — "

"Oh sure, thanks for calling, Mr. Concet. Also thanks for using that number, but you can use either the cell or my home number now. How can I help you?"

"Mr. Quinn, you should receive a Fedex by the end of the day that will include your government travel order, the company travel authorization and reporting instructions. I am here to answer any questions you may have."

"Great! So when am I supposed to report to the company? Reston, Virginia, right?"

"That is correct, Reston," Concet said. "Yes, our company headquarters is certainly located in Reston. That is why I, uh, wanted to contact you before the package arrives. Certain items in it must be explained. Mr. Quinn, I am sure you've been following the recent developments in Iraq. I'm referring to the debates in the news about the surge. My understanding is you recently returned from Iraq."

"Affirmative," Gabe said. "Is something wrong, sir?"

"No, not at all. A check of our records shows that your contractor combined access card (CAC) is still valid. Can you confirm that for me?"

"Hang on two seconds while I check." He pulled the card from his wallet and verified the expiration date. "I'm good for another seven months. What's going on, Mr. Concet?"

"Nothing nefarious, Mr. Quinn, I assure you. It's just with the surge starting, the company has been pressured to comply with the contract expeditiously. In view of the new urgency, we have reviewed each candidate's package, and those who have already been to Iraq and have a top secret clearance — we have decided to skip the orientation and send those candidates directly to a unit preparing to deploy."

"Fine, Gabe said. "I have a few questions. More than a few. Are you in a position to answer questions, sir?"

Sounding relieved, Concet said, "Fire away! If I don't have the information, I'll track down an answer and get back to you. But allow me to anticipate some of your questions and fill in the gaps."

"You caught me away from my desk. Can I put you on hold for a minute so I can find some paper and a pen?"

"Please be quick, Mr. Quinn. I must make several more calls this morning."

Gabe grabbed his cargo shorts and rolled off the tailgate landing on his butt. He rubbed his behind, and then, barefoot, dressed only in his polka dot skivvies, stumbled toward the front door. Still holding his shorts and phone in one hand, he turned the door handle with the other. It was locked. "Shit!"

He dropped the shorts and stepped back down onto the driveway. Jogging to the pea gravel path, he made his way to the back yard. Turning the corner, he surprised a woman. Probably in her fifties, but dressed to look like she was in her twenties, her poodle was doing its business on his lawn. He was not sure if it was she he recognized, or her stunned expression. "Morning, ma'am."

Her surprise turned to disgust. "Come, Pierre! He's a shameless and evil man!" She scooped the dog into her arms and stomped off.

"Get a cat, lady, they're better than dogs!"

Gabe crossed the bridge over the *koi* pond, continued through the pergola that connected the lower patio to the upper patio and the screen porch. He hurried up the steps, flung the screen door open, let it slam shut behind him, and tried the door to the house. Locked out again. He reached up, located his back-up key hidden on top of the lantern, and unlocked the door. Stepping inside, he saw a pen near the wall phone. He grabbed it, ripped a blank page from the phone book and sat by the breakfast table. Waiting long enough to slow his breathing, he finally pressed the talk button. "I'm back, Mr. Concet."

"Good, good. As I said before, allow me to give you the details that will most likely answer most of your questions."

"Go ahead, sir."

"You are to report immediately to the 82nd Airborne Division's 5th Brigade Combat Team (BCT), Ft. Bragg, North Carolina. When I say immediately, I mean take two or three days, you know, take care of family issues, et cetera, et cetera. The travel order only kicks in from the continental United States (CONUS) to Iraq and covers such necessities as billeting, DFAC, medical, clothing and weapon privileges while in-theater. While in CONUS, the company authorizes you to rent a car, actual expense for lodging, and $42 per diem. Once you receive the package, you can review the fine print that will detail other expenses you can claim while stateside. How does it sound?"

Gabe placed the pen on the table. "Mr. Concet, all nice to know information, but my questions go more to the mission. First, how do I fit in? What is my mission, not the generic stuff in the proposal, but me, Gabe Quinn?"

"You've read the mission document, haven't you?"

"Of course I have. Several times, sir, but — "

"Then perform under the guidelines of the contract," Concet snapped.

Gabe looked up at the ceiling. *I'm talking to a bean counter.* "Have you read the mission document, Mr. Concet?"

"Actually I have not, but that is really not my department. I am responsible for handling travel, cost and revenue projections. Well, the revenue side of it is not your concern. Your responsibility is to do the company proud, sir. Furthermore, let me also say — "

"Mr. Concet, where do I report when I get to Bragg?"

"That's an appropriate and easy question. Report to the headquarters company S1. I think that means personnel. Are we finished?"

Shaking his head in disbelief, but also ready to conclude this debacle, Gabe said, "Just a few more easy ones for you. First, do you have a contact name? Second, does the Army know I'm coming? Third, do they know my mission? Fourth, do they support the mission? You know, well, maybe you don't, but there's a natural dislike of civilians, especially civilian contractors, who enter into their domain. I'm assuming the company has laid the groundwork so I won't be perceived as pissing in their rice bowl. Do you understand the gist of my concerns, sir?"

"Mr. Quinn you sound like….Well, allow me start with number one. As I said, report to S1. I do not have a name for you. Number two, of course they know you are coming. In fact, they look forward to your arrival and the expertise you bring. Third, they are well versed in the mission document, and as I said for number two, they are anxious to use you in this deployment. As to your last question, I believe you are being overly sensitive. While I've not been in the military, and of course, never Iraq, the Army command has endorsed and embraced the REDDI concept. Is that all, Mr. Quinn? I really need to make some more phone calls."

"Mr. Concet, I'm sorry that I took up so much of your time. I think I understand my role and the company's goals. I'll be on the lookout for the package. Thanks."

"Good-bye Mr. Quinn. And of course, good luck!"

Gabe looked over his almost, non-existent notes — 5 BCT, 82nd ABN DIV S1. "This is going to be a cluster." *Dog Shit, you were right, damn were you right. The company goal is all too clear. The mission, well, who gives a shit about the mission. Revenues, baby.*

*****

Happy to conclude another unpleasant task with another unpleasant jerk, in fact, he believed all of the law enforcement types were jerks, Concet retreated to the familiarity of his Excel spreadsheet. Frowning, he looked over the list of other names on his contact list. He decided to play with numbers before making any more calls to distasteful brutes. The stateside overhead charged the government for Quinn alone would net the company at least 150% for each dollar charged in direct costs. After Quinn was in the war zone, the company would bill the Army four times his six-figure salary, plus additional overhead on other direct expenses. Concet stopped frowning. He would receive a healthy bonus at the end of the fiscal year, not only from Quinn's contract, but also for the other sixty-nine contracts. Then he grinned. *If Quinn is killed, I'll receive another bonus for processing his replacement.*

Startled by the sound of his office door opening, Concet looked up.

"How's it going, Clyde?" Bensen asked.

"Oh, Russ, it is so good to see you." Concet sat upright, folded his hands in his lap and smiled. "I have a few more calls to make. I just finished with Gabriel Quinn. The man is really an awful — "

"Yes, Gabe is an awfully good man. I don't want to hold you up anymore, so I'll leave you to it. Keep up the good work and I'll see you at the afternoon round-up, Clyde."

After Russ left, Concet frowned again. *Quinn, a good man? I think not, Mr. Russell Bensen. Quinn is an ass. Why are the good ones like Russell always married?*

Brigade Commander's office, 5 BCT 82nd ABN DIV, Ft. Bragg, June 11, 0735 hours

Colonel Gunnar 'Gun' Erickson, known by his soldiers as 'Viking Warrior 6,' was still cooling down. He had led his troops on an eight-mile run up to the 'hill' and back. Assembled in his office were the Command Sergeant Major, David Hacker, executive officer (XO) Lieutenant Colonel Harry Simms, First Sergeant Fred Bell, and the operations officer, Major Julian Royce.

Erickson stared through the window at the soldiers doing calisthenics on the parade field on the far side of Ardennes Avenue. "Gentlemen, we're not ready. The joint readiness training exercise (JRTC) at Ft. Polk was a disaster. A damn, pitiful, unadulterated train wreck. Worse than two monkeys and a damn football. Do you get my drift? Do you feel what I'm saying?"

"Sir," Major Royce said, "there are some minor issues, but I think — "

"Think!" Erickson shouted. "It's too damn late to think. We go to war in less than three weeks. We have a patchwork, cannibalized brigade, thrown together in a rush for this surge. Half of these soldiers are straight out of advanced training. This is an airborne unit, we're the devils in baggy pants for God's sake, yet they send me legs. Hell,

68

we'd be lucky to be ready in six months, much less three weeks! Less than half of the brigade have seen combat and all of that in Afghanistan. Different war, different enemy. Most of the Brigade's on block leave. Our equipment hasn't been refurbished or replaced since our re-deployment from Afghanistan. So Major Royce, are these the minor issues you're talking about?"

"Sir, I — "

"The question's rhetorical, Major." Erickson looked at each man before he continued, "I need a shortened timeline. One that will get our soldiers, our equipment, and us from here to Kuwait, and then down range. I need it now. No, disregard that, I needed it yesterday. Am I clear?"

Royce, Bell and Hacker, jumped up and said, "Airborne, sir. All the way!"

"Well, get to it. Are you still here? Dismissed." As they were leaving, Erickson stopped Lieutenant Colonel Simms. "I need you to stick around."

"Yes, sir."

"Harry, cut the 'sir' crap. That speech was for their consumption, not yours. You know that."

"Gun, I know. What do you need from me?"

Erickson closed the door. "Take a seat. Harry, I need your help with the other problem — our mission. I can't believe the Eighteen Corps brain trust and the Pentagon brass have agreed to put my brigade in Iraq on a security force mission. We're airborne assault troops, find and fix the damn enemy, make 'em hurt. Yet, they give us escort duty for beans, sodas, toilet paper and who knows what else up and down the MSR with every damn *hajji* with a gun taking pot shots at us. They intend to spread us all over the southern, central and western provinces with a single brigade. It's damn near criminal. We'd need at least three brigades to accomplish that mission. On top of that, our only authorized battle space is five hundred meters either side of the MSR. We must give the fight over to our coalition partners. A bunch of damn pussies — don't want a fight and don't know how. Harry, I'm taking one more shot at Corps. If they don't change the mission, I'm going to the Pentagon. If the Pentagon doesn't change it, I'll take my argument to General Petraeus after we land in Iraq. I owe it to these men. We all owe it to them. They're soldiers. They deserve it. I would be a sorry excuse for a commander if I didn't stick my neck in the noose."

"I agree with you one hundred percent, Gun. How can I help?"

"Harry, I'm heading to Corps this afternoon. If I don't get the answer I want, I'll be at the Pentagon next week. Corps may not like it but I'll phrase it so they won't be able to stop me from trying. I need you to take over here. In my absence, get the troops ready to fight. I know it's a tall order, but you have my complete confidence and support. It's Super Bowl time but we're not playing for a damn ring. You know what's at stake and I don't mean to preach to you. You were with me in Afghanistan, so you know we lost too many soldiers there. I know we'll lose more in the desert, but I don't want to lose one more soldier than is necessary. These are our men, entrusted to us to use, not lose."

"Gun, understood."

Erickson smiled. "I knew you would, Harry. Two more things. Find out where in hell Major Neesom was this morning. I didn't see him on the run, and he sure as hell wasn't here. His performance at JRTC was…well, should I say…lacking?"

"Sir, that's an understatement. I'll check into it right away. And the other?"

Returning his gaze to his troops on the parade field, he said, "Harry, it's time to get their attention, shake things up, set the example. Better yet, make an example. I don't think our team has fully accepted we are about to go into harm's way. It's our job to set the bar high for them. Those soldiers out there deserve all of the support we can muster. I want you to set up a briefing to include everyone in headquarters, Brigade Special Troops Battalion…all of the battalions. Hell, take it down to company level. I mean every section head from S1, S2, S3, S4 and S6. Include the JAG lawyers, and you may as well get the God squad in there, too. Some may need His divine guidance after my little 'shock and awe' campaign. Set it up for Friday at 1300 hours."

Office of Colonel Erickson, Monday, June 11, 2007, 1535 hours

Tap, tap, tap….tap, tap, tap, tap….

Erickson looked up from the papers scattered across his desk to the closed door. *Must have been something down the hall.* He ignored the irritation and focused on his section of the operational order designed by Corps for the rushed deployment.

TAP, TAP, TAP, TAP!

"Enter!"

Major Neesom opened the door halfway, and stuck his head around its edge. "Sir, the XO said you wanted to see me. Uh — "

"Close the door and take a seat, Major."

Erickson gave Neesom a quick once-over. Tall and lanky, he looked more like Ichabod Crane than a warrior. Fit enough, however something else was odd about the man. Neesom struck him as the type that if he heard someone say 'boo', he would fall onto the floor in cardiac arrest. The major was also not jump qualified, not a paratrooper — one of the many glitches in patching this surge deployment together — 'legs'. *How did he end up in my command?*

Then he saw the ring. Neesom was a West Point graduate; a ring knocker, part of a different brotherhood. Erickson on the other hand, was a 'mustang', who rose from the lowest enlisted rank to his current position. He got his command the hard way, by actually being a warrior. He had little respect for the ring knockers. There were exceptions like his XO and some of the generals, but he was more comfortable with officers who had proven their mettle on the battlefield.

"Major Neesom, I did not see you on the run this morning or in my office afterwards."

"Sir-ah-ah-y-y-yes. My d-d-d-do-dog, a re-re-re-tr-tr-tr-triev-triev-er-retreiver w-wa-was ill, and I had t-t-t-to ta-ta-ta-take her to the ve-ve-vet's and m-my da-da-daught-er-daughter…um my daughter, my daughter…um…well sh-sh-sh-she…needed — "

Someone had told him Neesom was prone to stuttering when under the slightest pressure. Erickson contained his disgust and said, "Enough, Major. I get the picture. You've been in this man's army for what, fifteen years? Yet, I see from your file that you have never deployed. Why?"

Neesom, rubbed his hands together and avoided eye contact with the colonel. "Um, sir…I …um…g-g-guess…i-i-it is the l-l-luck, yes sir, the luck of the draw."

"Uh-huh, I see — luck of the draw."

Erickson had the gift he was looking for — Neesom. He would be the perfect example, the foil for his shock and awe Friday briefing. *Better a casualty off the battlefield than one on it.*

"Major Neesom, Friday, 1300 hours, all hands briefing. The S2, your shop, will start the briefing. I want an informative — make that a precise-briefing on what our brigade will face when we go down range. Do you understand what is expected of you, Major?"

Neesom jumped to attention and bellowed, "Airborne, sir! All the way, sir!"

Erickson winced. The response Neesom blurted was reserved for those soldiers who were actual paratroopers, not legs. He decided to let it go. Friday was only a few days off. "That is all, Major."

"Sir, yes sir!" Neesom, still at attention, said, "Uh…sir…um…m-m-maybe you need to look at this. Um…I j-j-j-just re-re-re-received it on NIPR, ah…ab-ab-about an hour ago." Neesom attempted to hand the colonel a sheaf of paper twenty pages thick.

"Major, I don't have the luxury of time to read that shit!" Erickson snapped. "Spit it out, and I do mean spit it out, mister. What's it about?"

"Sir, well, y-y-you see s-s-some — a pro-pro-program, REDDI. Um, well, bottom line is the br-br-br-brigade is p-p-pick-pick-picking up a civ-civ-civ-civilian. A con-contractor who is, well sir, the civilian is de-de-de-deploy-ploy-ploying with us to I-I-Iraq — "

"What!"

Erickson jumped out of his chair and ran around the desk, only stopping just shy of knocking Neesom to the floor. Veins throbbing, eyes popping, he said, "Another damn civilian! I hate damn shit bird civilians. I need another fucking civilian in my command about as much as I need a fucking vagina. They're nothing but pampered, sniveling, money-grubbing — they're a damn pain in the ass. I already have a ton of those leeches to baby-sit. Civilian safety officer, civilians fucking up our communication, civilians for our Warlocks, civilians to wipe our asses — shit! Bush is outsourcing this damn war. I ask for soldiers and they send me another civilian."

Red faced, Erickson leaned into Neesom and shot him a look that would buckle a resolute, hardened warrior. He spoke with a slow cadenced beat. "Major, when this civilian arrives, you will offer no support. You will assign him, her, it, a place in the latrine or a broom closet. I don't give a rat's ass. You will not allow him, or her, or it, to interfere with our mission. I will run the shitbag's ass back home to momma. I will not, I repeat, I will not allow another civilian cancer to corrupt my command, or our mission. Do you understand me, mister?"

"Sir, yes sir!"

"That is all, Major Neesom." As Neesom turned to make his long overdue escape, Erickson, as if a bolt from the heavens had struck him, barked, "Stop! Major Neesom, my order still stands, but if this civilian actually finds Ft. Bragg, I want that civilian at the Friday briefing. Understood?"

"Yes, sir! All the way, sir!" Then, as if the bolt from heaven had arced in his direction, he fled.

Looking at the empty parade field, Erickson smiled. He was pleased. Now he would have two examples, two sacrifices for Friday's briefing. "Providence!"

Chapter 8
Doors

Pawleys Island, SC, Monday, 0230 hours

Gabe traveled light so packing was easy. He threw together several sets of cargo pants, shirts, desert boots, Ziploc bag holding toiletry essentials, an outdated pin stripe suit with a black tie and four liters of Bacardi. He stuffed everything, except the rum, inside a backpack and placed it into the trunk of the rented convertible. Since he had been sleeping in the studio above the garage for several days, he was able to slip out without bothering Nicole. Before he started the car, he dropped an envelope for her on the front doorstep. Stuffed with an apology letter, insurance policies, a will and an updated power of attorney, it was his good-bye.

There were no long farewells left in him. He had begun the deadening process needed to ready for war. No more decisions about what to buy the kids for Christmas, paying bills, red or white wine with fish, tie or no tie, or inane conversation with neighbors he did not know. He was eager to trade all for a return to a life of raw instincts — sleep, food and not being splattered across the landscape.

Nicole had staked out her position about his leaving again in a clear, unequivocal manner — 'whatever.' He had staked out his position in an ambivalent manner, "see you in fifteen months. Love you." Gabe was unsure about either the love, or the fifteen months, so rather than muddle the issue with high drama, he decided to remove the letter. Conscience clear, he started the car.

Traffic was light. Top down, music cranked up, he flew through the sleeping beach town to highway 501, and in less than an hour, was on the Interstate. The only substantial traffic on I-95 was southbound; a steady stream of Army transport trucks loaded with shipping containers, Humvees and other weapons of war, all painted in desert camouflage. *Probably on their way to the Charleston port. Next stop Kuwait and then on to the 'suck'.* He hoped to join them in a few weeks.

When he saw the sign, he braked hard, slowing from ninety to sixty mph, and whipped the car onto exit 46 B for Fayetteville.

Fayetteville, home to Ft. Bragg and the 82nd Airborne Division, was known by some of the Vietnam War era as Fayette Nam. For too many young men, it was the last stop before transport to Ft. Lewis, Washington, and then a one-way flight to the Nam. The town became so popular during the war that Jane Fonda graced the area three times to crack the morale of the soldiers, the same soldiers who in their earlier brief adolescence had fantasized, worshipped and masturbated to the sexual goddess she portrayed on the big screen in 'Barbarella'.

Originally known as the 82nd Infantry Division, the All-American Division was formed in Georgia in 1917. It had many notable members, including Sergeant Alvin C. York, the conscientious objector who, during World War I, received the Congressional Medal of Honor; General James M. Gavin, the 'jumping general' of World War II; and the infamous Captain Jeffrey R. MacDonald. The only combat MacDonald saw was when he used his medical and Special Forces training to dice and slice his pregnant wife and two daughters.

Fayetteville is a southern city inundated with pawnshops, strip clubs, sleazy motels and seasoned con artists preying on every soldier with a dollar in his pocket. Other than the Army town's clientele, it was not much different from Myrtle Beach. The beach attracted golfers, college students, high school revelers and a slew of transients and dreamers looking for economic or other salvation. They sought pleasure and fortune, but many left broken. Yet, even in failure, most returned for another try.

Fayetteville's crowd was different. Young, testosterone bursting through every pore, they also searched for a release. Their search, however, was more profound — a craving to experience all in life immediately and leave a mark, a seed, on something or someone before going to war. Many reaped nothing more than a hangover, a tattoo, an STD, or a prostitute's promise that she would wait for him and someday have his baby, his mark, his seed. Some would not return for a second bite at the apple.

Thirty minutes after exiting the interstate, Gabe passed the fort's golf course, then saw the bright lights of the main gate. He slowed and turned into the visitor section. A civilian security guard stepped out from his booth and yawned. Tobacco juice slid down his chin onto the white uniform shirt. "Morning," he said in a molasses thick drawl. "You got business here, mistah?"

"I have an appointment at the 5th Brigade." Gabe handed him his identification.

The guard squinted at the card, then Gabe several times before he nodded and gave it back. Then he lumbered around the car using a mirror attached to a long handle to check the undercarriage.

"Open the trunk for me, sir."

Gabe got out and popped the trunk lid. The guard lifted the backpack and checked underneath the trunk's carpet. Finally, satisfied Gabe had no weapons of mass destruction, the guard waved him through the gate.

"Have a nice day, sir."

"Where is the 5th Brigade?" Gabe asked.

"Sir, what you wanna do is stay right here on this road, this being Butner. It's gonna wind around a bit, then you gonna turn left on Reilly until you come to Longstreet. Then you wanna turn left — no, I mean right on Longstreet and then a left on Ardennes. You'll be close to it. Ask any soldier and they is gonna point out the Brigade for you."

"There seems to be a lot of activity for five in the morning."

"It's usually not like this," the guard said, "but the Brigade you visiting is leaving soon, and some of the boys are gettin' ready to ship out. Things gonna be a little hectic around here for a few weeks."

The activity inside was brisk, but organized. It was the Army's way to bring order to chaos, and when necessary, chaos to order, whether a simple task like sweeping a floor, or as complex as flanking an enemy in defilade. Break it all down to its common denominator, then build it back up and paint it olive drab or desert tan. It was a process that mystified those not in the club.

The predawn buzz of busied preparation excited Gabe. He was comfortable in his skin, alive again — an army preparing for war, the realm of the believers — all of one mind and one purpose. Although he could not sing a note, much less match the lyrics with a tune, he broke into a mixture of muted singing, whistling and humming. *Damn, what was that song?*

"Fighting soldiers from the sky, fearless men who — "
That's not it.

"Give me an F, give me a U, give me C, something, something, yippee we all going to die, I don't give a damn, next stop is Vietnam."
Wrong again.

"Lock and load your M-16 and begin to slay, I wanna kill some gooks today."
Right sentiment, but wrong war and wrong song — it's hajjis'

76

turn.

5th Brigade Headquarters, Monday 0510 hours

The headquarters parking lot was empty. A solitary light stood sentry over the Brigade headquarters and the American flag that hung flaccid in the morning's calm. The light reflected back from a double glass entry door, the pathway to the world of the 5th Brigade. Some divine comic, borrowing from Dante's Inferno, had added a plaque above the door admonishing, 'abandon all hope ye who enter here.'

Entering through the gates of Hell, he saw a lobby resembling a museum. Glass-encased shelves displayed war trophies dating from WWII — a win with more than a million Americans killed or wounded — Korea, a tie with more than a hundred thousand killed or wounded — and Vietnam, a loss with two hundred thousand killed or wounded. Missing was any mention of Walter Cronkite's notorious editorial that sealed the fate of many of the thousands whose names appear on the Vietnam memorial wall — "We are mired in a stalemate that could only be ended by negotiation, not victory." Gabe wondered which clever pseudo intellectual would emerge to pen the Iraq War's epitaph.

More shelves paid tribute to other wars fought because of politicians' failed diplomacy — Panama campaign, a win with two hundred killed or wounded, Operation Enduring Freedom in Afghanistan and Operation Iraqi Freedom — still in play and numbers rising.

After taking in the Division's history, he looked up at a raised platform desk. Flanked by computer monitors, a drowsy looking soldier stirred when Gabe stepped closer. The private removed the iPod earplugs and wiped his reddened eyes. "Good morning, sir. Can I help you?"

Gabe saw he was wearing a combat patch and a combat infantry badge (CIB) next to the nametape on his Army combat uniform (ACU). "Good morning, Private Buzzard. Sorry to bother you this early, but is this Purgatory or the 5th Brigade headquarters?"

"Sir," the private said, "it's zero five ten hours." He pushed his more than six-foot frame up from the chair. Combined with the height of the dais, he looked like a colossus dressed in camouflage. "I'm on company quarters duty (CQ) and the only person here this early. The rest of the Brigade's on a five-mile run. Is someone expecting you, sir?"

"Gabe Quinn's my name. Maybe a little early, but I didn't know the Brigade's battle rhythm. I was told to report to the S1. Should I come back later?"

"Sir, yes, sir. Command will probably start drifting in at about zero eight thirty. I can make a note in my report and let Sergeant Walker, the NCO in charge for personnel, know that he has a visitor. Do you have any ID?"

Gabe gave him his CAC. The private jotted down the information on a legal pad. Without looking up, he said, "Sir, on the subject of names, it's no big deal, but my name is pronounced Boo-sard. It's a common mistake, sir."

"Got it. Won't happen again. Haven't had my coffee yet and my eyes don't focus this early, but now I can see your name clearly. Bussard, is that French?"

"Don't know, sir. Never met my parents so didn't get to ask." He returned the card to Gabe and said, "Sir, I've noted your name and the time. I'll give it to my relief if Sergeant Walker does not get in before my shift ends. Regarding coffee, there's a mini PX about a mile down Ardennes on the left. They sell a good cup of joe. The main PX has a Starbucks, but doesn't open until later."

Gabe stuck the card inside his wallet and then looked up at the standing soldier. "Can I ask you a question?"

"Yes, sir."

"You're displaying a CIB. Aside from my deep respect for what it represents, it also tells me you've probably been in the Army at least two years, maybe more. Yet — "

"Let me interrupt, sir. You want to know why I'm a mosquito wing private."

"Yes."

"Sir, I don't do too well when we're stateside. Down range, I can handle myself. Here I get into trouble, and with trouble goes a stripe. It's all good though, sir. We'll be back in the shit in a few weeks."

Gabe considered the private for moment, searching for something prophetic to tell him. Not one to give advice, he let it go. "I understand. Can I pick you up a cup of coffee, soldier?"

"Sir, I hope to be in my rack in about thirty minutes. Last thing I need is caffeine. Thanks for asking and good luck with your appointment, sir."

Gabe stood on his toes, reached across the desk and held out his hand. "Private Bussard, I'd like to be the first person today to thank you for your service."

*****

Bussard smiled as he watched Gabe leave. After the door closed, he continued to stare through the glass. Somewhat disarmed by his bluntness, but at ease talking to the harmless civilian who was probably some sort of salesman hawking a new fangled, whiz-bang product to the Army, he thought Gabe was a man he would like to meet again. Still smiling, he returned the buds to his ears and amped up the volume.

5th Brigade Headquarters, Monday, 0900 hours

Three soldiers, busily engaged in the paperwork of war, crowded the dais. Gabe approached and without addressing a specific soldier, said, "Good morning, gentlemen. Private Bussard told me earlier this morning that I should see Sergeant Walker."

The apparent leader, a staff sergeant whose uniform lacked jump wings, a CIB and a combat patch, put a temporary hold on the paper war and looked up. "Yes, sir. Dirty Bird mentioned we had an early morning visitor."

Confused, Gabe frowned at the sergeant. "Dirty bird?"

"Yes, sir. He has jump wings on his uniform, name sounds like buzzard and everyone knows that's a dirty bird. His note says your name is Gabriel Quinn."

"Correct, Sergeant."

"Well, Mr. Quinn, I checked with Sergeant Walker and he hasn't the foggiest about who you are. Do you have any paperwork I can show him?"

Gabe, looking through his manila envelope, said, "Not much, other than reporting instructions from my employer directing me to your Brigade S1." He handed the entire file to the sergeant.

"Mr. Quinn, if you allow me to make a copy of these, I'll make sure Sergeant Walker gets it. Nothin's gonna happen today, so come back tomorrow and he should have this all sorted out."

Gabe thought he had pissed in somebody's rice bowl, nevertheless he thanked the soldier for his time. "Any motels nearby, Sergeant?"

"There're plenty of flophouses outside the main gate in Spring Lake." Then he added, "Several with bars, sir."

A mind reader.

5th Brigade Headquarters, Tuesday, 0700 hours

Balancing two cups of coffee, Gabe used his foot to jar the front door open. Then he stuck his elbow in the opening, gave the door a quick push and stepped through sideways before it had a chance to slam back. "Good morning, Private. Tagged again for CQ duty, I see."

Bussard looked up and smiled. "Good morning, sir. CQ is the price I must pay for....Well, not important. How'd your appointment go yesterday?"

Gabe handed him a double latte and said, "It didn't, but maybe today. Your Sergeant Walker must be a busy man."

"Sir, Sergeant Walker is and always will be a REMF playing at looking busy. When we're down range, he'll still be here on rear D keeping our personnel jackets in order. All good, though. One less POG to clutter the Iraq countryside. Mr. Quinn, you're early again. If I could sit on Sergeant Walker for you, I would. Problem is he'll show up long after I've been relieved."

"That's fine. I've settled into a one-half star motel, found a pizza place, and I'm mastering the layout of Ft. Bragg. You ready to deploy — less than three weeks, right?"

"Sir, I was ready to deploy two weeks after we returned from Afghanistan. Nothing here for me." Bussard squinted at him and asked, "Mr. Quinn, what do you do? I mean, why you are here?"

Temporarily distracted by Manuel Noriega's uniform encased beyond the private, Gabe returned his attention to Bussard.

"Besides running a coffee service for one of America's finest — that being you, private — I'm a man in search of a mission. I was hoping that Sergeant Walker could enlighten me. I've a question for you. What will the mission be for the Brigade once we arrive in Iraq?"

Bussard spilled his coffee on his uniform and the desk. He jumped up from the chair and brushed the hot liquid off the legal pad. He looked down at him and said, "We, sir?"

"You'll need coffee in Iraq, won't you?"

"Sir, you're a civilian and a little old — disregard, sir. Our mission? I'd like to think it's to rape, pillage and plunder, but I think I'll have to settle with just killing hajjis. Sir, I'm just a gun. Command doesn't let me in on the big picture. I like it that way. Simple. What I hear is we're taking on a SECFOR mission."

Gabe, thankful the green machine did not recruit only boy scouts and altar boys, but puzzled by the acronym, asked, "SECFOR?"

"Yes, sir, security forces. I hear our Brigade will pull security for convoys moving up from Kuwait to Baghdad and further north. That's about all I know, sir."

5th Brigade Headquarters, Tuesday, 1500 hours

After consuming three coffees and a half of pack of cigarettes, Gabe finally saw a sergeant exit from the guarded corridors beyond the lobby. He walked toward Gabe and while still moving, Sergeant Walker said, "Mr. Quinn, good news, bad news. The good news, I have found an officer who knows about you. Bad news, he can't see you until Friday. You are to return to this office on Friday for a briefing at 1300. Any questions?"

Suspecting he had bumped against a wall of silence and the pursuit of additional information would be futile, Gabe said, "Thank you, Sergeant Walker."

Lakeside Inn, room 407, Spring Lake, NC, Wednesday 2300 hours

Two days into his binge, Gabe was finally at the point where a good eight hour down for the count crash seemed prudent. Before nodding off, he decided one more night cap should get him where he needed to be. Pouring a double, he stepped through the opening to the balcony that overlooked nothing more than a full parking lot. Sitting on the only furnishing, a plastic ten-dollar chair, legs poised on the rail, he tried to focus on the light show above — Persied's meteor shower raining down from the northeast. Apart from its monochromatic palette, the display looked like a silent, slow motion firefight....

Dog Shit, let's go, man. They're inside the wire.

I'm with you, bro. Where's my damn weapon?

Keep your drunk ass down, Dog Shit. Let's get to the tower.

I'm with you, Monty.

Don't call me Monty. Shit, Dog Shit, they're hitting the wall with RPGs. Head down. It's coming from one o'clock. The tower, get to the tower. Down, Dog Shit...down...stay low. Can't see shit. All right, I see the muzzle flashes. Oh shit, they're at our three o'clock. Down, get down. Okay, get some fire on them. Getting low on ammo here, Dog Shit —

I'm bingo on ammo, Monty —

You seeing what I'm seeing, Dog Shit, no way — this ain't real, man. Middle of an attack and there's Stoddard, no weapon, in his skivvies pulling on his pud. Stoddard! Stoddard, get us some more ammo! Stop jerking off and get us some ammo. Dog Shit, he's laughing at us —

Boom...Boom...BOOM!

Mortars? Can't be. This ain't real. Dog Shit, you okay?

Thump, thump, thump.

Incoming, Dog Shit! They're bracketing us! Christ!

Thump, thump, thump.

"What the hell? Dog Shit, you here? Dog Shit, where you at, bro?"

Gabe looked around the empty balcony and decided that Dog Shit was real somewhere, just not on the patio. He heard a woman cry out, "Stop!"

"Thaz reeeal."

Sounds of shattering glass filtered through the paper-thin walls and sliding door. More sounds of a struggle from the room next-door put him into action. He jumped up and stumbled toward the sliding door — the closed one. Bouncing back, he raised his hand and rubbed the knot on his forehead. "Ouch!"

He stepped through the opening and picked a path through the minefield of empty bottles, pizza boxes and dirty laundry scattered on the floor. While he bobbed and weaved across the mess, the crescendo of the raging battle from the adjacent room reached a climax. A final earsplitting scream — then silence.

Committed to his mission, he found the front door and prepared to charge. Sobriety began to creep back just as he was about to step out of his room. "Key, dumbass."

Armed with his room key, rampant adrenalin, a few remaining brain cells, one sandal protecting his size eleven right foot, shower robe covering his Hanes blue and red polka dot boxer shorts, he teetered right, left, up, followed by a dizzy downward gawk at his bare left foot. Time being of the essence, he resolved that a badly dressed knight clad in blue and red polka dot skivvies and one sandal was better than a no-show knight wearing bright shiny armor.

Gabe pounded on his neighbor's door. He heard feet stomping across the floor just before the door flung open with a whoosh, followed by a loud crash when it hit the seventies era wallpapered sheetrock. He stared up at least four inches at a red-faced giant. Naked, except for gold wire rimmed spectacles that seemed to keep his bulging eyes from popping out, the man with short-cropped hair stared back.

Still feeling the ten-foot tall syndrome that usually goes hand in hand with a spirits fueled, multi-day cruise, Gabe leaned forward. "I'm trying to get some sleep here, friend. We're in a motel. A place people pay to sleep. Do you fuckin' mind?"

The man bent down and went eyeball to eyeball with him. "We

aren't friends. Mind your own damn business, you little shit. Get the hell out of here."

A retreat would be prudent, but not one of my qualities. Compromise works sometimes. Go with compromise. "You're absolutely correct, Mr. Giant. I am a little shit and I don't belong at your door. But, you know what, bro, your life's problems don't need to be shared with the rest of the fuckin' world."

"Now you think we're brothers?" The naked man laughed, then said, "You're unfucking believable. A count of five and you live. Got it?"

Gabe looked between the giant and the open door. He saw the back of a girl sitting on the bed. Fair skinned with jet-black hair, she was nude, except for a torn red dress twisted around her ankles. She did not turn around to watch the rum fueled jousting, but instead stroked her mouth with the back of her hand. Then he saw the blood.

Tired of compromise, he pressed his body halfway through the door. "Miss, are you okay? Do you need help?"

She answered in a soft, numb voice, "I'm fine. Please leave us."

Skeptical of her response, but from decades of dealing with domestic disturbances, Gabe knew the eventual outcome — no winners, only losers, and the gallant knight in the middle getting the worst of it. He turned to the giant. "Where are you with your five-count?"

"Six. Get out of here, asshole."

Still hoping to see the girl's face, he leaned in further, but the naked man pushed him back. Finally, Gabe said, "If I hear any more noise coming from this room that is not a shower running or a toilet flushing, I'm counting nine-one-one. We registering, brother?"

The naked giant slammed the door against his face, instantly doubling the size of the egg on his forehead. "Damn doors."

Chapter 9
Kabuki theater in digital camouflage

Afak, Iraq, Friday, 2200 hours
The boy pushed the toy tractor with a missing wheel across the earth floor. When it hit a rough spot, he picked it up and changed direction. He stopped pushing when he felt a slight vibration. He sat on his haunches, looked up listlessly as a big person with short hair, bent over and took the toy from him. The big person spun the wheels several times before handing it back. Then he tousled the boy's hair and smiled at him.

The eight-year old was used to this big person, as well as a shorter one with longer hair. The long haired person, and another smaller person with long hair, gave him things he would put in his mouth and chew. They poured cooler things in something, that when he put it inside his mouth, he did not need to chew.

The boy watched the big person walk to the long haired ones who were standing over something hot inside a big thing that was the color of night. He knew hot, he knew pain. Once he had touched the big thing that the long haired ones made circles in with sticks. He did not scream, but it caused a sensation in him that was not nice like the cooler thing he sipped. The long haired persons were making circles again. The smell coming out of the big thing was familiar. It smelled like the stuff he put in his mouth. Soon, the long haired persons would give him things to put in his mouth to chew and the other cooler one to drink.

The big person touched the taller long haired one on the hand. The long haired person turned toward the big one and looked up. Then they touched their mouths together. He had seen them do the same thing many times. The big person never touched mouths with the smaller long haired person.

The boy turned away from the big persons that were touching each other and pushed the tractor. When he neared the opening to another, darker room, he felt a tremor, this time stronger than before. He turned toward the pulse. The door opened and a big stick poked through. This stick was bigger than the ones used by the long haired persons to make circles. Once he had seen a stick like it spit fire. It looked just like the one the big person with short hair carried across his back when he left the house. The three persons he knew all did the same things — their lips moved many times, they shook, and they raised their arms and hands to cover their heads.

Many big persons with the same type of sticks that sometimes spit fire came inside. Some of the big persons looked a little like the big person he knew because they wore the same things. One of the big persons hit the one he knew with his stick.

Something seeped out of the mouth of the big person he knew. Then the big person he knew went to sleep.

The other big persons threw the long haired ones on the floor and touched them many times with their hands and feet. They put something across their mouths and something else around their hands and feet.

The boy hungered for the stuff he would put in his mouth to chew. He looked away from the big persons and pushed the tractor across the floor.

5th *Brigade Headquarters, Friday, 1245 hours*

Squinting at the civilian dressed in a wrinkled suit and food stained tie, he held out his hand. "Mr. Quinn, I am Major Neesom. You're just in time for the briefing. I think you'll find that our staff is all about teamwork, efficiency and mission oriented. I understand you are the expert on improvised explosive devices — knowledge we'll definitely need in Iraq. You're a welcome addition to the team."

Pleased he was welcomed by someone, and a decent someone at that, Gabe said, "Major Neesom, I'm happy to be here, but I need to correct you about my expertise. I have a basic understanding of IEDs — I'm sure a lot less than you and the soldiers. Other than being on the receiving end several times, I'm no expert."

"Hmm, I see. Well, that puts you ahead of me on the learning curve. After the brief we need to sit down, go over your scope of work and see how we can get through this deployment and bring democracy to the Iraqi people."

Nice enough fellow, but a boy scout. Democracy in Iraq? Ain't happening.

"I look forward to it, Major Neesom."

He led Gabe through the corridor until they reached a door labeled S2. "Mr. Quinn, I'll join you in a few minutes. Continue down the hall to the conference room, last door to the left. Find a chair and make yourself comfortable. I expect the brief should not last more than a couple of hours. It's more of a routine update and nothing of significance will be accomplished. However, it will be a fine opportunity for you to meet the team."

Neesom smiled, then stepped inside his sanctuary. Before the door closed, Gabe heard him mutter, "I'm off the hook now. P-p-pro-v-vi-d-d-en-den-den-ce."

What'd he mean by that? Gabe shrugged then looked down the hall. Several soldiers were standing near the entrance. He walked past them and stepped inside. The conference room was abuzz with chatter, packed to the gills with more than fifty officers and a smidgen of enlisted soldiers. The talking ceased as soon as he entered. Judging by their expressions, he thought perhaps the team might not be as pleased to meet him as Neesom was. He overheard one say, "You believe that joker — needs a haircut, shave, and probably a bath. He must've escaped the crazy ward when Nurse Ratched was changing her Kotex."

Gabe ignored the slight because he had locked on something more important — a heavily annotated map of Iraq taped to the far wall. Covered with icons, some he understood, but many were Greek to him. Key highways, bases and outposts highlighted in red, green and blue looked familiar. He recognized most of the camps around Baghdad and Mosul, but those in the Anbar province, the turf assigned to the Marine Expeditionary Force One, were foreign to him.

Several soldiers pushed by him in the crowded entrance, so he stepped aside and searched the room for an empty chair. One against the back wall was available. He stumbled over the legs and feet of a dozen officers before he reached the seat next to the wall.

Cramped in the corner, he looked at the map again, racking his brain to decipher the meanings of the icons and the alphabet-soup of Army acronyms. Although not a military strategist, the placement, color intensity and relationship between icons told him a story — the Brigade's area of operations (AO) once in Iraq, and the extent of its mission. The story scared the hell out of him.

Satisfied he had a basic understanding of the battle space, he took in his surroundings. Adjacent to the wall map was a lone enlisted soldier fiddling with a computer and the large screen anchored to the wall above it. The specialist, still showing signs of adolescent acne, hurried to bring up a Power Point presentation. To the right of the soldier was a conference table surrounded by six executive style

86

chairs.

More soldiers filled the room — men and women all younger than Gabe, several young enough to be his children. As they streamed by, he thought he recognized one from the motel incident several nights before. *Sure, the glasses, the haircut — he was there when Dog Shit and I were clobbered with RPGs and mortars. I'm damn glad he was there. We sure needed his help. What's his nametape read? Laddick, Major Laddick. It looks like he remembers me. Yeah, he does recognize me. Don't know why he's frowning, though. After this is over, we'll have some coffee and reminisce. Good to have at least one battle buddy here.*

"Excuse me, sir. Can I pass by and take that empty spot in the corner?"

Laddick's frown changed to startlement when he saw the girl who had spoken to Gabe.

Still smiling at the major, Gabe turned away to answer the pleasant voice. What he saw shocked him also — a pristine, angelic face, risqué and innocent at the same time — a perfect Madonna, except for a swollen and cut lip. Long forgotten carnal desires flooded over him.

He stood and moved against the wall. "Um, Lieutenant Loving, ah, please ma'am, take my chair."

Speaking softly in a voice that could stir the most pious of men, she said, "Thank you, sir, but that's not necessary. Keep your seat, I'll stand."

Consumed by overriding guilt for his un-gentlemanly thoughts, Gabe fought his tongue and mind, hoping to recover. "I insist. If an old man like me sits for more than ten minutes, it could turn into a nap. That would not be a pretty sight. Lieutenant, you'll be doing me favor if you take my chair."

"Chivalry's not dead. You know my name and rank, yet all I know about you is a voice I seem to recognize, but a name I don't recall. Other than sir, how do I address you?"

Her smile sent him reeling again. Extending his shaking hand, he said, "Quinn, um, Gabe Quinn."

Afak, Iraq, Friday 2215 hours

Ghazi looked at the bound prisoners on the floor near the boiling kettle, then at the boy pushing the toy tractor. He scratched at the scar that in the heat of the desert night and the adrenalin pump caused by their dynamic entry, had turned purple against his brown skin. He stepped toward the child, stopping only when he was within an arm's reach. Staring down at the boy, he clapped his hands several times. The boy continued playing. Ghazi turned to the others and told them to move the unconscious Kaseem and his daughter to the adjoining room. He looked at the boy and rapped hard against his head. The boy jerked his head up and frowned. Ghazi smiled and offered his hand.

The boy picked the tractor up, then, together they walked into the darker room. Ghazi dropped his hand and pointed to a corner. The child shuffled to it and squatted. He looked up, opened his mouth and raised his hand to it several times as if begging for food. Ghazi shook his head. The boy pushed the toy across the dirt.

Ghazi stood his AK-47 against a wall and sat cross-legged on the floor. He spoke loud enough for the six police assembled in the room to hear, as well as the two in the kitchen guarding the trussed wife. "*Allah* commands we must wipe out the infidels to the very last."

Annoyed by his moans, Ghazi glanced at the bloodied, gagged man splayed across the floor. He looked back at the police and spoke louder. "We fight the infidels, the Jews, the Christians. They are apes and swine."

Several police peeked nervously at the unconscious officer and the boy still pushing the toy. When the boy bumped Ghazi's leg with the tractor, he took the toy from him, tossed it to the other side of the room and then pointed at it. The boy scooted across the floor on his butt until he reached it and then pushed it around in circles.

"Look at Kaseem," Ghazi said. "He claims to be one of us, our brother in Jihad. He lies. I gave him a simple task and he failed. His stupid, useless son follows orders better. *Enahu laysoo aghbeia,* our enemy is strong but not stupid. Today we will set a course to destroy the infidels. We all have a part, yet Kaseem forgot his part. We will not forget. We will not fail."

Ghazi Codar el Ahmar, section leader for the Dhi Qar and Al Qadisiyah provinces of the *Jaish al Mahdi,* the Sadrist militia, turned to Nazmi. "Bring in the *zawgah* whore that sleeps with this cur."

Nazmi jumped up and placed a hand over his heart. "*Nam, Ghazi, nam.*" He moved quickly to the kitchen and within seconds returned, dragging Kaseem's wife by her ankles. He cut the electrical wire binding her feet and ripped the duct tape from her mouth and eyes.

She shrieked at the sight of her battered husband. Hands still bound, she stood and ran toward him, shouting, "Kaseem, Kaseem!"

Ghazi kicked her in the stomach with enough force to knock her headlong into a quarried stone table. He jerked her up and tore the *hejab* off, revealing the face of a woman in her early thirties. He spit on her, and then slapped and punched her until she coughed up blood and broken teeth.

"Forget him, you whimpering whore," he shouted. "Soon he'll be martyred to *Allah* and dead to you. You have guests. Have you not thought of our needs? Where is your hospitality, you mongrel slut? Feed us, woman! Get on your feet and feed us!"

He unleashed another flurry of kicks aimed at her abdomen and groin. Soon, tired by the effort, he said, "Nazmi, take this whore to the kitchen. Watch her as she prepares us a feast. If she is slow, beat her. If she is quick, beat her. When our feast is ready, bring it to us. As we eat *Allah's* gift of food, feast on the flesh of this wench. Enjoy her the way only Kaseem has enjoyed her. Treat her like the farm animal she is and when you are spent, kill her."

Within minutes, the police were eating vegetable stew. There was no talk among them, only solemn expressions and occasional glances at Kaseem and his daughter. Ghazi had their attention. The woman's screams helped. He needed an example, a sacrifice to harden them to the months, possibly years of battle ahead. He chose Kaseem, not because he was a bad fighter, just too meek. All of his excuses had worn thin. He showed heart to the villagers when steely coldness was required. In death, Kaseem would serve a higher purpose. Kaseem would thank him if he could, because Ghazi would give him an immediate place in Paradise through forced martyrdom.

"Now we will create the hell that will defeat our enemy. I have studied the *Amerikee*. I know their weaknesses and their strengths. Whatever I say take to heart. Commit my words to memory and to action. Do not be weak. Learn from Kaseem's failure."

All stopped eating.

"Do not attack in the open. We can't match their weapons or their numbers. Ours is a war of the people. I have studied Vietnam. The *Amerikees* are weak — their journalists are strong. We must play to the media who will send our message to the *Amerikee* people. We must send dead soldiers home. Gruesome, hideous deaths; deaths that will bring the horror of their atrocities against our families to theirs. Bring me *Amerikees* and I will cut off their heads and send them to their families across the ocean. They fear nothing more as losing their heads. We will feed on that fear. They are fools. They should fear *Allah*. The *Amerikees* want out. We must keep their desire to leave in front of them each day. They — "

The boy pulled on Ghazi's pants and mimed that he wanted food. He picked up the child, set him in his lap, and gave him the leftovers from his bowl.

"They feel safest when they sleep. We must deny them their dreams. Attack them at night with katushas and mortars. Use the bombs our brothers from Iran give us to kill their trucks. Spread the word in the villages that we will pay a thousand *Amerikee* dollars for each soldier killed. Moqtada al Sadr knows the *Amerikee* better than us. He and the Iranian *Quds* force will help with money and weapons. Tax the villagers. If they will not pay, destroy them. If they are *Sunni*, kill all of them and take their money. If they are *Shi'ite*, tell them we need their sons. If they refuse, kill the fathers and take their sons. Tell those who work for the *Amerikees* we need information. If they don't help in Jihad, kill them."

He put the boy down and pointed to the corner. The child grabbed the tractor and moved away. Ghazi stood and using the butt end of his rifle drew a map of southern Iraq. He identified weapon caches in the villages between Diwaniyah and Basrah. Reaching to the small of his back, he withdrew a Khanjar dagger and used it to draw a circle inside the map. Then he stuck the blade in its center.

"Here is where most of them will be. They call it Adder. They will feel safest at this big fort. We will concentrate the battle here and attack their monster trucks as they move north and south. We must stop the supply of weapons they use to kill our families."

He placed a hand on Abdul-Hakim's shoulder and said, "I need Suq ash Shuyukh. We hold most of Nasariyah, but Suq ash Shuyukh is close to their fort. It will be our impenetrable refuge, close to the battle."

Ghazi let go of him and scanned the faces of the other police. "New *Amerikees* will arrive in three weeks and will be led by a man called Erickson. He fought our brothers in Afghanistan. We have many eyes among the *Amerikees,* so soon we will know all of their names and types of weapons. We watch their television and read their newspapers. They don't know how to keep secrets. We will know where and when they will attack before they do. They are paratroopers and pride themselves in being fierce warriors of the 82nd Airborne Division. Before these new devils come to our lands, we must kill many of the *Amerikees* they will replace and send these tired animals home with fresh memories of *Allah's* justice. If we do this, they will not return. When the fierce warriors of the 82nd arrive, we do nothing. Nothing, until I give the order. They will be strong until the dogs they replace run home with tails between their legs. Watch the new *Amerikees* — learn how they move, where they go, what they do. Learn how they think. I will become their friend. When I know them as I know you, we will attack and bring the sword of Jihad across their necks."

Ghazi looked at Kaseem. He was almost ready. "We need the village elders and officials to join us in Jihad. Talk to them. If their ears do not hear, bring me an ear. If the remaining ear does not hear, bring me a head. Any villager who accepts gifts from the *Amerikee* will be an example. Do it in sight of his friends and family. Show them the importance of jihad. Do not martyr yourself. That day will come. We must first kill many *Amerikees*, only then will we seek *Allah's* grace."

Sweating, he had worked himself into a frenzied mess. He took several deep, quick breaths, then slower ones, until the fire in his eyes calmed.

"For now, finish eating and drink *chai*. We have one more duty to perform for *Allah* before we leave."

Ghazi unzipped his pants and urinated on Kaseem. "Awaken."

Office of Colonel Erickson, Friday, 1255 hours

Three days after he returned from Crystal City, Colonel Erickson was still upset that he failed to change the Pentagon's plans for the Brigade.

"Gun, it's time," Lieutenant Colonel Simms said.

True to his Norse ancestry, Erickson mumbled a quick prayer to Odin, and then to his Christian God, asking both for help with the impending sacrifices. He did not cherish the role but as a leader, it was his duty.

He ran his hand through his reddish-blonde hair, cropped closer than required by the Army. "Harry, did that civilian show up?"

"Don't know, Gun. If he did, he'll be easy to spot. No others are slated to be at the brief."

"Neesom better have kept him in the dark, or he'll get more of an ass chewing than the one he's about to get."

"I can assure you he has not had access to anything. I reinforced your order to Neesom in very clear terms."

"Good." Erickson collected his papers and stood.

Simms paused at the door. "Sir, do you want *Brynhildn*?"

"Of course, can't forget her. Thanks, Harry."

Erickson reached up, took *Brynhildn* from the wall and hefted her to his chest. The replica Viking battleaxe, given to him by the troops when he was just a captain, had been adorned with miniature battle flags and campaigns ribbons covering the decade of his rise from company to brigade command. The soldiers revered her and would be disappointed if she were absent. *Brynhildn* had become synonymous with Viking Warrior Six.

Looking at his prop and then at Simms, he said, "Harry, muster the troops. Time to shake them up and kick some ass. It's show time."

*****

Major Neesom rushed into the conference room and handed the specialist a last minute Power Point handout. He said something to the enlisted soldier before finding an empty chair near the podium.

Gabe was surprised that the senior S2 intelligence officer would not be at the table with the other staff officers and senior NCOs.

As soon as Neesom sat, Command Sergeant Major Hacker marched in and said, "Attent-hut!"

Every soldier in the room jumped up from their chairs and stood at attention. Immediately following the call to attention, Erickson said, "at ease." He strode through the doorway with posture rigid, chin tucked down to chest, *Brynhildn* balanced on his shoulder. Ten feet inside the room he stopped. He glared around the room at the soldiers as if daring them to match his fierce stare.

Although already standing when the order of attention boomed throughout the room, Gabe straightened his posture and assumed a civilian version that approximated the military one. Not yet challenged by the colonel's searing gaze, he was impressed. The colonel was not a large man, but clearly a scrapper who had paid his dues to society and looked like he was ready to pay some more. He looked like a warrior — one who commanded respect. His uniform was a résumé — Combat Infantry Badge, jump wings, combat patches, Ranger tab. Yet, Gabe was sure if he crossed paths with him in a bar, at the beach or anyplace else where he would be out of uniform, the colonel would still command respect. Rarely awed by anyone, he had an instant like for this man.

When their eyes met, the colonel's expression changed from a mere challenge to one of outright contempt. Almost a minute passed before Erickson looked away from him and marched to the table. He laid *Brynhildn* on the table, then again glared at Gabe.

Gabe lost sight of him when the rest of the procession walked into the room. Major Royce, Sergeant Major Hacker, First Sergeant Trujillo and Lieutenant Colonel Simms took their places around the table in some mystic hierarchy known only to them.

Facing the wall map, back to the soldiers, Erickson said, "Sit!"

After the sound of more than fifty butts hitting fifty chairs stopped echoing through the room, Erickson leaned toward Simms and whispered. The executive officer turned in his chair, looked briefly at Gabe, then turned back toward the colonel and nodded.

Gabe heard Erickson make a low noise that sounded like, "humph."

Erickson nodded to the specialist and said, "Begin."

The enlisted soldier stood at attention and said, "All the way, sir. I am Specialist Weiner, intelligence analyst and I will brief the S2 portion today, sir."

Relying on his Power Point slides and scripted monologue, Weiner began what should have been a tedious brief of what they could expect when they deployed to Iraq. Following standard mission, enemy, terrain, weather, troops, support, time available and civil considerations format (METT-TC), he moved quickly through several slides covering the Brigade's mission. Then he began the enemy portion of the presentation.

Four slides and less than five minutes into the brief, Erickson said, "What in hell does that mean? Who is our enemy?"

Weiner froze. He looked at the colonel and then down at his notes. He fumbled around the podium's surface, flipping through the printed version of the slides and his script for some clue as to what he screwed up. He looked pleadingly at his boss, but Neesom ignored him. Then he looked awkwardly at Erickson. "Sir, uh, sir... um, I don't — "

"Stop!" Erickson shook his head. He turned and looked at Neesom. He fixed his rage on him with an expression that could only be misinterpreted by a dolt — hell was about to be unleashed.

Erickson's voice grew from barely audible, to a roar clearly heard in the corridor behind the closed door and likely to the parade field beyond. "I'm not asking you, soldier!"

Neesom had been smiling, probably musing about how Weiner's briefing was an obvious success. Now, he was in the throes of an ice cream brain freeze — powerless over the forces of anatomical function. His mouth opened wide, as if ready for the incoming shit sandwich. His eyes took on that thousand-yard stare peculiar to soldiers who had seen too much combat, or the cherries who realized that momma was not there anymore to kiss the boo-boos, or the officer who botched a mission. His bladder released a trickle that spawned a darkening spot on the crotch of his uniform. Motionless and speechless, he gawked at the colonel.

Erickson's neck veins throbbed to the point of explosion as he continued his lethal stare at the brain dead major. Disgusted, he turned his chair away from Neesom, and the others in the room, and faced the empty wall. "Damn!"

Before moving on to act two of the improv theater, Erickson sat silent for several minutes, repeatedly shifting his hands from his thighs to his forehead. One sacrifice easily behind him and one remaining, not quite sure how act two would unfold, but confident he could manipulate the setting, he threw down the gauntlet. "Anyone!"

Gabe had seen his style before. He doubted the colonel ever heard about 'Theory Y' management or Maslow's hierarchy of needs. The colonel was old Army, a theory X leader — coercion and belittlement. The proverbial pin dropping would sound like a jackhammer meeting concrete in the room. Staff and junior officers alike, studied the floor between their feet, avoiding eye contact with Viking Warrior Six. Relying on lessons probably learned at the academy, ROTC or Officer's Candidate School, and fighting an urge to disappear through the carpeted floor, they wisely decided to let the gauntlet stay right where it was.

"Airborne, sir. Lieutenant Loving, sir."

Startled at first by the brazen act of courage, a collective sigh filled the conference room. Gabe understood their appreciation for this god-sent act of bravery, well beyond the call of duty. The officers looked up from the carpet to her.

Erickson turned his chair around and said, "Continue, Lieutenant."

"Sir, the enemy we will face downrange is al Qaeda. Sir, our other problems — "

Erickson raised his hand. He smiled at her like a parent watching his child's first step. Then he saw the man standing next to her. The smile was gone. "Lieutenant Loving, thank you. Take your seat."

Gabe, still pondering the act of seppuku performed by Neesom moments earlier, and failing to grasp that his situational awareness sucked, locked eyes with the Viking warrior. Not realizing his mistake, he returned the easy, but sometimes inappropriate smile, to his face.

Erickson pointed at him. "Who are YOU?"

Still grinning like an idiot, he pushed off the wall and said, "Good afternoon, Colonel Erickson. My name is Gabriel. Well, um, Gabe

Quinn, sir. I've been assigned to your Brigade as a law enforcement advisor, sir."

Stroking *Brynhildn*, Erickson summoned all his hostility toward civilians and fired for effect, "Well Gabriel, um, Gabe Quinn, who do you think is our enemy?"

"Sir, I agree with Lieutenant Loving. Our enemy is al Qaeda, and I'm sure she would have detailed other enemies you will encounter in Iraq, if given the chance."

"Continue."

"Sir, you know, and certainly the lieutenant knows, al Qaeda is a real threat. It may be easier to identify your enemy by first identifying your friends."

"Okay Gabriel, um, Gabe Quinn. Who are my friends?"

Clueless that he was walking blindly into a trap, Gabe ambled into it, rather than a headlong charge. "Sir, I think Bush, Cheney and Rumsfeld are with you. The Brits, Aussies, Poles, Rumanians, Kurds and probably half of Congress are with you. I'm sure the companies that mass-produce the 'we support you' yellow ribbons are with you. Oh yeah, I'm with you. Fox News, still a friend, but if you lose them, you're FUBAR. Network news, Hollywood and the academia were never with you."

"Thank you for enlightening me about my friends Gabriel, um, Gabe Quinn. Now enlighten me about my enemies."

"Your enemies...well, not being clear about your mission or your battle space, and looking at the map, there's much I can't interpret, but it appears the largest icons are concentrated north of Basrah around FOB Adder. Continuing north along MSR Tampa and ASR Boston, they're clustered around Diwaniyah, FOB Echo, Hilla, Rustimayah south of Baghdad, and some at Al Assad, Balad, Victory and Speicher. I'm swagging, but it looks like your main forces will be at Adder and smaller units at those other locations."

"Colonel Erickson, can I interrupt and direct a quick question to Mr. Quinn?"

Erickson looked at the young pixie looking ivy-league schooled lieutenant sitting near Neesom. "Go ahead, Lieutenant."

"Thank you, sir." She turned toward Gabe. "Mr. Quinn, I am Lieutenant Shelton, public affairs officer (PAO) for the Brigade. Sir, I pride myself in my command of the English language, yet I'm unfamiliar with the verb you employed. I believe it was swagging.

What does that mean?"

Erickson rolled his eyes. Then he looked at Gabe and chuckled.

Thrown off by the question, Gabe did his best. "I'm sorry, Lieutenant Shelton. Swagging is a technical term we use in law enforcement, ma'am. It's a technique used in the early stages of investigations when leads and witnesses are few."

Seeing that she still looked puzzled, he continued. "Ma'am, I thought the term had migrated to military lexicon, but I guess not. Quite simply, swag is a scientific wild ass guess. Does that help, ma'am?"

"Thank you Mr. Quinn, I will remember that word. Regarding FUBAR, sir — "

"Lieutenant," Erickson said, "see me after the brief and I'll personally show you what fucked up beyond all recognition looks like. But, now, sit. Gabriel, um Gabe, continue."

"Yes, sir. My swagging...I mean surmising, shows your main force will be at Adder with other units spread around the country. If that's the case, your main force will operate south of the capital, with some smaller units in Tikrit and Baqubah. The units in Tikrit will definitely rub up against Al Qaeda Iraq (AQI), but not with the intensity of our soldiers fighting in Mosul and Talifar. When I left Mosul six weeks ago, that was all we saw. In fact, the entire time I was there from '05 to '07, it was AQI. Thank God for the Marines, but when they kicked ass in Fallujah, they pushed the enemy our way making them the number one headache in Ninevah province. It's been an under-equipped, under-manned battle ever since.

"AQI will stand up and fight when cornered. They're made up of the hard cores from the *Sunni* Wahhabi sect, mostly foreigners from Saudi, Yemen, Syria and parts of Africa — true Osama bin Laden followers. They want martyrdom. Probably a bad way to phrase it, but there is a softer side of AQI — the *Sunnis* who fell under the *Salafi* currents encouraged by Saddam. He spent a fortune building a shrine in Baghdad for the Sufi saint, Abd el-Qadir al-Gaiani. Saddam was a shrewd man. Hoping to buttress his stranglehold over the *Shi'ites*, he encouraged *Sunni* radicalism in his faith campaign. Thanks to your excellent organization, Saddam is dead. Now you're probably dealing with one of his protégés, Izzat al-Douri. As you know, he was a senior *Ba'athist* and former vice-president of Iraq. I don't know who is heading the *Wahhabist* side of al Qaeda now that Zarqawi's dead, but I'm positive your intelligence folks will have a name soon. Aside from al Qaeda around Tikrit, you'll be dealing with sectarian violence that erupted after they blew up the golden mosque in Samarra last year. A stroke of genius, that really pissed off the *Shi'ite*."

Gabe paused to study the soldiers' faces for tells indicating understanding. Several seemed bored, but most appeared to follow his impromptu brief. He looked at the colonel and the executive officer — both showed signs of interest. Not wanting to bore the troops, Gabe picked up the pace.

"It's not a major one, as far as mosques go, but it does house the al-Askariya shrine. Whoa, I mean that's very important to the *Shi'ite* hajjis, more important than the shrines in Najaf and Karbala. Besides housing the tombs of two ninth century imams, supposedly direct descendants of the Prophet Muhammad, these folks believe the site is connected to the 12th and final imam — the hidden imam. They believe he hid under the shrine and when he's ready to return, he'll do it there. Sir, to the *Shi'ite*, this is heavy juju. Nothing really compares in our country. Around Tikrit, Baqubah and Baghdad you'll have to deal with all the shit…excuse me, trouble al Qaeda stirred up."

"Who the fuck is this guy?" Gabe looked at the man who had made the derogatory comment — Major Laddick. Doubts began to form whether he was a battle-buddy, or a buddy-fucker. He looked at the closed door, wishing he could sneak out for a smoke. Then he glanced through the window, and seeing a passing beer truck, thought he needed a drink more than a cigarette.

Erickson also heard the comment and looked at the man responsible. He jotted a quick note on his pad, and then said, "Proceed, Mr. Quinn."

"Yes, sir. Don't get me wrong — the *Shi'ite* and *Sunni* love to kill each other, and if it was just hajjis killing other hajjis, great. Let's pack up and go home. I'll chase down that Budweiser truck and the beer is on me. There's more to it, though. Killing Americans is a bonus to them, *Sunni* and *Shi'ite* alike. I don't think they'll get together and fight, but they seem to be aware of each other's goals, and have a tag team approach to killing us. Before the golden mosque went 'boom,' and even now, the main *Shi'ite* threat was from the religious quack, Moqtada al Sadr. Cashing in on the name recognition of his father

97

Ayatollah Muhammad Sadiq al-Sadir, he set himself up as the head of the anti-occupation Sadrist movement JAM, excuse me, the *Jaish al Mahdi*. His benefactor, Iran, is our real enemy in this war. Iran currently houses him while he racks up some brownie points with the *Shi'ite* by getting phony religious teaching. It uses him as a proxy to keep us involved in Iraq and them off the radar. If Congress ever tires of arm wrestling and actually makes a decision, you'll be knee deep in a war that'll rival the big one. Iran's our biggest threat. Sir, I don't mean to go political on you and cover stuff you already know. Do you want me to shut up?"

"Charge, Mr. Quinn."

"Yes, sir," Gabe said. "When I was in Sadr City in '04 and part of '05, Moqtada's minions were a real headache. It seemed like we took one-step forward and two in reverse. His propaganda machine had convinced the locals that Americans were responsible for every death in Iraq since before we were a nation. Let me put it this way — if your PAO and psy-ops could duplicate his information operation (IO), CNN, ABC, CBS, hell, even MSNBC, would be in your corner. The sad thing is the Marines had the bastard cornered in Najaf in August '04. They had him — I mean they had him and his followers dead in their sights. I know it wasn't the Marine Corps' decision to botch a chance of ending the insurgency in its infancy. It was our ambassador John Negroponte, who brokered a bravo-sierra settlement between Grand Ayatollah Sayyid al-Sistani and Sadr. What a grand opportunity pissed away. Over the years, JAM has grown. It has rivals; rivals you can exploit, sir. Bottom line, the bulk of your soldiers, based on where they're positioned on the map — their enemy is JAM, and ultimately Iran. Sir, what your map doesn't show is where your other two brigades will be positioned. Not knowing the provinces they'll secure, I can't address who they'll fight, Colonel."

Erickson released his grip on *Brynhildn* and mumbled, "My missing two brigades." Speaking louder, he said, "Mr. Quinn, I have one brigade. No supporting units."

"One brigade?" Gabe was stunned. Erickson had *gravitas*, a true warrior, but a warrior hamstrung by the politics of war. He felt sorry for him.

"Sir, that's mighty thin."

Afak, Iraq

"Nazmi," Ghazi shouted, "bring me Kaseem's wife."

Nazmi dragged Sanaa's battered corpse into the room by her feet. As he did, her head bounced along the floor. When he reached Ghazi, he let go and stepped away.

Ghazi nudged the body with his foot and rolled her over so her face was in the dirt. "Let us not forget our other guest. Place her next to her husband."

Conscious, Kaseem fought against the bonds in a futile attempt to comfort his dead wife. Duct tape covering his mouth muted the screams. His wild eyes tried to escape from their sockets. The fury soon turned to surrender, a concession that gave way to tears streaked with the blood from many cuts and contusions covering his face.

Ghazi stood over him. Upset with the abruptness of his surrender, he hit him in the face. Kaseem's head fell to his chest. Soon he roused and looked up at his captor with a deference that only infuriated him more.

Ghazi moved the body into a sitting position and draped her arm around Kaseem. He tilted her head until it rested against Kaseem's shoulder and turned her broken neck so her dead eyes could meet his. Kaseem did nothing, as if he had also departed this world.

Ghazi smiled at him, then looked across the room at the boy pushing the tractor. He looked beyond the boy to the boy's older sister. Bound, gagged, blindfolded, the child, who had yet to reach her eleventh birthday, was able to hear the assaults on her parents, but had no way of knowing the outcome.

Satisfied that all accomplices and victims for his sordid ceremony were gathered, Ghazi walked by the boy to the girl. He untied her hands and feet, then removed the blindfold. At first confused by the sight, she turned crazy. She yanked out the rag stuffed inside her mouth and shattered the somber quietness with repeated screams as she ran toward them. "*Abb, omm, abb, omn,* father, mother, father, mother."

Animated by his daughter's plight, Kaseem struggled to rise to his knees. She embraced his battered body with her tiny arms and hands. Helpless, all he could do was weep with his daughter.

Ghazi ordered two of his subordinates to restrain Kaseem and a third to force his head up to watch. He took off his clothes, folded them neatly and laid them on the stone table. He grabbed the girl and shook her small frame before he threw her to the floor. He leaned down and pinned her wrists to her side. "My little flower, *Allah* will reward you. I will be kind and gentle. Do not fear me. I am your teacher."

5th *Brigade Headquarters Conference room, Friday, 1322 hours*

After a long silence, Erickson snapped back to reality. "Mr. Quinn, what will our enemies throw at us when we RIP (Reinforcement in place) in two weeks?"

Detecting resignation in the colonel's voice, and fully grasping his dilemma, Gabe paused to collect his thoughts. He decided to proceed with what he hoped would be a dispassionate analysis of the Brigade's immediate future.

"Colonel, the enemy will play from the shadows and won't attack head on. He'll protect his limited resources and fight the only fight he can. They know that head to head, they lose. Their war is a war of attrition, not unlike Vietnam. To them a win is just not quitting. There won't be any charges to attain martyrdom, at least not by JAM. He'll pick at your forces all up and down MSR Tampa. Their weapon of choice is the IED — low risk, great reward. Sir, when I was up north they hit us with roadside bombs made from ordnance left over from Gulf 1 and Operation Iraqi Freedom. Most were 105 and 155 artillery rounds — survivable, unless it's a direct underbelly impact. They got smart and started digging down, burning the asphalt with tires, so they could bury AT-6 mines stacked three high. Then they'd reheat the asphalt and cover it up so our soldiers rolling down the highway could not see them. I saw those stacked mines take out a Stryker once — not an easy feat. Side blasts are not as effective as an underbelly one. I was hit twice in Mosul this year and we were riding in an up-armored Suburban. Had some damage, but we're all still ticking.

"We operated primarily in an urban environment that gave the enemy plenty of cover and concealment, so he mostly used command wire improvised explosive devices (CWIED). Sometimes, if he could reasonably control the terrain, he'd use pressure plate ones (PPIED). Both tactics present some risk. Their preferred detonation — radio controlled (RCIED) — well suited for the terrain where the bulk of your soldiers will patrol. I'm not familiar with the terrain in the south, but I do know it's mostly flat desert with a few *wadis*, canals, overpasses and culverts. Bottom line, they'll be somewhat exposed if they go with command wire and they shouldn't be able to control the traffic flow to make pressure plates practical.

"In Afghanistan you were probably hit with CWIEDs using home-made explosives (HME) made from ammonium nitrate and fuel oil (ANFO). Easily accessible to any farmer using fertilizer and doesn't require a chemist or engineer to build it. Further, I'm guessing since Afghanistan is about twelve centuries behind even Iraq regarding infrastructure and paved roads, most detonations were underbelly buried in the dirt road or stacked in culverts. Sir, I've heard explosively formed projectiles (EFP) are showing up in your AO. Iran is supplying the plates, primarily copper, but some steel. The local insurgents can fabricate the rest in any bare bones equipped machine shop, but the plates need to be precisely engineered, otherwise they end up with a basic shaped charge — good but not as effective. Copper is the best choice because it is more malleable than steel and has less spalling when it detonates. They fit the EFP with a passive infrared device making it victim operated. Hell, he can stand off miles and just activate it with a cell phone when he sees your patrols coming. Very little risk to him."

"Mr. Quinn," Erickson said, "let me interrupt you. Where did you get this information? Have you been in our — disregard. Stand down for a minute."

*****

Erickson turned to Simms and whispered, "Harry, has Quinn been in our SCIF (Sensitive compartmentalized information facility), or had other access to our classified intelligence?"

Simms shook his head and said, "Gun, this is the first time I've seen him. One thing Major Neesom got right was following your order to shut him out. He had no direct or indirect access to any intelligence from our Brigade."

Erickson looked at Gabe and then Simms. "You're positive?"

"Gun, I am positive."

Erickson stared at the civilian. "I just learned about the EFPs in our AO last week, and his guesswork about what we faced in Afghanistan…how in the hell did he — Damn!"

Afak, Iraq

Ghazi lifted the sobbing girl and held her against his chest. He stroked her hair and wiped tears and dirt from her face. Her continued whimpers set him off. He slapped her. She cried out. He joined in her

101

screams and hit her over and over, until only soft moans escaped her bloodied mouth. He tore at her clothes reducing them to measly rags scattered across the dirt. Thrilled by her fear, he took her. Amidst her groans and muffled pleas, he brutalized her. Throughout the rape, he glared at her father.

Kaseem was mortified by his impotence to protect his daughter's innocence.

After twenty minutes of unrelenting torture, Ghazi lifted his spent manhood from the child. Turning to his soldiers, he said, "Enjoy her as I have under the approving eyes of *Allah*."

At some point during the repeated raping, the whimpers silenced. She was dead. Ghazi trembled in delight seeing her naked violated body soak the earth with blood. He looked at his blood-lust possessed men. They wanted more.

"Where is your modesty?" Ghazi said. "Do not offend her femininity. Cover her body."

*****

The boy had watched as the big persons touched the smaller person with the long hair many times. It was similar to the way the big person he knew had touched the other long haired person he knew, yet different. Now both of the long haired persons he knew were asleep. He hoped they would awaken and bring him the cool stuff he liked to sip. The cool stuff made him happy. The sleeping persons did not look happy. He pushed the tractor across the floor toward the big person who had first touched the shorter long haired person he knew.

5th Brigade Headquarters Conference room, Friday, 1340 hours
"Mr. Quinn, where did you get the information about— " Erickson looked away from him to the window. He shook his head and ran a hand across his hair. "Continue, Mr. Quinn."

"Colonel, do you mind if I move closer to the map?"

Erickson waved him forward. "Be my guest."

Gabe made his way through the narrow aisle, apologizing the entire way as he stepped on and over desert tan boots. He stopped in front of the map, found a pointer and tapped the end of it on Basrah.

"Sir, the EFPs probably transit north to the battle in Baghdad following the same route the Bedouin have used since the days of Abraham. They'll pass right under the eyes of your forces at FOB Adder through Nasariyah to An Najaf, and then further north. If coalition forces or Mother Nature blocks the route, hajji will take an alternate one through Al Amarah to the north and east of Nasariyah. Weapons won't move south since Iran is right next door to Basrah and easily supplies the insurgency against the Brits. Our forces north of Baghdad are fighting mostly al Qaeda and have yet to encounter EFPs. Iran, to date, has not brokered an agreement to supply them. That day may come, but I just don't see it — too many old scores to settle, and all of AQI are *Sunni*. In and around Baghdad you'll face the EFP, since the battle there is against diverse militias with mixed alliances, but some are allied with Ayatollah Khamenei and Amadinejad. The JAM forces in the south are also a mixed bag."

Looking at Erickson as if he was the only person in the room, Gabe said, "Sir, there will be the cell leaders, the hard cores, who will command a crowd of insurgents with varying degrees of loyalty to Jihad. Some of their militia will be in and out of the battle based on the time of the year and the harvest. Others will join only for the money. Sir, the key is the cell leaders. You must find and kill them. They operate independently of one another, but there'll be regional commanders, who may fall within provincial boundaries. More than likely, their commands are aligned along tribal influences and allegiances. All will be *Shi'ite* and heavily influenced by the decrees from Iran."

Turning back to the others in the room, Gabe said, "In the immediate area of Adder you can expect sporadic IDF (indirect fire), mostly 122 rockets because of their range. My guess is hajji will shoot from the suburbs of Nasariyah and from the canals south and southeast of the FOB, from thirteen to sixteen clicks out. The terrain west of the Adder is desert, sparsely populated and few navigable ratlines. If they were shooting 107 rockets, maybe the west would come into play since an enemy could probably haul one on a dirt bike. But not 122s. They're damn near nine-feet long. They'd need a pickup or jingo truck to move a rocket that big. Since he needs heavier transport, he must use firm trails. Hajji won't get close enough to attack your base with mortars, not even the 120s — maximum range of five maybe six clicks. No sir, he'll stay out and just piss from a distance at night with his big rockets.

"I'd expect incoming sporadically from a half hour after sundown to the same before sunrise. Iran wants results so it's not going to supply 122s willy-nilly. The rocket attacks will be in short volleys of only three to seven rockets. If he gets a kill, the intensity of the attacks will increase within one to two weeks of the kill — about as long as it'll take Iran to resupply the successful cell. The bad news, the unit you are replacing will be hit soon — a catastrophic hit. Hajji will want them to be further demoralized before they leave. It happens to every unit, and I'm sure the same holds true in Afghanistan. The good news, when you are in the middle of the RIP, you get a free ride for a couple of weeks. Hajji won't expose himself to an enemy that is double normal strength. Sir, do you want me to stop? I don't want to — "

Absorbed in the civilian's brief, Erickson waved off the question. "Continue, Mr. Quinn."

"Yes, sir. You'll get a couple of weeks to gain situational awareness before hajji ramps up to test your tactics. After the RIP is complete, he'll probe you. As I said earlier, he'll hit Adder with 122s, and possibly 240s. With the 240, there's no such thing as a near miss. If hajji gets those on you, well, well…you know, sir. Your smaller units operating at the outposts will be attacked with mortars. Looking at your icon just south and east of Diwaniyah, they should expect an attack early in the rotation. The Poles operate FOB Echo in Diwaniyah. Thank God for allies, but they don't want to join the fight. They'll only be concerned with securing where they eat and sleep, and not pissing off *Jaish al Mahdi*. The militia owns the day and night in that area. That means your small unit at the outposts will take the brunt of it. South of Adder, between outposts 8 and 9, sir, 8 should be all right. They're isolated with no substantial villages nearby. In addition, the indigenous tribes in the area, the Al-Montifig and the Al-Montairat, are mostly Bedouin goat herders content to let the war by pass them. 9…different story. It sits right next to area thirty-eight.

"I bumped into a contractor from Global Security who used to roll down ASR Boston through that area. He told me his company had the contract to secure the unexploded ordnance (UXO) in area thirty-eight missed by our advancing forces early in the war. He described it as several square miles of row upon row of bunkers bursting at the seams with ordnance. They tried to blow several bunkers, but had to stop. Too dangerous. There were secondary explosions lasting more than a week. Your soldiers at 9 are sitting on hajji's treasure trove of ordnance. Hajji won't look too kindly on your soldiers in their backyard. As you can see, the outpost is within range of mortar fire.

Sir, area thirty-eight is also in the backyard of a key village."

Gabe tapped the map with his pointer. "Suq ash Shuyukh is where I'd establish my base of operations if I was hajji. Close to Adder, MSR Tampa, area thirty-eight and could be easily defended. Hajji will control it and secure his safe haven. Sir, the tribes there are a mixture of al-Montifig, al-Montairat, but more importantly, al-Ribad. The Montifig and Montairat will roll over for the insurgents after they get their attention with a few key assassinations. The Ribad tribe — well, sir, they're already with them. Indian country, sir. Suq ash Shuyukh is the key to hajji…and to you."

Afak, Iraq

He had their attention, but still it was not finished. They were in a feeding frenzy. They wanted more.

The boy stopped pushing the toy when he reached Ghazi. He looked at his father, dead mother and sister, then up at him. He opened his mouth as if to speak, but speech was not possible. Ghazi looked down at him and patted his head.

"Take the boy like you did his sister."

He endured the sodomy in silence. Alienated from the world of the hearing and speaking, the assault on him by those in that world was one more outrage he could not understand. Physically stronger than his sister, he survived. When it was over, tears streamed down his cheeks. Still clutching the toy, he looked up at Ghazi. It was the last living person he saw before the butt of the AK-47 crushed his skull.

Ghazi laid the rifle down and wiped the blood spatters from his bare legs. The smile that curled at the corners of his mouth turned to a snarl when he looked at Kaseem.

"Did you enjoy the feast? It is time for the finale, the desert — the best part."

5BCT Headquarters Conference room, Friday, 1355 hours

After digesting what Gabe had said about Suq ash Shuyukh, Erickson shifted gears. "Mr. Quinn, what tactics should we employ against the enemy?"

Gabe looked up to the ceiling for guidance, wondering whether he should answer. He decided to play it safe. "Colonel, in this room of unequaled talent, and me, probably able to muster at most mere ounces of grey matter compared with the fifty-pound brains of your more than capable staff — I'm not qualified to answer the question. It is well outside my limited capabilities, sir."

Erickson chuckled. "Mr. Quinn, humor me and take a stab at it."

Gabe thought about tactics he knew would work, but surely garner him censure. "Sir, you know how the enemy fights. They seem cold and brutal to most, but they are effective. It's hard to compete with an enemy whose only notion of an atrocity is the atrocity of losing. In Mosul, we had trouble recruiting and vetting locals to join the Iraqi Security Forces. When we were finally able to lure in some recruits with money, decent food, appeals to national pride and probably the first real shoes they ever owned, we began to feel good about our chances for some success. Three weeks into the training cycle, over our protests, the Iraqi leadership yielded to the whining of the recruits, and allowed them to go home for two days."

Lost in his thoughts, Gabe fell silent. Images of that day suddenly overwhelmed him. He shook his head, clearing his mind of the barbarity, and spoke in a low voice. "Sir, on the day of their expected return, hajji kidnapped nine recruits, tortured them, and stuck their heads on pikes right outside our camp."

Gabe smiled. "You have to admire their dedication to the mission. One single act of savagery set us back on our heels. None of the other recruits came back — gone — in the wind. Contrast their sense of purpose and dedication to the rules of engagement and escalation of force (ROE/EOF) that our young men and women are saddled with when they go into battle. Colonel, I appreciate a fair fight when it's for sport. This ain't sport. When we manage to capture an insurgent, we question him with some damn rules dictated by ACLU, and end up sending him to Abu Ghraib or Camp Bucca, to await trial based on battlefield evidence. Unless you assign a CSI and an investigative team to every soldier in the field, you won't get anywhere near the bar set by the legal eagles. No sir, we place insurgents in what are the graduate schools for terrorism until some panel of Iraqi judges determine they're innocent or reformed, and then set them loose on the battlefield armed with new and better tactics. I don't know what the experts are saying, but I bet the recidivism percentage is over ninety. I'm getting a little off point, but I've lost a few buddies over the years because of this bullshit."

Again he stopped. Fearing he was about to display emotions meant for private times, he looked down. After a moment, he looked to the back of the room and saw Lieutenant Loving. To him, she appeared representative of all of the young soldiers readying to march into the meat grinder. It was then that he realized he had to answer the question — more was at stake than his contract. If he threw out enough nuggets he had mined over the years, she and the others in the room might take hold of one that would help them once in Iraq.

"As to your tactics, first and foremost is keeping the press out. They are not your friends. To be blunt, the military's operational security (OPSEC) sucks. Right now hajji knows the names, ranks, hell, even the hometowns of your key staff. When you mount an operation, hajji will know."

Erickson straightened. "Mr. Quinn, that's a pretty damning assessment of our OPSEC. We adhere to the rules and take security seriously. What is the basis for your statement?"

"Colonel, take a look at the 'Stars and Stripes,' any edition. You'll find accurate battle damage assessments about coalition losses, giving the names, units and hometowns of our dead. If you read issues within the past few weeks, I'm positive there is a story about you and details about the upcoming transfer of authority at Adder. There are articles about the superiority of our equipment — articles that give untold insight to our enemy about how to counter our weaponry. Stories about our added armor, leaks about the soon to be fielded MRAPs and their V-hulls. Watch the Armed Forces Network, Europe edition, and you'll be flooded with stories about current and future operations, be they tactical or merely civil/military operations (CMO). Down range, every unit has an internal newsletter that's supposed to make the soldiers feel good about their role in the war. You know, happy birthday to sergeant or private whomever, congratulations to lieutenant what's his name on the birth of blah, blah, blah. When the internal 'feel good' rag finds its way to the trash instead of a burn bag, hajji takes it home. But not to wipe his ass with it. Sir, that just scratches the surface of the leaks from military sources.

"When you consider our free press and all of those damn embedded journalists, well the information going hajji's way is considerable. When you get in country, take a close look at all of the local nationals (LN) we employ. We've got LNs filling the water tanks, driving the honeydew wagons, burning our trash and cleaning our toilets. Damn near every one of them has a cell phone — a damn cell phone! What's so important about cleaning shit from our latrines that they need to call someone? Sir, these hajjis leave the base every night. So in addition to real time intelligence about departing patrols, probably following the same SALUTE format your soldiers use —

each night they return to their village and provide a detailed after action report to their command."

"Mr. Quinn, one moment please." Erickson made more notes on his pad, then motioned him to continue.

"Hajji knows if he can disrupt the coalition forces communication lines you'll be forced to airlift supplies to the battle. Obviously, you don't have enough air assets. Therefore, your mission is vital to the success of the war. How do you win? Fight their game, play by their rules. I'm sure many in here are familiar with the Phoenix program and know it was criticized and eventually halted by Congress. Nonetheless, it was effective. Ask Charlie Cong. Between '68 and '71, the program neutralized over eighty thousand Viet Cong. Our people used the local nationals to get inside the VC to identify the leaders and later take 'em out. Very effective, but of course it was painted by Congress as being nothing more than an assassination campaign. In Mosul, we attempted a smaller version of the concept and had some successes. The Judas project was — "

Stunned, Laddick jumped out of his seat. "Colonel, as Brigade JAG officer, I can't allow this man's opinion to go unchallenged. Sir, with all respect to you and the soldiers in your command, you need to stop him from where he's taking this discussion. It's clear to me that he's advocating the suspension of our ROE. It smacks of a total disregard of how we, as American civilized soldiers, fight wars. Furthermore, his raising the Judas project is outrageous!"

"Thank you, Major Laddick, for reminding me what my duties are as the Brigade commander. You seem to be on a roll. Since the taxpayers are paying your salary to advocate..." With a menacing glare, the colonel barked, "Advocate!"

Laddick launched an attack on Gabe that resembled the best of Hollywood's superficial treatment of courtroom drama. He laced his arguments with Latin terms unique to the law profession, plenty of finger pointing and voice inflection that went up and down like an elevator. He attacked him with references to the 'Just war' theory, rules of war, and the Geneva Conventions. Ten minutes later, he neared his summation.

"You sir, are dead wrong. I am familiar with the Judas project. In fact, when there is an accounting to be made of that program's abuses, I hope to be a part of that review. That program was nothing more than death squads committing wanton murder. You are most likely a cheerleader for the tactics employed by General 'Black' Jack Pershing. You, sir...go home and leave the fighting to the

108

professionals."

Reeling, not from the expected onslaught, but from the unexpected assailant, Gabe tried to understand why his battle buddy slighted him earlier and now completely severed the bonds of brotherhood. Studying his opponent in this jousting it dawned on him this was a rematch. Major Laddick was not in the tower with him and Dog Shit during the attack. Laddick was the giant in the next-door motel room assaulting a young woman.

Gabe returned fire. "Major La Dick — "

The deafening laughter of his brother officers, sparked the Major to speak again. "It is Laddick, not La Dick. Laddick, Laddick, Laddick!"

Surprised by the ease of rattling him, Gabe decided to goad him further. "Of course, sir. Please excuse my error. It's Laddick, not La Dick. I won't make the mistake of calling you La Dick again. Major Laddick, let me begin with your last point that I should go home and leave the fighting to the professionals. Gladly, sir. I'm a peace freak, not a fighter. That's your job. Furthermore, if you give me your personal guarantee, that you, Major Laddick, can turn the tide of this war according to your concepts of justice, and you also assure me you'll wrap up this inconvenient little war in a civilized fashion before my grandson comes of age, I'll take my non-combatant candy-ass home and go fishing. Can you give me those assurances, sir?"

Laddick glared at him.

"Of course you can't guarantee diddly squat," Gabe said. "Regarding Black Jack Pershing and his tactics, I assume you're referring to the years between 1909 and 1913 when he was Governor of the Moro province in the Philippines. I'm also assuming that you refer to the alleged...alleged, counselor...slaughter of Muslims at Mount Dajo and the Taglibi camp and the subsequent desecration of their corpses with pig's blood. My reading on the subject disclosed conflicting anecdotal accounts about the incident. If you studied Pershing's contemporary memos and orders of that era, you would find nothing. Not a scintilla of hard evidence showing the incident occurred. I will accede that possibly one of his subordinates, Colonel Alexander Rodgers of the 6th Cavalry, partook in some form of pig bloodletting against the *juramentados*. If he did and it worked, well, that's just damn fine and dandy in my books."

He waited for a comeback from Laddick. It did not come. "Your references to the Just War theory are equally flawed. I think we are beyond the first premise of *jus ad bellum*. Central, and arguably the most important condition of *jus ad bellum,* if you follow the line of thinking espoused by Saint Thomas Aquinas, Francisco de Vitoria, Samuel Wolff and de Vattel, is that we as a country — you, me, all of us — have a just cause. Major Laddick, do you believe our cause is just?"

Hearing no response, he continued. "Outstanding. We agree our cause is just. Moving to *jus in bello,* or the 'just' conduct within war, that is where we part company, Major. You seem to hang your argument on proportionality and discrimination. During my youth, and through my various careers, I was guided by a simple axiom — don't bring a knife to a gunfight. I'm no Dirty Harry. Quite the opposite. I'm a die-hard, chicken shit coward, but one with common sense. Where is the honor in losing because you failed to pull that new high tech deadly arrow from your quiver and use it to kill the enemy? As to discrimination in combat — I'll buy into that precept if it doesn't mean American blood is spilled because of someone's benign, but inept decision made in the heat of combat. If you dig further into the writings of theorists, theists and academicians, you'll discover that even some of them argue that innocents die in war and their deaths do not abrogate the just cause of the perpetrator.

"Sir, I could go through *jus post bellum* with you, but to be honest, the entire discussion of the 'just war' theory bores me. The arguments relate to hostilities between standing armies, and in no way do they apply to the insurgents we're fighting. Your final point about the Judas project — what was it? Oh yes, wanton murder. I didn't murder anyone. How can one commit murder in the middle of the war? Sir, it is the Wild West over there. Iraqis ran Judas, with some American oversight. The program, well, how do I put it? The goal of the program was to reverse the mistakes made by Paul Bremer and Donald Rumsfeld in the days following the toppling of Saddam's statue in Baghdad.

"Bremer, as head of the Coalition Provisional Administration, recklessly purged the leadership of the Iraq army and police force with his de-Bathification program. In so doing, he created a void, a void that in the aftermath of his ill-advised policy was filled by the fifth column, the very same insurgency you now fight. I am not at liberty to discuss details with you, because I don't know your clearance. Moreover, I do not intend to defend the program or my part in it, with you or anyone of your cut until that 'gotcha' inquisition you mentioned is knocking at my door. Finally, your declaration that I am dead wrong — I may end up dead during this deployment, but wrong

— don't think so. If you believe that, explain it to the soldiers filling the body bags with their friends."

Gabe did not think himself to be a violent man, but he felt like jumping over the chairs to get at Laddick.

The room was as quiet as a crypt. The combatants glared at each other. Finally, Laddick broke contact and sat in his chair. Gabe could not, so he clenched his fists and jammed them inside his pockets.

Erickson covered his smile with a hand. He returned the trademark scowl to his face, and with final theatrical flair, stood and hefted *Brynhildn* to his shoulder. Slowly grazing the room with his chilled gaze, he stopped when he reached Neesom. Returning the piss and vinegar to his voice, he spoke to all, but directed the firestorm at him.

"When I ask a fucking question, I expect a fucking answer! It's time to grow some balls. People, we're going to war. This meeting is over."

The entire command jumped to attention as the colonel and the others at the table marched through the doorway into the corridor. Those left standing in the room relaxed when Erickson was out of earshot. Gabe heard some laughs, a few curse words, but on whole, each seemed pleased that a piece of his or her ass did not leave the room with Viking Warrior Six.

A young captain approached Gabe and held out his hand. "I am Captain Kowalewski, Mr. Quinn. Excellent brief, sir."

Gabe shook hands with him and said, "Thanks." Still irked by the confrontation with Major Laddick, and thinking Erickson would cancel his contract, he slowly moved through the soldiers toward the hallway.

Lieutenant Loving blocked him at the door. She grabbed his arm and pulled him in. Then she tilted her head up and whispered, "Mr. Quinn, thank you for what you tried to do."

Gabe broke free of her light grasp and took a step back. "Lieutenant, uh, ma'am, you're welcome, but it was nothing. Really, nothing at all. I believe the colonel was a bit premature in cutting you off, but I'm sure he didn't mean anything by it."

Puzzled, Loving hesitated before responding. "Oh, yes, Mr. Quinn. Thank you for that also."

Afak, Iraq

Ghazi pulled the knife dagger with its highly honed six-inch blade, from the dirt floor. Kaseem's unresponsive eyes widened as his leader waved it back and forth.

He stood over him and said, "It is your time Kaseem. *Lah ilaha ill Allah.*"

Ghazi grabbed a handful of Kaseem's hair and jerked his head back, exposing the flesh on his neck. Kaseem struggled against the two soldiers holding his arms, blinked rapidly, his chest heaving as he gasped. He kicked out with his bound legs, twisting his body as he did.

"Hold him!" Ghazi shouted.

Ghazi made a thin cut through Kaseem's neck to the thyrohyoid membrane and cartilage. He continued his lateral cuts until the hypoid bone was barely visible. He increased pressure and sliced through muscle until he severed the bone.

Kaseem broke the hold of his captors and tucked his head into his chest. He shook violently, gurgling sounds escaped from the gash, blood streamed onto his chest.

Ghazi stood and watched Kaseem writhe on the dirt, spilling his life out. In an uncharacteristic act of mercy, he cut Kaseem's throat and quickly severed the main branches of the external carotid artery and the anterior jugular, easily cutting through the superior thyroid.

Rapidly bleeding out, Kaseem blinked uncontrollably, incapable of screaming, merely emitting bubbling noises from the deepened wound. Ghazi furthered his act of mercy and severed his facial and accessory nerves near the anterior border of the sternocleiomastoideus. Tired from the exertion, he forced the dagger further into the neck, struggling to sever the muscles protecting the cervical vertebra.

Kaseem, now dead, but still reflexively blinking, had gone completely limp. After labored carving and hacking, Ghazi finally cleared all bone and muscle and used knife as a scythe to cut the thin strings of skin that barely connected the head to the neck.

Naked, Ghazi dropped the dagger and stood clutching the decapitated head in his right hand. Blood coursed over his chest and legs to the floor as he held it high above him.

"Kaseem's Jihad is complete. Take the bodies to Suq ash Shuyukh. Place his head at the entry of the chief elder's home for all to see. Be mindful of Muhammad's teachings and properly cover the females. When the *Amerikees* come to the village tomorrow, we will have another surprise ready for them."

Colonel Erickson's office, Friday, 1445 hours

Erickson dropped *Brynhildn* and his legal pad on the credenza and quickly skirted around the desk. "Close the door."

112

Simms held up a sheet of paper and said, "Gun, I was just handed this a few— "

"Couple of matters, Harry. First, prepare Major Neesom a glowing OER for my signature. Put in whatever's necessary to promote him out of my brigade up to Corps. He won't be able to get anybody killed from behind a desk."

Erickson chuckled so low it seemed it was for his amusement alone. "Second, Major La Dick, my JAG officer — assign him supplemental duties of the S1 shop until we get a replacement for Major Hedrond. It should keep him busy and away from the Joes. That man reads too much liberal shit. Third, Lieutenant Loving... find out what her job is. She showed more balls, or whatever the female equivalent is, than the others. If she's not in a critical position put her in CMO. Fourth, cancel that appointment of mine with the Stars and Stripes reporter. Tell him to reschedule for next year after we return. And while we're on OPSEC issues, when we get settled in Iraq, collect all cell phones from the locals. If they have a legitimate need for a phone, we'll provide it and monitor their calls. Fifth... disregard. Before we get to five, I need your input, Harry. What'd you think of our Mr. Gabe Quinn?"

"Sir, a bit eccentric, maybe even a bit dangerous, but Gun, overall I was impressed. Colonel, there's something I must show you — "

"Harry, my thoughts exactly. Hell, I like dangerous. Look at the profession we chose. That oddball knew more about our mission than many of our staff officers. His description about how to play the lousy hand we've been dealt damn near matches mine. And his off-the-cuff brief — shit, the only thing he missed in the METT-TC brief was the weather conditions, and I'll bet if asked, he would have known. I don't know yet how to use him, but — Harry, see what you can learn about this Judas thing. Don't go through Major La Dick though. I rather like that, La Dick. It grabs you. Also, assign Sergeant Walker to get Quinn outfitted for Iraq. I think he'll look good in a uniform after he gets intimate with a razor and a barber. We'll figure out how to use him when we get down range."

"Yes, sir. I'll let personnel find him a slot until we sort things out." Simms held up the sheet of paper. "Gun, there's something else you need to know."

"What is it, Harry?"

Reading the email silently for a second time, Simms said, "Sir, bad news from FOB Adder. Our advance team alerted me that the unit we're replacing took a major hit today. Actually a catastrophic hit."

113

"How bad?"

"Responding to a report from a village elder, a team was sent to investigate a possible assassination of an Iraqi policeman, his wife and two children. During the response, the patrol triggered daisy-chained IEDs, causing six KIA and at least four WIA. Comes at a bad time sir...them supposed to go home in a few weeks."

"Harry, you know there's never a good time."

Falling into his executive chair, Erickson stared through the window, lost in thoughts about the ambush thousands of miles away. After several anguished minutes, he turned back toward Simms.

"Where were they ambushed, Harry?"

"Suq ash Shuyukh."

ميزان

Balance

Part Two

War is cruel and you cannot refine it. War at best is barbarism.

— Civil War General, William Tecumseh Sherman

Dude, war is a video game.

— American soldier, Iraq

Chapter 10
The elephant

FOB Adder, aka Talil Air Field, Iraq, June 27, 2007, 0300 hours

"Damn, they're inside the wire! We've got hajjis on our right flank. Hit 'em! Hit 'em with the rocket. Damnit, I said hit 'em! You wanna fucking die? Good hit, Saunders. Good fucking hit, dude."

"Mop 'em up with the ma deuce, they're still moving. No prisoners baby. Nope, no prisoners today. Die mutha fucka, die!"

"Look out, look out. They've moved a PKM into position. On the rooftop at your eleven, Saunders. Oh shit, I think they have our number."

"Take it easy, Boykin. This ain't my first fucking rodeo. You worry about your sector. I've got mine covered."

"Got it bro, got it. Little confusing right now. How's your ammo doing? I'm getting low, may need to…oh damn, that looks like…it is, it is…hit that truck, Saunders…he's comin' in hot…VBIED for sure. That thing blows we're fucked."

"I've got it, I've got it."

"Damn, Boykin, did you see that thing blow? Beautiful, I mean whoomph, hajji heaven. Look at that. His leg must've flown fifty yards. Ha, this is fantastic. Bring it on, hajji. I'll kill every last one of you rag heads."

"At your nine Saunders, at your nine, four hundred, no, four fifty out. In that window, three up, yeah three up and two over. You see him?"

"I've got him, Boykin. Settle down, dude. I'm waiting for that son of a bitch to come out of the shadows. Once he takes a peek, it will be his last fucking look at this world. Time to freedom his ass and let him collect on those virgins. I hope he gets the clap and his dick falls off."

"Just a little bit more, a little bit, that's it, yeah baby, time to take his head off with the Barrett. Just a bit more...he's moving out now. I can see him in the window. Yeah, I have the shot, Boykin...I have it...I've got him now...I'm taking it...."

Bam, Bam, Bam...Bam, Bam, Bam.

"Aw shit! Hit pause, Saunders. I'll see what this asshole wants. Can't have any fun in this damn war! Jeezus fucking Christ."

Boykin jumped from his bunk and in two strides stomped the six feet to the barrack's door. He grabbed the handle and flung the door against the prefab's metal wall, then peered into the darkness with an 'I'm gonna tear you a new one' look. "What the fuck do you — First Sergeant, good morning. Uh, wha-what'd I do?"

Forty-three years of mean, twenty-five of them in the service of the Army, First Sergeant Thayer said in a deep voice, "You stumps shut down the fucking X-Box. Major Laddick has a mission for you. Go over to billeting. Find out where they housed our fucking civilian, Quinn, yeah, Gabriel Quinn. I think he's down at LA 7 with the other fucking war tourists. When you find this civilian, tell same he needs to gear up and be at motor pool 5 at 0630 for a patrol brief. SP (start patrol) at 0650 hours. Are you getting this, Boykin?"

"Sure, First Sergeant. Find Quinn and tell him to grab his gear and be at motor pool 6 for a 0500 hours patrol brief. SP at — "

"How the fuck you made it into my Army got a cherry fobbitt assignment to S1? Jesus Christ."

Thayer leaned in and flooded Boykin's senses with an odor that smelled of after-shave and mouthwash, tinctured with Jim Beam. He grabbed a handful of Boykin's t-shirt, drew him in even closer, and narrowed his stare to a squint. "Why you didn't do the honorable thing and commit suicide with the other million brain-dead sperm that ran down your momma's diseased ass after Jody dismounted — shit."

Thayer pushed Boykin to his bunk and said, "All right numb nuts, let's try this again. I want you and your chair-borne Ranger buddy — yeah, I mean you, Saunders...to find Quinn. Got that?"

Heads nodded at whiplash speed.

"Well, fucking fantastic. Tell Quinn he's to be at motor pool 6. Damnit, you two are like a fucking contagious bacterium. Now you got me doing it. Motor pool 5. 0630 hours patrol brief. SP at 0650. Tell him to hook up with the LOGPAC (logistical package) heading to COP 6. That's it. Well PFC Beavis, PFC Butthead, do you think you two can un-fuck yourselves temporarily and not fuck up this mission? Do I need to…screw it. You shit bags blow this one, I'll put your asses outside the wire wearing pink panties so hajji can tear you a new one."

In unison, convinced that Thayer might actually put their asses outside the wire in the, God forbid, real war, Boykin and Saunders assumed the position and shouted, "Roger, First Sergeant."

"Fucking wonderful. Leave a trail of bread crumbs." Thayer stumbled into the darkness mumbling, "I don't need two fucking DUSTWUNs (duty status, whereabouts unknown)."

Living Area 7, Room 217B, 0340 hours

Two hours before sunrise, yet Gabe streamed sweat. He nursed a cup of fresh brewed coffee as he sat on the stoop of his hooch. A faint sandy breeze tickled his crotch from under his well-worn blue and red polka dot skivvies. The only noise was the hum from the generators that powered the transient desert city oasis.

He felt lucky to have a room of his own. The French-made prefab contained three sleeping quarters, each seven by nine feet. His room had a bunk with a two-inch Iraqi mattress, a window air conditioner that struggled to keep the ambient temperature below 95 degrees, and his only luxury, a five-cup coffee maker.

A sodium light illuminated the toilet trailer seventy-five yards from his room. Fifty yards beyond the toilets was a shower trailer. The local Iraqis cleaned both prefab units at least once a day. Most cherished, however, was the bunker, a mere twelve leaps from his bed. Cherished because the concrete steel reinforced inverted U might save his life when the 122 rockets were flying.

It was all good — the worm had turned in Gabe's favor. He could get into this fobbitt life. The base camp had a Burger King, Pizza Hut and an old Saddam barracks used as a theater for the occasional USO show put on by some no name acts from the States. He heard he might get internet to his room. *Screw going outside the wire. Almost a week into this deployment and I haven't even seen the wire. The Army has forgotten about me.*

A pair of lights broke his pre-dawn solace. The beams weaved and crossed, making their way through the maze of the other hundred trailers and the labyrinth of perimeter and interior blast walls.

He heard two men talk and laugh as they stumbled over the gravel. Errantly or purposely, they kicked stones against the sides of the trailers, stirring the sleeping occupants. Common at most military compounds in Iraq, the gravel was a great way to control dust fifty weeks of the year and mud during the other two weeks. However, it became secondary shrapnel during a rocket or mortar attack. Which was worse, a few pounds of daily dust for the lungs to flush, or a golf ball sized piece of rock hitting a skull at warp speed? Gabe was not Mensa material but even he could answer that one.

First, the beams found the room number on his door. Then the blinding lights shifted to hit him square in the face. Their laughter and conversation abruptly stopped as the men took in the sight of a shaggy looking civilian lounging in polka dot shorts.

"Sir," Boykin said, "we're looking for a civilian named Quinn. You know him?"

Gabe threw his coffee to the ground as his contribution to the Coalition's dust control effort and stood. "I'm Quinn."

Dressed in full battle rattle, Boykin and Saunders kept their flashlights aimed at his face. "Good morning, sir. I'm PFC Boykin and this is PFC Saunders. We're from the 82nds S1. Sir, uh…the higher ups want you to join a convoy that's heading north to do a resupply of a combat outpost."

Boykin lowered the flashlight and checked the notes he had scrawled on his palm, then returned the beam to Gabe's face. "You are to report to motor pool 5 for a patrol brief at 0630 hours, SP at 0650."

"Fine." Blinded, Gabe pointed to the flashlights. "Privates, do you mind?"

"Sorry, sir."

After he regained some of his lost night vision, Gabe looked in the direction of the soldier he believed had spoken to him and asked, "What higher up do I thank?"

"That'd be Major Laddick," Boykin said. "Acting S1, sir."

Unsure why a JAG officer assigned to a temporary personnel billet could issue an order, Gabe decided to let the mystery slide to another time. "Where's motor pool 5?"

"It's about a half mile from here," Saunders said. "Do you know where Camp Terandak, the Aussie camp is?"

"I wasn't aware of its name, but I know where their TOC (Tactical Operations Center) is."

"Too easy, sir," Saunders said. "The motor pool is right next to the Aussie camp and has a bunch of those huge tents they use to work on our vehicles."

"Gentlemen, thank you. One more question. Is this a day trip or

119

should I pack?"

"Well, sir, the supply convoy usually pushes on north beyond the outpost when they do a resupply. Probably a week before they return south, at least a week, sir. I wish we were going with you. Damn, a chance to get outside the wire and get personal with the hajjis. Wow, I mean, dude, me and Saunders could do some real damage out there." With a dreamy look on his face, Boykin mumbled something about gettin' some. "Don't worry none though, sir. It should be a milk run."

Outside the wire, is a good thing? Can't forget the enemy also has a stake in the war.

Gabe was amused by their PX warrior gear queer appearance. The first thing that jumped out was the Rambo knives that hung from their utility belts. They looked John Wayne cool, but were cumbersome and had serrated blades. *A finely honed, double-edged boot dagger is more effective. From a crouched position, two quick slashes in an upward movement across the inside thigh — femoral artery and vein slashed. Continue up the torso with cuts under the armpits — sub clavian artery and axillary vein severed. When the target falls, two more cuts — carotid artery and jugular vein ripped. No bones to hang up the serrated blade — just flesh and sinew. Over in two, three seconds tops. Clean, perfect symmetry — poetry in red emotion. Mark him, then move on to another target.*

The next thing that drew his attention was their M4 assault rifles. Secured by three-point slings, they carried the rifles at the combat ready position and had added tactical flashlights, laser mounts and an extra ammo pouch to the collapsible butt stocks. Night observation device (NOD) rhino mounts were attached to their Kevlar helmets. The Interceptor Body Armor (IBA) was adorned with numerous pouches, First Aid kits, combat tourniquets looped through a Velcro strap, three standard double load magazine pouches, zip ties, neck and throat protectors, combat gloves and ballistic glasses, woven through one of the snaps on the side small arms fire protective insert (SAPI) plate carriers. Their ensembles were completed with forty-five ounce Camelback water carriers, kneepads, elbow pads and other assorted accoutrements necessary to the personnel section's war on an enemy they would never meet.

"You can take my place on the convoy," Gabe said. "In fact, why not join me? I'm on a first name basis with Major Laddick. I'm sure that he could call someone and add you to the manifest."

Boykin exchanged a panicked look with Saunders before he stammered, "Um, well, we'd love to, sir, but First Sergeant Thayer has another mission for us today. Yeah, another mission. And sir, that mission takes priority over everything. Sure appreciate the offer though, sir."

In a lowered voice, almost as if he was including Gabe in some grand conspiracy, Boykin said, "Sir, you don't need to mention this to Major Laddick. He's a real busy officer, sir. And, well, Mr. Quinn we really need to return to our unit. Good luck, sir."

Gabe knew these young men could easily become casualties of indirect fire or some non-combat related accident. Whether they died from combat or an accident wouldn't make an iota of difference to their loved ones. Dead is dead.

"Privates, I was kidding," Gabe said. "Not to worry. Major Laddick and I are barely on a last name basis. Can I offer you a cup of coffee before you leave? It's not as good as Greenbeans, but it's strong and it's free."

Saunders and Boykin declined, did an about face and began the return trek to their hooch. These soldiers had another battle to finish, a battle still waiting on pause.

"Stay safe, soldiers."

Motor pool 5, FOB Adder, 0610 hours

Still low on the horizon, yet visible above the Ziggurat, the red ball had raised the temperature to a hundred and five degrees. It promised to top one hundred and twenty-five before day's end. Sweat-soaked and almost spent from his half-mile walk with eighty pounds of gear, Gabe cursed the gravel that strived to trip him up and wrench a knee or an ankle. He pushed on until he saw several military cargo trucks and armored security vehicles parked near a trailer.

Four soldiers, stripped down to their army ACU pants and desert tan t-shirts, laughed as they chased and threw ice at a female soldier. Bowled over by the irony — a child's game of war in the middle of a real war — and envious of their youth and energy, he stopped and dropped his ruck-pack on the gravel. Probably their first deployment and yet to be blooded, he hoped they retained some of their youthful innocence after they returned home.

The female soldier took a direct hit to her head. She stopped dead in her tracks and turned to face her attackers. Teeth bared, eyes wide beyond crazy, the pint-sized soldier growled with a weighty Jersey accent, "You wanna fuckin' play? Let's fuckin' play."

She scooped a handful of gravel, targeted the nearest soldier and pummeled him with a perfectly aimed barrage that found its target

121

with such precision a firearms range coach would beam approval. Not one, but three direct hits to the soldier's groin.

The wounded soldier fell in a heap. He grasped his injured parts and fought an urge to cry as he writhed and squirmed towards the protection of a truck. Surrounded by his brothers in arms, the only aid he received was laughter and hollow reassurances.

One pointed at the stricken soldier and broke some more ice. "Dumb ass, you know not to fuck with Combat Barbie. She's a hundred pounds of whoop ass, a real Jersey ball-buster."

Combat Barbie approached the laid-out soldier and offered her hand to aid his return to the standing Army. "Gee, I'm really sorry," she said. As he reached for her hand, she planted a kick to his groin and howled, "I was aimin' for your left fuckin' nut."

Still laughing, the soldiers with un-bruised manhood dropped back to give Combat Barbie a respectful, wise and wide berth.

She triumphantly shouted, "Pussies."

Game finished, they returned to their vehicles and reclaimed their ACU blouses and boonies. Over several minutes, they fine-tuned their uniforms, gulped liters of water and devoured breakfast sandwiches. The attackers were soon joined by a dozen more soldiers. Together, they ambled toward the operations trailer and lined up in a loose military formation.

Gabe picked up his ruck and fell in behind.

Precisely at 0630 hours, a lieutenant emerged from the air-conditioned trailer. The ranking NCO in the formation shouted, "Atten-hut."

The order was soon followed by an 'at ease' from Lieutenant Lutz. She alternated her look between a notepad and the soldiers before zeroing in on Gabe. She acknowledged him with a curt nod then returned her attention to the formation.

"Listen up," she said. "The first part of our mission is to make a run to COP 6, refuel their tanker and drop four pallets of water, eight pallets of dry goods and some reefer supplies. We'll pull any required PM on our vehicles then push on to Scania where we'll overnight. Tomorrow morning at 0130 hours, we'll make a run to BIAP, pick up more supplies, then continue to several outposts between Baghdad and Speicher. With luck, good weather and no IEDs, we should return to outpost 6 in about ten days. Sergeant Fuller, what's the latest intel?"

Fuller looked up from the Brigade intelligence report and said, "Ma'am, in the last week there've been several SIGACTs (significant activity) including IED dets with casualties on MSR Tampa between checkpoints nine bravo and two bravo just this side of Scania. One of the explosions was in the vicinity of a catastrophic det that happened three weeks prior to our deployment. SAF (small arms fire) was reported just south of Scania two days ago following one of the IED dets. No casualties from the SAF. Hajji continues to limit his attacks between 2100 and 0500 hours meaning we should be all right on our run to the outpost. Our run from Scania to BIAP will fall within the window the enemy has taken a liking to. Our leg this morning is timed to follow an RCT (route clearance team) that's pushing through to Scania."

The sergeant gave enough time for the comforting news to sink in, then he kicked the legs out from under them. "Just because we got some bomb magnets clearing the path for us doesn't mean relax. Hajji can set up an IED within minutes of the clearance team passing, so if you screw up, you become a statistic on the nightly news. Stay in the game, stay awake and pucker up, people. That's all I have, ma'am."

"Thank you, Sergeant."

Lutz glanced quickly at the vehicles then at Combat Barbie. "You lost the lottery Specialist. You're taking the lead. Control the pace, this is not a race, but don't blow my timeline. When we get on the hardball, I want speed. We have a hundred and eighty clicks of potholes, washouts and pissed off indigenous types before we make it to the outpost, but that doesn't mean we blow my timeline. We should be there in five hours. Let me rephrase that — we *will* be there in five hours. Separation, keep it between a hundred fifty and two hundred meters once we get on the road. Stagger the formation, careful at the overpasses and culverts, don't bunch up. Remember the ROE and escalation of force rules. We don't need an incident to fire up the hajjis. If we get hit and you think you have PID, get my clearance first. I'll decide, not you. Let me repeat that one more time — if you think you have positive identification of a combatant, you get my clearance first. Clear on that?"

After she heard a lackluster, mumbled 'hooah' Lutz said, "All right, rock drills and roll-over drills."

Following several minutes of using stones to represent their vehicles covering maneuvers to counter an attack, Lutz said, "One more thing. We have a civilian riding with us to the outpost. Colucci, Mr. Quinn will ride in your vehicle. Get your pax to the outpost still breathing. All right, load up and let's get it done."

As the soldiers broke formation and headed to the vehicles, Lutz approached Gabe. "Quinn, I've heard about you."

Good or bad? Gabe looked at her and smiled.

"Follow instructions from your truck commander, sit back and enjoy the ride."

He reached back for some people skills he had picked up in the past. "Ma'am, I'm sorry that I got pushed on you like this. I know you don't need the headache of a civilian ride-along. It wasn't my doing."

"Mr. Quinn, you being here wasn't my doing either. I got word late last night that you'd be a pax on my convoy. Major Laddick suggested that you ride in the point vehicle so you can increase your situational awareness. He also told me…disregard. Whatever issues you have, keep them out of my convoy and we'll get along fine. This should be an uneventful convoy, at least the first leg that you'll be with us. Remember to hydrate. It's going to be a hot one. My timeline doesn't allow for an unnecessary stop just because you didn't hydrate properly."

Gabe noted he needed to drink water and also get a refund from the people skills seminar guru. He hefted his ruck, IBA, Kevlar and M4, then picked a path through the tire-rutted mounds of gravel to the lead Humvee.

Combat Barbie was near the rear of the truck shouting orders to her crew. After Gabe confirmed the name on her uniform, he grinned and said, "Good morning, Specialist Colucci. I'm your passenger, Gabe Quinn. Where do you want me?"

Barely taller than her assault rifle, she looked up at him and mustered all of the nastiness she could on short notice, locked eyes with him and shot a silent challenge. Before her eyes could leap from their sockets and bitch slap this new unwanted headache, she broke contact and turned to the gunner.

Unaware of the skirmish below him, PFC Nieves continued to mount an M2 to the turret and load assorted ammo cans inside the bowels of the Humvee. Colucci picked up a stone and threw it at the turret's armor. The clang of the rock against the turret mimicked the sound of a 7.62 mm round. Rather distinctive, an instant attention getter. Spooked, Nieves dropped down. Then he warily poked his head above the rim of the turret and sheepishly looked down at Colucci. "What?"

"Ass-wipe, put Pops' gear in the rear with the other rucks."

Colucci faced Gabe. She took a long pull from a water bottle, swished the liquid around her mouth, and amassed the sand from the morning's war games and those pesky leftovers from the breakfast sandwich. Taking aim, she jettisoned the potpourri concoction to the gravel at his feet.

"Pops, here are my rules. You sit behind the driver. Keep your pie-hole shut. Don't un-ass my vehicle until I tell you to un-ass my vehicle. If we get hit, do nothin'. Keep the muzzle of your weapon down and on safe. If you have an AD (accidental discharge), I'll kill you, then kill you ten more times. Combat lock your door once we leave the wire. If you gotta pee, use a water bottle. We ain't stoppin'. If the gunner gets hit, pull the red quick release on his harness and get him down. If we're attacked, give him ammo when he yells, give me some fuckin' ammo. Don't fuck with anythin' in the truck. The ice chest has water, Gatorade and Red Bulls. Don't touch the Gatorade or Red Bulls. Any questions, Pops?"

Unsure whether to laugh or shit, Gabe answered, "No ma'am."

Colucci beamed as if she had just rendered a performance worthy of an Oscar. She rotated her raised arm in a circle and shouted above the rumbling noise of diesel engines, "Mount up, ladies. Game on."

Pleased that he was such a big hit with Colucci, Gabe struggled to open the three-hundred pound armored door. Then he contorted his body, ballooned to twice its normal size by the IBA, ammo carriers and other attachments, and snaked into the rear seat.

The rear compartment, with ergonomics designed by AM General to torture even a dwarf, offered a hard, unforgiving seat that smelled of tobacco, sweat, urine and cordite. Littered with cigarette butts, spent shell casings of various calibers, empty water bottles and the ever-present sand, the floorboard had about nine inches of space for his size eleven boots. Strategically positioned at shin level to guarantee additional bruising discomfort, was a welded horizontal bar that secured the driver's seat. The door's fogged rectangular bullet-resistant glass window distorted the world on the other side.

Tied loosely to the center of the compartment were an ice cooler, combat life support bag, ammo boxes, a half full MRE box, additional headsets, two over stuffed patrol packs and a box of pen flares. Slung behind the driver's seat were ammo carriers that secured ten fully loaded thirty round magazines for the M4s, and linked ammo for the M240 that was mounted next to the M2 in the turret. The rear seat beyond the center transmission hump was jammed with backpacks, more ammo and other sundry articles of war necessary to the survival of the soldiers. Ventilated black boxes that contained electronic counter measures equipment (ECM), air conditioning components and an intercom plug-in panel were attached above and behind the rear seats. In the event of an IED detonation, RPG hit or a rollover,

125

all of the equipment would become flying debris and defile any flesh or bone in its path.

Gabe loosened his body armor so he could breathe. His hardened, salty sweat was strategically positioned to chafe the inside of his thighs, crotch and armpits with each miniscule movement. He accepted the minor irritation and relaxed, confident that at least his legs would go numb and get some sleep. He decided to buck the rules and keep his helmet and flame retardant gloves off until the very last second before leaving the wire. Out of the corner of his eye, he saw that his rebellious act had not gone unnoticed. Colucci shot him a disapproving look. He returned her stare, and with a touch of theatrical flair, inserted his protective earplugs, as if to say, not up for discussion. She wisely decided to ignore the infraction. His senses of humor and manners had their limits.

Ten minutes later, they passed through the next to last choke point before leaving the base camp.

Nieves waved and yelled 'Jambo' to the contract Ugandan security guards. They returned his salutation with repeated 'jambos', animated waves, smiles and laughter. Gabe didn't have a clue what the word meant. He was sure Nieves didn't either. It could've meant I want to be your bitch and bring you great pleasure under the moonlight — or just hello. Gabe didn't think Nieves cared because he heard him laugh when the Africans turned goofy.

The convoy slowed as it approached the weapons loading point and, being the driver of the lead Humvee, Private First Class Poppins drove forward to the last barrel, allowing enough space for the rest of the convoy to fall in behind. As soon as he stopped, Colucci opened her door and turned toward Gabe.

"Pops, you can get out now. Chamber a round, keep it on safe, and put your fuckin' helmet on."

Gabe, Colucci and Poppins got out of the truck and went hot with their M4s and M9s. Nieves stayed in the turret and chambered rounds in both the fifty-caliber and M240. When the rest of the convoy was loaded and ready to meet hajji, Poppins drove another two hundred meters to entry control point 3.

As they waited for another gaggle of Ugandans to raise the barrier arm and move the coils of razor wire, Colucci contacted command on the Sheriff's net. "Sheriff, this is Slayer 1. LOGPAC convoy with six vics and eighteen paxs. Destination, COP 6. SP at 0710."

Ten seconds later the radio crackled to life, "Roger Slayer 1, six vics, eighteen paxs, destination COP 6. Stay safe, lil' sister."

Colucci, known to be provoked by gender references, contained her disdain and responded, "Tango-mike." She switched to the internal frequency and muttered, "Fuckin' REMF."

After rapping her fist against the dashboard, she removed her headset jack-plug from the internal radio and stepped out one last time before leaving the relative safety of the base camp. Standing on her toes, stretching to reach a leverage point on the eight-foot adjustable Rhino boom mounted to the bumper, she muscled it to the horizontal, locked it in position and attached a teddy bear to the Rhino's black box. The stuffed toy, a gift from her seven-year old sister, was Colucci's pre-patrol ritual. She told her crew that it would keep them safe during the run north.

Back inside the truck, Colucci adjusted the view on the Blue Force Tracker and switched to the convoy's radio frequency. Brusquely, she instructed the other truck commanders to activate the Warlock, Duke and Jukebox ECM equipment. When she saw her Warlock amber light turn to green and the other ECM gauges come to life, she punched Poppins in the arm and said, "Go."

Nieves shouted a final 'Jambo,' waved to the guards, then lowered the barrel of the fifty-caliber and pointed it menacingly forward. He kissed a crucifix that dangled from the automatic weapon and gave an adoring pat to a photo of his wife's naked ass, proudly and prominently displayed in the turret.

Poppins stuck a plastic Jesus to the dashboard, mouthed a quick prayer and stomped on the accelerator. The truck slowly plodded forward as it fought to overcome the extra ton of manufacturer's and added hillbilly armor. The heat from the struggling transmission and the underpowered engine added fifteen degrees to the hundred and ten degree outside temperature. After the sun reached its zenith, the wheeled oven would warm up to turkey roasting temperatures exceeding a hundred and forty-five degrees.

Gabe also had an obsessive pre-patrol ritual. His began two hours earlier in the toilet trailer. Having experienced the physiological phenomena of an untimely bowel movement under high stress, he learned 'don't leave the wire without first leaving a gift to the hajji clean-up crew.' The ritual continued with the earplugs, hoping they would save his eardrums in the highly likely event of an explosion.

Next, as the vehicle left the wire into Indian country, he cinched the lap and shoulder harnesses to the max, meant to keep his body in the seat and not plastered on the headliner when the inevitable happened. He knew it would happen again — the only questions were when, where, how bad. After he finally resigned to putting on his helmet, he tightened its straps until they dug into his neck. He had experienced the effect a loose-fitting helmet had on the bridge of his nose and did not want a repeat. Last, as the vehicle crossed the 'oh shit it's gonna get real' line of departure, he instinctively raised his feet from the floorboard, irrationally hoping that his legs might survive a blast and not be turned into sausage. This ritual usually faded after several minutes. The labored effort and resultant aches overrode his base survival instincts.

He had encountered the full spectrum of the survival instincts. Fight, sometimes — flight, often — posturing, that never seemed to go his way. Endure was the one. In a long drawn-out war, a marathon of sorts, it was endurance, tolerance and suffering that ruled. Tomorrow would follow today — tomorrow becomes today — then with some luck, another tomorrow. Basic survival algebra. Repeat that routine three or four hundred times, board the freedom bird and return to the world. Get drunk, get laid, get another bottle and try to forget.

Gabe removed one earplug and inserted the radio's intercom cable in the panel behind him, then attached the headset's Velcro strap to his Kevlar and lowered the microphone boom so it would not get caught in the safety harness. He adjusted the volume to the lowest level, toggled the transmitter to the internal frequency and positioned it across his chest for easy access. Communication within the confines of the truck was impossible without the intercom. Somehow, overlooking creature comforts in an effort to keep expenses down and profits high, the manufacturer ensured that the decibel level inside the cabin hovered at, or exceeded, the noise of a jet engine at takeoff.

Now capable of tracking internal and external conversations, he settled in for the five hours of drudgery and moonscape ahead. He peered through the distorted glass window to the world beyond, occasionally straining to look past the driver's head for a clearer view of his immediate future.

Five minutes into the patrol, Gabe saw the Ziggurat of Ur at his nine. The temple, finished by King Shulgi in the 21st century BC, was but a shell of its former grand self. The mud and brick multi-tiered tower rose seventy feet from the desert floor and covered an area about the size of a football field. No longer used for worship, the antiquity continued to serve modern man. Visible for miles, the enemy used the Ziggurat as a natural aiming point for their rocket attacks on Adder. The soldiers used it as an unscientific measure to gauge route status. If you could see the Zig, patrols rolled. If a sandstorm obliterated the view, patrols didn't roll. MEDEVAC status was red. Red you're dead. You get hit and take casualties, you self-evac because the DUSTOFF angels in the Black Hawks ain't flying.

Gabe was roused from his National Geographic moment by a crackling intercom. "Slayer 6…Slayer 1."

"Send it."

"LT," Colucci said, " I just caught some traffic on the Sheriff's net from the RCT. They're blocked at Cedar Two by a southbound super cell comin' off the MSR and enterin' to refuel. Lookin' at the BFT, that convoy's at least three miles long. Wait one." After a short pause she continued, "I see the convoy now. LT, we're gonna be delayed for at least an hour."

"Roger, Slayer 1," Lutz said. "Contact the super cell and get us permission to push through. Timeline, remember the timeline."

"Roger, LT, but that means we won't have the RCT today to clear the way." Hearing only dead air, Colucci begrudgingly obtained permission to cut through the larger convoy. Then she told the Slayer convoy, "Close distance, cut speed to twenty-five and let's get through these guys. Don't flag 'em with your weapons. They're pissed at us for delayin' their breakfast. Don't give 'em another reason to go postal on us."

The super cell, with more than a hundred vehicles, stretched from Cedar's rutted dirt road to the main supply route entrance ramp and half a mile beyond. Probably headed to Kuwait, the convoy included half a dozen military security vehicles, but mostly empty civilian contracted cargo trucks. The few tractor-trailers not deadheading were flatbeds loaded with burned out Humvees, ASVs, and a Bradley fighting vehicle. Removal of the hulks from the battlefield served two purposes. First, some of the vehicles could be scavenged for parts to retrofit dead lined vehicles in Kuwait. Second, and more important, was to remove visuals that would remind soldiers that the war came at a price, a price that was not only measured in dollars.

As Slayer one made its way to the on-ramp, the soldiers were quiet as if paying homage to a funeral procession. Gabe, a marginal fatalist who clung to the tenuous belief that he could control some aspects of his life, ignored the procession. He was more interested in what was on the highway and more to the point, what wasn't — no civilian traffic. His years in Iraq had taught him that was never a good sign.

Also absent were the highway galvanized guardrails. Only the upright posts remained in the median and on the shoulders of the

129

divided highway. The reason for the omission was clear. The enemy used the terrain and any suitable man-made structure to hide IEDs. Coalition forces, in an effort to limit the hides available to the enemy, had removed most of the guardrails. Removal of the posts would have been a herculean task — too many and firmly encased in concrete.

He also saw meter-wide curb cuts nominally spaced about a hundred meters apart. Designed to channel the monsoon rains that occurred during Iraq's only two-week season that was not summer, they were exploited by the enemy. They fabricated IEDs to fit in the cuts and painted them to match the concrete curbing. Many patrols drove into the kill zone and joined the ranks of the fallen heroes. Coalition forces still struggled with that one. They didn't want to destroy the run-offs and upset the locals, so the military and civilian think-tanks labored to come up with a compromise that would fit in the new counter-insurgency warfare model — 'hearts and minds, people, hearts and minds,' the jingle recycled from the waning days of Vietnam. Gabe's solution was more tactical than strategic — blow the entirety of the curbing from Kuwait to Turkey, along with any hajjis who got in the way.

Thirty minutes north of Cedar Two, the patrol slowed for the Romanian bridge spanning the Euphrates River. The bridge's survival was critical to the supplies trucked north that kept Coalition forces in the game. It was guarded by a token force of rag-tag, undernourished, ill-equipped, unmotivated and unenthusiastic Iraqi Army soldiers. Titular supervision was provided by a platoon of Romanian soldiers, hence its familiar name.

Gabe chuckled when he saw the motley crew. *The Romanians, proud of their mission and contribution to bringing democracy to Iraq. Not!* Sitting atop their armored Cold War relics, they were happy about their extra combat pay, DFAC privileges, short tours, easy mission and low casualty rate.

The Romanians waved and gave the 'thumbs up' as the patrol passed. Slayer's gunners responded in kind, keenly aware that these were the last friendlies they would encounter before reaching the outpost. The fact that the Romanians returned daily to the base camp and had ready access to liquor and the promiscuous females within their ranks, may have also stoked the soldiers' enthusiasm. Maybe a little fraternization with these Coalition partners could open the door to wine and women. The Joes would be more than happy to provide the song.

One hour into the patrol, Gabe was ready to surrender to the unseen enemy in Iraq. An enemy that sucked out reason, resolve and spirit. During his years in the Iraq desert and more spent in African ones, he had never been able to adapt to this foe. He wrestled, confronted, and silently damned it. It was an enemy he couldn't escape. Heat. To many an inconsequential four-letter word, they mildly cursed in the summer when poolside sipping iced beverages. In the desert of perpetual summer, heat was a killer. It tempered thought, mood, and action. Simple physical movement became an epic challenge that had to be calculated weighing the benefit versus the risk. A mental calculus — more precise, a mental masturbation he was constantly drawn to in search of relief from the potential executioner.

Despite his effort, he teetered at the precipice. His head bobbed and bounced in rhythm with a surreal, dawdling melody. His heart pounded at a prestissimo tempo faster than a meth crazed rock drummer's assault on the skins. Lungs sucked in super-heated, sand-filled air that burned his windpipe and lungs.

He drained a tepid bottle of water, another, and then one more. The primeval part of him that prowled the recesses of his subconscious understood water would keep his body functioning. The here and now rationale caused a schism — *what the hell am I doing in Iraq?* Endure, tolerate, and suffer. Stay in the marathon. He would survive this skirmish, but he knew that he would confront this enemy many times in the coming months. Just had to get through this one.

Colucci also battled the beast. Her battle was not as harsh since she had not sullied her body with decades of alcohol overindulgence, added ballast, or the lack of serious physical exercise. She saw his struggle.

"Pops, you all right back there?"

Jolted from the chess match that was at play in his head, he returned to the truth of speeding down a highway in a rolling coffin, chasing doom. He took another swig to moisten his tongue and throat to make speech possible. He managed a feeble response. "Fine." With a skosh more spirit he added, "A little warm in here, Specialist."

"Pops, it's thirty degrees past fuckin' hot," Colucci quipped. "Drink one of my Gatorades. It's supposed to have some weird shit in it that makes it better than water. If there's any ice left in the cooler give yourself a thrill and shove some of it down your crotch. We're only four hours out."

"Thanks. I'm really encouraged now." Gabe mimicked Colucci's Jersey accent on the Army's favorite adjective, adverb, verb and noun, and said, "Gosh, only four more *fuckin'* hours."

The next three hours crept along as if time had swallowed a fistful of Quaaludes. Nieves stalwartly rotated the turret's chain drive with his weight and swept the mounted fifty-caliber in an arc from his nine to three o'clock. Initially he had called out potential threats in the awakened southbound civilian traffic and the nomadic *Bedouin* herders that flanked the highway. As the hours passed and the heat rose, his enthusiasm plummeted. His rolling monologue changed to sporadic transmissions that only served to break the droning engine noise and barren desert panorama.

Lost in his battle with the heat, Gabe was lulled into a stupor. His only movement was to adjust his position when the aches in his knees, back, neck, shoulders and legs became intolerable. The readjustments were frequent, the relief was brief.

"Abandoned Iraqi police checkpoint on the southbound side of the highway," Nieves laconically transmitted.

Stirred by the transmission, Gabe wiped the dust from his glasses and squinted through the window. The checkpoint was formed with empty fifty-five gallon steel drums, coils of razor wire and scavenged boulders placed to mark pull-off areas. Behind the last drum was a bunker built with Hesco barriers and topped off with corrugated steel roofing.

Common throughout Iraq, in theory the checkpoints were meant to stop the flow of weapons and insurgents and contain the spiraling death count. In reality they were used by the Iraqi police to supplement their paltry incomes by forcing donations from any hapless traveler who ventured out on the highway in anything other than an official vehicle. Distasteful to many westerners, but overlooked by the Coalition forces, the practice was the norm in this part of the world as it was in most third world countries. Firmly entrenched before the rise of Saddam, the custom did not skip a beat after his eventual fall from power. The system did nothing more than redistribute meager amounts of money from one set of have-nots to another set of have-nots.

Gabe first experienced this form of point taxation during his years in west Africa. Those transactions were typically initiated by a local African Gendarmes or customs agent. Usually the conversation began with an exchange of pleasantries in Wolof. *'Nanga def,'* response, *'Manga furek.'* Then the *impots,* or tax, was demanded in broken English interlaced with French. "You, mistah, make me *cadeaux.*" If the gifts were not forthcoming — better to pay.

He understood the importance of the checkpoints to the survival of the Iraqi police. Their absence made him jumpy. If the police were not at their assigned post, something bad was about to happen. Not to the police. His mind flipped from listless stupor to mushrooming anxiety. The sweat-dried shorthairs on the back of his neck instinctively stood at attention and his severely constricted sphincter puckered more.

"We're approachin' CP 9 bravo," Colucci announced to the convoy. "Slow it down to thirty so we can try to get a visual on any IEDs hajji may have hid in the columns."

Immediately, Lieutenant Lutz overrode Colucci. "This is Slayer 6. Disregard that last command. Keep it at fifty. We lost too much time back at Cedar. Slayer 1, remember my timeline. Timeline people, timeline."

Colucci shook her head, toggled the transmitter to the internal frequency and told Nieves to drop down in the turret when they neared the checkpoint. Many a gunner had been decapitated by a strategically placed roadside bomb.

Gabe looked over Poppins' shoulder and saw the checkpoint, still two or three kilometers ahead. More than just a map reference point, it was a notable terrain feature in the vast emptiness of this stretch of the highway — an incomplete overpass that would connect some future road from nothing to nothing.

As the gap between the overpass and the convoy narrowed, Nieves returned to life and declared that all was safe since there was a police vehicle on the overpass.

Colucci sounded relieved when she said, "We're one hour out."

Gabe was not reassured. His vision, already hampered by the distorted ballistic glass, was further blurred as tunnel vision kicked in. Tunnel hearing overtook his auditory sense. He interpreted any sound made by the tires chunking road debris as potential peril. The adrenalin pump was in full speed mode and his heart rate soared, sending extra blood to his muscles to counter the unidentified danger. Trapped in a speeding tomb, no place to run or hide, the only defense left in his arsenal was to master his heightened state of survival awareness and read the clues. He did not want meet the eternal zero just yet.

He scanned the highway and useless guardrail posts in front of the fast approaching overpass. As they raced under it he strained his neck and turned his head to allow a quick, fuzzy glimpse at the vehicle. His eyes' receptors caught a fleeting flash of a blue and white GMC Jimmy police vehicle and its lone occupant. The receptors absorbed the light and shapes and started the electrophysiological process that sent the raw data to his brain for analysis. Within seconds, his brain processed the raw data in one lobe, sent it to another and then spat out a disturbing deduction that further exacerbated his panic. His vision narrowed more until all he saw was the road's shoulder. He scanned the road thirty meters ahead and to the side, then broadened the search another hundred meters.

One hundred fifty meters.

Two hundred meters.

Two hundred fifty meters.

Three hundred meters.

After he had surveyed the two kilometers of highway beyond the overpass, he saw it. The procedure repeated. New information bounced around his brain. Processing completed, the brain sent an urgent message to his vocal cords and lungs. "Stop!"

Nothing happened — the truck plowed on. His out of control, racing brain commanded the vocal cords and lungs to increase the volume. "STOP!"

Again nothing happened....

Two hundred fifty meters..."STOP DAMNIT!"

Two hundred meters..."Please, please, PLEASE, stop, stop, STOP!"

One hundred seventy meters and they still sped toward the black beyond.

"DAMNIT STOP!"

Colucci turned toward him and raised her hands to her ears, shook her head and pointed at his intercom switch. She mimed that he had not toggled to transmit. "What'd you say, Pops?"

One hundred sixty meters..."I"

One hundred twenty meters..."don't"

One hundred meters..."want"

Ninety meters..."to"

Eighty meters..."DIE!"

Gabe processed the new data sent by Colucci, realized his mistake, toggled the mike and again yelled, "STOP!"

Poppins ignored the command and continued to rocket into the valley of death.

Colucci reached across the divide that separated them, smacked Poppin's helmet and shouted, "STOP!"

Poppins stomped hard on the brake pedal. The vehicle instantly reacted to the abuse and shook violently. Loose gear flew throughout the truck's interior. Brakes screamed, spitting fluids and rust, yet the inflexible forces of momentum continued to propel the truck and its human cargo closer to death.

Seventy meters...

Sixty meters...

The tires bounced and skipped across the asphalt. Close to a rollover, the truck fishtailed across both lanes. Like a shackled rag doll, Nieves was thrown from one side of the turret to the other.

Fifty meters...

Forty meters...

Thirty meters...

Twenty meters...

Fifteen meters...

Four meters short of oblivion the truck came to a tire burning stop.

Colucci pulled her chest and head from the dashboard, looked at Gabe, and then calmly asked, "What the fuck, Pops?"

Holding up a hand, he tried to regain control of his heavy respiration and out of control heart rate. He removed his glasses and wiped the salty sweat and desert sand from his eyes. Head in his chest, hands cupped over his nose and mouth, he gulped air. Finally, he raised his head and looked around the truck's interior. He was still alive. His heart pounded as if reacting to an overdose from too many espressos, and his brain throbbed so fast that a stroke was imminent. He fought back and returned a measure of calm to his voice. "Reverse, does this vehicle have a reverse?"

Colucci motioned Poppins to back up. After fifty meters she told him to stop.

Gabe shook his head and said "Not enough. More."

"Hold fast, Poppins," Colucci said. "All right, Pops, I'll repeat my question. What the fuck?"

"IED."

Colucci looked at the road and examined it from left to right in five-meter increments. "I don't see nothin'."

Breathing normal, but hands still shaking, Gabe toggled his microphone. "Back up another hundred meters and I'll show you."

Colucci stared at him but saw no change in his expression. "Do it, Poppins."

Nieves stood straight in the open turret well and shouted directions to the driver. Poppins slowly backed up another hundred meters.

"Why have you stopped my convoy, Slayer 1?" Lutz demanded.

Colucci attempted to buy some time with a lame, "Wait one,

Slayer 6." She pointed at Gabe and motioned him to remove his headset. In a low voice that neither the driver, nor the gunner could hear, she asked, "Where?"

Gabe pointed to a spot about one hundred fifty meters in front. "There."

Colucci removed her ballistic glasses and looked to the area where he had pointed. After several minutes of concentrated effort, she shook her head again and said, "Nothin'."

Gabe removed his safety harness and grabbed the combat lock release. "Give me permission to un-ass your truck, and I'll show you."

"Okay, Pops. Do the five-twenty-five drill and meet me on my side. I'm about to get an ass chewin' so do it quick."

Gabe scanned for booby-traps within his immediate area, moved around to the truck and saddled up next to her. He pointed at the threat. "Look to your eleven. A hundred and fifty meters, no a hundred and sixty, and a meter off the hard ball in the median strip. Now do you see it?"

Colucci raised her rifle and looked through the attached Advanced Combat Optical Gun sight (ACOG). She swept the area but failed to see the object that had the old-timer jacked up. "Nope, don't see it."

"All right, look to your left at the post immediately to the driver's nine." Gabe did a mental count of the posts between him and the threat. "Now count thirty-seven, no, count thirty-eight posts out. Do you see it?"

Colucci whispered a count as she looked down the road until she identified the thirty-eighth post. Again she searched the area with the ACOG. "Pops, you need to drink some more water. You're fuckin' hallucinatin'. There's nothin'."

She turned toward the truck and opened the door. "Let's go, Pops. I've got one pissed off LT to deal with, thanks to you."

"Wait." Gabe grabbed her arm and said, "Look at the post next to the driver again. What do you see?"

"I see a fuckin' post, Pops," Colucci groaned. "What do you fuckin' see?"

"I see a post too, Specialist." Gabe squeezed her arm tighter. "Now look at the next post, the next one and the next, all the way to the one I pointed out. Now what do you see?"

"Damnit, Pops, we're burnin' daylight and you got me lookin' at posts." Colucci broke his grip and backed away from him. "All right, I see thirty-eight fuckin' posts. Happy? Now let's fuckin' go."

"Specialist, I see an IED. Can't you see a difference between that post and the other thirty-seven, or the other thousand or so we've passed since leaving the FOB? That post has sand bermed around its base. Not the thirty-seventh, not the thirty-sixth and not the other posts behind us. Just that one, number thirty-eight. Get some binos and look closer. I spotted a glint in that berm. Just for a fraction of a second, but damnit, I saw it."

Like a crazed demon from Hell, he descended on Colucci, grabbed her arms and forced her to within six inches of his face. He bore through her with an intensity that she probably had never encountered in her twenty-one years. "You've got to trust me on this one."

He released her arms and again faced the terror at post thirty-eight. "Colucci, it's an IED."

Shaken by his zeal and arrest of her body, Colucci rubbed her arms bruised during his fanatical plea. She looked at the pavement, then the suspected hide, then back down at the asphalt. Finally, she looked up at Gabe. She shouted above the idling diesel engine, "Nieves, I'm comin' up. Get your binoculars."

Colucci climbed on the hood, grabbed the binoculars from the gunner and searched again for the threat. After several minutes, she jumped down and walked toward Gabe, stopping ten feet short. "I see the sand pile, but no glint."

He met her declaration with a rigid stare.

Colucci searched Gabe's stoic face, a face of certainty chiseled on a granite slab. "Pops, you sure about this?"

"I'm sure. When we drove under that overpass two or three clicks back I saw what you saw. One police vehicle, one policeman. One policeman, Colucci, just one. I don't know if this is your first deployment in Iraq, but these police are not like ours. They are as corrupt as they come. You think Camden police are bad. Hell, they're damn Boy Scouts compared to the Iraqi police. Their ranks are filled with insurgents. They're never alone."

He paused to weigh the effect his words had on her. "I mean never. Never will you see a lone police vehicle with a lone cop anywhere in this country."

Nieves leaned over the turret and shouted, "Colucci, the LT wants you on the radio. She's babbling about her timeline. She wants a SITREP."

"You know what, fuck her SITREP and fuck her damn timeline. Give her some damn excuse. Anythin'. I don't give a rat's ass."

Almost as soon as she finished her rant, she reversed herself.

"Disregard. I'll deal with her."

Gabe understood her predicament. She had to appease an irate lieutenant hell-bent on maintaining a petty, concocted schedule. He pushed a little bit more to tip Colucci in the right direction.

"I guarantee you that hajji cop is long gone from that bridge. Could've been a lookout. More likely he's a triggerman and used a cell phone to arm that IED at post thirty-eight just hoping to send Poppins, Nieves, you and me home in body bags. Colucci, it's not a game out here. It's real. People die. Damn, too many die. I don't know if you've seen what one of those things can do to a Humvee. Don't know if you've seen what one can do to a soldier. If you haven't, I hope you never do. It ain't pretty."

She probed his face for a crack that was not there. "Okay, Pops. You got me. Not convinced, but you got my attention. I need to call the 6 and let her know what's up. Convince her, Pops, and I'm off the hook. By the way, I'm from Newark, not fuckin' Camden."

Colucci hailed Lieutenant Lutz on the convoy frequency and explained the reason for the stop.

Within moments an M1117 armored security vehicle (ASV) sped from the rear of the convoy and stopped ten meters from Colucci. Lutz jumped from the air-conditioned comfort of the rear compartment and briskly closed the distance between her and Gabe. She shot a malevolent stare first at Colucci, then Gabe. She looked back at Colucci and spit venom, "Where is this IED that has blown my timeline?"

Colucci gave the lieutenant the binoculars and walked her gaze to post thirty-eight. Lutz surveyed the area for less than ten seconds. She spoke to Colucci but looked directly at Gabe. "Bullshit! Get this civilian back in your truck and let's roll."

Trained to follow orders and respect the rank, if not the person behind the rank, Colucci did what most soldiers would do when issued a direct order. "Yes, ma'am." She returned to the Humvee.

Gabe was not a soldier. "Lieutenant that would be a major mistake — your fuck up, my life."

"Quinn, I told you to keep your issues out of my convoy. Major Laddick warned me about you. I haven't got the time to be jawing with a washed-up drunk who thinks he knows something, but doesn't know jack shit."

He didn't move, didn't blink and didn't speak.

Lutz's anger boiled over. "Get in the truck or I'll drop you where you stand. You tracking me, mister?"

Gabe suppressed an urge to lay her out. He was unsure sure how far he would push his point, but he damn sure wasn't getting in the truck and becoming a statistic just so this anal-cranial-loopback could add a medal to her uniform.

Colucci got out of the truck and returned to the pair of combatants. Politely, she asked, "Ma'am, you remember our missin' RCT that was held up back at Cedar?"

Lutz continued to glare at Gabe.

"I just caught some of their radio traffic," Colucci continued, "and I can see them on the BFT about ten clicks behind us rollin' at about forty. They'll be here in fifteen, ma'am. Maybe, well, you know since they're gonna be here anyways, maybe we could hold put awhile and let 'em check it out. What ya think, LT? Give us a chance to take a piss break and stretch our legs."

Grinding her teeth, Lutz redirected her rage to Colucci. "Fifteen, Colucci, fifteen. Timeline, Colucci, timeline." She turned snappishly and marched double-quick to the security and comfort of her ASV — air-conditioned and always on the left side of cold.

Still in mild shock over the atypical, incompetent display of leadership by any officer he had met, Gabe turned to face the IED. *Our blood, our guts, your glory. The LT would make a fine poster for that bit of soldier's sarcasm.* Shaking off the clash of egos he told Colucci, "Thanks, Jersey girl. I owe you one."

"It's fuckin' nothin', Pops. She's PMSin'."

*****

Seventeen minutes later, Sergeant First Class Pickens directed his four-vehicle route clearance team through the staggered vehicles of the Slayer convoy. He stopped his mine-protected Buffalo, with its large articulated arm used for ordnance disposal and numerous antennae for the added ECM equipment, behind Colucci's truck. After he removed his headset he jumped down from the truck. Spotting Colucci, he nodded and cautiously approached, surveying the road's shoulders near and far.

Lutz reemerged from her ASV and shouted an order at Pickens to stop.

Pickens turned to face the shout. He noted the rank insignia on her uniform, performed a quick assessment of her probable command worth, and said, "Yes, ma'am."

Without skipping a beat Lutz began firing questions at the

Sergeant as she jogged to him. "I'm on the wrong side of my timeline. How long is this going to take? What is it? Can we pass by? What are you going to do? I was told fifteen minutes. What took you so damn long getting here?"

Command worth assessment completed, Pickens repositioned the wad of long-cut chew in his cheek and delayed his response until the Lieutenant was within five feet. He drawled his speech to the point of tedium. "Well, I don't rightly know just yet. Give me and the boys a few minutes to set up, ask some questions, study the situation, chew it around a little bit and I'll be able to get back to you on that."

After a long pause just short of insubordination, he threw in a belated, "Ma'am."

"Be quick about it, soldier," the lieutenant ordered. "I'll be in my vehicle."

Pickens nodded his head and sent her a tortoise paced obligatory, "Yes, ma'am."

After Lutz was out of the picture, Pickens turned to Colucci, dropped his country bumpkin routine and asked, "What do we have, soldier?"

"Sergeant, do you mind if my civilian joins the conversation?"

Pickens looked at Gabe leaning against the Humvee. "If he has something to contribute bring him over."

They gave Pickens an overview of the situation and pointed out the suspected hide.

"You did good," Pickens said. "Specialist, have your vehicles back up another hundred meters. Tell your team to pull security to west, east and south. Contact Adder, explain the situation and advise them that I may need a no-fly window if I have to BIP (blow-in-place) this puppy. Tell your soldiers to stay inside, or behind their vehicles and not to approach any closer. My team will take the north security and determine what we're dealing with. Tell your LT that she should only be inconvenienced for about an hour. If that doesn't satisfy her, tell her…disregard."

While his men assembled, Pickens studied the hide and possible approaches. Orders were few since his team was well versed in the procedures needed to not go boom. One soldier readied one of the two Pack Bots that had been stored inside the Buffalo. Another soldier maneuvered the other robot to the site.

Pickens viewed the images transmitted from the robot's camera and assessed that he was dealing with a multi-array radio controlled IED, probably an EFP. He told his team to get the second robot ready and armed.

After the first robot was recovered, the second robot, outfitted with a disruptor charge needed to shoot the power source and initiator, was guided to the hide.

Pickens instructed Colucci to take cover in the unlikely event that he made a mistake and detonated the bomb's main charge. He checked the area behind him to insure all were behind cover. Then he did a ten count before taking the shot with a water projectile shape charge at the bomb's initiator. Once the smoke cleared and the muffled sound of the explosion died in the desert, he reengaged the bomb with the robot's camera. Draining the last juices from the chew, he spit the remnants to the road and squinted at the video images. Failing to see secondary bombs, he suited up in the bulky bomb suit.

Before he advanced to the site, the explosive ordnance disposal team (EOD) split ranks and moved out on both sides of the road. They made their way to the flanks of the site in a serpentine movement. As they advanced, the soldiers probed the desert with rods and passed mine detectors over the ground. Fifty meters from the bomb, they stopped.

The team leader gave Pickens a thumbs up indicating that neither secondary IEDs nor command wire were found. The soldiers returned to the ad hoc command center behind the Buffalo, popping smoke canisters the entire way so Pickens' approach would be masked from enemy snipers and cloud the tactics he used to disable the threat.

Pickens labored against the heavy special helmet and the bulky suit as he walked toward the killer. He also randomly threw smoke canisters. For the next twenty minutes, he moved around the hide on his belly and meticulously studied, probed and poked the entire area. Then he did it again.

He stood and removed the helmet. Now with a distortion-free view, he repeated the process, this time on his knees. Satisfied the device was safe, he slowly waddled to the Buffalo. He removed the suit, secured the helmet in the rear of the vehicle and then downed three bottles of water in quick succession to replenish the eight pounds of sweat he gave to the desert. Thirst temporarily sated, he walked around the Buffalo, stopping when he saw Colucci.

"The IED's cleared."

*****

Gabe had strained to watch through the smoke and wind-whipped sands as a master tirelessly labored against the elements and the enemy's trickery to save the lives of people he didn't know. There was a word for it, but he suspected Pickens was a man with real sand, a man who would never describe himself with that word. It would be counter to his being. He waited until Pickens drained a fourth bottle of water. "Sergeant, was it a radio controlled IED?"

Pickens squinted against the noon sun to see the civilian. "Yes sir, an eight-array EFP. The spread would've defeated your Rhino. Your Warlock, Duke and Jukebox would've been useless. A definite killer, sir."

Gabe narrowed his eyes to slits peering at the hide through the lingering smoke and heat squiggles radiating from the highway. "Sergeant Pickens, thanks for risking your ass. You've got balls that clang louder than those at Saint Abbey's cathedral. I don't know how you keep them in your pants."

He turned and saw the sergeant grinning. "I have a small request."

"Name it, sir."

"No more sir. The name's Gabe." He talked faster when he saw the ASV move closer. "Sergeant, when you recover the device I assume you'll send it off to CEXC (Combined Explosive eXploitation Cell) for analysis."

Pickens nodded.

"I'm also guessing the bomb was activated by a cell phone?"

Again Pickens nodded.

"Sergeant, if you can manage it without getting your ass in a sling, do you think you could drop the cell phone off on the SIGINT (Signals Intelligence) experts long enough for them to exploit the SIM card before you package it off to CEXC?"

"That's a Roger, sir. I mean, Gabe. What're you thinking?"

"Nothing sneaky, Sergeant. CEXC's final report will probably take weeks, if not months and we both know that intelligence is only actionable if it's current. Ask the SIGINT boys to forward their analysis to S2 at COP 6. Anything the experts come up with may mean something to the soldiers there. Won't mean shit to the folks back at Adder."

Gabe saw the lieutenant's ASV slow near Colucci's truck. He quickly shook hands with Pickens and said, "Again, thanks for what you do, Sergeant." Gabe walked to the far side of the truck to be clear of another confrontation with the Lutz.

Before the vehicle had completely stopped, Lutz shoved the rear door open and leapt to the pavement. She stormed in like a category-five hurricane and blustered, "Sergeant, you told me it would take an hour. It took you seventy minutes."

No atta-boy, or thanks for the sergeant who had risked instantaneous atomization.

Pickens recycled his earlier routine. He placed a healthy wad of Skoal inside his jowls and turned it over several times. "Ya know, ma'am, what we do is part science and what we do is part art. Sometimes the art part of it, well, sometimes it gets a little messy and you just have to adjust your brush strokes. We had to do some adjusting. But ma'am, you is good to go now. Whoever spotted that thing, well, let's just say if it hadn't been spotted it would've been a bad day for y'all. I don't know how close y'all got to that thing, but you were damn lucky."

Pickens winked at Colucci and pushed a little more. "As a matter of fact, ma'am, if someone got within say, thirty meters of it, well, she would qualify for a Combat Action Badge. That's according to the new guidelines put out by our very own General Petraeus."

Gabe watched the drama unfold. He had completed his command assessment of Lutz's abilities long before they had left the base camp. She was a genuine, certified, real McCoy, 'what's in it for me' type. He knew a Combat Action Badge would bode well for an up and coming junior officer and he was positive she would strain the bounds of credulity to turn the harrowing event to her advantage.

"Specialist Colucci," Lutz said, "how close would you say I... I mean how close did we get to the IED? Ten or fifteen meters?"

Confused, Colucci looked at Pickens for help.

Pickens adjusted his position slightly to be out of the lieutenant's line of sight. He answered her puzzled expression by conspicuously shaking his head and silently mouthing the words, "Don't say it, Specialist."

Inner turmoil written all over her face, Colucci sagged, as if she had been sucker punched. Shame and defeat resonated through her softened voice. "Ten meters, ma'am."

Smiling and sounding like a wizened sage, Lutz said, "Well I certainly would have put it closer to twenty, but perhaps you are correct. Yes, I guess ten meters sounds about right. Ten meters. We were within ten meters when I stopped. Sergeant, put that in your report and send it to me through channels. Now get your team out of my way so I can push on." She performed a perfect about face and marched back to her air conditioning.

Pickens shook his head. Watching the lieutenant hustle to her vehicle, he muttered, "Report my ass. You can fucking blow me, bitch." As she was about to get in the vehicle he shouted, "You're welcome, ma'am."

He turned to Colucci and placed his hand on her shoulder. "Look at me, Colucci. You did real fine. Keep up the good soldiering. Don't let that buddy-fucker LT of yours get you killed. Stay safe, lil'sister."

Colucci, not upset by this soldier's gender reference, looked up at him and managed a weak, "Thanks, Sergeant."

An hour of somber silence passed as they covered the last miles to the outpost. Gabe had seen it before. The young soldiers had just encountered the reality of war — somebody wanted to kill them. No holding hands while singing around the campfire, or blathering about transgressing cultural boundaries and getting to know and understand each other better. Just kill. Not someone else — more personal than that. Hajji wanted to kill them. They were here, they were convenient. *Allah* had commanded death to the infidels and they would do just fine. Shocking. A life changer. They had been reduced to mankind's prehistoric struggle to survive. Kill or be killed. They would rediscover the same emotions each time they faced that reality. It was their time to contemplate the human condition. It was their time to search for a rational answer. It was their time to find anything to help them cope with the next fifteen months in this cauldron named Iraq.

Nieves broke the silence and blandly transmitted, "I see it."

The outpost sprouted from an unbroken lunar landscape, previously scarred only by the highway and the debris of past battles. Home to fifty soldiers, it resembled a medieval castle, complete with towers and seven vehicle fighting ramps. The rectangular perimeter covered about two acres and was protected by fourteen foot high T-walls. It had four outer towers. Those facing northwest and southeast were manned by a soldier armed with either a fifty-caliber, or an M240, along with his M4 rifle. The southwest and northeast towers were empty.

The inner redoubt was protected by more walls and towers. These thirty-foot towers would remain vacant unless an attack breached the perimeter walls. Then it would become their Alamo — and they would become a postscript in some dusty military journal, an unremarkable memorial shunted to the sands of time, forgotten within a generation.

The combat outpost was a staging point for daily patrols on the MSR and a refuge for any friendlies that happened by in need of assistance. It was tethered to Adder by a one hundred-eighty kilometer umbilical cord braved by the convoys to deliver the soldiers' sustenance. Everything was trucked in.

The lives inside the walls depended on the grit of the soldiers, and in the event of a complex sustained attack, any air support that could be mustered from Adder or BIAP. The thirty to sixty minutes needed to get support could seem like an eternity, or it could be over in a New York minute. Throw in a few more body bags with the next supply convoy, please. Every soldier inside the castle knew this. They didn't dwell on the subject. No point. Where could they go?

There was no Pizza Hut, Burger King, PX or theater.

No USO shows.

No Morale, Welfare, Recreation facility, other than years old magazines, a few lousy romance novels and playing cards missing the aces.

No privacy.

No escape.

No time off, unless you counted the few brief hours of sleep.

No latrine trailer. They burned their shit here.

There was a unisex trailer with two shower stalls. Non-potable water was always in short supply so combat showers were standard operating procedure. Turn the shower on — get wet. Turn the shower off — lather up. Turn the shower back on — rinse. Turn the shower off — towel off — no need. Do it all in one minute. Damn, that was refreshing. Two minutes later, need another shower. Wait a few days.

Constant noise from diesel generators. Almost daily suffocating sand storms with visibility measured in feet instead of kilometers. Scorpions and camel spiders thrived in, under and above the trailers, shitters and every other nook and cranny in between.

There were sporadic care packages from the Girl Scouts or some other do-gooder organization. By the time the packages made it to the outpost they had already been cherry picked by the fobbitts, leaving only the throw-aways.

These soldiers were out there, really out there. Combat <u>out</u> post. Fifty forgotten creatures surrounded by a sea of empty desert. Empty, except for hordes of jihadists hell-bent on hastening their demise. This was hajji land.

The monotonous routine was broken by the supply convoys and other random travelers. Sometimes the soldiers needed a reminder that God and Jesus were on their side so occasionally a chaplain stopped by with his magic show. God made this hell. Whose God? Hajji's God? It couldn't have been an American God. Jesus would

145

not be caught dead in this desert shithole. Nazareth was a resort by comparison.

In spite of the Spartan conditions, most of the soldiers thrived in the outpost. To them it was preferable to the fobbitt routines at Adder. No sergeant major to jump in their shit for a minor uniform infraction, haircut or a few days' stubble. The outpost only had two officers who suffered the same miserable conditions as the enlisted. Clear of the Army's sometimes mundane and dubious policies, the occupants concentrated on the essentials. Mission — staying alive — and ticking off the days to the freedom bird.

Poppins maneuvered the truck along a twisted path shaped by concrete barriers and double strands of razor wire to the outpost entrance. He stopped briefly before reaching the final barrier. A soldier emerged from behind the protective walls, waved and then raised the barrier arm. Poppins drove another thirty meters to the first wall that formed the outer perimeter and put the transmission in park. Silent, each soldier got out, ejected the magazines and cleared live rounds from their weapons, topped magazines off with the loose rounds and reinserted them in the wells.

Colucci paced ten steps in front of the truck and directed Poppins where to park.

Once inside the outpost Gabe, who had chosen to walk behind the truck after he cleared his weapon, leaned it against the parked Humvee's rear tire. He gulped down two bottles of water, removed his Kevlar and let it drop to the gravel. Next he unsnapped his throat protector and ripped the Velcro release on his body armor. He raised an arm and struggled to rid himself of the sixty pounds of armor and ammo. Gymnastics completed, he dropped the IBA next to his helmet.

He pulled a third bottle of warm water from the iceless cooler and moved to a blast wall near the Humvee. Old age and the punishing trip had almost done him in. He flexed his legs and rotated his back side-to-side, hoping to circulate blood to the parts of his body that had gone numb, which was pretty much every part of his body that needed blood. Then he squatted, braced his back against the wall and allowed his butt to plop to the ground. Exhausted, he reached into his cargo pants thigh pocket, found his cigarettes and lit one. The poison was hot to his throat, but took immediate effect.

He relaxed and watched the others quietly perform the same ritual, same except for the 'plop' maneuver. Somehow, the young soldiers looked different from the kids he had watched roughhousing earlier at the motor pool. At first, he could not pinpoint the difference. Then it hit him — they had seen the elephant. Their brush with death had stolen the naivety of youth. The days of seeing a world through rose-colored lenses were gone. No turning back. If they survived the suck they would return to a home that would be foreign. Whatever years remained for them, these warriors would discover they never fully returned home. Their families and friends would have moved on down life's highway, but not them. They had taken a detour on that road. A part of them would always remain in Iraq. With luck, they could tame the elephant and control their spontaneous psyche trips to the desert. Without some luck, they would meet the same end of too many of their peers — self-inflicted ruin, be it substance abuse, lost fervor for life, or suicide.

Scared by this newest brush with the zero and scarred from previous encounters, Gabe was nevertheless euphoric. Panic and fear always entered into the equation, but after having survived yet another near miss, a surge of dopamine rushed through him, a surge more addictive than heroin. He feared the next one, yet he craved it.

Colucci raised the trunk lid, climbed on the bumper and gingerly stepped into the compartment, momentarily disappearing in its cavernous space. Reemerging with a patrol pack, she dispersed her weight on other unseen gear, nimbly negotiated the trunk and placed one leg, then the other on the bumper. Maintaining a firm grip on the pack she performed a perfect airborne jump to the gravel. She spotted him, and with the patrol pack held at chest level, said, "Mr. Quinn, here's your ruck, sir."

"Thanks, Specialist." Gabe pushed away from the wall and wobbled to a stand. He pointed to his helmet and IBA, and said, "Drop it there."

With great care, she placed the ruck on top of his body armor. She rose and looked hard at him for a full minute. Her lips began to quiver as if trying to speak, but nothing came out. She ran to him, threw her tiny body against his and tried to wrap her arms around him. She cocked her head and looked up at him. Tears formed at the corners of her eyes. Just as she was about to speak, he pushed her away. He was uncomfortable with outward displays of tenderness. Wasn't raised that way, couldn't change.

With an expression of bewilderment muddied by sandy tears, she backed away. "Mr. Quinn, I didn't mean...Mr. Quinn I'm sure sorry, sir."

After waiting for a response that did not come, she blurted, "Sir, thanks for today. Sir, we owe our lives to you. If there's anythin' I can ever do for you Mr. Quinn, I will, sir."

Gabe regretted his gaffe. Callousness had already cost him his children's love and Nicole was headed in the same direction. He searched for a response that might ease the tension of the moment and the trauma from the earlier near tragedy. He held no animosity towards this child. In truth he admired the reticent courage that enabled her to face death each day. He respected the ballsy way she stood up to the lieutenant. He was in awe that she had heard the call to duty, a call few understood, few appreciated and fewer answered. He felt honored and privileged to walk amongst all of the young Coluccis who wore the uniform. They were the very best of American youth, and towered over their pampered, narcissistic, sniveling peers, who only answered a call to feed self-indulgent hedonism. He wished Colucci was his daughter, a daughter he could protect and nurture. The passion was there — he just did not know how to voice that passion.

Stumped, he decided to punt.

"Jersey girl, there is something you can do for me. Don't call me Mr. Quinn. Don't call me sir. To you my name is Pops. I've gotten rather accustomed to the way the word just rolls off your tongue."

It worked. Colucci wiped the tears from her eyes and smiled. "Pops. Okay. Won't make that mistake again, Pops."

"Well, I guess I better find the concierge and check into this five star establishment."

He slung his ruck over one shoulder, the IBA and Kevlar over the other, and moved to his weapon. He stopped short of the truck and turned to Colucci.

"Stay safe, Jersey girl. See you in ten days."

Chapter 11
Blood lust

 *Suq ash Shuyukh, Iraq, 200 km southeast of COP 6, 32 km southeast of FOB Adder, June 27, 1130 hours*
Where is she?

Ghazi glanced from his watch to the map of southern Iraq spread across the faded green, recycled-plastic table. He fought an urge to leave the room and search for her, but the map was more important — she would have to wait.

He highlighted FOB Adder with a yellow marker, then using a blue one, drew a circle. Centered on its airfield, the circle represented eighteen kilometers, the maximum effective range of a 122 mm Katusha rocket. He used his index finger to measure the distance from the village to the center of the airfield. Thirty-two kilometers.

Again he looked at his watch. *Where is she?*

"Father, what are you doing?" Mohammed asked.

The eight-year-old lay crumpled on the floor, one shriveled leg tucked oddly beneath the other. The crutch Ghazi had made for his son was on the floor by his side. He frowned at both abominations. Mohammed was useless and had become a liability. He should have sent him to al Kufah with his daughter, but his cousin had no more use for a cripple than he. He needed a solution to rid himself of the slag. If God willed it, *insha Allah,* an answer would come.

The other repugnance, the outgrown crutch that emphasized his son's twisted deformities, was the lesser of his problems. He would ask his cousin to find some more eucalyptus and shape a new one. He wished his son would stop growing.

"Silence," Ghazi said. "Go in the other room. Looking at you sickens me."

"Yes, father." Mohammed straightened his limbs, rolled to his side and grasped the crutch. He crawled to the nearest wall and, with the aid of the gnarled and weathered wood, rocked and wobbled his way to a perverse standing position. His face showed no emotion as he hobbled to the front room.

Ghazi was drawn to his watch again. *Where is she?*

149

Thirty-two kilometers was too far. He would order his men to fire the rockets from the east side of the river near Awdah al Wahabi. It was well within the range of the 122 mm rockets. It was time to wake these new American devils of the 82nd Airborne Division.

He taught his comrades to make a simple rocket launcher from used lumber, six-penny nails and a car's scissor jack. He trained them to use a handheld GPS and compass to determine the range and bearing, and gave them basic trigonometric formulas to calculate a rocket's flight path. Because of him, they knew how to rig a delayed fuse with a simple oven timer. It was time to test the men and to trust them. Since the Americans first arrived four years earlier, his role had evolved from being a mere fighter to a leader and strategist. No longer could he enjoy the pleasurable task of killing individual Americans. Now, he would bring the full weight of *Jaish al Mahdi* on the infidels and kill many Americans.

His new quarters, better than his village home, were well secluded for his work. A recent acquisition, a Cummins C-11 generator, powered the nearby underground workshop along with the few lights and one appliance inside the mud-brick house. Maja al Din had let him the three-room structure for less than thirty American dollars a month. His cousin was a believer and a supporter of the cause, but he did not want him in his cell. He would fulfill a different need — a need almost as powerful as Ghazi's lust for American blood. *Where is she?*

Just as he set a second map onto the table, the cell phone rang. He checked the caller's number.

"*Marhaban,* Dhul Fiqar," Ghazi said. "*Asalaam aleekum.*"

"*Aleekum asalaam.*"

"You called me with good news, yes?"

"Today we failed," Dhul Fiqar answered.

Ghazi dropped the phone and jumped up causing the plastic chair to skitter and bounce across the uneven dirt floor before it tumbled. Mumbling a curse, he moved to the chair and kicked it to the far side of the small room. He pounded his fists repeatedly against his head, veins pulsed from the blood rushing through his neck. Hungry for the facts, he calmed himself and righted the chair. He shoved it nearer to the table and collapsed into it. Glaring at the phone, as if it were the face of the person who had called him from two-hundred kilometers north, he picked it up and said, "Explain."

"The bomb did not explode. The Americans must have stopped before they passed it. Ghazi, I do not know what went wrong. It was well hidden. I sent Mansur into the desert to watch and learn why the bomb did not explode, but he saw nothing. The Americans used smoke to hide what they did. Ghazi , I am sorry, I — "

"*Yalal gaheem*! You are an idiot," Ghazi shouted. "You are sorry? You have failed me as Kaseem failed me. You remember Kaseem. Do you remember Kaseem's mongrel slut and her screams when Nazmi took her, when Nazmi killed her? Do you remember his children? Should your fate be any different? Should I ravage your daughter as I did his? Should I take your wife as you do? Do you think the bombs are free? Our brothers in Iran will not help us in our *jihad* if you continue to fail me."

He glimpsed his son watching silently from the open doorway. "Get out!" he yelled. "You have heard nothing. Get out and close the door, you grotesque offense to the eyes of *Allah*. You are no more than a monstrous pest, an irritation that I must bear. Get out now, or I will beat you with your crutch and then I will — be gone."

Mohammed answered his father's outburst with a blank, expressionless stare. No shock, no reaction, as if his father's behavior were normal. Without a word he turned to leave, but as he did his legs became entangled with his crutch and he crashed headlong onto a chamber pot. The contents splashed over the floor and on the torn and ill-fitted *dishdasha* he wore. Covered in urine, he awkwardly straightened his legs and rose, balancing himself against the wall. Although pained by the simple task, he was able to close the door.

Ghazi again heard Mohammed collapse. "*Allah*, what have I done to offend you, the one God, the only true God? *Allah*, what have I done to deserve a horrific curse like Mohammed?"

He scourged his son and Dhul Fiqar. He stepped over to the ancient electric stove and poured hot *chai* into a clear shot glass. Mixing the steaming tea with a large dose of sugar, he drained it in a single gulp. Calm again, he returned to the room's one chair. He did not need more than one — his living dishonor would only fall from it.

"Give me the details, all of them. Leave nothing out."

Dhul Fiqar explained how he had scouted the site, armed and camouflaged the bomb. Defeat resonated in his voice. "*Allah* is my witness, I swear, Ghazi. I hid the bomb so well that not even I could see it. I don't know how the Americans saw it."

Ghazi needed him — for now. "It is okay. *Insha Allah, Amerikees* will soon die."

Speaking that hated word aloud unleashed another rampage. "I will send you another bomb in a few days. You will personally set the bomb and then you will tell me that *Amerikees* have died, many *Amerikees*. You will collect mortar shells from — you know the place. Use them and attack the *Amerikee* camp. *Amerikees* martyred my father. *Amerikees* caused my wife's death, my daughter's death. *Amerikees* are the reason my only heir is a living sin. I want blood. I want *Amerikee* blood. I want rivers of *Amerikee* blood and I want it now."

"Yes, Ghazi, it will be done."

"I chose you to replace me in Diwaniyah so I would be free to bring the battle to the *Amerikees* at their big base. I cannot be in both places at once. My fight is here. Here is where I will create the hell they deserve. Do not fail me again."

"I will not fail you, Ali Sabah," Dhul Fiqar said. "I will die before I fail you. This I promise. I will — "

"You brainless idiot!" Ghazi shouted. "Never use my birth name when we talk. *Amerikees* listen, *Amerikees* hear!"

"I am sorry, I am sorry," Dhul Fiqar said in a whisper. "I forgot, Ghazi Codar el Ahmar."

Ghazi waited a long time before he was calm enough to continue. "I need a new phone now that you have compromised this one. When I have it, pass my new number on to our friend. You know who he is."

"Yes."

"Soon we will meet again, *insha Allah.*"

Ghazi ended the call and placed the phone on the table. Consumed with thoughts of blood — American blood, Dhul Fiqar's blood and — he looked at his watch. *Where is she?*

He heard a thin knock at the front door. Soon after the taps, the sounds of Mohammed's slow, arduous trek to the entrance could be heard. *She is here.*

Mohammed jubilantly greeted the guest. "*Asalaam aleekum.* Cousin, I am so happy, oh so happy. Please cousin, please, please come in. Oh cousin, you are so *jameela*, so, so beautiful. *Allah* has been good to you. I have missed you so much. It has been too, too long. *Chai*, can I get you some *chai*, Lutfiyah? Or water?"

Ghazi opened the door several inches and peered into the room. Her name mirrored her delicate and graceful appearance. Lutfiyah had developed in thirteen years to become a budding adolescent on the cusp of womanhood. The odd mixture of dated western garments that hung from her body could not cloak her feminine allure. Still a child, however, she giggled as Mohammed fawned over her. She tried to mask the joy of seeing her cousin by clasping a hand over her

152

mouth, but her fingers could not silence the childish laughs.

Mohammed continued to beam as he steadied himself against the doorjamb with his crutch thrust forward. He reached for her, clutched her hand and laughed until tears formed.

"Mohammed, leave us," Ghazi said as he entered the room. "Go to the street and beg *dinar* for your supper. Do not return until tomorrow."

Mohammed's face went blank — the joy was gone. "Yes, father." He looked at Lutfiyah and started to speak, but said nothing. He released her hand, grasped the crutch in both hands, and lamely shuffled outside.

"Lutfiyah, come in," Ghazi said.

"Yes, Ali Sabah."

He took a firm hold of her and led the way to the third room. Once inside he dropped her hand and backed away several feet. He ogled her from her uncovered head to her bare feet. "Maja al Din told me you were a woman, yet you do not wear a *hijab*. Are you a woman, Lutfiyah?"

"I do not understand, Ali Sabah," Lutfiyah said.

Agitated, Ghazi raised his voice and demanded, "Have you started menses? Have you bled?"

Lutfiyah instinctively clasped her hands and covered her femininity. Blushing, she bowed her head to the earthen floor and whispered, "Yes."

He leered at the diminutive, desert princess. "Are you *adra*?"

Tears formed. Voice quaking, she whispered, "Yes, I am a virgin."

"Do you know why you are here?"

"Father ordered that I must come. He did not say why." The tears gushed, her body heaved gasping for air. Between sobs, she whimpered, "That is all he said, Ali Sabah."

He studied her bone structure. Her full hips would serve his purposes well. "Why the tears woman? Are you not a good Muslim? Do you even know what Islam means?"

She looked at him and dutifully answered, "Submission."

"Yes, Lutfiyah. Have you submitted to the will of *Allah*?"

"*Allah* is the true God, the only God. He is my God," Lutfiyah answered robotically. She wiped her tears, looked to the floor and sighed. "Why do you ask me these questions?"

He caressed her hair, then forced her chin up. "Lutfiyah, you can see Mohammed is not one of *Allah's* blessed. Your father has promised you to me. You will submit to *Allah's* will and you will

153

submit to me. Take my seed and after your menses stops, you will return to the house of your father and mother. If you bear me a son, we will marry. If you birth a girl I will — "

He saw no advantage in telling the fate that would be hers if she failed to produce a male heir. He turned away and looked at the room's only furnishing — a thin, rancid mattress lying bare against the dirt floor. He released his grip on her and unbuckled his police duty belt.

"Remove your clothes, Lutfiyah."

Chapter 12
Hold the mayo

 COP *6, June 27, 2007, 1218 hours*
Gabe turned away from Colucci. It was time to make his presence known to management and find out what he was supposed to do for the next ten days. Eighty pounds of gear precariously hanging from his shoulders, weapon in his gun hand, Kevlar in the other, he plowed through the mounds of gravel in the direction of a trailer sprouting numerous antennae and satellite dishes.

Ten meters into his journey, he cornered an inner perimeter T-wall and tripped over a clock and compass. It was not a standard clock, with a dial and sweeping hands, or a compass with a metal needle pointing north. He had stumbled over a bare-footed human timepiece-compass, prostrate on a piece of cardboard in the midst of his noon *salat* — the *zuhr* — one of five punctual daily prayers devout Muslims recited to insure a place by the prophet's side on Judgment Day.

"I'm sorry," Gabe said as he untangled himself from his gear. "I didn't see you."

The man ignored him and continued his trance-like recitation of the prayer, "*Allahu Akbar, Allahu Akbar.* All praise to God, the Lord of all the worlds, the Compassionate.... "

Gabe reclaimed his scattered belongings and moved away from the true believer. He stood silent, mesmerized by his dedication to a seventh century huckster's pitch.

Dressed in a camouflage uniform left over from the first Gulf War, he rose from his makeshift prayer mat, keeping his arms by his side and continued the incantation. "*Allahu Akbar, Allahu Akbar, Lah ilahus ill Allah.* God is greater. God is greater."

The Iraqi bowed one last time southwest towards Mecca, put on his shoes and picked up the cardboard mat. Then he turned to Gabe. "I am sorry, sir. Are you injured, sir?"

He looked like he belonged behind a professor's lectern instead of on a combat outpost in the midst of a brutal war. The baggy uniform

155

did nothing to counter his bookish appearance. Shorter than Gabe, and slightly built even by Iraqi standards, he wore thick, silver-rimmed glasses that highlighted his clean-shaven, childlike face. Despite his youthful appearance, Gabe was sure he was in his mid-thirties, if not early forties.

"No, no, it's nothing," Gabe said. "It's my fault. Sometimes, well most of the time, I walk around with my head up my — "

He moved closer and extended his hand. "I'm Gabe Quinn. My apologies, sir. *Asalaam aleekum.*"

"*Aleekum asalaam,*" the Iraqi said. "Mister Gabe Quinn, I am called Hercules. It is my very deepest pleasure to make your acquaintance, Mister Gabe Quinn."

Gabe knew that many American soldiers had problems pronouncing Arabic names and sometimes assigned a pseudonym that was easier on the tongue — *but Hercules.*

He lightly wrapped Gabe's hand within both of his and guided him nearer. Gabe was uncomfortable with the Arab custom of invading his personal space. In his mind, there were only two reasons to be that close to another human being — sex and killing. He broke the light embrace and retreated to a distance more in tune with his Western standards.

"Mister Gabe Quinn, the name Gabe is familiar to me." Hercules scrunched his face in deep thought and continued in his singsong, soft voice, "Does your name, Mister Gabe Quinn, have another meaning, sir?"

"Gabriel."

"Oh yes, sir. Gabriel, but of course." Hercules dropped his quizzical expression and nodded at Gabe's revelation. "In Arabic we say Jibrail. Very similar, very similar indeed, sir. You have the name of an angel, sir."

Gabe laughed and sang a lyric from a seventies song. "I'm no angel, I'm no stranger to the streets — " He saw the puzzlement on Hercules' face and stopped mid-lyric. The song could turn into a clash of cultures, or at a minimum, an enigma to his male audience, who, if he understood the song, might question his intentions. "Hercules, what do you do around here?"

"Sir, I am one of the translators. You American soldiers call me a terp. I believe it means interpreter."

"You're batting zero today. I am certainly no angel, and Hercules, I'm no soldier, but I understand your confusion. I'm sure you see a bunch of out of shape old men around these parts wearing Army uniforms. It has been my pleasure to meet you. Can you point me in the direction of the TOC?"

"Yes, sir, Mister Gabriel Quinn." Hercules pointed to the trailer with the antennae and said, "The Tactical Operations Center is there, sir. Do you need assistance with your luggage, Mister Gabriel Quinn?"

"It shows, huh. No thanks, Hercules. I packed it, I'll hump it."

Gabe stopped in front of the trailer, dropped his gear to the ground and slung the rifle over his shoulder. When he opened the door, he saw the back of a seated soldier, hunched over a computer keyboard.

"Afternoon, soldier. I'm Gabe Quinn reporting in — "

The soldier jumped up from his chair and blurted, "Mr. Quinn, great to see you again, sir."

"Well I'll be damned if it ain't Dirty Bird," Gabe said. "Sorry Private, no coffee this time. The convoy wouldn't stop at that Starbucks we didn't pass on the way here. Private — well, I'll be damned again. Congratulations on your promotion, Private First Class Bussard. How the hell are you?"

Bussard pumped Gabe's hand, and said, "Living the dream, sir, living the dream." He released his grip and then frowned. "I caught the radio chatter earlier about your near-miss this morning. Sounded close, sounded real close. How are you doing, Mr. Quinn? You okay?"

"I damn near messed myself, but that's why we get paid the big bucks."

"That's a Roger, sir. Big bucks ninety-nine percent of the time. It's that other one percent when it gets real ugly, not enough money in the world, sir. About that coffee, Mr. Quinn, I can scrounge up a cup from the kitchen trailer if you want. It's nothing like the PX coffee, but it works out here."

"Maybe later. Right now, I need to check-in with the CO and get situated. Is he around?"

Bussard looked around the empty trailer. "I'm it for now, sir. Captain Ski, I mean, Kowalewski is on a village patrol. He should return by 1800 hours. Let me give you a hand with your gear and I'll get you a rack in one of the hooches. I can put you in with White Meat and Dark Meat for now."

Confused by the names, Gabe said, "Should I ask?"

"PFC Jefferson and PFC Jefferson, sir. You'll figure it out."

"Whatever you say, but it sounds like one of those Dirty Bird handles to me."

Bussard grabbed the ruck and IBA in one hand and hoisted them as if they were feathers. He led him through the maze of T-walls and trailers to a dorm prefab. Once inside, he turned on the fluorescent and surveyed the eight bunk beds arranged against the walls. He moved to an empty lower rack in the far corner and placed the gear on its bare mattress.

"Your home, sir. If you need sheets or anything else, I'll look in my hooch for extras. Nothing exciting will happen until the patrol gets back. Settle in, take a nap or whatever. Chow is around 1830. Mexican night. It'll clean out your system by morning for sure."

"Bussard, I really appreciate your help. That sir business, drop it. The name's Gabe, REMF, fobbitt, or whatever else you want to call me. Just not sir."

"Roger that, Gabe."

"Got time for a few questions?"

"Sure."

"I bumped...check that. I tripped over a terp, Hercules. How many terps do you have?"

"We have two. The one you met and the other is Dawud. He's out with the patrol." Bussard chuckled, then added, "We keep one here just in case some hajji shows up with intel about Usama bin Laden."

Gabe pushed his gear to the foot of the bunk bed and sat on its edge. "What's Hercules' story? I mean, he struck me as being a nice fellow, but maybe a little out of his element."

"Looks can be deceiving." Bussard sat on a nearby bunk and continued, "I don't know a hell of a lot about the guy. We inherited him from the unit we replaced, but from what I've heard, he hates the locals and is a real asset. He can get aggressive and is a real animal when he gets outside the wire. I guess he's a devout *Sunni* and really likes to crack on the *Shi'ite* every chance he gets."

"*Sunni*? You sure about that?"

"That's what we were told. I can't tell the difference between one hajji and another. Dawud's a different story. He deployed with us from Bragg. Global Language Incorporated, the company that hires our Cat 3 terps with top-secret clearances, found him in Chicago working at a clothing shop. He'd been employed there since before I was born. Problem is he don't know shit about Iraq or Iraqis. I don't even think he understands the local dialect. He's a Lebanese born Christian, older than Bush or you." Embarrassed, he added, "Sorry, sir. I don't mean anything by that. I mean, not that you're that old, sir."

"Don't worry about it. No offense taken, unless, you're comparing me to George H and not George W. What's Hercules' real name?"

"Not really sure, sir. Damn near every one of 'em is named Ali or Mohammad, but I think his is Mutahhar Sabah something and something else, then al Amarah. You know how their names can be. Why they can't have a first, middle, and last like the rest of us is a mystery to me. That'd be too fucking simple."

"Tell me about it." Gabe placed his Kevlar at the head of the bed as a pillow, laid back and said, "Well, my friend, I'll take that nap you think this old fart needs. Thanks for your help. Wake me if we're attacked, or if George W calls and asks for my advice. On second thought forget the latter. Can you hit the lights on your way out?"

"Sure thing, Gabe"

After Bussard left, Gabe closed his eyes and drifted. Just before he crashed from his earlier adrenalin high, he replayed the memory of Hercules praying. Something about those images was eating at him. *Sunni?*

He opened his eyes when he heard a screeching voice.

"Do I look like I give a flying fuck? Ya don't know shit, Dark Meat. Ya think ya is the subject matter expert on everything. Bro, ya just anotha fucking ghetto nigga. You can suck my balls."

"Boy, who are you calling nigger? You're nothing but an Alabama honky-cracker. White Meat, you're a — oh shit. Cool it, White Meat. Um, sir, we didn't see you there sleeping. We're sorry, sir."

Gabe rubbed his eyes and adjusted his vision to the brightness of the fluorescent light. He swung his legs over the bunk's edge and squinted towards the commotion. Framed by the doorway he saw two dusty, gritty soldiers wearing uniforms that had not been laundered for at least a week. Still half asleep, he blinked several times and focused on their nametapes. Jefferson and Jefferson. One short and lily white, one gargantuan and the color of ebony.

"Gentlemen, sorry I disrupted your conversation." Gabe yawned then grabbed the upper bunk's end rail to support his rebirth. "I'm Gabe Quinn, your roomie for a couple of weeks. Am I okay in this bunk?"

Dark Meat, taller than the trailer's doorway and almost as wide, stooped for clearance. He flashed the only white he had in an exaggerated grin and said, "Sir, you just upped the class of this neighborhood. That bunk's fine. We keep it available for VIPs just like you." He looked at his shorter battle buddy and in a deep bass voice said, "Don't mind White Meat, sir. He's a bit touched in the head and smells like ass. I'll clean him up and improve the stink factor in here. Nothing I can do about his affliction, though. No sir, not a damn thing."

White Meat dropped his patrol pack and leaned his M4 against the wall. He threw a shadow punch at Dark Meat and said, "I smells like ass? I'm touched?" He wiped a crocodile tear from the corner of his eye and in a shrill voice that was a dead ringer for Pee Wee Herman, said, "Dark Meat, ya makes Forrest Gump out to be like a fucking highway schooler. Sir, I've been stuck with this shit bag since way back in boot camp. He thinks he's all educated because he had a lil' college. I've done tried to educate him about how the civilized world be, but he such a shammerai warrior it's a lost cause."

Dark Meat pushed the heavy fifty-caliber machine gun off of his shoulder and tossed it to the nearest bunk. He turned on the smaller soldier, placed him in a headlock and gave him a spirited noogy. "Cracker, that's Rhodes Scholar, not highway schooler." He kept his hold on White Meat and grunted, "Humph, humph, humph," as he simulated a sex act, an act unnatural to most.

Gabe laughed at the duo's impromptu comedy and approached them with an outstretched hand. "Well I'm glad to see that I'm in a political correctness free zone."

White Meat broke the hold and shook Gabe's hand. "Welcome to paradise, sir."

Dark Meat shoved White Meat to the side, threw a protective arm around Gabe and pulled him in. He whispered, "Don't worry, sir, I'll keep you safe from him. He's scary for sure, but cute in a cracker sort of way. But if he gets all cuddly with you, watch your six, sir." He stepped back and pointed at White Meat. "Sir, I'm sure he's one of those 'don't ask don't tell' rainbow warriors. He'll do you for real."

Gabe placed both of his hands protectively against his buttocks. "I take it you just returned from a patrol?"

Both soldiers nodded.

"Successful?"

"You know how it is, sir," Dark Meat said. "Nobody got hurt, so yeah, it was successful. We didn't learn anything, though. We went to this village because some hajji told the captain a generator was stolen. We tried to follow up with the elders but they were too afraid to talk. Just another ride in the desert. One more day in the suck down."

"Is Captain Kowalwuewalaski, or whatever, is he available?"

"Sir, I think Ski's in the shower trailer getting the sand out of his cracks. Soon as it's free that's where my little bro here is going." Dark Meat pulled off his shirt revealing arms as thick as tree trunks.

"The captain will be at the kitchen trailer by 1900. Mexican night, sir. You can't miss Mexican night. Guaranteed shit bombs by tomorrow morning, sir."

The combination kitchen-dining-recreation prefab was full and loud. Twenty soldiers were crowded into the small trailer and huddled around folding tables. Some sat in the flimsy plastic chairs, others stood behind them, or to their sides, and harangued them with taunts. All wolfed down burritos and tacos that oozed grease. Generous portions of salsa, hot sauce and mayonnaise made the food palatable. Captain Kowalewski sat at the head of one table.

If not for the captain bars on his blouse, one could mistake him for just another young enlisted soldier grab-assing with his peers. He was at the center of a heated debate about the merits of using mayonnaise on tacos as a substitute for sour cream. The argument was moot since sour cream was not available within a hundred miles. Most of the soldiers used mayonnaise on tacos, burritos and just about anything else heading for their bellies.

Kowalewski ended the debate with booming finality. He banged his fists on the table causing a bottle of Texas Pete and a saltshaker to take flight. "If you use mayo on a taco you're one sick bastard. You're a disgrace to the Army, the United States of America, and by-God, Kraft Foods, Incorporated." A broad smile covered his face.

With grease, mayonnaise and salsa streaming from his mouth to his chin, White Meat pointed at the gallon jug of mayonnaise on the table. "Sir, I be using that there mayo on my ass-sores when they be hurting. Do ya think sour cream be better?"

The room fell silent. Soldiers stared at the half-eaten tacos and burritos that remained on their paper plates. One studied the taco he was about to chomp into. Shaken, he dropped the shell on the table. "White Meat, did you use a clean spoon?"

"Spoon?"

A communal "ughh" sounded through the room.

"What the fuck?" White Meat said as he used his free hand to clear the goop from his chin. With his other hand, he shoved half of a taco inside his mouth. Eyes wide with delicious enjoyment of the grease and mayo, he managed to slur a few words between bites. "I used my clean hand."

Nobody touched another taco. Nobody looked at another taco. All eyes were fixated on the scrawny human garbage disposal as he shredded, pureed and macerated the mayonnaise-laden taco.

Dark Meat chuckled.

Dirty Bird was next with a muted laugh.

Kowalewski, recovered from the after-shock of White Meat's bombshell, grinned slowly at first. His grin broadened until it covered the lower half of his face. Then he burst out laughing. The floodgates opened and the room exploded in gut-pained laughs that shook the walls.

Gabe watched from the trailer's entrance, half expecting a follow-on quip from Dark Meat, but even the best improv would be bunged after White Meat's candid line.

The captain stood when he saw Gabe in the doorway. "Mr. Quinn, come join us. There's plenty left, but hold the mayo."

Gabe walked to him and shook his hand. "Good to meet you, Captain."

"We've already met, Mr. Quinn." Kowalewski said. "I was at the briefing when you eviscerated our JAG fag, Major Laddick. Or should I say, La Dick. I'm glad you're here."

Gabe remembered the briefing, but could not place the captain — too many young faces to consider. He had difficultly remembering his home address, so he lied. "Sure, I remember you, Captain."

"Mr. Quinn, after the Joes clear out, I'd like to run a few ideas by you, if you have the time, that is. Grab some food and I'll get us some coffee."

"I should check my day planner first, but I think I can fit you in. Captain, the name's Gabe. That Kowalewski tag of yours is quite a mouthful. Do you mind if I just keep it at Captain?"

"Gabe, this ain't the FOB." Kowalewski, whose name was about as long as he was tall, said, "Ski works just fine around here. This place'll empty out in ten minutes. Now, about that coffee."

Ski returned holding two Styrofoam cups. He set one on the table in front of Gabe. "What happened to your convoy this morning is a change in hajji's tactics. That's the first time we've seen a daylight attempt on a convoy."

"I'll take your word for it, Ski. I haven't been privy to intelligence, so I don't know what's been going on in your AO." Gabe sipped his coffee, then said, "If the change is radical, my guess is the enemy cell in your area is under new management. Time for him to make a statement."

"That's exactly what I think," Ski said. "Hell, we don't have a clue about the old leadership, how many we're dealing with, where their rat lines or weapons caches are located — *nada*, zip. Gabe, let me ask you a question, more of a request."

"Let's have it."

"I received a heads-up about your arrival via SIPR internet last night. No details about your mission — just that you'd be on the LOGPAC and our guest for a couple of weeks. Since you're here... well, some of what you said back at Bragg made sense. Gabe, I don't know how your contract reads, but I could use some help to get a handle on this enemy. If that's contrary to your contract, you're welcome to just hang out here and pass the time. I'll understand."

"Captain, my scope of work reads like a.... Let me put it this way. It's like my company gathered every member of the American Bar Association, locked them in a room where they took a group dump and out plopped a contract. Plenty of thin-print, a myriad of cryptic CYA statements, lofty goals, appendices, sub-appendices that need appendices, but no mission details, other than the United States Army is my boss and vague platitudes that the mission is to help save American lives." Gabe grinned and said, "Ski, those are the important ones. I'm yours to be used and abused. What do you need?"

"Help."

"You've got it."

Gabe looked away from Ski when he heard the door open. Hercules stepped inside and grabbed a Coke from the cooler and then sat a nearby table.

"Mister Gabriel Quinn, are you finding our accommodations pleasing to you, sir?"

"Yes I am, Hercules. The cuisine, um, food, is perfection, the company even better. So good I may never leave."

"Good, sir, good," Hercules said. "We have much to talk about. I am very interested to learn about your family, your home, what you think of my country — and what you do, sir."

"We'll do that sometime, but the captain and I must leave you now. *Mas allama.*"

Gabe looked at Ski and winked, "Captain, I'll take you up on your offer to see the TOC."

It took several seconds before Gabe's intent registered on Ski. "Sure thing, Gabe. I think you'll be as overwhelmed with the set-up as you are with our food. Follow me."

As they stepped inside the operations center, Gabe asked, "Captain, do your terps have free access to the entire camp including the TOC?"

"Well, yeah. Sometimes we bring one of them in when we need

to call a village elder to set up a meet, but we control the cell phones. They can't have their own, only ours, and the calls are strictly mission oriented and monitored. We stand right by them when they make a call."

"I understand, Captain. You can never be too careful. Back to what we were discussing. Not knowing exactly what you want, how about this? I saw one of the LOGPAC sergeants refer to an intel log this morning— "

"That would've been the trail-book," Ski interrupted. "The Brigade S2 updates it nightly and puts it out there for every patrol leaving the wire."

"If I'm to get a handle on your situation that seems like the logical starting point. Can you get me a copy of the trail-book that goes back to, I don't know, three, maybe four months before you ripped with the prior unit?"

"Not a problem."

"Along with that — well, let me ask another question first. When your patrols return from a mission, I assume that an after action review (AAR) is conducted?"

"Affirmative."

"Are those AARs reduced to writing?"

"Every one of them," Ski said. "We even keep a file on the prior unit's patrols."

"Do the reports detail the map grid references, times and any activities that stood out?"

"I'd need to look at the prior unit's reports, but ours do."

"Captain, if you could get me those, the trail-book and a map of your AO, I'll find a place where I can wallow for a day or two and see what I can come up with."

COP 6 TOC, June 29, 2007, 0645 hours

"I don't know how you managed to hide out in this camp for two days, but you did," Ski said. "I thought you lost it, crossed the wire and had gone 'Lawrence of Arabia' on us."

"T. E. Lawrence was an egotistical faggot," Gabe said brusquely. "Captain, you have a problem, an OPSEC problem."

Ski lost his smile.

Gabe's sunken eyes, three-day beard and uncombed hair telegraphed that he had not slept in days. Stripped down to ACU pants, a sweat-stained tee shirt and shower sandals, he teetered at the entrance to Ski's office, bracing himself against the doorjamb. "Sorry 'bout that. I didn't mean to come off so — I missed my morning coffee and haven't taken a dump in two days. Let me reboot. Good morning, Ski."

Ski looked past him and shouted, "White Meat, need a cup of coffee and a laxative from Doc for Mr. Quinn."

Seated in front of the radio, White Meat repeated the order, "Crap medicin' and a cuppa Joe for Mr. Quinn. I'm on it, suh."

Ski walked by Gabe and closed the door. "Take a seat and tell me what you found."

"Captain, you do have a leak. I can't tell you who or how, but…let me go over my analysis." He remained standing as Ski moved behind his desk and sat. "During the fifteen months the prior unit covered this AO and your three weeks here, not a single enemy has been captured or killed. Until a few days ago, no IEDs had been discovered before detonation. It should be good hunting here. I realize you're working with too few soldiers and a huge area, but even a blind whore finds an occasional John. It's early, Ski. That should've been something about a squirrel."

"I get your point," Ski said. "I guess I'm the whore in your metaphor."

"Captain, in some way we're all whores. What I'm saying is the desert has eyes, the desert has ears, the desert knows. I don't know how often Iraqis come to your camp, don't know their reasons, but intelligence is getting out somehow. Rule number one — never trust a hajji, any hajji. I'm convinced an Iraqi cop tried to hit us on our way in. Forget all that feel-good crap you learned in cultural awareness training. Leave it back at Bragg. They all want something. Could be just your money, water, food, or maybe your life. Take Prime Minister Maliki, our friend, our supporter, and our partner against the insurgents. Bullshit! He was a *Dawa* leader before his back-room brokered appointment and still gets support from Iran and Syria. While we pour our blood and treasure into this shit-hole, he's out there courting our enemy, Moqtada Sadr. I read in the Stars and Stripes that Maliki promised amnesty to insurgents if they killed only Americans and not Iraqis. Damnit! Killed only Americans! And we support this clown. He's the biggest whore of all and we're the over-charged trick who doesn't even get a nut off."

"All right, Gabe. I get it. What can I do?"

Gabe fought a yawn as he rubbed his glazed-over eyes. He steadied himself on the captain's desk and said, "Sorry Ski, I'm losing it. I need a drink…I mean sleep. What I'm trying to say…listen, you strike me as being a fine officer, your soldiers love you, and if you follow the rules and play it safe, you'll probably get through this deployment with minimal casualties. Ski, I don't have many answers, just a lot of questions. But I know that if you follow the rules and play it safe, it only means one thing. Your tactics suck."

"Gabe, I'm all about getting my soldiers home in one piece, but I also realize I have a mission to complete. If you have ideas how to accomplish the mission and keep me from writing those damn letters to loved ones, well you have — "

"Ski, let me go out on a few patrols and maybe suggest some ways to ramp it up a bit. When I was up north I learned a few things that aren't in the manuals."

Gabe's vacant stare went beyond the captain to a vanishing point conventional metrics could not measure. "The kill, Captain. That's the reason I…you came here."

Chapter 13
The butterfly awakes

Isfaban, Iran, May 4, 2005

The soldier's death had been decided when he still had a first name and was repeating his junior year in high school. An argument could be made that his fate was fixed 13.7 billion years ago, at the time of the singularity, when all elements were formed, for it was the inert elements dug from the earth and shaped by man that would end Jeremiah's life. A more contemporary timeline places the beginning of his end in this century, and at its core, Iran.

Iran, and an unwitting co-conspirator, which also happened to be its enemy, manufactured the death that would fall from the sky on July 4, 2007. The *Hadid* HM16, 120 mm, smooth bore mortar launcher, SN 33-4718س ت-17-و, was an exact copy of a standard K6. Iranian spies had stolen the design from the arms manufacturer, Soltam Systems, a subsidiary of the Mikal Group, Yokneam, Israel.

The launcher rolled off Iran's production line in May 2005, at a cost of less than two-thousand American dollars. A pristine HM16 could fetch as much as eighteen thousand dollars in the weapons black market. This one, however, had a flaw — a slight pitting and scoring inside the unrifled tube. Because of the imperfection, quality control had culled it from the production line. General Ataollah Salehi, commander of Iran's *Pasdaran*, had decreed that defective weaponry would be warehoused until it could be fixed, or, if not cost efficient, scrapped. Thus began the tangled and prophetic journey of SN 33-4718س ت-17-و.

Twenty months later, a more detailed inspection disclosed that although the defect was minor, the mortar tube was unsuitable for fielding by Iran's army. As with other imperfect weapons, and for a discount, the heavy mortar was acceptable to Iran's proxies. The mortar, a bipod with attached cross-level elevation and traverse mechanisms, a twin recoil-buffer unit, a rectangular base plate and a re-conditioned NSB-4A optical elbow telescope, were packaged for a cross-border incursion into Iraq.

167

Khorramashahr, Iran, February 1, 2007

The six feet by three feet crate, weighing nearly three hundred pounds, was tracked from *Isfaban* to the Iraq-Iran border town by a bar code affixed to its side. An Islamic Revolution guardian in charge of the sub-warehouse, opened the crate and inventoried the contents. Satisfied nothing had been pilfered, he supervised the movement of the components, still dripping with cosmoline, to a wooden coffin. He dropped the head of a slaughtered goat inside a burlap USAID rice sack, tied it with twine and placed the bag inside the casket.

Another guardian, dressed in traditional *Bedouin* garments, signed a release form and took possession of the container and SN 33-4718س ت-17-و. He nailed the coffin's lid shut and ordered his two assistants to load it onto a truck. Then he called Iraq.

"*Aleekum asalaam.*"

"*Asalaam aleekum,*" Ghazi said. "Is it ready?"

"It is, my friend. I hope you will use it wisely and bring much glory to our cause."

"*Insha Allah*, much glory will be ours together," Ghazi said. "I will meet you before the sun rises tomorrow. Will we meet as we did last time?"

"Yes. *Mas allama,* go with God."

17 km southeast of Basra, Iraq, February 2, 2007, 0350 hours

Ghazi navigated the rutted desert *wadi* in total darkness. He slowed the rusted station wagon when he saw two flashes from a distant vehicle. He flashed his light three times. After he saw the countersign, one short and two long flashes, he cautiously narrowed the two-hundred meters that separated them. When he was close enough to recognize the Jingo truck and its occupants, he stopped the car and tightened his grip on the *Kalashnikov*. He needed his Persian brothers, but he was wary of them. He opened the door, moved the rifle's selector to full auto and got out.

"Ghazi, it has been too long," the driver said. After a brief exchange of cheek kisses, he continued, "We must be quick. I have another delivery to make further north to your friend. We could not fit the mortar rounds and fuses in the same container, but this way will be safer for you. The money must— "

"I understand," Ghazi said. "You are wise to be careful. I too am careful, my friend. When I arrive at my destination, I will make a call and your money will be ready at the same *hawala* we used before.

Once you have secured the package to the roof of the car, I will be on my way. I have many kilometers to travel and many checkpoints to evade."

Ghazi didn't worry about Americans discovering his cargo because they had grown complacent. The numerous coffins moved around the war-torn country had become commonplace and to them, expected. Their timidity and beliefs about not violating the sanctity surrounding the handling of a Muslim corpse made it easy to deceive them. The putrid stench emitted from the goat's head would satisfy most soldiers' curiosity about the casket's contents.

He was concerned about his *Sunni* enemies, as well as his *Shi'ite* brothers who had ignored the dutiful path of *jihad*. He had taken precautions that would negate most of the challenges ahead. Being an Iraqi police officer gave him an edge. Although he did not wear his uniform, he had his badge and knew the location of the fixed checkpoints between Basra and the safe house in Afak. He also knew where the *Sunni* strongholds were. His familiarity with the terrain would enable him to skirt around both hazards undetected. His only concerns were the snap road checkpoints of government loyalists and those of fellow *Shi'ite* insurgents. The American dollars he carried would satisfy most loyalists. If not, there was the AK47.

For the benefit of his fellow *mujahedeen*, he had tied a piece of fabric to the outside mirror. The cloth displayed three green dots formed in a triangle and a crescent moon — a sign his *Jaish al Mahdi* comrades would understand.

al Qunar, Iraq, February 2, 2007, 0558 hours

Just as the sun peeked above the drained marshland thirty-three kilometers northwest of the first weapon transfer, Dhul Fiqar accepted five wooden-plank crates from the Iranians. The smaller crate held thirty Iranian manufactured, AZ111A2, super-quick impact fuses indistinguishable from the German *Junghans* DM111. An Iranian intelligence officer had purchased several of the *Junghans* and secreted one off to the Democratic People's Republic of North Korea to be reverse-engineered.

Three medium sized crates safeguarded twenty-four, 120 mm mortar bombs, each weighing 12.6 kilograms. The fourth wooden box protected twenty-four, donut shaped, eight-charge propellant systems that would be needed to boost the rounds into flight.

Dhul Fiqar was not concerned about his trip north. Like Ghazi, he was an Iraqi police officer, but unlike him, he openly wore his uniform and displayed his badge. He instructed the Iranians to load the crates in the back seat and rear cargo area of his 2006 GMC Jimmy police vehicle.

As the Iranians transferred the last crate to the SUV, they lost their grip. The impact of wood slamming against pavement shattered the container's side panel. Eight high-explosive bombs careened across the highway.

After praising *Allah* for their continued existence, he and the Iranians positioned the loose projectiles between the gaps of loaded crates and the SUV's interior sidewalls. One bomb, Lot 7B, produced April 1, 2004, and numbered 7B3169, was slightly damaged. One of its eight fixed flight-stabilizing fins was slightly bent inward seven millimeters.

Awakened, the butterfly was ready to flap its wings.

82nd Airborne, Ft. Bragg, NC, February 2, 2007, 2315 hours

After three attempts, Jeremiah finally earned a GED. Two weeks later, on September 11, 2005, his first name changed to Private. Five-hundred and nine difficult days later, during a brief company level ceremony, his name changed again — Private First Class.

February 2nd was the proudest day in his nineteen years. He celebrated at a nearby Fayetteville gentleman's club by drinking several O'Doul's beers with his older, legal-aged and bombed Army buddies. Then he called his mother. She hung up. Jeremiah would cry out for Momma once more.

Chapter 14
Walk with me Jesus

COP 6, July 2, 2007, 0423 hours
" Oooooh...Sabirra. Too many holes."

"Gabe, wake up."

"Wha-wha-what?"

"Get up," Bussard said.

"Is it you? Are you him? You bastard, why'd you put those holes in her? Why so many damn holes? Why'd you do that? What kind of an animal are you?"

Gabe grabbed the Beretta from his patrol pack. He instinctively flicked the safety off then clumsily raised the 9 mm and pointed it at Bussard.

Bussard blocked his arm and wrestled the weapon from him. "Gabe, it's all right. It's me, Dirty Bird."

"Dirty Bird? Bussard? How'd you get here? It's not safe here. Don't stay here."

"You're safe Gabe, I'm safe. You okay, brother?"

"Sorry, sorry...I'm sorry, I — " Gabe adjusted his eyes to the dim light and saw the Beretta in Bussard's hand. "Give it back."

Bussard thumbed the safety and returned the handgun to him. "Gabe, we move out in twenty. You gonna be all right? I mean, damnit Gabe, you scared the shit out of me. I can tell Ski something to get you out of the patrol."

"Fine, I'm fine, Bussard. Twenty minutes...I'll be ready in five. Where we going?"

"Afak, thirty clicks out. The captain wants to try the elders one more time about that missing generator. Gabe, that didn't sound like a wet dream. Who is she?"

"Was."

Afak, thirty-three kilometers northeast of COP 6, 0640 hours

Gabe followed the captain and Hercules into the village's main *kulat*. Surrounded by mud-brick walls topped with broken glass, the courtyard consisted of several outbuildings, a small stand of date palms and a meeting hall. With temperatures already nearing one hundred degrees, the promise of slight relief beckoned from the hall's cooler interior.

Weighed down with body armor, weapons and radios, Ski and Gabe also carried cases of warm, Kuwaiti bottled water. The water was meant as a *quid pro quo* gesture. Iraqi customs dictated that a gift required a matching, if not a grander offering. Information was the hoped for tit-for-tat. As they worked their way through the throng of children, goats and peddlers, each focused on the perimeter, possible defilade, escape routes and the hands of all military aged males they encountered. The *dishdasha*, or man-dresses in soldier lingo, worn by the Iraqis could hide a handgun, AK 47, suicide belt or a thermo nuclear device.

Hercules carried nothing other than attitude. His job was to create an authoritative aura that would play on another Iraqi trait — obedience. He wore dark goggles over his prescription glasses, and a *shemagh* covered his face and head. Not even his hands were visible, hidden underneath black gloves. The only sense the village elders could use would be hearing. They would not know the speaker's tribe or sect, only his voice. In addition to cloaking his identity for security reasons, the charade would feed the elders' deference to power. Having suffered under *Sunni* rule for centuries, the *Shi'ite* were used to the big-stick approach. Saddam had understood and had kept them herded for decades — sheep for shearing and slaughter.

Once inside the hall and after the customary exchange of salutations, cheek kissing and handshakes, Gabe sat cross-legged with his back against a wall near the room's exit. Before he had gotten out of the Humvee, and against Army policy, he had pushed the safety on his M4 to the off position and moved the selector to three-round burst mode. Mindful of the sage advice spoken by the renowned American philosopher, Dirty Harry, Gabe was a man aware of his limitations. He was a terrible shot. At close range, however, he could unload a thirty-round magazine in seconds, reload six more times and hit something. Gabe believed that in a firefight, it was speed and sending volumes of lead down-range that could be the game changer, not precise target acquisition. Spray and pray, or in his case, spray.

Twenty minutes into the *shura* council, unsure of Hercules' questions or the elders' answers, Gabe thought nothing was being accomplished. Contrary to his law enforcement style of asking open-ended questions to elicit candid responses, it sounded like Hercules was lecturing. His soft, melodious voice was absent, replaced instead with a crusty, jagged one Gabe did not believe possible from such a frail looking man.

The fear on the villagers' faces was obvious. Their attention shifted nervously between Ski and Gabe, as if looking to them for protection and understanding. The few times the elders looked at Hercules they soon diverted their glances to the floor.

Gabe leaned over and whispered into Ski's ear. "We wasting time here?"

"Don't know, Gabe. The little bit I'm getting when Hercules bothers to translate is they know nothing. I did catch that they want another generator from us so they can pump water from the river. If we don't, livestock will die, children will get sick and they'll starve."

"That's our problem? Captain, can we talk?"

Ski stood and touched Hercules' arm. He whispered something to him, then motioned Gabe to follow him outside.

"What's up, Gabe?"

"Captain, we're talking about a Cummins C-11 generator. Weighs about three hundred-fifty kilos, bigger than a breadbox, smaller than a Volkswagen. Didn't sprout wings and fly away. Kind of hard to misplace. Somebody knows something but they aren't talking. It's clear they lack the stones to fend for themselves. Easier to ask for another generator since the Iraqis and every damn stateside liberal believes we're stealing Iraqi oil and have all the petro-dollars we need to fix every one of their problems without killing an occasional hajji."

"What can I do? I agree a hundred percent but nothing I can say to these folks is going to shake them out of their shared amnesia."

"I know that, Ski. I'm just tired of the hajjis' answer to everything — *insha Allah*. If *Allah* doesn't will it, we gullible Americans patsies will."

Gabe paused to formulate another option. "We know it was stolen. We know they know. We know they know who did it. We know they won't say. There's a lot of knowing going on in that room but those candy-asses — Screw it. Let me move around the village and talk to the ones who aren't afraid...the kids."

"Give it a shot, Gabe. I can't spare Hercules, so you won't have a terp."

"I'll manage. I know some Arabic. Can I borrow your photo of the stolen generator?"

"Sure, I'm done with it. As soon as I wrap up inside I'll send Hercules your way. Let me get you some security."

"Don't worry about me. Haven't you heard that I'm Gabriel, the

Archangel? I walk with Jesus, and besides, if he forsakes me and something happens, I won't count against your stats. Remember, I'm just a money-grubbing civilian war tourist. Ski, you need some backup in there. I'll hang until you get someone. Some of those old guys are eyeing your tush like you're a chaste sheep that needs to be bedded. Give you the Hershey highway thrill ride."

Ski laughed and said, "Damn, you're one sick dude." He keyed his radio and ordered Sergeant Sandoval to rally Bussard to the *shura* council. When Ski finished he said, "Gabe, stop by my Humvee and see the gunner. We carry a booty box with candy, MRE leftovers, dolls and other stuff the kids like. May help some. Stay in sight of security and don't stray too far. If the shit hits the fan, we move fast, angel or no angel."

Gabe saw several soldiers near the parked convoy handing out water and MREs to a small group of boys. The kids were tugging on every exposed limb of the soldiers trying to get little hands inside big pockets for more baubles. He could not decide who was enjoying the fracas more, the boys or the soldiers. Iraqi children could always be counted on for comic relief. They distracted the soldiers from the monotony of daily patrols and the hardship of being separated from their own clans on the other side of the planet.

He skirted by the cultural exchange to the captain's Humvee and lifted the trunk lid. Perusing over the pogey-bait, he filled his cargo pockets with candy, pencils, crayons and several children's trinkets, including a cheap, but colorful Mickey Mouse necklace. He was amazed at the items home-front suburban philanthropists dumped into care packages after they failed to reap a dime or a quarter from their Saturday garage sales.

Gabe sought virgin territory away from the pandemonium. He saw an inviting alley and decided to walk its deserted path between the houses. Less than a hundred meters into his recon, he came to a small clearing. Besides the swarms of flies and the ubiquitous goats and disease-carrying, mangy dogs picking through the heaps of garbage, the only other thing recognizable was a police vehicle parked next to a more affluent abode another seventy meters away. The wall surrounding the house was topped with razor wire instead of the broken glass usually seen on the walls of most *kulats*.

An Iraqi policeman wearing mirrored aviator sunglasses and sporting a thick, Saddam style mustache, stepped through the open gate toward the police vehicle. As he opened the car door, he looked up and saw Gabe.

174

Gabe lowered his rifle and waved. The policeman froze and stared back across the garbage-strewn field at him. Gabe took a few steps toward the him, but the Iraqi turned away. Dismissing him like he was a trivial vermin one ignores or puts under the boot heel, he got inside the SUV, started the engine and disappeared in a cloud of dust.

"Asshole!" Gabe shouted. "No candy for you."

Checking his surroundings, he decided he had wandered too far off the beaten path, so he did an about-face. On his return trip he caught occasional blurred forms peering at him from inside the huts along the alley. Never a word or other form of human acknowledgement, just staring eyes — eyes that once contact was made would hurriedly disappear into the shadows.

When he neared the patrol vehicles, he saw the soldiers were still hamming it up for the kids. Thirty meters from them, he glimpsed three young girls doing the hajji squat near a hut's entrance — a metal door painted in a psychedelic lime-green color hanging from rusted hinges.

The girls' laughter made it clear they wanted to join in the one-sided gift giving, but to do so would violate some male driven Islamic taboo.

Gabe ignored the cultural vulgarity and approached the girls. Ten meters from them, he removed his sunglasses, pumped up his smile, and greeted them in Arabic. Shocked, they stopped giggling.

From his long hours of pouring over the Qur'an and books about Arab culture, he knew a line had been crossed. These children, whose world extended no further than the *kulat's* walls, reacted to his blunder in a predictable manner. They saw him as *Shaytan*, the evil supernatural *jinn* sent to prey upon their souls.

Gabe saw them as the silent victims of a superstitious, poorly thought-out religion that guaranteed their servitude and miserable lot in life. The lucky ones died in the womb. The unlucky ones entered life with odds stacked against them by a stifling religion and an ignorant, male dominated society. Born into a fundamentalist sect, these unfortunate girls would be virtual prisoners behind real and imagined walls built by their brothers and fathers, and later, the husbands chosen for them. They would be entombed in the heavy, black, veiled body-covering *niqabs* they were forced to tolerate from puberty until the day they escaped in death. The only thing these poor souls could take comfort in was they had not been born in Afghanistan and forced by the *Pashtun* Taliban to suffocate behind *burkas*.

Aside from their malnutrition, filth, brown eyes, dark hair and skin, Gabe saw, or liked to imagine that he saw, semblances of his granddaughters in these children. *To hell with the prophet, his self-indulgent, debauched teachings and hadiths. To hell with the hordes of chauvinistic Islamic imams and other supposed religious scholars who piled on the fatwas that justify everything from pedophilia to fast-track martyrdom though suicide.*

Undeterred by any absurdity, much less one shrouded in religion, he moved closer and reached inside his pocket. He rummaged through the bulging thigh cargo pocket until he found some Twizzlers and Skittles, then placed the candy at their feet. He patched together several words and phrases from about a dozen he could butcher with ease. "*Sabah al-kheir* — a present for three, beautiful, precious gifts from *Allah*."

Their subdued expressions transformed into wide smiles and even wider, disbelieving eyes. The oldest of the children said, "*Shokran, shokran laka,* mistah."

"*Ahlan wasahlan,*" Gabe said. He reached inside another pocket and pulled out pencils and crayons, then laid them near the two younger girls. They quickly grabbed the offerings and hid them beneath their clothes.

Gabe squatted near the oldest girl, un-slung his assault rifle and laid it on the ground next to him. He pulled the folded photo of the generator from underneath his body armor and held it up for the girls to see. Searching his sodden memory for an Arabic phrase to ask who stole the generator, he settled on pantomime, grandfatherly charm and what he hoped was the universally understood expression for a thief — *Ali Baba*. He failed miserably, so he brought out the last of the big guns, the *piéce de résistance* — Mickey Mouse. He dangled the shiny object in front of the older child and pointed to the photo.

"*Hal yumkin an tosa' dany? Min fadlik, mann 'Ali Baba'* the generator?" Gabe asked.

The older girl hesitated, showing the same fear he had seen earlier on the elders' faces.

The youngest girl, four maybe five years old, grabbed the necklace and hung it around her neck. She swatted the hand of the older one as she reached for the invaluable treasure purchased from an over-priced novelty shop at the mystical Disney World, the very existence of which they would never know. Undeterred, the older girl reached over a second time and tore it from the child's neck.

Fiddling with the clasp, she fixed the necklace and draped it around her neck. Beaming like she was a beautiful, bejeweled young

176

princess, she paid the price for the prize. "Ghazi Codar el Ahmar."

Hercules ran towards Gabe's unorthodox, kiddies' *shura* council and shouted in Arabic. Gabe repeated the girl's response as a question. "Ghazi Codar el Ahmar?"

"*Nam,* Ghazi," the child confirmed. Then she said, "*Enahu shorty.*"

Gabe was disturbed by her candid addition, but not shocked. *Enahu shorty* — a policeman.

He could not decipher Hercules' Arabic rants. Too fast and too many, but he could see the effects they had on the girls — eyes cast down, bodies trembling, panicky glances among them — a panic closer to dread.

Hercules stood over the girls and continued to scold them with heated admonishments. He ground the candy into the sand under his knock-off, Nike running shoes. Gabe couldn't understand the words, or why Hercules' apparent sectarian-fueled hatred was so viciously unleashed on innocents. He had validated Bussard's precocious characterization of him — an animal when outside the wire and in the presence of *Shi'ite.* Gabe, thankful that Hercules was not armed, questioned the military's wisdom in using a *Sunni* interpreter in a *Shi'ite* dominated province.

The two younger girls bolted across the opening and disappeared down the same alley Gabe had recently reconnoitered. The oldest and newest 'Mouseketeer' opened the lime-green door just enough to slide through the gap and into her sanctuary.

As she did, Gabe said good-bye. "*Ala-al-leka'a.*"

The girl looked one last time at him and gave him a parting gift, his tit-for-tat — a beautiful, unforgettable innocent smile.

Hercules scowled ominously at the retreating child, still barely visible through the slightly ajar, lime-green door. "Mister Quinn, you cannot talk to the girls. It is against our tradition, sir. It is bad, sir, really bad, not permissible. This is scandalous, dangerous, *ma ahlah, ma al-amal.* Good heavens, what is to be done, Mister Quinn? Come sir, we must leave now."

"Hercules, take it easy. Get a damn grip, friend," Gabe said as he rose from his squatting position. "It's not like I'm asking them out on a date."

Gabe looked inside the house's murky interior and fought an urge to reach in, scoop the child up in his arms and somehow spirit her off to civilization six thousand miles across the ocean and centuries ahead of this mayhem — *a chance Jesus, give the innocents a chance.* He dropped any pretense of civility from his tone and said, "Okay terp, blow me away with your damn terping abilities. What does Ghazi Codar el Ahmar mean?"

"Nothing, sir, nothing. It is, how do you say, gibberish, Mister Quinn. Just childish gibberish. We must go, sir. The *shura* council is finished. We have been here much too long. The captain is anxious to leave, sir."

"Childish gibberish," Gabe repeated. "How about — "

The first RPG struck ten meters in front of the captain's Humvee. A deafening explosion spewed hot, jagged shrapnel forward in a deadly arc that shredded the truck's left front tire and penetrated the engine compartment. The second RPG rocketed wildly above the Humvee and exploded with a muffled 'ka-whoomf' about one hundred meters farther down the alley Gabe had explored. He reacted as he always did on first contact — like a coward. He dove to the ground and fought an overwhelming urge to defecate and disappear. Before the noise of the explosions finished echoing, he heard bees ripping and cracking through the air far above and to his sides.

Dark Meat slung blood from his face and swung the fifty-caliber, blasting away indiscriminately creating a rhythmic, reassuring deep bass sound similar to a small caliber howitzer — thump, thump, thump, thump, thump, thump.

White Meat grabbed two small boys in his arms and tossed them behind the damaged Humvee. Again, he jumped into the withering fire, effortlessly snatched three more boys, and then sprinted to the cover of the smoking vehicle.

Sandoval shouted unheard orders while he unleashed a long burst from his M249 at seen or unseen targets, filling in the baritone — ratat, tat, tat, tat, tat, tat, tat.

Enemy AK 47s responded with the steady, terrifying alto pitched maelstrom of 7.62 mm rounds cracking through the air hitting metal, sand, brick.

Ski, recon-by-fire, shot three-round bursts, expending two magazines in seconds, reloading a third, filling in the harmony — ratat, tat, tat — ratat, tat, tat — ratat, tat, tat.

Dirty Bird emptied his SAW's linked ammo in a rock steady tenor.

Caught in the open, Gabe tried to be small, looking for a target, seeing none, ducking, rising, enemy fire continuing to create angled geysers in the sand far to his right and left, shouting in a fear-induced, unnatural soprano, "Stay down, White Meat, stay the hell down!"

Hercules stood tall as if immune to the deathly music flying through the air, acting like an orchestral conductor enjoying and directing a discordant row he had scored.

Gabe leapt from a crouch and knocked Hercules to the ground, rolled over him to a prone position, firing frantically at muzzle flashes and dark shapes darting between houses and open doorways.

Dark Meat, with no time to swap out the fifty-caliber's glowing hot barrel, switched to the M249 and banged away with more concentrated fire.

A lone enemy insurgent stepped out of a doorway, took direct aim at Gabe and Hercules with an RPG.

Staring at sure death, Gabe cursed his empty weapon and awaited the inevitable. The Iraqi abruptly raised his weapon, smiled at him, then disappeared into the shadows.

Soldiers leap-frogged left and right trying to flank the continuous flashes and tracers, dropping, rising, running to new cover while continuously firing to overcome the enemy advantages of surprise and superior firing positions.

Enemy fire slackened, becoming sporadic. Blistering American firepower reacted to the slowing tempo of the concert and tapered off to single shots.

Eighty-three seconds after the opening salvo the frenzied melee ended.

"Check fire! Check fire! Accountability check! Who's hit? Anybody down? Sound-off! Report!"

Slowly, one by one, the soldiers radioed or shouted their status. Miraculously not one soldier was killed. Dark Meat, the only soldier wounded, had suffered a superficial, barroom-bragging-rights gash on his cheek.

Ski ordered four soldiers to change the blown out tire and attach the disabled Humvee to another vehicle with a tow bar. He and the rest of the squad pushed out in all directions to expand the security perimeter, provide cover and look for enemy killed or wounded.

Gabe rose and scanned the battlefield. It took a few seconds for his senses to register, but he awakened to the fact that none of the enemy fire came anywhere near him or Hercules, almost as if they had been inside an invisible, protective cone. Why did the insurgent not take the shot that certainly would have killed them? Was the Jesus he didn't know but whom he wasted too much time on introspection — was he with him that morning? Or was it something else, a more earthly explanation? He would muse over the paradox later after he emptied his bowels, controlled the shaking, had privacy and a clearer, calmer thought process.

"Are you crazy or just plain fucking stupid?" Gabe shouted at Hercules. "You don't survive in war by making yourself a damn target."

"Mister Quinn, I am fine, sir. *Allah* protects me. *Allah* protects you."

Gabe heard it first — a distant, shrieking howl, followed by screams, then a continuous, haunting wail. He turned toward the direction he thought it was coming from, the alley he had walked. He swapped the empty magazine for a full one and raised his M4 to the firing position. Slowed by the weight of his armor and other equipment, he jogged down the alley checking converging narrow walkways, door openings, windows and rooftops for hidden threats. Eighty meters into his search he stopped.

Faceless behind *niqabs*, several Iraqi women were attempting to coddle two lumps of flesh he could not readily identify.

He took a few more apprehensive, short strides. *Why would these women grieve over a couple of dead dogs?*

He braved several more cautious steps until he saw splintered yellow-orange pencils and shattered crayons scattered chaotically across the ground.

With swelling unease, he ventured closer to the carcasses, still steaming and smoking from the RPG's white-hot slivers of death that had ripped them apart. He cringed.

He wished he were blind.

Chapter 15
Toilet musings

COP 6, TOC, July 2, 2007, 1915 hours

"Mr. Quinn, you missed your ride," the duty sergeant said. "The LOGPAC rolled through earlier when you were at Afak. Couldn't wait. Sorry about that, sir."

"Fine." Gabe stepped through the open entrance, closed the door behind him and placed his M4 in a wooden gun rack. He walked to the trailer's small refrigerator and grabbed two bottles of water. He quickly drained the first, threw the empty bottle in the garbage can, uncapped the second and fell into a chair near the sergeant. He looked at the nametape on his uniform and asked, "Sergeant Knowles, do you know why they were five days early?"

"No, sir. But we have convoys passing by all the time, most heading to the base camp. Don't worry, we'll find you a seat on one of them."

Gabe chugged the second bottle of water and then repeated the word he preferred for most adversities he encountered. "Fine." It wasn't. He glanced over the maps that covered most of the walls in the office — Iraq, Quadissiya, Thi Quar and Maysan provinces, street maps of Diwaniyah and Nasariyah and a layout of his other home, FOB Adder. The base camp was one hundred eighty-three kilometers south. Too far to walk at this late hour. Another city grabbed his attention. Al Amarah was familiar to him, but he didn't know why. He shook it off expecting that the answer would hit him the way trivia always did, when least expected. "Sergeant, do you know any of the soldiers on the convoy I missed?"

"Sure do, sir. Known most of them since before the readiness exercise at Fort Polk. Anyone in particular?"

"Specialist Colucci, a foul-mouthed firecracker of a gal who is about — "

"Who doesn't know Combat Barbie? Firecracker hell, she's a damn munitions depot fused and ready to blow. She wasn't with the convoy. There were some issues, sir."

"Issues?" Gabe leaned toward Knowles. "Serious issues, Sergeant?"

"Sir, I don't know the details, but she's sitting in the brig up at Camp Cropper pending charges for insubordination and striking an officer."

"That's serious. Let me guess, Lieutenant Lutz?"

"Roger that, sir," Knowles said. "Again, I don't have the details, but PFC Poppins told me Lutz had been riding Colucci's ass since you were dropped off here. I guess things sort of went south after that."

Gabe looked at the floor and shook his head. He got out of the chair and replaced his dour look with a smirk. "Fine, just fine. This is shaping up to be another fine mess of a day. Sergeant Knowles, please keep me posted about that ride. Time for me to go drop a deuce and clean up before I get monkey-butt."

"Been there, done that, got the t-shirt." Knowles reached under his desk and produced a partial roll of toilet paper. "Sir, this should help. Birthday gift from the wife. Super soft, double-ply and scented, better than that John Wayne paper we keep in the shitters."

Gabe pocketed the toilet paper in his cargo pants, grabbed his rifle by the barrel and stepped outside just as the last of the sun's rays dipped below the perimeter blast walls.

Since he was in a combat zone, light-discipline rules were in effect. He pulled a red-lens, mini-mag flashlight from his ankle pocket, turned it on and pointed the beam at the rudimentary, triple-stall wooden outhouse near the southern perimeter wall. He paused to adjust his night vision and then walked carefully over the thick layer of gravel. As he neared the mixed aroma of feces and diesel fuel he saw a faint, green glow barely visible through cracks in one of the end stalls.

When he was less than twenty meters from the structure, he tripped over an exposed power cable. Falling to his knees, he dropped his rifle and sent rocks flying in all directions. Fortunately, noise discipline was not a factor because his clumsiness would have awakened even the sorriest of enemies if they had been within a quarter mile. He pushed up from the gravel, found his weapon and reoriented himself to the stalls. The green glow was gone, yet he had not seen a soldier leave.

Although privacy under any circumstances was nearly impossible at the outpost, he hoped to maintain some dignity and chose the stall farthest from the one he thought might still be in use. His gastrointestinal turmoil could not be relieved in stages so he decided to violate outpost and outhouse protocol and take care of business in a single sitting. Per post rules — liquid number one down the angled PVC piss tubes located at the opposite end of the outpost one hundred and fifty meters away — solid number two through the cut out plywood seats balanced above the halved, fifty-five gallon drums sitting directly in front of him. He would grace the half-drum with all of his waste, rationalizing his breach of etiquette with rapier sharp logic. All of the alcohol he had consumed in his life must have left a flammable residue in his bladder and it should mix well with the diesel in the burn barrel. When lit, kaboom, a massive fireball.

He surveyed the stall with his flashlight searching above, below and to the sides, even peering into the barrel. A few surprises there, but not the type that scared him. He had an innate fear of the dreaded 'S' words — shark, snake, spouse, spider and scorpion. Sharks were not in play, snakes not likely either. His spouse was well entrenched in her idyllic life as a gracefully aging, Carolina southern belle. Scorpions and camel spiders, however, were a different story.

His inspection of the field toilet stopped at head level. He saw numerous cracks, cubbyholes and other dark spaces in the wood above him that could hide an army of the critters. Not his hand, or the hand of any sane soldier would venture anywhere near those potential hides.

Satisfied that all was relatively clear, he dropped his pants, parked his butt on the wooden throne and struck a pose reminiscent of the meditative Dobie Gillis statue ingrained into the sub-consciousness of the black and white TV generation — otherwise known as Rodin's sculpture, *The Thinker.* He swept the flashlight's beam across the ground in a continuous arc, constantly on the alert for any multi-legged intruders. Occasionally he dipped his head and swung the light underneath the door's two-foot gap scanning for enemies massing for a frontal charge.

Confident that his inspection of the area had been thorough, he decided to hatch a plan while dropping his deuce. He could help Colucci, but needed an idea and an actionable plan. Midway through his primary business of eliminating body poisons, an idea struck him with brilliant clarity as he watched a tiny spider in the rocks attack one of its own and then suffer the same fate at the end of a scorpion's stinger. The seed of inspiration had been planted. The incident five days earlier on the main supply route would be the grist. He just needed to work out the Machiavellian details. With a solution to one problem in the works, he slipped into the next — the girls' deaths.

That tragedy was more difficult for him to wrap his brain around. He had seen many of the blameless die during his years in Iraq, and a quarter of a century earlier, in the jungles of Zaire and on the Angolan savannahs. The African affair was a different type of war, acted out by the proxies of the Cold War super-powers on the killing fields of Angola. It was brutal. Before Africa, he was Gabriel, bound by a belief in ancestral sin. After Africa, he was just Gabe. The religious shackles had been broken, all thoughts of penitence to naive superstitions were gone — buried with the rotting corpses of the blameless.

Although the African and Iraqi children may have had different shades of skin color, different languages and cultures, they were the same. Innocent. He had learned to push thoughts about them into the dark, rarely explored corridors of his mind and deal with the horror later when he was far removed from the events, both physically and emotionally. The innocent counted, but they could not be considered when in the middle of another horror. To do otherwise would mean his demise. He would ponder their deaths when it was done, when he was anesthetized in the company of his friends, Bacardi Dark and Bacardi Light. Until then they were gone, didn't exist, and never did.

In the midst of his profundity, he heard the end stall's door creak. Through the diffused red light shining outward, he caught a glimpse of a Nike logo stride by his stall.

He wrapped up nature's calling, snatched his weapon and stepped into the night. On his way to the dorm trailer waves of nauseating tsunamis crashed over him from epicenters positioned at his crotch, armpits and feet. He raised his arm and sniffed. He knew what he had to do next.

Back at his temporary home, he quickly stripped down to his skivvies and t-shirt. He replaced his bloodstained boots with shower sandals, plucked a towel and hand soap from his ruck, stuffed his Beretta under the mattress, then grabbed his M4 and headed for the shower trailer.

Unlike the toilets, the trailer belonged to him. He was alone. Similar to his toilet rebellion, he disregarded the rules and took a luxurious five-minute shower instead of the permitted one-minute drill. Again, relying on his wits, he rationalized that skipping a shave justified the extra water he used to bathe. Bathing complete, and already sweating as if the shower's cooling water had been merely a perverse tease, he contemplated his next action.

Nature came through again. He felt a rumbling on the move inside

184

his gut. It was either the Saddam-trots sequel or his belly screaming out for more punishment to replace the questionable contents he recently purged. Deciding it was hunger, he returned to his quarters.

Once inside, he put on the last of his clean uniform pants over soiled skivvies, changed to a fresh tee, swapped the shower sandals for formal Jesus cruisers and sat on his bunk. He was forgetting something. *Proper dinner attire? Check. Flashlight? Check. Cigarettes and lighter? Check. Weapon? Weapon?* No check. That was it. He had committed the big one, almost a capital offense no-no. He had left his M4 in the shower trailer.

Gabe raced across mounds of gravel and exposed cables toward the showers. He grabbed the handle and flung the metal door so hard it crashed against the trailer's exterior with a bang. Propped against the opposite wall was his assault rifle, exactly as he had left it.

Weapon secured, he turned to leave, but before he took a step, someone shut off a shower faucet. He saw a thin, light brown arm reach out from behind the plastic curtain and grab a towel off of a hook. An expected occurrence in the crowded neighborhood, but one could always hope for a naked woman. Not to be. He was in Iraq.

This arm belonged to a man and had a unique tattoo just above the wrist — three green dots and a crescent moon. Gabe had seen similar ink somewhere within the past three years, possibly in Iraq. Tattoos in Iraq, however, were a rarity usually reserved for the criminal class as an artistic visual resume or as a badge of honor.

As he walked to the door, Hercules emerged wrapped in a towel. Startled, he quickly gathered his *dishdasha* and pants stacked on a wooden bench near the shower, then stepped back into the stall, pulling the curtain behind him.

His skittishness suggested Gabe may have violated another Arabic taboo. He wasn't sure. He was sure he had glimpsed numerous scars on Hercules' back. Diagonal scars that criss-crossed other scars, not a few, but many. The flesh had been scourged by the lash over several years. Fresh scars had hardened on top of older ones.

"I'm sorry, Hercules. I didn't mean to surprise you like that. I guess I should've made more of a racket when I came in."

Hercules stepped out from behind the curtain completely dressed, except for his shoes. "Mister Gabriel Quinn, how good to see you again. It is nothing, sir."

"I'm sorry about this morning too, Hercules. Sometimes when I get excited I say some pretty stupid things."

"Again, sir, it is not important. Do not bother yourself with

185

misgivings, Mister Quinn."

"You have a date tonight? You're looking pretty sharp there all dressed in black. Looks like you're James Bond incognito getting ready to go on the hunt and snatch some unsuspecting babe and put some night moves on her, if you catch my drift."

"Hunt...snatch...babe...night moves, sir?" Hercules nervously shifted from one foot to the other. He hesitated before letting out a long, uneasy laugh.

The laugh Gabe heard in response to his lame attempt at humor seemed inappropriate.

"Oh no, sir. I do not have a date. I am returning to my home for a few days, sir. That is all, sir. Perfectly innocent, I assure you, Mister Quinn. I have not been to mosque in weeks. I must go, sir."

"Now, Hercules? It's not safe at night and besides I think a curfew's in effect. Can't it wait until tomorrow?"

"I must go now, sir," Hercules answered tersely. He turned away from Gabe, picked up his shoes and sat on the bench. Fully involved in the banal task of covering his feet, he said, "I will be safe, but thank you for your concern, sir. Captain Kowalewski observed me as I used the cell phone to call my cousin. He is a policeman and has the authority to drive at night. He will take me to my home, sir."

"Where's home, Hercules?"

Hercules focused on tying his shoes. Once again, he hesitated before responding. "My home, sir?"

"Yeah, Hercules, your home. You know, the place you hang your *dishdasa* and park your Nike's when you're not stuck here."

"Of course sir, my home, where I hang my *disdasha* and park my shoes." Hercules stopped his shoe-tying marathon and looked up at him.

The long silence struck Gabe as being weird. Hercules appeared to be considering his question as a matter of life or death instead of idle chitchat between friends.

"Yes, sir, my home." Hercules bit his lower lip hard enough to draw blood. He rolled the tip of his tongue over the cut flesh. "My village is north, sir. It is near al Habbaniyah and al Fallujah, sir. Do you know the area, sir?"

"Not too well, but I think that's in the area of one of Saddam's old strongholds. *Sunni* territory, as I recall."

"Yes, sir, Mister Quinn." He dropped his gaze to the floor and covered his mouth with his hand as if he was ashamed. In a wavering voice, he said, "I am *Sunni*, sir."

"Well that makes sense, Hercules, a *Sunni* from a *Sunni* village." His nervous affectations reminded him of deception mannerisms exhibited by the guilty during an interrogation. Gabe was confused. These were simple questions about the man's home and religion.

"Watch out for those *Jaish al Mahdi* clowns. Hate to see you lose your head to those *Shi'ite* butchers. Sorry I'm holding you up. When you return to the camp we need to talk about something…something that was said in Afak today."

"Certainly, Mister Quinn. I will look forward to our conversation and seeing you again, sir."

"Be safe. *Mas allama*, my friend." Gabe shook his clammy hand.

He followed Hercules out of the shower trailer and set a leisurely pace to the dining trailer. As he turned the corner near the trailer's entrance, he saw White Meat and Dark Meat coming out.

The pair laughed and gave each other backslaps and feisty high-fives. White Meat looked his usual self — scrawny, dirty, face and uniform covered in food drippings. The boy could eat.

Larger than life Dark Meat blocked the narrow path between the trailers with two hundred and forty-three pounds of muscle and sinew. In the dim light, Gabe saw his brilliant, white teeth framed in an expressive smile. He also saw a dull, white bandage stuck on the left side of his face, held in place by tape and dried blood.

"Good evening to the Jeffersons. How things in the hood?" Gabe said, hugging the trailer's side to avoid saying hello to the gravel again.

Both stopped and in unison blurted, "Mr. Quinn!"

"Hell of a morning, sir," Dark Meat said. "Hell of a morning. We scared the bejeezus out of hajji. Damn, we gave them some shit."

"Yes you did, gentlemen. Let me shake hands with two of America's finest," Gabe said. "Dark Meat, you looked all Audie Murphy up there on that fifty. White Meat, what can I say? That was either the dumbest or bravest example of soldiering I've seen. Haven't decided yet. You looking to get a medal?"

"Sir, I doan need no fuckin' medal. Doan mean nothing. They be kids, sir, jus lil' kids. Mr. Quinn, one these days, ya know, I hope to has me some kids. That's all, sir."

"I hope you do. You're a damn fine soldier and I know you'll make a damn fine father. When you two get stateside the first, last and all rounds in between are on me."

"That'd be illegal, Mr. Quinn," Dark Meat said. "Cracker and I aren't of age yet."

187

"Gentlemen, gentlemen, gentlemen. Hold on there now. You misunderstood. I certainly would not want to break the law and corrupt you, the sheltered, fragile youth and future of America.... Are you kidding me? We're gonna get hammered in a titty bar of your choosing. I'll be carrying a fistful of dollars and I'm going to stuff those dead Presidents in the g-strings of every sexy harlot in the saloon. Sort of, prep the battlefield for you two fine, incorruptible youths. And while I'm crawling on the floor contemplating the carpet, those beauty queens will hammer you in ways you never thought possible. Positions so risqué they were banned from the Kama Sutra. And gentlemen, just like today, I expect you two trigger-pullers to have my six. Understood?"

White Meat grinned and said, "Roger that, sir. I doan be knowin' nothin' bout that risky camee shoota thang, but we be followin' all legal and illegal orders and neva, sir, neva do we goes and leave a buddy behind."

"Good. I'm glad that's settled." Gabe pointed at the dining trailer and asked, "Anything good in the roach coach tonight?"

"According to my little buddy here, it's all good, sir," Dark Meat said.

"I'll take White Meat's recommendation as gospel, then."

Gabe passed by them and opened the dining trailer's door. He stepped inside and paused long enough to adjust his eyes to the bright lights. Captain Ski was seated at a table laughing as he talked to a civilian.

"Gabe, join us," Ski said. "Have you met Dawud?"

"No, Captain. Haven't had the pleasure."

Never in Gabe's life had he imagined crossing paths with such a unique, eccentric persona, much less one in the outback of Iraq — or for that matter anywhere. Before Dawud had a chance to utter a sound Gabe knew he liked him. It was impossible not to. In front of him sat a dapper, distinguished looking gentleman. Dapper, a word he believed was from a dead language used by the Edwardian age aristocracy was, in Dawud's case, a perfect fit.

The man did not sweat. Ninety-three degrees inside the trailer and Dawud, unlike Gabe, had not even a hint of perspiration. Rotund but not obese, the man had a swarthy complexion complimented by an agreeable mixture of Middle Eastern and Mediterranean features. His grey hair was coiffed to perfection and his mustache was trimmed pencil-thin.

Even here in the wild, Dawud was a man who took pride in his

188

appearance. He wore pressed pleated khaki pants, burgundy wing tips that glistened from the layers of shoe polish and the labor that brought out the luster. A silk patterned ascot billowed from his open collared, finely tailored and monogrammed shirt. Tinted, frameless bifocals were pushed high on his forehead and kept in place by deep wrinkles. His exotropic left eye, or what Gabe's grandmother had mistakenly called a lazy eye, acted as an erratic pointer that was constantly drawn to the right as if seeking shelter behind his regal nose, a nose with Greek or possibly Italian input.

And the finishing fashion accessory, a *Gauloises Brunes* cigarette smoldering at the end of a jade quellazaire that jutted from the corner of his mouth. Dawud looked like he had just stepped off the set of *Casablanca* and then tossed inside a Greek-Italian-Lebanese cultural blender, with a dash of Kafkaesque lunacy thrown in for good measure.

Dawud uncrossed his legs, got up and shook Gabe's hand. With the cigarette holder still clenched between sparkling white teeth, he said, "Cheers, my good man. A forty regular. Yes, definitely a forty regular, sir."

Caught off guard, Gabe said, "Excuse me?"

"Your suit size, sir, a forty regular. Am I correct?"

"At one time you would've been right." Gabe chuckled as he grasped Dawud's dry hand. He avoided staring at his dizziness inducing, roving eye. "It's been years since I was a forty anything, suit size or age. Not positive but I think I'm closer to a forty-two short."

"Perhaps, but I could certainly fit you in a proper manner and you would be a forty regular with a stylishly exquisite and skillful cut. After this bloody desert drama ends you must visit me in Chicago at my brother's shop, sir. I will take care of you and highlight the best of your attributes."

Gabe laid his weapon under the table and sat across from Dawud and Ski. Smiling at both, he said, "I didn't know I had any attributes, but I'll be sure to look you up after we finish this bloody desert drama, Dawud."

"Jolly good, mate. It is agreed then. I will bring out your ruffian personality and make you look even more dashing, my good man." He pulled a business card from his wallet and handed it to Gabe.

Embossed in gold print, the card read, *Aladdin's Discount Haberdashery, DVDs, Cigarettes, Lamps, Novelties and more... where your every wish is granted.*

"It is a date then, sir," Dawud said. "Our shop is located on West Lake Street near Union Park. It can't be missed. We adorned the edifice's roof with a sign of subtle tastefulness, and certainly not boorishly garish as some would have you believe. Sir, it is a refined yet dramatic and eclectic combination of Art Deco, Fauvism and Art Nouveau unlike any treasure your eyes have ever feasted upon. Yes, Mr. Quinn, the sign is charitably proportioned, not overwhelming as some of the uninspired would claim. It is perfection, my good chap, perfection defined. A brilliant and delightful blinking neon billboard, crafted in the likeness of an Arabian oil lamp that emits lovely plumes of pinkish smoke clearly visible from the CTA line and from the many exceptional neighborhoods nearby."

"Dawud, you've sold me. Aladdin's has definitely made it onto my bucket list." His knowledge of Chicago's west side was limited, but the area Dawud had described was known throughout law enforcement circles as having the highest crime rate in the country.

Recovering from Dawud's spellbinding discourse, he corralled his amusement and returned to thoughts of the war. "Captain, that was a pretty complex attack hajji threw together, too complex for them not to of had some time to think tactics through. You think you were set up this morning?"

"Gabe, I'm still reveling in the fact that I didn't lose any of my men, but I have thought about it. I just can't see how they could've known. It was an impromptu *shura* meeting, and I only told the squad and the terp, sorry Dawud, I mean interpreter, about an hour in advance. Just enough time to top-off the vehicles, load up the crew-served weapons and grab some quick chow."

"You did the right thing, Ski," Gabe said. "Not only about operational security, but out there this morning. Your boys performed honorably. Was it their first time seeing action as a unit?"

"As a unit, yes, but some saw action in Afghanistan. My first time. I'll never forget."

"Sort of like the first time you had sex," Gabe said. "You'll never forget, always there, unforgettable. Savor every detail, Ski, and learn from them. Could've turned into some serious carnage this morning."

"Gabe, there was carnage. The children — "

"Don't go there, Ski. Leave it alone."

"Look, all I'm saying is those two little girls died this morning. You saw them. You were — "

190

"I know the girls died, but do we really need to talk about it now?" Gabe's icy expression chilled the room. The uncharacteristic coldness in his voice sounded like a neural circuit breaker had been tripped. "They weren't American so they really don't count, now do they?"

Ski was frozen, staring at the Gabe he didn't know seated across the table from him. The conversation was finished.

Then, almost as if his Jekyll and Hyde moment never happened, Gabe spoke. "Ski, do you have a secure line I can use to call a sergeant back at the main base?"

"Uh, sure thing, Gabe," Ski answered in a muted voice. "See Sergeant Knowles and he'll set you up. Anything else you need, I mean, if you need to talk anything through about what happened out there this morning, I am — "

"Thanks," Gabe said. "I do have one more request, Ski. I was hoping to ask Hercules a few questions but he was in a serious rush to get out of here. Didn't get the chance. Something was said to me this morning that has raised some questions. Mind if I ask Dawud?"

"Of course, Gabe. I don't mind. Like I said, if there's anything you need to discuss about the girls — "

"Dawud...Ghazi...Ghazi Codar el Ahmar. Does that mean anything to you?"

"Ghazi Codar el Ahmar?" Dawud looked anxiously at the captain, then down at the table. He raised his head and focused his controllable eye on Gabe, while the rover darted about on a wild roller-coaster ride.

"Could be meaningless, but the word Ghazi, loosely translated, means the conqueror. The Codar el Ahmar part does not immediately register."

Dawud looked up at the ceiling as if in deep thought. After an extended pause, he said, "In Hebrew history there was a similar name. Chedorlaomer, who if their mythology is to be believed, smote the remnants of the seven profane tribes in the land of Canaan. If he is one and the same, Muslims believe he destroyed the troglodytes of Thamud by killing the sacred camel of Saleh. Codar el Ahmar could be a transliteration, but in all honesty, it is probably just a made-up name. Or it could be absolutely nothing at all."

"Made-up name...like a nickname?" Gabe asked. "You know, Dirty Bird, White Meat, or Dark — "

191

"No, not that. Something else, Gabe. Quite possibly a *kunya.*"

"*Kunya?*"

"Yes, *kunya*. Not a simple nickname, but an honorific name. Sort of like Rommel the Desert Fox, Old Blood and Guts Patton, or from your civil war, Stonewall Jackson. A *nom de guerre,* Gabe. Quite possibly mate…a bloody name of war."

"Ski, I think we know who the cell leader is. Well, at least we know — " Gabe stopped mid-sentence and nodded his head. He alternated his gaze between them before he spoke again. "The game is afoot, gentlemen."

Hunger forgotten, his minor outburst having never registered long enough in his thoughts to be forgotten, Gabe reached under the table for his rifle. He stood, hefted the weapon to his shoulder, pushed the chair to the table and walked to the door. Midway he stopped and looked back at them. Sometimes an acerbic cynic, sometimes a Pollyannaish idealist, but many times both, his face was wrapped in a quixotic grin.

"War…war could be fun if it weren't for the pain and dying." Then he was gone. In more ways than one.

Gabe stepped into the darkness, closed his eyes and tilted his head toward a dark, moonless night sky. He didn't bother to turn on his flashlight. Didn't need it. He was basking in enlightenment.

The Afak incident wasn't about a generator. The villagers' fear was not spawned by a mere property crime. He knew it went deeper, much deeper and was more sinister. Iraq was ground-zero for duplicity, locked in the chaotic state of civil and external war. Conspiracies played out from the lowest levels of government to the Prime Minister's office. Corruption was endemic, expected by the public and condoned by the American and Iraqi governments. In that environment only an accomplished and careful enemy would create a *nom de guerre* to cover a simple theft.

Don Quixote had his evil magician. Sherlock Holmes had Professor Moriarty. The Americans had al-Qaeda and al-Qaeda had the Americans. Every person, every country, every living creature needed an enemy to help define them and drive them — and sometimes there was a symbiosis in the pairings, an interaction so close and interdependent that the religious would see the hand of God in the matchmaking. For the first time since returning to war, he again had a *raison d'être,* his Enchanter — Ghazi Codar el Ahmar.

192

He rejected any thoughts that he might be attacking windmills like the ingenious gentleman of La Mancha.

Gabriel knew there was only one path to end the madness of this war — sound the trumpets loud, unleashing an 'end of days' nightmare so ghastly, even the insane would be horror-struck. Crush the demonic jihadists using their depraved methods. The balance would be returned. He vowed to pursue this faceless and immoral foe and score him with the mark of Judas.

Chapter 16
Behind the green door

COP 6, July 2, 2007, 2018 hours

Gabe entered the operations trailer allowing the door to slam shut. The noise startled Knowles. He had been looking at a photograph taped to the wall above his desk.

Although Gabe's view was partially blocked by a chair and a file cabinet, he thought he detected some action going on in front of the sergeant.

Knowles spun his chair around and said, "You surprised me. Guess I need to fix that damn door closer brake thing. Were you successful, sir?"

"The launch went off without a flaw," Gabe said. "Thanks to you the mission's after action paper review, although not spotless, was a pleasurable experience." He reached into his oversized thigh pocket, pulled out the remaining toilet paper and was about to hand it to the sergeant.

"Keep it for future emergencies," Knowles said. "I've got plenty, sir. The wife, I love her dearly." He looked over his shoulder and pointed at the water stained glossy photo of a woman wearing a swimsuit that advertised a well-endowed chest. "I really do, sir. She keeps me satisfied in the bed...I mean paper, sir. She keeps me well stocked with shit paper."

"Well thanks, Sergeant. I'll have to think of something else besides toilet paper for your Christmas gift, but it's impossible to top what a good woman can give a man." He sat in a folding chair near the sergeant and balanced his weapon across his knees. "Sergeant, I need to call someone at FOB Adder on a secure line. Ski told me you could make it happen."

"Can do, sir. I'll set you up in his office so you'll have some privacy. You got a number?"

"Need your help with that one, too," Gabe said. "All I know are rank, last name and specialty."

"Big base, sir. What's the name?"

"Pickens, Sergeant First Class. He's an EOD — "

"Pickens, Pickens….Sir, wait one." Knowles opened a desk drawer and rummaged through several files until he found the right folder. He pulled out a piece of paper, scanned it quickly. Then he read aloud, "Pickens, Sergeant First Class, EOD, FOB Adder, Subject, IED found and cleared, MSR Tampa, 27-June-1030 hours, SIGINT exploitation, attention Staff Sergeant Knowles, COP 6, S2. Does that sound like your man, Mr. Quinn?"

Gabe smiled. "That's him."

"That was easy, sir. His contact info includes a number. I'll get you up on the secure line — "

"Sergeant, anything interesting from the SIM card exploitation?"

"Sir, the results are classified. I don't know if I can tell you — "

"Understand, Sergeant. I understand completely. I don't want to cause you any grief, but I have a top-secret clearance. Run me through JPASS and confirm it."

Knowles hesitated, staring at the paper. Then he grinned. "What the hell. Pickens mentioned you in his email and wrote you are a man who could be trusted. Sir, the report showed there was only one incoming and no outgoing calls."

"Was the number for the phone used to call the cell phone identified?"

"Just the number. I've run it through SIGINT and my databases for hits, but nothing, sir. It's an unknown and hasn't popped up on anybody's screen yet."

"Does the analysis show the time of the incoming call?"

Knowles tapped his finger on a line near the bottom of the page and said, "June 27 at 1002 hours, sir."

It had been the Iraqi policeman on the overpass who activated the IED. He tried to remember how the policeman looked, but his glimpse that morning was less than a flicker. The Iraqi was one of more than a hundred thousand other policemen stealing from the people of Iraq. All hajjis looked alike to Gabe.

"Sir, FYI," Knowles said, "we have a field kit here and I can do basic exploitation on cells phones and SIM cards should the need arise."

"Good to know, Sergeant. About that secure line — "

"Follow me, Mr. Quinn." Knowles stood up and led him into Ski's office. He pointed to a phone labeled with a red sticker, SVOIP. "If you need anything else, I'll be right on the other side of the door."

"Thanks, Sergeant." After Knowles closed the door Gabe leaned his rifle against the wall. He sat in the chair then picked up the phone. He had forgotten his three-dollar reading glasses so he held the paper at arm's length and squinted. As he deciphered each number on the sheet he pushed the corresponding number on the phone. It was a struggle.

"Sergeant First Class Pickens," a gruff voice responded.

"Sergeant Pickens, Gabe Quinn. I don't know if you remember me, but — "

"Gabe, how the hell are you, sir?"

"I'm whooping it up at outpost hell having a grand time. A bit of dysentery, but it's all good. The old system needs to be cleaned out occasionally. Sergeant Pickens, you staying out of trouble?"

"Always, sir."

"Fine, that's just fine, Sergeant...but I'm calling about someone who isn't doing fine. You remember Specialist Colucci?"

"Lil' sister, are you kidding?" Pickens said. "Hell, if I weren't a married man and if I was ten years younger, I'd be trying to court that lil' Kewpie doll. Amazing girl, amazing soldier. She definitely has her shit together. What's her problem, Gabe?"

Gabe provided him an overview of her situation based on the limited information he had. "Sergeant, I wish I had more details and I wish I knew the ins and outs of the UCMJ, but unfortunately I have only a basic understanding of military justice. Not enough to know how deep of a hole she's dug for herself."

"Shit, ain't that the fucking shit," Pickens said. "Lieutenant Lutz, what a....Gabe, I can read people and that LT, a damn princess prima donna that one. I wish there was something I could do to help Colucci, I mean anything — "

"There is," Gabe said. "Have you submitted an official report about the IED incident?"

"Sure have. Internal and external."

"Did you include the Lutz version with the added details about her heroic leadership that morning, the details that would get her a Combat Action Badge?"

"Right, Gabe, right." Pickens laughed hard. "Hell no, I didn't put that crap in the report. She's already called me three times and told me to include her spin in the report. She even put the full court press on me and sent Major Laddick to my shop. That Major, what a dick. Birds of a fucking feather, Gabe. He damn near ordered me to amend the report to include that made-up shit. I think he's pushing her for a Bronze Star. Like I said, I can read people, and guaranteed, right as rain, you can take it to the bank…Major Laddick is tapping that piece of ass. I've seen the two of them cavorting around here like a couple of love struck teenagers, not even trying to hide it. No way this side of hell I'm gonna falsify a report for the likes of them lovebirds."

"Change the report, Sergeant."

"The hell you say!" Pickens shouted, almost loud enough for Mrs. Pickens to hear in North Carolina.

Gabe jerked the phone away, stuck a finger in his ear and popped his jaw several times to clear his ear canal. Then he lifted the phone to his good ear.

"Hear me out, Sergeant." For the next ten minutes, he went over his plan and how he hoped it would play out. When he was finishing he said, "…and Sergeant, make sure when you do the rewrite you only use her statements, just as she told you. Make it crystal clear that you did not witness the event, but are only repeating her words."

"Roger that." Pickens laughed and said, "Gabe, you are one conniving, devious mother-fucker, but I love you, brother."

"What, me devious and a conniver? All I can I say is thanks for the compliment. That love part though, you're not really my type. See you on the trail, my friend. Stay safe and stay left of the boom."

Gabe hung up the phone and stood. He owed Pickens a beer, a truckload. As he was slinging his rifle, his eyes were drawn to the map of southeast Iraq, specifically Al Amarah. *What is it about that name?* Still bothered by the mystery, he opened the door.

Knowles was bent over at the waist doing the two fingered hunt and peck drill on the computer keyboard, frequently glancing at the monitor for encouragement.

"Thanks for the help, Sergeant Knowles. You mentioned you're the S2 for the outpost."

"Roger, sir. Some SIGINT and also commo."

"I know the Iraq-Iran border area is outside of your unit's area of operations, but there is a city near the border, al Amarah. You know anything about it?"

"Al Amarah's *Shi'ite* country, also a *Jaish al Mahdi* stronghold," Knowles said. "We can't touch it, that area belongs to the Brits. They've pretty much given up, declared it pacified and skedaddled back down to Basrah, sir."

COP 6, Dorm trailer, July 2, 2007, 2330 hours

Sleep was impossible. Gabe closed his eyes for the hundredth time, only to open them again and stare at the empty bunk above him.

197

Three long and hard years in Iraq, fifty-five years old, reaching fifty-six questionable, more life behind than ahead, and here he was trying to keep up with teenagers. *Why?*

Maybe it was because of the hypocritical, pious, intoxicated jihadists devoted to a false cause evoked by a phony prophet. Maybe it was because of Islam — a religion that was about everything except peace — a religion that had been on a cultural and civilizational slide for seven centuries. Possibly it was because of an enemy that prayed to a god wanting blood, an enemy that had no qualms about butchering its own to advance Islam. Or maybe it was because the enemy believed that the only atrocity in a war was the atrocity of losing. Perhaps the answer was Ghazi, and the thousands of others like him, who were trying to kill the dreams not yet dreamt by young soldiers. Conceivably it was for all of those reasons, but Gabe believed he stayed in the game simply to do what he could to help a few American soldiers make it home.

Less than a month in country, shot at, almost blown up by an IED, yet all he had to show for it were questions. Was the policeman on the overpass the same as the officer he saw in the village? Was he Ghazi? How were the insurgents alerted to the patrol's arrival in Afak? Why did Hercules stand up during the firefight and why did they come through the fight unscathed? Why didn't the insurgent take the kill shot with the RPG? Who, or what caused the scars on Hercules' back? What did his tattoo mean? Why was Hercules nervous? What bothered him about how he prayed? And his name, Mutahhar al Amarah. *Al Amarah.* The answers were in the village. He had to talk to the child again.

Gabe envied the villagers. They had a tough life, not one he would want, but it was their culture. They were not burdened by the same problems that plagued the soldiers sent to help them. When the sun disappeared each night so did most of the villagers' problems. They could sleep and dream of better days. The children could not dream about much, but one child could at least dream about Mickey Mouse.

Gabe also hoped to dream — a dream that would give him answers.

Afak, July 3, 2007, 0215 hours

In the darkest hours before dawn, three men dressed in black spoke in hushed tones. The *kulat's* thick walls muffled their conversation.

"Dhul Fiqar, are your men ready for the *Amerikees'* Independence Day celebration tomorrow?"

"*Nam*, Ghazi. They are ready and I am ready," Dhul Fiqar whispered. "We will start the attack just before the sun sets."

"You have done well. *Allah* commands that we must slay the infidels who are the friends of *shaytan. Insha Allah*, we will send a message to the mothers' of these *Amerikees* on a day that holds much meaning for them. Make it their hell. For he who believes in the Trinity, the fire will be his abode. Bring the fire, Dhul Fiqar. Target their dining hall and many will be slaughtered as they feast on the unclean meat of their pigs. Hit the headquarters building and their means of communicating will be destroyed. In your prayers ask for *Allah's* blessings and pray that he will guide our bombs."

Ghazi turned to the third man. "The hour is late. We are ready?"

"All is ready, brother."

"Is this necessary?" Dhul Fiqar asked. "Is this wise? I beg you, these are our people, they are *Shi'ite*. They are not our enemy. Where is the wisdom in turning our own against us and against the cause?"

"You are weak," Ghazi's brother said. "They are our people and it is true they are not *Sunni*, but some must die, examples to keep others focused on the path to paradise. The Qur'an says a painful doom awaits all believers who will not fight. It also written we must only protect Muslims who fight jihad and all Muslims must fight united to make Islam victorious."

"Listen to my brother, Dhul Fiqar," Ghazi said. "He is a wise, brave warrior who understands the Muslim's duty to make *jihad*. We are not mindless robots who butcher our own without reason. Read the Qur'an, study the *hadiths* and be guided by the *fatwas*. Everything that will ever be has already been written. We are the sword of *Allah*. We have the blessings of Muhammad."

Ghazi picked up a canvas satchel and handed it to Dhul Fiqar. "We do this now."

Even in the darkest of dark they were quick and silent. Each was familiar with the alleys and knew which *kulats* were protected by unclean mongrels. The few dogs they encountered remained muzzled as if afraid to bark, hoping death would pass them by.

"Is this the one, brother?" Ghazi whispered.

"*Nam.*"

"When we are inside be quick." Ghazi drew his Khanjar dagger from beneath his *dishdasha*. He leaned forward and placed his ear against the door. Hearing nothing, he nudged the lime-green door slowly inward, but stopped when he heard the hinges creak. A slight stirring sound came from inside the house.

Behind him, Dhul Fiqar reached into the satchel and pulled out a flashlight and a roll of duct tape, then passed the bag and the tape to Ghazi's brother.

Ghazi pushed the door a few more inches. Met with silence, he inched the door more until he had enough clearance to slip through the opening into the three-room house. Dhul Fiqar and the third man followed. Once inside, they moved with the precision of a Swiss watch. Each knew the layout of the house and their assignments.

Ghazi and Dhul Fiqar tiptoed left into a small bedroom. The third man, armed only with duct tape, placed the satchel on the floor and slithered silently to the only other room in the house.

Dhul Fiqar flashed the dim beam on the room's two sleeping occupants. The husband awoke. Startled, he was about to scream. Ghazi was on him in an instant. He straddled the man's chest, pinning his arms with his legs and covered his mouth. Using his other hand, he slammed the blade through the man's windpipe and twisted, then repeatedly stabbed, ripping and tearing his heart and lungs until they were nothing but jellified waste.

The gurgling sounds loosed from the man's opened neck emboldened Ghazi. He pulled the dagger from his chest and turned to the traumatized, silent wife. He drove the knife through her open mouth, penetrated her larynx and the brain stem behind it. The impact of his thrust was so powerful that an inch of the knife's tip broke off when the blade hit the tiles beneath her sleeping mat. For several minutes, he laid on top of her to control her death rattle, all the while slashing and plunging the knife into nearly every inch of her body. Finally, after her eyes stared emptily at the fiend who had stolen her days, he stood. Blood-soaked from head to sandals, he wiped the damaged blade across his *dishdasha*.

Dhul Fiqar stared at the desecrated bodies. They had been friends since childhood. The woman was his cousin. He vomited.

The death squad had been in the house for less than four minutes. It was time to dispatch the remaining occupant.

Shaken, Dhul Fiqar followed Ghazi to the smaller bedroom.

Ghazi's brother had been proficient, restraining the child without a sound. She had been stripped, then gagged and bound with duct tape. Even in the low light the horror was visible in her darting eyes.

"You have done well, brother," Ghazi said. "Dhul Fiqar, go into the other room and fetch the bag and a blanket." He leaned over the girl and stroked her hair.

Dhul Fiqar returned and placed the satchel at his leader's feet.

Ghazi reached inside and removed an eighteen-inch piece of rebar. Then he took out a cordless drill with an attached three-sixteenth inch steel bit.

"Dhul Fiqar, hang the blanket over the doorway." Ghazi waited until the door was covered and then he knelt beside the girl. He set the drill speed to its lowest setting and squeezed the trigger. The whirring sound panicked the child more. She thrashed futilely against the tape that bound her. He eased off of the trigger and placed the drill on the tiled floor, then struck her face once, twice, a third time, finally drawing blood from her broken nose on the fourth strike. He grasped the drill and restarted its motor. As he lowered the spiraling bit toward the girl's foot a hand grasped his arm.

"No. She is mine."

Ghazi released the trigger and handed the drill to his brother. The room came alive with sounds of a low-pitched hum and muffled screams.

The girl's death could have been mercifully quick, lasting no more than a few seconds. The third man was methodical. It took her hours to die. When finished, he tore the necklace from her neck.

Ghazi gave his brother a piece of cloth marked with three green dots and a crescent moon. He wiped perspiration from his brow, then removed his glasses and used the same cloth to wipe the blood splatters from its lenses. He could do nothing about the Nikes.

Chapter 17
Turning the eye inward

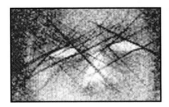

COP 6, July 3, 2007, 0430 hours
"You're up early, Mr. Quinn," Sergeant Knowles said. "Take a seat and I'll get you in with him in a minute, sir. Just need a moment of Captain Ski's time for some bravo-sierra business."

Knowles raised his voice and said, "Captain, Second Lieutenant Bishop jumped me last night with an urgent, bona fide, broken-arrow situation."

"Right. Okay, let's have it. What's my LLMF's crisis this time?"

"Sir, he was complaining that none of the men completed his survey about what to serve for tomorrow's July 4th celebration. He was pissed, yes sir, livid."

Knowles winked at Gabe. "The choices are hamburgers and hotdogs, mac and cheese, beans, cake but no ice cream. Or if we skip the dogs and just go with burgers we can have mac and cheese, beans, cake and ice cream. Or we can choose steak and get the mac and cheese, beans and cake, but we'll lose the ice cream. That's a tough one, sir, losing the ice cream. Or we can — "

"You're killing me here, Sergeant," Ski said. "Tell him to shove his survey form up his — disregard. Sergeant, do you know what you want for tomorrow's cookout?"

"That's a Roger, sir. I would like the — "

"Enough already! Whatever you want, I want. How's that for a command decision? Anything else, Sergeant?"

"Yes, sir. Mr. Quinn's waiting to see you."

"Why didn't you say that in the beginning? Send him in."

"LLMF," Gabe said, "that's a new one on me, Sergeant."

"Lost like a mother fucker, sir."

"Roger that." He passed by the sergeant and stepped inside the office. "Morning, Ski."

"Gabe, you look like a damn train wreck. Sit down and take a load off."

Gabe looked more like an aging hippie than a train wreck. He

202

was dressed in an unauthorized mix of military and civilian garments — Army combat uniform pants, a paint-stained, moth-eaten Buffalo Springfield t-shirt, flip-flops, beginnings of a bandito style mustache and sandy hair flecked with grey that was skewed to all compass points.

He sat in a chair facing the captain. He searched for a way to begin the conversation, finally deciding to start with an apology. "About last night, possibly I came off a wee bit odd."

"Your word, not mine. This place can get to the best of us. Sometimes it helps to sit down and talk things out. Yesterday, you know, it got to me, too. Hell, it would be a gut check for anyone. Is that why you're up this early, to talk things through about the girls' deaths?"

Gabe was puzzled by his question. "Uh, not really, Captain. Another time, maybe. Ghazi, he is or was the cell leader in your area."

"You have my attention. Talk to me."

Gabe recounted the previous day's exchange he had with the children. He told him about the fear on the other girls' faces when the oldest one said Ghazi was a policeman and had stolen the generator. He also told him about the other Iraqi cop's reaction when he encountered him during his recon of village.

"We need to follow up and we need to do it now," Gabe said. "If a lead goes cold it's no longer a lead. Just another lost opportunity. People shut down. If we can talk to the parents of the girl maybe we'll get something useful."

"You're convinced?"

"Absolutely."

"I'll tell you what, I was going to let you take it easy today and sleep in, but since you're already up — " Ski got out of his chair and walked to the doorway. "Sergeant Knowles, join us."

"Yes, sir."

Knowles brought in two cups of coffee and handed one to Ski and the other to Gabe. "I figured with all of the deep cogitating going on in here you'd need these, sir."

"That's why you're my top, always anticipating. Sergeant, is the patrol ready?"

"Will be in about fifteen minutes, sir."

"New mission," Ski said. "Brief Sandoval and the rest of the squad. We're not going south, we're returning to Afak. Get up with Dawud and put him and Gabe on the manifest. They'll ride with me."

"Roger, Captain."

"Ski, there's another matter," Gabe said.

"Be quick, Gabe."

"We can get into it later, but you need to know something's not right about Hercules. He isn't *Sunni*, Captain. He's *Shi'ite*. A devout one."

Lead Humvee travelling north toward Afak, 0520 hours

"Gabe, what's this about Hercules being a *Shi'ite*?"

"Captain, I know this will sound strange, but in my dream — "

"Dream?" Ski laughed. "Gabe, a dream! What's next? Tarot readings, séance with burning incense, Ouija board session?"

"I know, I know, but things have struck me as odd about Hercules. I couldn't put my finger on it and I still can't grasp all of it, but follow me on this one, Ski."

Gabe explained his observations and how they were interrelated. Hercules prayed with his hands to his side, a *Shi'ite* practice. *Sunni* crossed their arms over their chests during prayer. He told him the little he knew about Arabic naming conventions. Hercules' personal name, Mutahhar, was typically a *Shi'ite* name. The last part of a name was sometimes a geographical or tribal reference, depending on context within the full four to seven components that made up a classical Middle Eastern name. If the prefix 'al' or 'el' was used, it generally indicated the person's birthplace or tribal affiliation. Al Amarah, a *Shi'ite* dominated city, was not the *Sunni* area near Fallujah that Hercules claimed as his home.

He described the scars on his back and then gave a brief history lesson about *Ashura*, the mourning day commemorating the death of Muhammad's grandson, Imam Hussein, killed by armies of the caliph Yazid. Many devout and crazed *Shi'ite* reenacted Hussein's death by engaging in bloody self-flagellation processions, hitting their backs with knife-covered chains and cutting their heads with swords.

"Ski, he has a tattoo. That one, well, I can't explain that one yet, but I've seen it before. It'll come to me eventually."

"Maybe in another dream," Ski said. "We'll kick it around later when we have time, but not now. There's the village. Pucker up, people."

The four patrol vehicles idled slowly into the village center and parked in a half-circle with crew-served weapons pointing toward the alleys. The truck commanders got out and took up protected positions nearby while the drivers stayed inside with armored doors closed and bullet resistant windows buttoned down. Turret gunners slowly rotated their fifty-calibers and M249s within their overlapping fields of fire. One readied a MK 19 grenade launcher for another clash. After the recent firefight nobody was taking a chance.

In the pre-dawn hour the village looked deserted. As soon as the sun topped the distant dunes and the village awakened, the dirt streets would come alive with children, peddlers, herders and women dressed in black *niqabs* traveling in small groups of two or three. Already sporadic dog barks and the crowing of roosters could be heard both near and far.

Gabe knew from previous battles, the Iraqis, with their memories still fresh, would keep their distance from the American bullet magnets. He and the captain got out of the truck and scanned the village for threats. Seeing none, Gabe pointed to the house with the lime-green door. "There, Captain. How do you want to handle this?"

Ski whispered into the handset attached to his armor. "Bussard, Dark Meat, rally on me."

Loaded down with gear and weapons, they did the soldier shuffle and hustled to the captain and Gabe. Dawud got out and joined the group huddled behind the Humvee.

"Bussard, Dark Meat, when we reach the house pull flank security," Ski said. "I want your eyes on rooftops, alleys, doors, windows and any hajji that approaches. Dawud, you'll attempt to rouse the occupants. After contact is made, get them to invite us inside. The entire village doesn't need to know what's going on. Gabe, you and I will make entry with Dawud. Everyone clear? Any questions?"

There were none.

Guns raised, they spread out in a right-strong-side wedge with ten to fifteen meters separation between them. Bussard and Dark Meat took the flanks, Ski the center and Gabe to his right. Dawud followed closely behind the captain. As they neared the door they collapsed the formation and moved quickly to the outside wall. Bussard and Dark Meat hugged it and moved three meters to either side of the door. Gabe and the captain stacked to the right side of the entrance, Dawud stood to the left. Ski pointed at Dawud and nodded.

Dawud knocked on the door. "*Marhaban, sabah al kheir*, hello, good morning." No response.

He knocked louder. "*Hul la' ahad an yaftah al-bab*, would someone please come to the door?"

Dawud looked at Ski and said, "Captain — "

Ski cut him off. "Try again."

Dawud raised his voice. "*Hal yomken an taftsh al-bab*, would you open the door?"

Ski stepped around Gabe and banged on the door jarring it open several inches. "Again, Dawud, again."

"*Hul sawfa natahadath alaya*, are you going to talk to me?" Dawud shouted.

Ski raised his weapon.

Gabe dropped to his belly and inched forward to the entrance. He jerked his head and took a quick peek in the opening created between the blood stained door and its jamb. Through the home's dark shadows he glimpsed a room straight ahead with its entrance covered by a blanket. As he backed away from the gap he heard a faint buzz sound coming from inside. Clear of the opening, he stood with his back to the wall, looked to his right and calculated the distance from his position to the far corner. He reasoned there was enough space for at least one room, possibly two, on that side of the house. He looked expectantly at the captain awaiting orders.

"Dawud, tell them to open the damn door."

"*Eftah al-bab!*" No response came from behind the green door — nor would one come that morning.

"That's it!" Ski said. "Dawud, go back to the Humvee and stay put. Bussard, Dark Meat close in tighter and no matter what you hear, stay out. I don't want any fucking crossfire. If anyone runs out, it ain't us. Gabe, you ready?"

Gabe flicked his tongue over his parched lips and changed his stance to face the door. He pocketed his ballistic glasses and raised the assault rifle to a firing position. "Ski, there's a room at your twelve, five meters in. Nothing to your right. At least one room maybe two on the left, couldn't tell. I'll cross over high and go left, you buttonhook low and go right. The main threat is the room at the twelve. You'll see a blanket covering its doorway. When we go, cover down on that. I'll clear whatever's in my way. Don't flag me with your weapon."

"It's a plan, let's do it."

Gabe backed off a meter from the door and kicked it hard enough for one of the hinges to snap. The door flew inward and hit the wall, but before it had a chance to bounce back, he was through the void and inside the sparsely furnished room. He moved with short, heel-to-toe steps toward the open room on the left. Looking above the gun sight, he constantly adjusted his field of vision to see any threat from the right side. Hearing a scurrying noise behind him, he glanced quickly over his shoulder and saw Ski take a kneeling position in the corner and point his weapon at the far room.

Gabe quick-stepped toward the open room but midway through he slipped on something liquid and fell hard against the tiled floor. He recovered and stood up, then advanced on his target. The barely audible buzzing noise he had heard earlier was now louder and coming from inside the bedroom. He rushed to the wall left of the opening, braced his back against it and took three quick peeks into the room. He paused long enough to allow the distorted kaleidoscope snapshots to register in his mind and form a useful panoramic image of what he had seen. Image registered and satisfied that there was no living threat inside, he crossed the open doorway and pointed his weapon at the final room. He turned and saw that Ski was still in a kneeling firing position. He waited until he glanced in his direction, and when he did, signaled him to cross over to the other side of the cleared room.

Ski crab-walked across the open space, weapon aimed at the far room. He put his back against the wall, looked at Gabe and whispered, "What?"

Gabe pointed to the room's interior.

Ski looked inside. He dropped his rifle, but the sling stopped it from crashing on the tiles. Jaw dropped, eyes wide — he was Edvard Munch's *The Scream*.

Gabe focused on the next threat area and moved fast. He stuck the muzzle of his weapon between the wall and the blanket, moved the gun barrel slightly and pushed the cover enough to take a brief look inside the room. He lifted the blanket more and surveyed the room in a zigzag, three-dimensional quadrant pattern from chest level, to the floor and then up to the ceiling. Seeing nothing that could harm him in this world, he reached over his head and grabbed a handful of the heavy, wool blanket. With a quick tug, he ripped the cover from the duct tape that anchored it and let it fall to the floor. He saw more flies and the same coagulating liquid that caused his earlier fall. The unmistakable familiar odor filled his nostrils.

He lowered his assault rifle and stepped into the room. Then he reached inside his ankle pocket, plucked out a cigarette and lit it. Inhaling deep, he coughed. He inhaled deeper and forced his lungs to absorb the mixture of smoke and death. Squinting hard until his eyes peered through mere slits, he was fascinated with the butchery that had played out in the room.

He stepped into the larger room and casually said, "Clear."

The captain was slumped on the floor by the first bedroom.

Gabe walked over and placed his arm around him. "The other room, Captain — you gotta see this."

Ski looked up blankly. "Ga-Ga-Gabe, Gabe — "

"It's fine, Captain, it's all fine. I'll help you get there."

"What's going on?" Bussard shouted from outside. "Everything okay?"

"Fine, everything's fine," Gabe yelled. "Stay out."

Ski dropped his head to his chest. Bound together, he surrendered, allowing Gabe to be his ferryman, his Charon, and guide him through the stagnant rivers of red to Hades.

"Let their way be dark and slippery," Gabe spoke softly as they made their shaky journey to the gates of Hell. "Let the angel of the Lord persecute them…let destruction come upon him unawares."

He stopped at the doorway. "Ski, look and see the genius that took place here. Break their teeth, O God, in their mouth…let them be cut to pieces."

Ski kept his eyes tightly closed as Gabe moved him through the opening and stood him against the wall.

Gabe let go and allowed the wall to take Ski's weight.

"Whoever that does not seek the God of Israel should be executed. Open your eyes, Ski. You must see what we fight, why we fight."

Ski shook his head as he slid down the wall to the floor. Gabe unsnapped the captain's helmet and set it on the floor beside him. Then he placed a hand under Ski's chin and forced his head closer to his. "Open your eyes, Captain."

Gradually he did. He looked around the room until he saw her. "Uhhhh, ohhh, God, oh God… Gabe, Gabe…who, what, how…ohhh God…why?" He fell sideways to the floor.

"Breach for breach, eye for eye, tooth for tooth, as he hath caused a blemish in a man, so shall it be done to him again. This morning you asked if I wanted to talk things through. Now I do, but you seem to be in a different place. Cat got your tongue, Captain? Can you see the beautiful simplicity and the truth before you? Can you hear the screams that never left her mouth? My God, it is, it is…Zen."

He left Ski sobbing in his fetal position and stepped across the large room's red pools toward the other bedroom. He studied the corpses from different angles — sometimes standing erect, other times lying flat. At one point, he knelt by the woman's body and stuck his gloved finger through her mouth to the floor beneath. Satisfied he knew the sequence of the events that unfolded inside the room, he walked back to Ski, all the time scrutinizing the blood smears that covered the tiles. When he reached the girl's room he surveyed it like the crime scene it was.

"Captain, if you can't even look at what they've done...if you can't accept their methods...how will you ever become like them? Can you become your enemy, Ski?"

Ski barely opened his eyes before he locked them down again. "I...I could never...never do that."

"Then you will lose, Captain. If America can't do this, America will lose. With this single, low-risk tactic, hajji now owns this village. We could spend years trying to win the villagers' support and in the end we would fail. They are lost to us. The enemy violates our self-imposed morality and ethics with ease. He's ready to sacrifice more, suffer more, kill more. He that killeth any man shall surely be put to death, so sayeth the Lord. Ski, man endeavors to kill. It's what we do so well. We have swallowed the Pabulum of the revisionists and the pacifists who can't accept when an Islamist jihadist says he wants to kill us all, he actually means it. If we can't match their cruelty, we are doomed. Do you want to lose, Ski?"

"I...I...I just wanna go."

"Stop your crying. Be a man and accept what this war is. You are not just a disinterested spectator, but one of the privileged few who can see death in its rawest form and partake in its splendor. Stamp the images in your memory, Captain. When the weak, the uninformed, the peace fucks say you are in the wrong, remember today. Know you are right. Know you are the sword of God. If those not in the game keep busting your balls, don't just jump down their throats, but rip out their damn throats and piss in the gash. They can't see with clarity the truth that lies at your feet."

Gabe rolled the girl's body over to examine the injuries. "Forty-five holes in her, Captain. I'm sorry, I missed the one in her ear. Make it an even forty-six. My God, they were skilled and patient. Look, not one of the wounds touched a vital organ or artery. They used a small drill bit to drag it out and had hours of fun with her."

He looked at the child's tongue that had been thrown against the wall. "Our Hollywood elites and the new crop of Jane Fondas, the academia, the students, the preachers, the housewives — they are the enlightened, the wise ones. They sit in their Malibu Beach homes, college coffee shops, classrooms, churches, eat-in kitchens, wringing their hands, torn by all that they know about this war. Yes, they know everything. They mull over and struggle with the brutality of the immoral, evil, American soldiers who stripped, blindfolded and even photographed those poor, young innocent Iraqi men and boys at Abu Ghraib. Oh the shock, oh the cruelty, oh the horror of it all. They croon, 'American soldiers must be better than that. The bad, bad soldiers must be punished.' That's right, *el Capitan* — we must follow the rules of war made up by those academic whores, liberal think-tank whores, preacher whores, housewife whores, network whores and the righteous political whores. We must follow their rules so we can lose this fucking war. And ye shall perish among the heathen, and the land of your enemies shall eat you up."

Gabe picked up the piece of rebar, turned it over in his hands touching the spot where the blood stopped on its shaft. Then he dropped it. The noise it made hitting the tile startled the captain.

"Captain, are you back with me and my quiet little friend here? Good. Let me give you an overview of what happened in this house. Keep in mind, I'm not a forensic expert or a pathologist, but I've been around a few crime scenes over the decades."

He moved to the room's opening and pointed at the lime-green door. "Three came in there. Two moved left to the first bedroom, but only one did the killing. He used a knife to take out the main threat first, then the woman. The second one watched from the doorway. Did you see the puke on the floor, Captain? He was the weak one, not a leader."

"Look at the blood in the other bedroom. Only two sets of sandals smeared that blood, the leader and his weak-kneed friend. The same sandals trailed from the other room to here. The pussy stood at the doorway, never entered. The third one, now this guy knows war. He didn't bother with the first bedroom, didn't hesitate at all. Not him, no, sir. He's done this before, a professional. This hajji came straight here, subdued his quarry and stayed put until he was finished. Look at the shoe prints and you can see how he moved around her and drilled from different angles. This one enjoys his work."

Gabe rolled the body so it faced the ceiling. "I think she emptied her bowels and bladder early on, probably when her nose was broken. You can see her shit and piss right over there."

He picked up the severed tongue from the floor and held it close to Ski. "This was post mortem, Captain. If they did this too early in the game she would have asphyxiated on her own blood. It's a clear message to the villagers — don't talk to the infidels. Prophets and dreamers are to be executed if they say or dream the wrong things. I'm not sure if that gem is from the Old Testament or the Qur'an. Captain, do you know? Don't know? Fine, it's not important. So

210

what do you think finally killed her, Captain? Still no comment, huh. Could've been the loss of blood, but I don't think so."

He picked up the rebar and held it close to Ski's blank eyes. "He used this on her rectum and vagina. My best guess, this is the culprit, Captain. See how far the blood extends up its length — must have made it all the way to her ribcage. Again, I'm not an expert on the human body, but there are all sorts of vital organs that were ruptured by this. So what do you think, Captain? Have I talked things through? You know, sort of gotten things off my chest."

Curled up in a ball, Ski appeared to be catatonic, incapable of speech.

"Well, now you know." Gabe stared at the listless boy-soldier on the floor. "If you want to survive the madness you must learn to put this shit out of your head while you're in the thick of it. Save it for when you get home. Save it for those many times you'll be alone. Alone even when you're surrounded by friends and family. You'll be alone, Ski. Nobody can appreciate what you've seen today so don't even try to explain what can't be explained. If they haven't experienced it, there's no point. Think about it when you are alone… and never, never again fucking ask me, or anyone else who has been in that place, do you want to sit down and talk about it."

Gabe leaned Ski's weapon against the wall. He repositioned his own rifle to lay flat against his back and then secured the captain's helmet on his armor.

"Let's go, son."

Ski looked up at him with a flicker of recognition. Gabe helped him up and steadied him against the wall. He grabbed the other weapon and placed his free arm around Ski. Together they retraced their steps through the red ooze of the Styx.

"Dark Meat, take the captain to the vehicle and get him some water. Get him out the armor and cool him down. He's got to stay cool. Don't ask him any questions, but make damn certain he's not left alone."

"Roger that, Mr. Quinn, but what's up?"

"A crime scene. Nobody comes in…not you, not Bussard. You don't want to see."

"How much longer?" Bussard asked. "The hajjis are getting restless. Look at 'em." Bussard pointed at a group of ten to fifteen men, women and children pushing up against several soldiers blocking their attempt get closer to the house.

"Not long, five minutes. Just keep them out, when I finish…just keep them the fuck out."

Gabe returned to the girl. He stopped at the opening and picked up the wool blanket. Moving closer, he knelt by her side. After shooing the flies away, he stroked her bloody, matted hair. Then he kissed her violated forehead.

"He who pleased God was loved. He who lived among sinners was transported, snatched away, lest wickedness pervert his mind or deceit beguile his soul. Having become perfect in a short while, his soul was pleasing to the Lord, therefore he sped him out of the midst of wickedness. Dream now, innocent child. The wickedness is over."

Gabe covered the obscenity with the blanket and then moved away from her. He flung his helmet to the opposite side of the room. It bounced off the wall, then wobbled on the floor like a spinning top. He rested briefly against the wall before sliding down its rough surface to the floor. Staring at the mounded blanket, he smoked a cigarette. Finished, he pitched the smoldering butt to the tiles. He dropped his head to his chest and cried.

Chapter 18
Noise
July 4, 2007

"Across America, our citizens are going to come together for parades and pyrotechnic displays, and readings from our Declaration of Independence. It's a grand celebration. It's a great day to be an American.....We need for people to volunteer to defend America. Because in this war, we face dangerous enemies who have attacked us here at home. Oh, I know the passage of time has convinced some — maybe convinced some that danger doesn't exist. But that's not how I see it, and that's not how many of you see it. These people want to strike us again. We learned on September the 11th that in the age of terror, the best way to do our duty, which is to protect the American people, is to go on the offense and stay on the offense. And that's exactly what we've been doing against these radicals and extremists...." *President George W. Bush, West Virginia Air National Guard, Martinsburg, West Virginia, July 4, 2007*

Republican fundraiser, Inez, Kentucky

Ruftus Biggs sat large in the chair. The summer heat was tempered somewhat by the giant oak's shade and a breeze rolling across the horse pasture behind the sprawling, country house. Even so, sweat poured from his forehead and temples. Sometimes he stopped the flow with the back of his hand, other times not. If the briny seepage made it to his chin and mixed with the juices escaping from his mouth, he'd scoop it up with his fingers and then lick them clean. He had stuck a white linen tablecloth inside the top of his shirt at the neck and allowed it to drape down across his imposing belly. Sauce and grease had dripped, dropped, spattered and smeared across the cotton canvas with the *panache* of an abstract expressionist. Spread out in front of him were a bucket of bones and several plates heaped high with his fifth serving. He attacked his food as he did everything

213

in life — taking no prisoners.

Ruftus had honed his skills over four decades. He first cut his teeth selling reconditioned mobile homes and then hawked vinyl replacement windows, followed by the pest extermination business. Bugs, he thought, were his true calling. He was so successful selling services folks didn't need, he started a franchise and amassed a small fortune marketing insect killing to other 'get rich quick' schemers across Kentucky, Tennessee and southern Ohio.

A chance meeting with a political consultant in a hotel lobby changed everything for Ruftus Biggs. For several years he became the scion of the reputed rogue known for running hard-edged campaigns. During the 1980 South Carolina congressional run, he understudied the master and watched as he destroyed his candidate's opposition. Ruftus was introduced to push polling and other tactics that exploited an opponent's weakness. If there were no weaknesses, one was created. Phony pollsters implied the challenger was a member of the NAACP. In the home of the only 'Dixiecrat' presidential nominee, the slightest hint of any tie to the 'colored people' spelled an end to a campaign for a national office — it just wasn't white.

Not one to pause and consolidate gains in the midst of an attack, the bad boy of politics also sent out last-minute letters telling voters that the Democrat foe would disarm America, and turn it over to liberals and communists. Always the one who had to drive in another stake, he placed a shill in the audience to ask an epochal, loaded question, along the lines of when was the last time you beat your wife. "Is it true that the Democrat running for Congress has had psychotic treatment for being suicidal?" Later the 'dirty tricks *extraordinaire*' told reporters the opposition candidate was quite nutty and had been hooked up to jumper cables to fix his 'loony toons' antics.

That same evening at a Five Points nightclub near the University of South Carolina, Ruftus listened and watched as the political strategist picked up a guitar and hit a chord progression that topped the blues boy's best riff. Who taught whom the solo repetition was one mystery, along with many others, that went to the grave with him. Neither Lee Atwater, nor his friend and fellow bluesman, B. B. King, ever revealed the answer.

Before Atwater threw Ruftus into the deep end of the pool he made some key political introductions for the large man to set him on a new path in life. Ruftus discovered that buying and selling influence as a lobbyist to the dimwitted elected marks in the capital was much easier than killing imaginary bugs for country folk.

Ruftus Biggs' head bobbed in synch with the music of the blue grass band hired for the fundraiser. Like a great white shark, his eyes rolled back inside of their sockets as he gnawed on a fresh rib. Some stray meat strands were trapped between his upper front teeth so he cleared the debris with his fingernail then wiped his hands on fresh linen. "This must be a mustard based sauce," he said to the Republican National Committee chairman. "Damn, they're scrumptious! Tell that colored boy of yours he did good on these ribs."

Ruftus threw the naked bone into the bucket and pushed away from the table. He forced a belch to show his appreciation for the feast, yanked the napkin from his neck and dropped it next to the bone pile on the checkered tablecloth. He pulled out a pair of Cuban *Cuabas distinguidos* from his shirt pocket and offered one to Mike. The chairman shook his head and politely declined. Ruftus forced his chubby hand into his pants pocket and removed a solid silver guillotine cutter. He clipped the end of his stogy, licked the length of the cigar's shaft and fired it up with a matching Xikar torch flame lighter.

"Mike, you haven't got a prayer next year," Ruftus said. "You lost everything in the midterms and this damn surge is going to cost us the White House. We have too damned much at stake to back a loser. The country doesn't care about this war, I don't care about the war, but most important, my clients don't give a shit about the war. It's a distraction from the important money issues. You don't have a doable candidate so we're hedging our investment this time around. Mike, it isn't just me, everyone's jumping ship."

"Ruftus, I've been in banking and politics since the seventies," the chairman said. "I know how the world turns and it's turning left now. You're right, we're going to lose and lose big. It's a damn shame about the soldiers and Marines — "

"They don't factor into our decisions," Ruftus said. "Grow up and see the world for what it is. This isn't about some boys and girls playing soldier in Iraq. Hell, they're all volunteers anyway. This is about the real money, the real issues and the real people who count in this country."

Ruftus winked at a mini-skirted high school cheerleader as she pranced around the festivity teasing the crowd's waning enthusiasm with patriotic cheers. The pair of golden metallic pompons she energetically whipped about complimented her healthy set of mammary pom-poms. She smiled, he smiled. His thoughts turned to carnal desserts he hoped would eclipse the carnivore delight working its way through his gut.

"Mike, where you hiding that fine Kentucky bourbon I paid for?"

Kenwood community near Chicago, Illinois

"Sir, I think you're on the right track. The surge is the issue, the winning issue," the former Freddie Mac director said. "You came on strong with your senate floor speech. That bit about you opposing dumb and rash wars was genius."

"Yes, it was good. I'm thinking of a follow-up, perhaps a strongly worded letter to Bush, or even — "

"We need to go slow on that," Rahmbo said. "Damnit, put out that cigarette. We've talked about that before. It's all about perception."

"Sorry, sorry, I know," the first term senator said as he stubbed the cigarette out in an onyx ashtray. "All right, if not a letter, how about another book? I've been kicking around an idea. Something along the lines of the audacity of change, change is audacious, maybe hope is audacious, or — "

Rahmbo shook his head. "That's nice, Senator, but let's keep our eyes on the prize. They stole the office seven years ago. It's ours to steal this time around. It's going to come down to you and that political slut, but we've got her. When she voted to support Bush's crusade in 2002...how did she phrase it? 'I cast my vote with conviction.' We're going to crucify the bitch with that blunder."

"Yes, we definitely own the high road on that issue," the senator said as he lit another cigarette.

"Don't get smug, Senator." Rahmbo pulled a folded piece of paper from his coat pocket and read it in silence. When finished, he looked up at the senator. "I keep a copy of your speech from the Chicago anti-war rally. Everything was going great guns until you ad-libbed the part about Saddam being a bad guy and Iraq would be better off without him. Do you know why I keep this speech in my pocket?"

"Because you like the way I can read a speech off of a teleprompter?"

"I keep a copy in my pocket so I won't forget the challenge of how to overcome your screw-up." He reached across the kitchen island counter and plucked another cigarette from the senator's fingers. "Every time you wing it...damn...'we live in the greatest nation in the history of the world. I hope you'll join with me as we try to change it.' Where the hell did that come from? You must learn to

216

stick with the script, Senator. This is not the time to — "

"I've changed. You know I'm all about hope and change. Why I've even — "

"Time-out for a reality check, Senator. I'll flood the media with the message that you were against the war and the surge before she was. We've got all of the majors on our side except that Australian bastard at Fox. Hollywood's lining up nicely. Steven, Barbara, Robert, Susan, Sean — when it's crunch time they'll be there. Did you read the statement Tim Robbins made on Air America?"

"Was it included in my talking points about how much of our nation's greatness we owe to the patriotism of Hollywood and — "

"Uh, Senator..." Rahmbo rolled his eyes. "Robbins said because of Hillary's votes on the war she could kiss his ass! If the man wasn't so principled we could offer him a speech writing position. Kidding, of course. We'll save a plum like that for patronage payback time."

Rahmbo's pupils narrowed to pinpoints as he picked up a steak knife from the countertop. He plunged it into the maple cutting board and whispered, "That bitch is dead, dead, dead...dead."

"Now, now, calm down," the senator said. "We'll handle Hillary, but it must be done with an appearance of decency. Rahmbo, no more deliveries of dead fish wrapped in newspaper. I'll have enough problems with the born-agains, the military, the NRA. I can't afford to lose the female vote, too. I'm more worried about the Republicans than I am about her. I'm sure it won't be that preacher, Huckleberry, but the war veteran...wasn't he in the Marine Corpse during the Korean War?"

Rahmbo looked up at the senator in disbelief. He pulled the steak knife out of the butcher block and contemplated its other uses for a few seconds. Left-brain dominance kicked in and he set it down on the countertop.

"Senator, it was the Vietnam War and he was in the Navy."

"I was against that war, too."

"You were two years old when the war began and in middle school when it ended." He grabbed yet another cigarette from the senator's hand. "Senator, while we're on the subject of gaffes, you just go ahead and give our opposition their 'nucular' moment. It's the Corps. Not a fucking corpse."

Pacific Heights, California

The study was furnished as one would expect for a mansion meant to sustain a person of means. The estate, located near the family's

217

twenty million dollar vineyard in St. Helena, was only a short limo ride to the congresswoman's 8th District office. On this day, the study had an additional piece of furniture that was normally stored in a third floor suite — a padded dentist chair, complete with adjustable legs, arms and a telescoping headrest. She was sitting in it.

The physician leaned over her and maneuvered the small gauge needle to pre-marked dots on her forehead. "We must be conservative and wait at least two months before I perform additional Botox treatments."

Although only the slightest movement of facial muscles could be detected, a noise escaped through her pursed lips that resembled a chuckle. She looked at the doctor with an unblinking, mannequin stare and said, "Conservative Botox treatments? You must be a Republican."

"Madame Speaker, I'm apolitical."

"You should vote Democrat. We're the party that looks out for your type," she said. "Nevertheless, I have the money so there will not be any cutbacks in my personal entitlement plan. Today is about me. I'm treating myself to a full facial, massage and pedicure. I deserve it for what I am tirelessly giving to my constituents. After you work your magic I'm off to the Napa Valley Auberge Du Soleil Resort we own. I think we own it. I'll check with the hubby. Where was I? Oh yes, a wine tasting event I am graciously sponsoring, and, of course, tax deductible!"

She raised her right arm and shook her fist in a delayed, spasmodic, *Dr. Strangelove* gesture that seemed to emphasize the tax deduction. After recovering from her paroxysm, she said, "Make me look vibrant, make me look young, make me beautiful."

"A wine tasting event on Independence Day. That's an interesting choice, Madame Speaker." The doctor placed the needle on the side table attached to the chair. He pulled an oblong piece of metal from his white smock and turned away from her. His eyes instantly swelled as he stared at Thad's dented dog tag — Thad, one of three sons, but the only one killed in Iraq. "I would have thought something along the lines of a visit to the Presidio or even the Camp Pendleton Marine base would be more appropriate on a special day like today. Possibly a trip to Iraq — "

"There you go with Iraq!" She jolted to an upright position and hissed, "I visited Syria earlier this year. In Damascus my name is a household word. They love me there and besides, it's right next to Iraq. Everything's Iraq, Iraq, Iraq, or the surge, or our troops, blah,

blah, blah. They're all volunteers anyway. If they had any intelligence they would get a liberal education and go find a real job. Also, if they — Yikes!" she shrieked.

"Sorry, Madame Speaker."

"My God! Did you intern under Mengele? You have the hands of a butcher. I hope you have a license to practice in this country."

"Yes, Madame Speaker."

She released her death grip on the armrest and continued. "The military know I support them, but that doesn't mean I must visit them, talk to them, touch them, and smell them. At least once a session I see their generals and admirals, festooned with those absurd ribbons and medals, walking stiffly around the capital. I smile at them even though they don't support my majestic agenda. I know what's best for them, but do they show any appreciation? Of course not! One of those same generals referred to a sister colleague of mine on the other side of Congress as ma'am. After Senator Barbara Boxer worked so hard to get that title, and him, nothing more than a tin soldier, calls a well-respected senator ma'am. Unbelievable! It's absolutely scandalous. Regardless, I pay you twice the going rate to buy your discretion and silence. So stop talking!"

She relaxed, allowing her body to fall against the padded chair. She shot the doctor a contemptuous look then closed her eyes. "Finish up quickly. It's going to be a wondrous occasion."

He rummaged through the items on the tray until he found what he didn't need — the largest diameter needle the AMA would allow, short of ethics repercussions.

"Madame Speaker, did I say I was apolitical?"

Brentwood Estates near Hollywood, California

"I'm listening, Guillermo, but I really don't care if we lose a few million. We'll get it back in distribution fees." Steve switched the phone to his other ear and continued, "We had some winners last year. Hell, we even had an Oscar nomination…Yes, I know that most anti-war films have not done well at the box office, but do you want a Bush-cloned idiot to win next year?...That's the point, though…I know, I know. Paul missed big with that *In the Valley of Elah* disaster. But think about it, Gui. Who could relate to a movie title like that? It sounded like a *Lord of the Rings* sequel. And that other big, big loser, *Lions for Lambs*, I don't know what Bobby Redford was thinking. I thought it was going to be another Hannibal Lecter gore-fest. My movie will be serious and send a message that…I know, but we have a duty to get our views across and change the minds — hang on a second, Gui."

Steve pushed the mute button and adjusted his position on the sofa. He cupped his hand under her chin and forced her head up. "Honey, your audition is progressing nicely and I'm sure I'll have a part for you. It's between you and Reese, but you need to slow down. Tempo, it's all about tempo and much too early for you to bite down. Slow down, get some rhythm, go a little deeper and stroke. Oh, yes, that's much better."

"Where was I, Gui...right, Bush. Okay, try to get that writer, what's his name...yes, Allejandro. Get him on board and have him punch up the script, take out that positive bullshit. Also see if Jake Gillenhale, Gellanwhore, whatever the hell his name is, see if he's available.... No, he's not typecast. America's almost there, but it's just not ready yet for gay cowboys having sex on a broken back mountain. They'll forget his role in that movie before the next blockbuster numbers are in. He's not really a homosexual is he?...You don't know? Doesn't matter. But if he's not open, see about Matt or Ben...who the hell is Chaz...okay, okay, fine."

Steve used his free hand and forced her head down farther. "We're making an oral, I mean a visual statement with this piece...I know... ooooh God...I know, but...the...ooooooa... the timing's...perfect.... with this surge...surge...babe...oh goddamn...suuuuuurrrrrrgggge."

Beach house, Santa Monica, California

He looked at his naked lover asleep on the chaise lounge next to his. It had been a frantic lovemaking session that began and ended hours before the sun rose above the Hollywood hills behind him. He snorted more cocaine before he picked up the script. He had read it many times — in front of the mirror, to his lover, to his agent, to his cat — he even imagined reading the part in his dreams. This was the one. This could be the role that would win him the Oscar he deserved.

"Wake up, Roger," Chaz said. "I need your brutish and honest opinion about me."

"Huh? Okay, okay, sure lover, but let me do a line first."

Roger opened his eyes and yawned. Then he got off of the lounger, stretched and then walked past Chaz to the wrought iron nesting table. He bent down and took a hit of the *primo* Columbian spread out on the table's glass top. "Good fucking shit, dude. Best aphrodisiac known to man." He rubbed Chaz's back and kissed him on the neck below his ear. "You ready to go again, stud-muffin?"

"Oh, Roger! You silly, silly man. It's this part. I was made for it. My name is all over it."

"You mean that war film?"

"War, western, comedy, horror, musical — what does it matter."

Chaz eased out of the recliner and treaded softly to the deck's rail. He closed his eyes when he was within an arm's reach of the polished metal tubing and inched nearer to the edge of the cantilevered deck jutting from the cliff. When his stomach brushed up against the railing he opened his eyes and looked nervously over the solid acrylic half-wall to the beach below.

"Boo!"

Chaz squealed and almost fell over the wall. "You're terrible, Roger. I could have been hurt."

"Sorry, dude."

"Oh never mind, you gorgeous, lovable muscled ox. You're forgiven. Yes, Roger, it is a war movie, but look at me. I'm perfect. I work out five days a week, eat the right foods, not a wrinkle to be seen, not a scar or bruise on my body. I even take yoga. It's almost like that manly jiu-jitsu thing, I think. I can almost grow a beard. I would make a perfectly heroic looking soldier. What else is needed besides a dimpled chin, straight nose, Nordic expressive eyes, high cheekbones, proper diction and an understanding of the character's inner turmoil? I ask you, Roger, who could play a grizzled, hunky, sympathetic, disturbed war veteran better than Chaz Rock Van Dickens? Jake G, that bitch — I know he's their first choice, but my God, who can even pronounce that abortion he calls a last name? Seriously, Roger, can you pronounce a name with so many consonants?"

Chaz shivered then his body tensed as he looked at the beach below the cliff. He carefully pushed away from the edge and slowly backed up several feet before he turned around. With his nerves of steel regained he said, "Jake beat me out on that other role. I would have been a dandy cowboy, and oh, my God…can you imagine the love scene with Heath? We would have sizzled and lit up the screen. What do you think, Roger? And don't play coy with me. I want the unvarnished, heartfelt truth, and for goodness sake, don't let the fact that I pay for everything sway your opinion. So, Roger…."

Breakers Resort Hotel, Suite 1103, Myrtle Beach, South Carolina

Amber Reeves, naked in front of the bathroom's vanity mirror, fought tangles in her wet, shoulder length blonde hair with a wide-toothed comb. When she hit a particularly nasty snag she dropped the comb to the sink, grabbed some strands and yanked hard. Tangle cleared, she reached down to pick up the comb, but stopped when she saw her reflection in the mirror.

Staring back at her was a girl barely out of her teens, saddled with two young children. She wept.

Amber's only prior experience with high finance was pocketing tips at the strip club and stretching the monthly allotment checks from the Army to cover rent, daycare and food. Her unexpected windfall, a two hundred and fifty thousand dollar death benefit she received after her husband was scattered across Iraq a month earlier, overwhelmed the hill-country girl. She allowed Bonar Peterson to *invest* her sudden fortune until she could come up with a plan that would put her on the path to the good life. She thought her nights at the gentlemen's club were behind her.

Tears daubed dry, she wrapped herself in an oversized bath towel and stepped into the adjoining living-dining-bedroom suite. "Bonar, I needs some money to cova' my kid's babysittin' and I needs some money to git me a new tire for ma car."

"I'll see what I can do, but you must understand your investment in me...I mean with me, is for the future, not the present."

Bonar poured Scotch into a tumbler and moved back to the king-size bed. "Later, you take yourself a couple of twenties from my wallet."

He smiled and held out his arms. "Baby doll, the Viagra's kicking in so get that fine little ass back in this bed. It's the Fourth of July, sugar. Time for some more fireworks."

Small clearing near the wharf across from the Royal Street Junkyard, Mobile Bay, Alabama

"Yeah, baby, baby, baby...ooooh baby, you're so biiiiig," she whispered in his ear. "Don't stop, please don't stop...that's it...oh, oh, oh...come on, baby... you can do it...cum, cum, cum, baby, oh God, baby, I'm comin' too...."

The dockworker grunted and moaned repeatedly before he made one final, deep thrust. Then he fell silent and allowed his three hundred and ten pound mass to collapse against her.

"All right, big boy, you's crushin' me."

He rolled off of her emaciated body, reached behind her head and grabbed his fouled jeans. "Ten bucks, right?"

"Bull-shit, stud! It's twenty." Naked from the waist down, she jumped up and brushed dirt and sea grass off of her bruised buttocks.

222

She looked down at him and screeched, "Pay up!"

"Ten, you skank ass crack-whore."

He did not see the underwear on the newspaper spread out over the dirt. He picked up his pants then rolled across the ground fighting to get his grossly overweight legs and ass to fit inside the tortured denim. After nearly the same amount of time and same number of groans it had taken him to reach an orgasm, he won the battle against the Levi's. Then he saw the Hanes with brown skid-marks, still laying on the newspaper. Faced with the conundrum of another protracted skirmish removing his jeans, he decided in favor of free balling and tossed the underwear into the bay.

"It's ten or I tell the boys your cooter's all dried up."

The longshoreman dug into his pocket and pulled out several crumpled bills. He pitched a torn five-dollar bill and four ones to the ground, then zipped up his jeans and pulled his grease-stained work shirt from a nearby bush. He fumbled around in his other pocket until he found some loose change, counted out several coins and dropped them near the bills.

"You ain't no twenty dollar hooker. I owe you a quarter."

Whistling the theme from the Andy Griffith show, he walked between bushes and weeds, kicking empty beer cans along the path. When he reached the chain link fence, he peeled back a loose edge and labored to get through the opening.

The thirty-six year old snatched up the bills and stuck them inside her brassiere along with the other thirty-three dollars she earned earlier. She picked up a section of the *Press-Register,* Mobile's only daily. Unable to read, she did not have a literary use for the newspaper — her need was of a sanitary nature. She tore off the front page that headlined partisan criticism about the Iraq surge, and used it to wipe the jizzum from between her legs and the load that was sliding down her thighs.

It had been a good morning, almost good enough to warrant some type of celebration. So far she had enough for four rocks of crack. Ten to twelve more tricks and she would have the money to feed her habit through the following evening. If she worked hard today, there would be time in the morning to take a short break and visit the public health office. She had to know for sure. The last thing she needed in her life was another Jeremiah.

Savannah Street residence, The Plantation, Pawleys Island, South Carolina

Nicole Quinn sat by the breakfast room table that overlooked the screen porch and the golf course beyond the *koi* pond. Spread out in front of her was a sheaf of papers tabbed with inch long, pink sticky-notes. She thumbed through the stack until she reached the first highlighted section, picked up the blue fine-tip Sharpie pen and signed the document. Her attorney had told her that all of the documents had to be signed in blue ink, not black. The originals of the divorce papers had to be distinguishable from the copies that would be mailed to Gabe.

82nd Airborne parade field, Ardennes Street, Ft. Bragg, NC

The young mother and her daughter smoothed out a blanket across the grass directly in front of the Army's eight-piece band and near the barbeque. They had arrived early so they would have an unobstructed view when the Golden Knights parachute team jumped in from above the west side of the parade field.

Another early arrival, carrying a beach chair and a small cooler, stopped at the edge of her blanket. "Mrs. Kowalewski, what do hear from your husband?" the chaplain's wife asked. "All good news, I hope."

"Oh, hello, Mrs. Phelps," Sarah said. "He's fine. We do the on-line chat thing almost on a nightly, or maybe it's a daily basis, I'm not really sure with the nine-hour time difference. We haven't spoken today, but I'm sure we will later. On special occasions I'll wake up Brianna so she can say hi to her daddy."

"She's certainly a precious little darling," Mrs. Phelps said. "Brianna, honey, how old are you?"

The child twisted behind her mother's sundress and squeezed her hand.

"Don't be shy," her mother said. "This nice lady's husband is serving with daddy in Iraq."

Brianna peeked from around her mother's hips, held up her hands and splayed six fingers. "I'm four."

"My goodness, four years old," the chaplain's wife said. "You are a big girl now. You must miss your daddy very much. I bet you are proud of him and all he's doing to help all of the little children in Iraq."

"Can they be my friends, Mommy?" Brianna asked. "Can I play with them, Mommy?"

"Not today, sweetheart. Daddy says they are special like you and want to be your friend. When we talk to daddy tonight, we'll ask him to tell us all about the little Iraqi boys and girls and what they do to have fun. Okay?"

COP 6, Commander's office, 1700 hours

Captain Kowalewski had not left his office since returning from Afak the previous day. He had not eaten, slept, showered or spoken to anyone. Wearing the same uniform, a uniform stained with the blood of the child and her parents, he sat motionless behind his desk. Ski had been staring at the photo of his wife and daughter for twenty-three hours.

LA 2 dorm trailer, Forward Operating Base Adder, 1702 hours

"Wear the red, open-shelf bralette with the caged lace panties and garter belt. Don't forget to put on some of that black-honey lipstick and those dangling earrings."

"Yes, sir, Major Laddick," Lieutenant Lutz said.

COP 6, Tactical Operations Center, 1710 hours

Bussard had relieved Sergeant Knowles and was busy on the non-secure computer. He happily accepted the additional duty when it was offered because it allowed the internet time needed to find the answer.

His adoptive parents were silent about the specifics surrounding his origin, either out of genuine ignorance or some novel belief that the truth would be harmful to him. He believed he plopped into this life somewhere near New Orleans in the spring of 1988. He had researched birth records for most of the city's hospitals and many of the outlying parishes. Finding no leads, he decided to increase the parameters of his search to include coastal towns east of New Orleans, through Mississippi, all the way to Mobile Bay.

Bussard had already spent thousands of dollars on sham search organizations. Recently he found a website through *Quest America Adoptee Search* that seemed to offer promise. This new site included testimonials and pictures of adoptees' reunions with their biological mothers. He was sure this one was reputable and that he could cover the fees with his extra combat and jump pay.

COP 6, dorm trailer, 1720 hours

He braced his back against the wall behind the bottom bunk and picked up the worn book. It was his third reading of the epilogue's second part, but he was confident he could master and then debunk the novelist's theorem. The writer's philosophy mirrored his until he infused the concept that there was a great divine force behind history. That's where he and the author parted company.

Dark Meat thought the force behind most notable events was not a god. He saw the error in the EPR paradox and believed quantum entanglement was deterministic and measureable. Einstein, Podolsky and Rosen had gotten it wrong with their 'detached observer's view' of physical theory.

Dark Meat's grand view was more aligned with the 'many-worlds' interpretation and the seemingly conflicting, but actually supporting, quantum logical approach that emphasized non-Boolean structure. When quantum systems became entangled they were no longer unique but remained in a quantum superposition and shared a single quantum state until a measurement was made. Everything in life was a result of these random collisions and had nothing to do with spirituality. Man was a biological machine destined for oblivion and nothing more.

Although he had missed the target with his God fantasy, Dark Meat respected Tolstoy's service during the Crimean War and enjoyed his take on Napoleon's invasion of Russia.

COP 6, kitchen trailer, 1721 hours

Second Lieutenant Bishop sat in the vacant dining trailer sipping chocolate milk through a straw. He was quite pleased that the captain's bad fortune had turned into his good fortune. He was in command now, albeit temporary. The cherry, butter-bar lieutenant was self-intoxicated with an air of hegemony. He had convinced himself that only he could bring order out of chaos. Discipline was slack, so slack that the soldiers referred to the captain as Ski. He did not have a clue what 'LLMF' meant, but from the way the soldiers looked at him and laughed when they whispered the acronym, he was positive it was an insult. He had been called names throughout his childhood, even well into his later teenage years. His older brothers had tried to drown him when he was eight.

It was payback time. The bullies of the past were not available, but he had close to fifty soldiers under his command now. Also, there was that eccentric interpreter, Dawud, and that civilian curiosity, Gabe.

"I've got the grill fired up," PFC Jeremiah Barton said when he stepped in from the adjoining kitchen. "When do you want me to start the steaks?"

226

"Steaks!" Bishop shouted. He blasted out of the chair like a human cannonball shot across the arena of a three ring circus' big top. "There will be no steaks while I'm in command. And when you talk to me you will address me as Lieutenant Bishop."

"Yes, sir, Second Lieutenant Bishop," Jeremiah said. "But Sergeant Knowles gave me the menu and I'm supposed — "

"The rank insignia on my blouse is a gold bar, not chevrons with a rocker! A gold bar outranks a sergeant and furthermore, I'm almost a first lieutenant so you will address me as lieutenant, not second lieutenant."

"Yes, sir, Lieutenant Bishop. I'm sorry, sir." Jeremiah stared at the floor, nervously rubbing his greasy hands together.

"There will be no steaks, no ice cream and no cake. One hamburger per soldier, one serving of beans and one serving of macaroni and cheese." Bishop turned when he heard the sound of the door open.

White Meat came be-bopping into the trailer. He made it several steps before he recognized the threat. He executed a fluid one-eighty and tiptoed back toward the door.

"Halt!" Bishop said. "The uniform in the Army and on my post is bloused boots, clean tan t-shirt, clean ACU pants, clean ACU blouse and a clean boonie hat that you will remove when under cover. What army do you belong to, soldier?"

White Meat stopped dead in his tracks, did an about-face, slapped his hands against his thighs and stood at attention. "LT, I wuz just, I means, suh, I wuz — "

"LT!" Bishop screamed. His face turned tomato red, blue veins throbbed on his temples, hands clenched into fists. "I'm a lieutenant, not an LT. Consider yourself to be on report, soldier. I will get with Sergeant Knowles after the celebration — a celebration that you will not be allowed to attend. Now get out of my dining facility, go to your room and put on a proper uniform."

COP 6, shower trailer, 1727 hours

Running from the dining trailer, White Meat slowed as he neared Sergeant Knowles, who was almost moving as fast as him. On a trajectory toward the shower trailer, the sergeant was carrying a towel and a plastic bag.

"Hey, Sarge. Date night agin'?"

Knowles passed by him without saying a word. He just nodded and grinned.

Once inside the trailer, Knowles locked the door, affixed the Ziploc bag on the shower stalls' wall with tape, and then quickly stripped. He stepped into the shower and ogled his wife's photo, secure and waterproof behind the plastic. He placed a bottle of Jergens hand lotion on the soap dish. He hoped eight ounces would be enough — it was going to be a heavy date.

COP 6, laundry area, 1738 hours

Gabe was not enjoying his date. His was more of an obligatory outing, required every week or so, to keep him in the good social graces of the surrounding soldiers. He sat outside the laundry trailer, with its one working, water-wise, washer-dryer combo, waiting for his entire wardrobe to be rid of blood and sand. He could not launder his combat boots, so he wore them over sockless feet. To protect his head from the late afternoon sun, he cocked his soiled boonie hat down low on his forehead, just above his sunglasses. The only other garment he wore was a set of dirty, red polka-dot skivvies. He had contemplated going with the full Monty look on this date, but reconsidered when he discovered the grubby boxer shorts underneath his bunk bed.

He sat in a broken canvas chair on the east side of the laundry shack. The shade helped some, but at one hundred and twenty-three degrees, with only a slight breeze, he was hurting. He spread his legs wide and occasionally flapped the boxer's slit opening to cool his crotch and air out the rot that was flaring up. His belly still hung out over the edge of his shorts, but he was down about fifteen pounds since he stepped off of the C-130 less than a month earlier. He didn't care. He would gladly bloat up another twenty pounds if the added calories came from healthy doses of rum.

The dog tags and the jagged piece of iron that hung down across his chest were hot to the touch so he swung them around his neck to rest against his back. The ball-chain and the attached stamped metal identification tags had left an impression on his scarred chest. He didn't think much about the scars or the other milestones that marred his skin. They were just insignificant reminders of the parts of him that had already died. The scars, however, bothered Nicole so much she insisted he cover up when they went to the beach or to the clubhouse pool.

Gabe fell into a deep funk thinking about past celebrations. The Fourth of July, on the beach, the grandkids whispered and shouted 'oohs, aahs' and 'wows' as they watched the fireworks. Nicole's smile when the kids romped through the home as if it were an actual fun house instead of the deathly quiet, marital mortuary it had become. He yearned for the days when Nicole would sneak a peek at him with a spark in her eyes. He missed burning the steaks on the barbeque, chasing the grandkids across the 5th fairway in a game of touch football, then passing out on the sundeck lounge chair — not from liquor, but from the gratifying exhaustion brought on by all of the love and attention spent on him by the children. He wanted his past back, but all that was left inside was war. Finally, reaching an uneasy peace, he slumped lower in the chair and slept.

Dry riverbed, 4565 meters northwest of COP 6, 1812 hours

Normally they would have stayed inside when the sun burned, but today, Dhul Fiqar and his four-man crew had been busy throughout the afternoon preparing for the celebration. They had placed a series of rocks in the shape of an arrow that pointed at the outpost. Three of his best men had assembled the *Hadid* 120 mm mortar and laid out twenty rounds in orderly groups within easy reach of the weapon.

Dhul Fiqar adjusted the mortar's sight and set the approximate range and direction for the first shot. He inspected the tube, SN 33-4718س ت-17-و, and the projectiles. During his inspection of the round numbered 7B3169, he saw that one of its fins was bent. He picked up the bomb and set it aside. Then he phoned the fifth member of the team, the spotter. "Are you in place...no...call when you are set."

COP 6, vehicle-parking area, 1845 hours

Bishop stopped walking when he came across Gabe asleep in front of the laundry. He was about to speak, then thought better of it. The second lieutenant was unsure about his status if Gabe got up and decked him. Aside from getting hurt, he could be prohibited from bringing charges against a civilian. He pulled out a pad and jotted down a note to get clarification about his legal standing from his friend, Major Laddick, the Brigade's JAG officer.

Bishop resumed his walk to the nearest Humvee. He opened its door, reached inside and grabbed the handset. He turned the vehicle's starter knob to 'accessories only,' switched the radio to the loudspeaker position, and said, "Test, test, test...one, two, three."

Buoyed by the sound of his commanding voice echoing between the perimeter's blast-walls, he admired his reflection in the vehicle's mirror one last time and then cleared his throat. "It is now 1848 hours. There will be a mandatory formation in front of the latrine at 1850 hours by order of the outpost commander…me…Lieutenant Bishop. I repeat…a formation at…"

COP 6, laundry area 1849 hours

Gabe, the enemy and every other living creature within a kilometer was blasted awake by Bishop's broadcast. He sat up in the chair and watched the ensuing flurry of activity as soldiers scrambled toward the open area near the toilets. The men were in varying stages of dress that ranged from gym shorts and sneakers, to partial or full military uniforms. All of the soldiers except Captain Ski, PFC Jeremiah Barton, those pulling security and maintaining the TOC's radio, fell into a hurried formation.

He smiled at the unfolding Chinese fire-drill and the soldiers' blurted comments — "Formation in a fucking combat zone, LLMF, whiskey-tango-foxtrot, ass-hole, get off my foot mother-fucker, dress-right not left shit-bird, this is a damn goat-fuck, who you calling a fucking goat, I ain't re-upping for this shit."

White Meat fell in at the rear of the line-up, dropped his head below the shoulder of the man in front of him and turned to look at Gabe. He smiled with his boyish grin and cupped a hand to hide the middle finger he aimed at Bishop. Gabe lost it and cracked up. This was much better than passing out on his lounge chair back home. If the enemy could see they would throw in the towel and surrender.

Bishop slowly strode through the ranks, looking like a young General Patton who had swapped a riding crop for a notepad. He stopped after every other soldier and wrote on the pad. With a satisfied smirk, he marched to the front of the formation.

"I did not say at ease." He pointed at Dark Meat and shouted, "PFC Jefferson, did you hear me say parade rest? Uniform infractions. PFC Sturdis, un-bloused boot. Specialist Gomez, unauthorized sunglasses. Sergeant…."

After he recapped his list of the soldiers' violations, the real torture commenced. Bishop, in an unwavering voice, delivered a monologue at a mind-numbing, tortoise pace. "Soldiers of the 82nd Airborne, 5th Brigade Combat Team, combat outpost 6, this is a very special day. It is an important day in the history of our republic, and an important day to…uh, where is my note…disregard. Before we begin the planned festivities I want to read from a speech General David Petraeus, Commanding General of Multi National Force, Iraq, made today at Camp Victory. First, by conducting what surely is the largest reenlistment event ever held in Iraq and perhaps in our Armed

Forces' history...."

Gabe slid farther down in his chair. Within seconds, he nodded out. Within minutes, he was snoring.

When Bishop's tone changed twelve minutes later, Gabe perked up, praying that the daunting oration had about run its course.

"...and we certainly cannot put a price on the freedoms you defend or those we are trying to help the Iraqis establish and safeguard here in the land of the two rivers."

Bishop lowered the piece of paper and said, "Gentlemen, that concludes General Petraeus' comments. Shortly we will begin — what is it Jefferson?"

"Suh, I means, Lootenant Bishop," White Meat said. "Them there two rivas... is he be talkin' about tha Missoura and Misippi, suh?"

All military order crumbled as the formation reacted to White Meat's penetrating inquiry. Bishop threw his note pad to the ground and stomped his feet like a toddler throwing a hissy fit. He placed both hands on his hips and shouted, "Order, order in my formation! That's enough. Stop laughing and straighten up. I said attention! This is not a laughing matter. This is...this...this...."

Tongue-tied, Bishop paced back and forth in front of the disintegrating formation. Finally he stopped and looked directly at White Meat. "Jefferson, in addition to your uniform demerits, I'm adding disrespect to an officer of the United States Army in direct violation of UCMJ code section...section...whatever the damn section is."

The soldiers, struggling to contain their laughter, gradually returned to attention. Dark Meat punched White Meat on his upper arm and said something to him. Grinning, White Meat turned toward Gabe and gave the 'thumbs up' sign.

"That's better," Bishop said. "Stand tall, men. Before we enjoy the bountiful feast I have prepared, I want us all to sing a few songs to get us in the proper spirit of the occasion. Sergeant Sandoval, start us out with the Star-Spangled Banner."

Cell tower 812 meters northeast of COP 6, 1904 hours

He hid the Iranian manufactured, 125cc *Arman Taksaz* motorcycle behind a dune forty meters from the cell tower. Just before he started to climb, he removed his black *dishdasha* and Nike running shoes, then placed them near the ladder.

After climbing thirty-four rungs he paused to glance southwest at the outpost. The Iraqi hurriedly curled his legs over a rung and wrapped his arm around a tower support beam. In his excitement he fumbled with the lanyard around his neck. He took several deep breaths and steadied his hand enough to grasp the Nikon binoculars and raise it level with his glasses. He turned the diopter ring to adjust for his prescription hoping to confirm what he thought he had seen. When the target came into clearer focus he froze. He released his grip on the field glasses and allowed them to drop to his chest. Then he pulled out his phone and called Dhul Fiqar. "Shoot now! All of the American soldiers are exposed in the open. Shoot, shoot, shoot!"

COP 6, 1905 hours

"...the rockets' red glare, the bombs bursting in air — "

The pressure wave blew Gabe out of the chair a millisecond before the sound rushed in and ruptured his left eardrum. Confused, he fought his temporary loss of equilibrium and uncharacteristically tried to rise up from the gravel. The second explosion inflicted the first real damage. The round landed fifteen meters behind him, well within the kill zone of a 120 mm mortar round. Fortunately, he had only risen to one knee and was below the bomb's cone of death. The blast knocked him to the ground again, pummeling him with secondary shrapnel created by shattered gravel that rocketed outward at a velocity slightly slower than the steel fragments shot out by the exploding mortar.

Cell tower located 812 meters northeast of COP 6, 1906 hours

"Drop fifty, left twenty, fire for effect," the spotter shouted into the phone.

COP 6, 1907 hours

The soldiers' harmony from the seconds before the big bang, changed to a discordant chorus of shouted warnings and expletives. "Incoming! Oh shit, incoming! Find cover!"

The third explosion lifted Gabe three feet off of the ground and blew him several meters to his left. When gravity smacked his body against the rocks, he frantically clawed through them to dig his shallow grave in the hardened earth. A block of C4, or a jackhammer, would have been needed to break through the sun-baked dirt with physical properties rivaling concrete. Wishing he was a mole, he gave up his mining dig, closed his eyes, curled up in a fetal position, reducing his signature to that of a whimpering, frightened child — exactly what he had become. He resigned his immediate future to the freakish fancy of chance, settled in for the ride and used his good ear to start the count and determine the direction and intensity of the attack.

"Three."

A few quiet seconds later, his future looked brighter. He opened his eyes and triaged the damage. Blood oozed from his legs — a good thing. Had it been an arterial spurt, things would have gotten ugly real fast. Satisfied the wounds were not life threatening and that the pain would not register until his adrenalin pump returned to the idle position, he relaxed. Nicole would be pissed about the fresh scars and he would probably need to buy a surfer style-bathing suit that extended below his knees, but he would live.

He broadened his field of vision to take in all that could be seen in his small world. His view was obstructed by trailers, blast walls and the smoke and dust kicked up by the explosions. The closest bunker was out of sight and much too far for him to risk a mad dash. Survey completed, he realized he was alone in his little space. He hoped the others had made it to safety.

He drove the pings and sparks from his brain and adopted a '*que sera, sera*' state of mind so he could continue his assessment. He loved the calming effect simple math had during times of elevated stress. Ball parking the intervals between explosions, he deduced the enemy had a mortar team of at least three, possibly four or more members. Based on their exceptional accuracy, they probably had a forward observer calling the shots.

One round short, one long, and the fact that he heard the third round's whoosh before it impacted southeast, he reasoned the enemy was zeroed in and shooting from the northwest. He had not seen the angle of the impacts' blasts, nor did he have a chance to perform a field expedient crater analysis. Therefore, he couldn't guesstimate the enemies' range or accurately compute a back-azimuth to the point of origin, or in military parlance, the POO site.

He recalled enemy tactics and outcomes from prior mortar attacks that he had weathered. History, at least from the annals of Gabe, had shown that a third of the rounds would be duds. He reasoned the bombardment would last less than two minutes since the enemy normally fired five to seven projectiles and then *didi mau* the hell out of Dodge.

With a failure rate of thirty-three percent, coupled with the three shots already taken and a maximum of seven tries to kill him, he felt much better about his chances — 7 times 33% = 2.331, minus

7 maximum rounds in an attack = 4.669, minus the 3 shots already taken = 1. 669, rounded to the nearest whole number = 2. The enemy had two more chances to kill him. Gabe could live with those odds. He loved numbers, especially when they added up to his advantage. If the insurgents rolled snake eyes, he would be able to put a couple of band-aids on and get back to his laundry in less than five minutes. He hoped hajji flunked math.

"Four! Okay, two maybe three more and it's over."

"Five! Two more and they should be duds. Gonna make it, keep it together."

"Six! That should have been a damn dud!"

"Seven! It's gotta be over now."

"Eight — shit!"

"Nine — shit!"

"Ten — shit!"

"Eleven — holy shit!"

"Twelve — fucking numbers!"

"…seventeen — shit, shit, shit…eighteen — I'm so fucked!"

"Nineteen — forgive me, Nicole, for all of the dumbass things I've done in life, especially coming to Iraq."

Then silence. Three minutes later and still silent. Five minutes later — all quiet.

Gabe rolled over on his back and managed to sit upright. Encouraged, but still drunk from the ringing in his ears and the pain that was creeping in, he stood. He thought he was going to pass out so he stumbled three meters until he was next to the laundry shack. He leaned his back against the wall and slumped. He could feel something moist trickling down from his left ear. Arms, legs, stomach, neck and head felt like they were being pricked from the inside by scores of needles.

"All clear!" someone shouted. "Accountability check. Anyone hit?"

"Two down over here," another soldier yelled.

"Where's Gabe? Anyone see Gabe?"

Just as his mind was about to slide into a dark place he saw White Meat corner a trailer forty meters from him.

"I sees him, Sarge," White Meat shouted. "Aw, Mr. Quinn, you be hit, suh. I'll help you, you jus stay put. I be comin' to you, suh. MEDIC! MEDIC!"

Cell tower, 812 meters northeast of COP 6, 1925 hours

The spotter scurried down the ladder, but in his haste he missed the last six rungs and fell hard against the ground. The sudden impact caused the trinket he was saving for his daughter as a gift to celebrate the end of *Ramadan* to fall from his pocket. Recovered from his fall, he put on his Nikes and *dishdasha*. When he stood he saw a glint on top of the sand near the ladder. He reached down and brushed the sand away from the Mickey Mouse necklace. He picked it up and then ran to the motorcycle.

Dry riverbed, 4565 meters northwest of COP 6, 1926 hours
Dhul Fiqar saw smoke rising from the desert four and a half kilometers southeast. The attack was finished. He was about to order his team to break down the mortar when he saw the damaged round laying near the tube. He went to it and with both hands, hefted the twenty-eight pound projectile to his shoulder. Body bowed down by the weight, he steadied it with his hand and took several erratic steps toward the *Hadid* 120 mm. He carefully lowered the instrument of death to the sand.

The four cell members looked at him questioningly. He pointed to the youngest, who also happened to be a dolt, and said, "You."

Dhul Fiqar, and the three men not chosen, backed away fifty meters and crouched behind the police SUV.

Dhul Fiqar shouted, "Shoot."

The young Iraqi struggled with the round, first lifting it to his bent knees, and then lumbered to raise it against his chest. Muscles strained from the weight of the missile, he balanced it precariously on the tube's end. Before he propped the round vertical on the edge of the weapon, he looked at his *Jaish al Mahdi* comrades and yelled, "*Allahu akhbar.*" Holding the bomb with both hands, he turned his head away and dropped it down the barrel.

The mortar tube had been set at a sixty-five degree quadrant elevation. After the round completed its short, one-point-seven-six meter slide to the gun's base, the donut shaped propellant charges ignited. The detonation at the base of the mortar sounded the typical 'thoommf,' associated with this type of an indirect fire weapon system. The expanding gas shot the bullet out at an initial muzzle velocity of three hundred-eighteen meters per second.

Normally a *Hadid* 120 mm launched a projectile flat, that is, no spin. This weapon, however, because of the scoring inside the tube caused at the point of manufacture, took on the characteristics of a rifled mortar. The one bent fin on the bomb also caused anomalies

235

in its predicted flight path. The round had been manufactured as a *fin-stabilized* shell. When it had been dropped, bending the one fin, it took on the properties of a *spin-stabilized* bomb. These two factors caused the round to rotate through the barrel and exit as a spinning bullet much like a sniper's bullet does when shot through a rifle.

Since the round exited as a spinning projectile, versus a flat one, the 'Magnus' effect kicked in. The trajectory of the bomb drifted perpendicular to the spin axis causing it to follow a curved flight path. The normal yaw angle of three degrees and pitch rate of one point eight rads per second were dramatically altered. When it reached its maximum altitude of three thousand four hundred and eighty-seven meters it had already drifted two degrees right of its projected trajectory.

Because the wind was calm, thereby having no effect as a correcting variable aerodynamic coefficient, the bullet continued to drift right as it plummeted to earth after reaching its apex. Had both the round and mortar barrel been pristine, the bomb would have followed its predetermined flight path and landed outside of the outpost's perimeter walls. Had the fuse been a graze or inertia type, instead of a super quick contact fuse, it would have detonated when it brushed against the CAT-5 wire strung above and between the dining trailer and the TOC. Had the initial quadrant elevation been forty-five degrees, instead of sixty-five, most of the fragmentation would have been wasted, either directed downward into the ground or upward in the air.

Had the butterfly been splattered against a car windshield in Beijing on May 4th, instead of surviving to flap its wings on May 5th, hurricane Katrina would have missed New Orleans on August 29th. Maybe.

Sycamore Inn at Williamson, eighteen miles from Inez, Kentucky

Ruftus picked up the pompons from the easy chair next to the room's vinyl replacement window and placed them on the mobile-home quality, simulated wood-veneer covered particleboard desk. Recalling golden memories from his former life, he smiled as he squished a roach that skittered across the carpet. Then he squeezed his butt down, around and over the chair. He couldn't bend over enough to untie his shoes, so she helped. Ten minutes later, in the midst of her, 'hey, hey what do you say, shish-coom-ba' cheer, Ruftus exploded.

Cabana behind a Georgian-style mansion, Kenwood community near Chicago, Illinois

The senator found the cigarettes he had secreted in the towel drawer and was enjoying his third, uninterrupted smoke. The legal pad set on the table in front of him included a list of seventeen survivors. He had already lined through twenty-one other book titles that just didn't have pizzazz.

Suddenly his eyes widened when he had a flash of genius. He quickly penned a real attention grabber that shouted, 'I'm the one, I've arrived, read me, vote for me!' He dropped the pen on the tabletop and grabbed the matchbook, but the cerebral exhilaration was too much to bear — he couldn't control his shaking hands enough to light the cigarette. His brain's chemical synapses overdosed. He exploded.

Auberge Du Soleil Resort, Napa Valley, California

Madame Speaker tilted the *Riedel Montrachet*, twenty-four percent lead crystal stemware under her nose and carefully swished the liquid around the broad bowl to take in its sensory titillating, aromatic bouquet. It was her fourth glass of the richly colored red with exquisitely proportioned tannins that enhanced its astringent qualities. The *vite vino* gave her a tingly sensation that triggered her collagen-injected lips to pucker even more.

The wine had eased the swelling of her forehead and the pain was nearly gone. She was determined to find a new physician, one with a delicate touch, quieter bedside manner, and of course, a registered Democrat.

As soon as she saw it she knew it had to be hers. She spun the bottle around in anticipation until she found the numbered black seal.

"Oh, my God," she gasped.

Her right hand involuntarily leaped to her breast with a whoosh. She commanded the *sommelier* to uncork the valued treasure. Although it was not from her winery, she could not resist sipping the wonderful Spanish *Gran Reserva,* one of the few wines worthy of *Denominación de Origen Calificada* status. The whisper of the grape's nectar across her tongue and palate was heavenly. Madame Speaker's taste buds exploded.

Brentwood Estates near Hollywood, California

Steve dropped the phone and exploded in her mouth.

Beach house, Santa Monica, California

Chaz was a versatile lover, so today he was pitching. Temporarily relieved from the enormous pressures of preparing a mental draft of his Oscar acceptance speech, and not having to worry about make-up or lighting, he concentrated on action. He exploded all over Roger's back.

Breakers Resort Hotel, Suite 1103, Myrtle Beach, South Carolina

Amber stared at the ceiling and wondered if Cialis was less potent than Viagra. Bonar pulled out and exploded on her belly for the fourth time.

LA 2 dorm trailer, Forward Operating Base Adder, Iraq

The open-shelf bralette with the caged lace panties and garter belt proved to be the magic bullet. Major Laddick yanked one of her dangling earrings, ripping through her ear lobe.

Lieutenant Lutz screamed.

Major Laddick exploded.

COP 6, shower trailer

Sergeant Knowles exhausted the hand lotion and had switched to shampoo. His face turned Japanese. The shower stall erupted in an explosion of bubbles.

Clearing across from the Royal Street Junkyard, Mobile, Alabama

The sixth longshoreman of the day didn't mind that the crack whore's cooter was dried up. He discovered necrophilia worked better with a lubricant, so he carried, in addition to the ligature, Vaseline. Yet even with the petroleum-based jelly, it took him more than an hour to explode inside the corpse of Jeremiah's mother.

COP 6, 1926 hours and 23 seconds

Gabe heard the air sliced by the earth bound mortar shell. Instead of following his instinct to get low and hit the dirt, he looked to the sky. At first, it was a mere speck, smaller than a diving gnat. A split second later, it had grown to the size of a football. Just before it impacted, he thought it had swelled larger than the Chicxulub asteroid that ended the Cretaceous period sixty-five million years ago.

During his rag-doll flight, or possibly when he slammed against the blast wall, he was knocked unconscious. Bits of gravel, metal shavings the size of microscopic flecks and fingernail sized steel splinters riddled his flesh. The largest gash was made by a piece of leg bone.

Gabe stirred back into a disoriented reality seconds, maybe minutes later, he did not know. Blinking rapidly to flush the sand and cordite from his eyes, he fought back against the work crew pounding sledgehammers inside of his head. Then he forced his muscles and bones to roll his battered body over from his back to his side. Peering through the flames, smoke and falling sand, he saw him. Gabe clawed at the gravel and crawled several meters before he detected any movement from him.

"Jefferson," he whispered.

White Meat tried to go to his knee. He pushed off the ground with his left hand and dug his knee into the gravel for leverage. He managed to get half way up before falling. Again he tried, this time planting his charred left arm and the stump of his other into the gravel. For a second, he was almost erect. The one-sidedness caused by his missing right leg toppled him.

Gabe rose to an unsteady crouch and leaned against the blast wall for support. Back arched, legs straightened, he managed a tenuous standing position. Then he shoved off of the wall and leaned forward to gain momentum so as not to crash to the ground again. He closed the gulf separating him from Jefferson with a drunken gait. Almost close enough to reach out and touch him, Gabe stumbled over something and fell. He elbowed his way nearer and managed to roll him over.

White Meat tried to smile, but with half of his face missing, he could only manage a slurred whisper.

Gabe inched closer and placed his good ear near his lips. "What, Jefferson?"

Before White Meat died, Gabe thought he heard him say, "Momma."

He looked away from the dead soldier to the object that had tripped him. It was Jefferson's severed arm. Inked below the elbow was a heart-shaped tattoo that read, *Mom & Jeremiah Forever*.

He was about to pass out. Frustrated with his failing senses, he pulled a crushed pack from his unlaced boot. He freed one of the flattened smokes, raised it to his lips and pulled matches from the pack. He tried to light it, but blood had thoroughly saturated the tobacco. He gave up on the cigarette and let his mind absorb what it was trying to forget — White Meat.

No doubt, Americans were busy celebrating, firing up the grills, shooting fireworks, hitting the booze, giving patriotic speeches. Some of the few who had skin in the game may have taken a moment

239

to think about those fighting in faraway lands. Yet, Gabe believed most Americans were focused on their trivial, invented troubles and could not give a rat's ass that nineteen-year-old, Private First Class Jeremiah Jefferson, made his mark in blood on the sands of Iraq, Independence Day, 2007. If they had any thoughts at all about the war, they were niggardly, egocentric and lacked any empathy for the thousands of Jeremiahs who had made the ultimate sacrifice on their behalf. Who could blame them, though. The soldiers were volunteers and too stupid to get a real job.

The only people who would grieve the death of a scrawny cracker from Alabama were his brothers in arms at combat outpost 6, and if they had known, maybe the village children whose lives he had saved — and surely his mother. White Meat's epitaph would be a fast, scrolling blurb across the bottom of some cable network's news broadcast. Even then, it would be a number. Just a number.

Almost delusional before he blacked out, he mustered enough strength to whisper to an imaginary audience — an audience, that in his mind, was almost as contemptible as the enemy.

"America — his name was Jeremiah."

Chapter 19
Meat glue

Captain Kowalewski picked up the cracked picture frame from the floor, blew off the ashes and plucked glass shards from around the inside edge. He placed the photograph on the remnants of his desk, then looked regretfully at the singed images — his strawberry blondes — Sarah, and her smaller version, Brianna. He turned from his family and waded through the twisted and torn debris to the inferno raging inside the communications office.

Bussard cursed as he sprayed fire retardant at the base of the flames licking the wall behind the radios. Contents depleted, he threw the extinguisher on the melted linoleum floor, grabbed the last charged one and emptied it. Then he pulled off his shirt and beat the fire away from the stacked radio equipment. Exhausted, he turned from the blaze and saw Ski.

"Sir, all satellite communication's fried. Sandoval got a nine-line CASEVAC out to Echo on VHF. He's in contact with the inbound MEDEVACs. Should be here now. Sir, did you hear me? Captain, you okay?"

Oblivious to the danger surrounding him, Ski stared at the soldier. He turned away and slogged through the foam and crackling cinders to the exit. The door, looking more like aluminum Swiss cheese than a portal, hung precariously canted. He barely touched the knob, still it broke free from its feeble anchors and fell. The captain stepped over it and went into the night.

wump...wump...wumP...woMP...wOMP...WOMP... WOMP...WOMp...WOmp...Wump...wump...wup...WOMP... WOMP...

womp...womp....

His boonie hat was sucked into the vortex and sailed up toward an OH-58 Kiowa racing across the outpost pulling pedal turns in a low

241

sweeping pattern. He saw two Blackhawks hovering a kilometer to the north, their red crosses barely discernible in the darkening sky. A thousand feet higher and several kilometers to the northeast, infrared countermeasure pyrophoric flares shot out in multiple clusters from a lumbering AH-64 Apache flying top cover for the defenseless MEDEVACs.

Isolated pockets of flames enveloped the camp in a pallid cloud of smoke. Staccato sounds of outgoing rounds mixed with the helicopter's beating roar and soldiers' shouts. Like a rootless specter, Second Lieutenant Bishop materialized out of the fire's miasma and iridescent shadows.

"Captain Kowalewski, several of the men cussed and called me an LLMF. They won't follow my orders to police up cigarette butts around my dining facility and my inventory has conclusively shown someone pilfered toilet paper supplies. I've started a detailed list of their violations and the shortages. Captain, I — "

WHOP...WHOP...WHOP...whop...Whop...Wup...wup

Bishop closed his eyes against the wind-charged granules, held the hat tight against his head and bent nearer to the ground to escape the whirling eddies formed by the Kiowa's low pass.

Ski sauntered by him to the nearest inner perimeter tower. He hunched down to clear its opening and climbed forty-five metal steps to the top landing.

From his elevated parapet, he watched the July Fourth celebration in full swing. Soldiers in a gun truck on the west side lit up the night with tracers fired in long bursts from its fifty-caliber. To the southeast, another was killing sand and rocks with 40 mm high explosive grenades lobbed from a MK19. The noise oscillated in multiple sonic booms, as other soldiers joined in the revelry ripping the air with lead from long and short spurts shot from their M249s and M4s. Several soldiers illuminated the desert with star parachute and white cluster rounds fired from M203s. Shadows created by the slower falling parachute flares drew more fire from the paratroopers.

The untold number of bushes, boulders, scorpions and spiders slaughtered reached genocidal levels. The enemy was never there. The sound of the gunfire was sprinkled with the shouts of frightened soldiers and some others wanting payback — "Check fire, at your nine, shoot at your nine, I don't see nothing, put out the fire, the fuel bladder's ruptured, it's gonna blow!"

Beyond the north perimeter, headlamps raced and bumped through the darkness across the rock-strewn sand. As soon as the lead vehicle shuddered to a stop, several soldiers jumped out to prep the area for the extraction. One popped green smoke and threw the canister to a clear patch of the desert while two others ringed the impromptu landing zone (LZ) with blue Chem Lights. Another waved green Cyalume light sticks and guided the cautious UH-60 pilot for his approach. The chopper flared, nose raised in a combat assault landing.

Three more Humvees stopped sixty meters from the waiting aircraft. Once the helo touched down, drivers toggled go-light joysticks. The white light cast the LZ in a ghostly pallor of churning sand and made the chopper a silhouetted, sitting duck. A security team dispersed around the site and blindly pointed their weapons toward the non-existent enemy.

More soldiers pulled two stretchers from a truck retrofitted as an ambulance. The litter-bearers crouched low against the blast furnace rotor wash, while medics, holding IVs, stood over the wounded. Both litter teams hustled to the MEDEVAC.

The aircrew quickly took the stretchers from the soldiers and secured them to the deck of the bird. The crew chief spoke into his microphone and flashed the thumbs up sign toward the cockpit. He looked at the wounded warriors' buddies and raised his hand in a quick, smart salute. In less than a minute, the chopper and the damaged human cargo were airborne.

The second DUSTOFF repeated the landing procedure. Soldiers hefted the dead weight of the zippered, black sack and ran through swirling silica to the high-pitched whine of the aircraft. The aircrew snatched the body bag and tossed it on the floor of the chopper like garbage instead of a fallen hero.

A dark giant, with what looked like a toy gun hanging low across his massive back, reached inside and yanked a crewman to the sand. As the hulk was about to stomp on the prostrate aviator, two soldiers hit him with body slams.

The obscure flyboy, face hidden behind a full helmet visor, stood and brushed off his flight suit. The giant engaged him in a highly gesticulated exchange. The chastened aviator scampered back inside the flying ambulance followed by the mocha-colored colossus. The oversized soldier sat cross-legged, placed his hands on the dead warrior and bowed his head.

The moment the portside door closed, the pilot pulled up hard on the collective and the pitch of the twin-turbo engines intensified. Shuddering, the chopper shot up as the pilot gained altitude to clear the blowing sand. He pushed the cyclic forward — the rotating meat cleavers bit into the desert air and grabbed vital airspeed. Fighting gravity with added power, the pilot gained enough elevation to dip the chopper's nose and transition to forward flight. Within minutes, the helicopters were out of the range of small arms fire, RPGs and nervous GIs.

Ski stared at the blinking red lights until they disappeared from sight. Once again, calm ruled the airspace above the outpost. Chaos still reigned on the ground. Someone shouted at him. His thoughts turned from heaven to the earth as he strained to see the distraction beneath the low hanging smoke. Before he descended the stairs, he looked above the western wall at the darkness blanketing the horizon.

"Sir, one KIA, three WIA," Knowles said. "White Meat's dead. I gave Dark Meat permission to accompany his body to Adder. Specialist Johnson, PFC Vitters and Gabe, wounded. Johnson's ambulatory, probably spend a few weeks at the base camp hospital before he returns to duty. Vitter's war is over. After he's stabilized he'll be headed to Landstuhl."

Ski looked beyond the sergeant to the smoldering operations center. Indifferent to the sergeant's presence, the captain returned his gaze to the empty night smothering the outpost.

Knowles searched the hazy blackness as if trying to see what fascinated him. "Gabe refused to leave, sir. He's afraid of heights."

Brigade TOC, Forward Operating Base Adder, July 4, 2040 hours

The sixteen-foot-wide digital screen, split between a large pixilated map of the task force area of operations in southern Iraq and a smaller fifty-kilometer square grid surrounding the lonely outpost, covered the wall of the electronics alcove. Static one moment, hopping the next, four blue helicopter symbols moved away from the outpost toward the base camp. Within minutes, they faded from the boundary of the smaller map and slipped inside the edge of the base camp's air space. The map encircling the isolated encampment disappeared, replaced by a depiction of Adder's multiple grids.

Non-stop chatter inside the operations center was barely audible. Some soldiers spoke in hushed tones on radios or secure phones, others updated information on the big screen through computer links. Major Phelps, the Brigade chaplain, leaned on a long desk taking notes while speaking with the liaison officer from the combat hospital.

Lieutenant Colonel Harry Simms saw Viking Warrior Six enter the top-secret room. He set the phone on the table, stepped down from the dais and rushed to meet the commander.

"Colonel, we have a developing situation at outpost six. Details are sketchy, but we took some casualties. DUSTOFFs dispatched from Echo are inbound with one KIA and some of the wounded."

"Some?" Colonel Gunnar Erickson said. "Harry, what the hell do you mean by some?"

"Gun, two soldiers and a civilian were wounded. We've got a preliminary CASEVAC report — "

"A damn civilian!" Erickson's words reverberated against the walls like the boom from a 105 mm howitzer. Conversation inside the room abruptly ceased. Eyes shifted from computers, phones and the wall mounted screen, to the two field grade officers, particularly the one holding a battle-axe.

"We've got a civilian out there? What civilian?"

"Mr. Quinn."

"Who in hell authorized him to be at my outpost?"

"According to Major Laddick, you did, sir. The order must have come down when you were at Victory meeting with Petraeus."

"Negative!" Erickson barked. "I didn't authorize Quinn or any other civilian personnel to be at any of the outposts. Get me a vehicle, Harry. When the wounded land I want to see the soldiers and Quinn."

"That could be a problem, sir. Not the vehicle, but Mr. Quinn. He's not on the chopper. Something about he's afraid of flying."

"Damn chicken-shit!" Erickson hoisted *Brynhildn* from his side and held her close to his chest. Caressing the gleaming, Norse blade, he turned from his executive officer and set his sights on the staff. The stunned soldiers averted his angry glare and returned to their tasks.

The pissed-off colonel spoke to his XO in a low, raspy voice, "I still need the vehicle. I'll sort out this cluster fuck about Quinn later. Harry, how bad are my boys hurt?"

COP 6, July 4, 2007, 2042 hours

Mimicking a racehorse doped on elephant juice, a soldier zipped past the sergeant and Ski. Knowles yelled at the disoriented, galloping Mexican, "Over here, Speedy."

The combat medic altered course on the run and sprinted toward the sergeant. He slid to a stop sending gravel flying toward the pair.

"Where the fuck do you think you're going, Gonzalez?" Knowles said.

"*Yo iba a buscar usted!*" Gonzalez blurted. "*Tenemos grandes problemas, el sargento!*"

245

"Speak American damnit," Knowles said. "You're not in the *barrio,* home-boy!"

"*Si, sargento*! I speek *Inglés.*

"How's Gabe?" Knowles asked.

"I make *Señor* Gabe okay for now, but he neez to had be *pasado* on zee *helicóptero.*" Panting heavily, the specialist continued, "He eez say some crazy *gringo* sheet about zee war be here and if he leevz he eez never come back. *Sargento*, he eez a fool in zee head."

"Is he going to die, Speedy?"

"He eez hurt purty bad but he eez no go to *muerto. Jesús Cristo sargento*, theez eez a fokking outpost and me no real doctor. *Dios mío*, I only can do some theenz — "

"Well get it done and quit your damn bellyaching!"

"*Si sargento*, but he eez *loco*. He eez yell somzing about putting he back together with meat glue. *Sargento*, what eez theez fokking meat glue he eez talk about? What you want me to do — "

"Find some fucking meat glue and put him back together." Knowles turned from Gonzalez and faced Ski. "I'll get a nine-line to Brigade about the casualties and follow up later with a battle damage assessment. Captain Ski — "

The captain looked at the winded medic and smiled. "It's a beautiful evening. Don't you agree?"

Knowles grabbed Ski's arms and forced him to look at him. A non-responsive officer stared back. Perplexed, the sergeant said, "Sir, we've got a genuine broken arrow situation here. What are your orders, Captain?"

"I must leave now and put my family back together." Ski looked away from the sergeant and again searched the ebony painted sky. "Can I have some meat glue?

Chapter 20
Maintenance

COP *6, aid station trailer, July 9, 0412 hours*

One light pulsed, its brother was dead. Gabe heard, or imagined he heard, the steady hum of excited electrons colliding with mercury atoms as they raced through the glass tube in a game of kinetic combat. Between the flickers of the trailer's one surviving fluorescent bulb, he saw a familiar sight — clean boxer shorts covering his manhood.

Resting against his chest was a vaguely familiar furry face with fixed, black button eyes. Tan colored gauze swathed his calf and a white compress was taped to the left side of his stomach. Smaller bandages, exposed sutures, bruises and bee sting-like welts dotted his chest, arms and legs.

He had survived the collisions of war. Not through skill or godly intrusion, but by the arbitrary interplay of numbers. Foiled by the calculus of space and time, the grim reaper had been cheated. A smile crossed his face — he had beaten the psychopomp again. His smile was soon replaced by a grimace. Reality crashed in. Gabe pulsed, a brother was dead.

He tabulated the scorecard. His undisciplined pursuit for information cost the lives of three young girls, a mother and a father. Because he placed himself in a time and a space he didn't need to be, Jeremiah Jefferson had been ripped apart. Since he was exactly where and when he needed to be, Colucci, Nieves and Poppins lived. Six to three, not a noble accounting in games or war. Something was missing from the balance sheet. It was time for a reckoning, a dead reckoning with the enemy.

Gabe swung his feet over the bed's edge to the floor. He yanked the needle and tube from his arm letting loose a trickle of blood and pus to the floor. Then he pushed up from the mattress. Favoring the good leg with most of his weight, he stumbled toward the door.

Specialist Gonzalez stirred, then raised his head from the desk.

"Señor Quinn, *que quieres?* Eez no *bueno por tu pasado. Tu eres bién chingado."*

Gabe stopped and looked through drooping eyelids at the medic. He turned away from the soldier and opened the door.

"Señor Quinn, *alto!"*

"Gotta piss."

He broadened the slit in his underwear and dribbled a thin, reddish-yellow rivulet to the rocks below. Eyes heavy from the weight of drugs coursing through his veins, he teetered at the door frame.

Gonzalez was at his side. He wrapped an arm around Gabe's waist then helped him struggle back to the bed.

Gabe fell backward on the mattress, legs suspended in mid-air over the edge. Gonzalez lifted his patient's battered legs up to lay flat on the sheet, and then covered him with fresh linen. Finally, he placed the teddy bear beside his ward's head.

Gabe's hooded, vacant stare, like that of a cannery row drunk, was only broken by sleep — a deep sleep that lasted for forty hours.

COP 6, aid station trailer, July 10, 2007, 2012 hours

Unforgettable smells seeped into his clouded, stimuli-deprived, hypnopompic state. He crossed over consciousness' threshold and opened his eyes. Gabe saw a man sitting next to the bed.

A cigarette stuck between the man's nicotine stained fingers, filled the small room with a pungent, yet to an addict, sensory pleasing, caustic blue smoke. The other aroma emanated from a golden liquid he swirled around the inside of a glass tumbler.

"Bloody good, mate," Dawud said. "You have rejoined the living, none the worse for wear. In fact, with the pounds you've shed I can most certainly fit you in a forty regular now."

"Dawud, wha-what day is it?"

"Night, actually. Tuesday, July tenth, my good man. It's the night you get out of bed and join a remarkably sophisticated cohort in a toast to your long overdue transformation."

Dawud reached inside the jaws of a tanned alligator skin shoulder purse and rescued a silver flask. He poured two fingers worth of the liquid into another tumbler and held the glass up to the sputtering light.

"Ah, its brazen luminescence," Dawud said. "Ambrosia worthy of the gods, infused with rich and indulgent toffee sweetness. For months, this exceptional twenty-one year old, single malt Scotch was finished in barrels that once ferried rum from the Caribbean. The oaken casks were fabricated, some say, from the very same stock used by your infamous rumrunner of yesteryear, the Baptist bootlegger. The story of why the Irish Catholic patriarch to the Kennedy clan was labeled a Baptist is fascinating."

He leaned toward Gabe and handed him the drink. "Cheers, mate."

Gabe sat up in the bed and accepted the offering. He downed the contents in a single gulp. Before the burning liquor cleared the frenulum at the base of his tongue, he gagged. Eyes glowed wide and hot as he suffered an extended coughing fit. He managed to sputter one word between his spate of coughs and gasps. "Smooth."

"Nurture it, Gabe. William Grant aspired to create the best dram in all of Glenfiddich valley, and he did. True appreciation of an exquisite enemy of lucidity requires one to sneak up on it, not heroically charge like the ill-fated Light Brigade. Don't swill like a common bloke."

Dawud took the tumbler from Gabe's trembling hand, poured slightly less than two fingers and returned it to him.

"How in the hell did you get alcohol in this place, Dawud? General order one prohibits — "

"Gabe, never underestimate the prowess of gentility. Fools' rules need not apply equitably. We may be in uncivil surroundings, and certainly embroiled in an ungentlemanly war, but you cannot strip a nobleman of all comfy delights and expect him to uphold any measure of courtliness."

"I'm not questioning your lineage." Gabe sipped the liquor, yet still coughed. "I didn't come from nobility, but reared well enough, I guess. I'm used to cheap wine and cheaper rum. Jesus Christ, Dawud, this stuff, it's fantastic. You here to give me some bad news, or just to get me drunk?"

"Perhaps both. We shall see. That fine young man, White Meat, the poor lad, well...I think you know," Dawud lamented. "Several others were injured. The good news is we now have a new operations trailer with a functioning air conditioner. It arrived two days ago on a convoy from Adder along with Dark Meat, a mortar team and their rather impressive, but thunderously loud gun. The big gun brings up another topic, Gabe."

"What topic?"

"Hmm, how do I address this delicate subject with a modicum of decorum? Almost around the clock for the past several days you have been tended by Bussard, and after his return, Dark Meat. You seemingly made a positive impression on those young lads.

Completely understandable. I have taken a liking to you myself. In your days of unintentional turpitude, you lounged in bed quite exposed to all passer-bys. Also reasonable, given your present physical and mental condition. I am not a connoisseur of the forbidden arts, but I am not blind to them either. Gabe, as measurements go, you are… shall I say, slightly above average, but nothing extraordinary. Usually I am a word meister, but how can I phrase this euphemistically? How about…your *down under* does not merit porn star status. Perhaps, when mustered to duty it rises to the occasion, but — "

Gabe laughed hard, then winced and reflexively placed a hand on his stomach. Fighting through the pain, he smiled and said, "I'm sure my wife would agree with your paltry assessment. My dad's sperm count was low when my number came up, so the biggest, best and brightest had already left the gene pool. With fewer competitors, my little swimmer caught a break and won gold. Where in hell is this going, Dawud?"

"I cannot fathom why, but you seem to be quite the ladies man. The fairest wench I have ever seen, I daresay an angel, accompanied the new trailer from the base camp. She seemed quite smitten with you and overly concerned about your trifling injuries. Unfair, chap, really quite reproachable. Disgustingly unsporting to conjure up a few wounds to tip the odds in favor of oneself. I relentlessly fawned over the lass but she ignored all of my wily, calculated ministrations and snubbed me as if I were a gelded puissant or a solemn court jester. You must tell me how you won the favors of such a delectable creature like Lieutenant Loving."

Stumped by his exposé, Gabe said, "Loving? Lieutenant Loving?" He smiled when he remembered his brief encounter with the enchantress, Mira. "Let me get this straight. You make a pun about my privates, and you want me to give it up. I'll drink your Scotch, also wouldn't mind one of your cigarettes since you're in a gift mode, but the secret? Ain't happening, my friend."

Dawud lit a cigarette and handed it to him. "I assumed as much. Ah, but the saga continues and becomes ever more intriguing. Four days ago, a military police convoy in transit to Adder from Camp Cropper stopped by. Another beautiful vixen, indeed a diminutive Sophia Loren, was unquestioningly, yes I would say, thoroughly overwhelmed, by your fabricated predicament. Tears flowed from her eyes as she watched you pitch and roll about the bed in your delirious state. I believe she would have comforted you under the sheets if not for the handcuffs. And before the guards pulled her away, she managed to kiss your forehead and imparted an extended gift on your unappreciative lips. Passion wasted. Absolutely a senseless crime against mankind. I get chills in my…well, the anatomical specifics are unimportant. She also left you the stuffed animal. Apparently, it held some sentimental value for her. Colucci, I believe. Yes, Specialist Colucci."

"Jersey Girl," Gabe said. "I've got to help her."

"Gabe, you are in no condition to help anyone. The order of the day is get well. After you heal, then, by all means, rescue the fair damsel in distress. I will enlist in your chivalrous cause as a loyal servant, and together we will slay the evil that haunts her."

"Thanks, Dawud. I wish it were that easy."

"You had another visitor who was also quite distraught over your current pickle. Hercules — "

"Hercules!" Gabe shouted. He tried to stand, but Dawud forced him back down to the bed. "Son of a bitch. Where is that little lying piece of shit?"

"Calm yourself, or you will tear out your stitches. I spoke to the young man concerning your revelation of his true religion. He seemed nonplussed by your disclosure, more concerned about your injuries. Gabe, in Muslim societies, particularly in Iraq, sectarian lines can sometimes become muddled. It is not always a black and white delineation. His explanation to me made sense. Talk to him with an open mind and an open heart. I think the man worships you. War is always difficult for the participants, but Hercules' role is much more complicated than our small part."

Dawud reached inside his bag and retrieved an unopened bottle of Glenfiddich. He placed the Scotch on the bed next to the teddy bear.

"A parting gift for a comrade and *circumspect* confidant," he said, stressing the word circumspect. "Keep it well hidden from Second Lieutenant LLMF. He wanders about our little borough like a horseless dragoon in search of his lost steed. Certainly, he is a loutish chap of dubious intelligence and breeding, nonetheless not one to engage in a squabble."

Dawud stood. "I must be on my way. Mother Nature is beckoning me to attend to scatological necessities."

When he was about to open the door, he turned around. Dawud looked over his shoulder at Gabe and said, "By the way, are you hoarding toilet tissue?"

"Huh?"

A smile snuck in at the corners of Dawud's mouth. He shook his head and said, "Forgive my folly, an inexcusable breach of etiquette. Of course, being the proper gentleman you are, never would you stoop to such an act of chicanery. Tally-ho, mate." He winked once, then was gone.

July 13, 0915 hours

Gabe hobbled down the dorm trailer's steps and hopped around a few times until his bad leg could take its share of the load. Seeing the new operations trailer, he had a ping of remorse. It had been more than a week since he had done anything to earn his keep.

Then it hit him. Neck arched back, he sniffed the air like a dog smelling a bitch in heat. Guilt forgotten, he followed his nose. The nearer he got, the stronger the aroma, the faster his pace. Sensing the reward was within his grasp, he climbed the steps as best he could and opened the door. The smell of the bean brought a smile to his face. Before he had a chance to close the door, the smile was gone.

"My dining facility is closed."

Gabe looked around the trailer until he saw the only soldiers present. Second Lieutenant Bishop, seated at a table near the kitchen, was holding a green and white lined columnar pad. Next to him, Private First Class Barton.

Gabe smiled weakly and said, "Fine." He opened the door to leave.

"Mr. Quinn," Barton said. "I can get you a cuppa coffee. Ski's orders, I mean Captain Kowalewski's, are we keep a pot brewing twenty-four hours a day."

"Great." His smile returned.

Bishop frowned at Barton and muttered something, then threw a ballpoint pen on the floor. The missile shot across the linoleum on a wild ride, stopping only when it hit Gabe's sandal.

Gabe bent down, picked up the pen and limped toward the pair. He set it in front of Bishop, turned and searched the room of empty tables to find the one farthest from the officer. Target sighted, he shuffled over and placed his assault rifle on the floor.

"Remove your hat when in my facility," Bishop ordered.

Gabe stuffed the boonie hat inside his cargo pocket, moved to the opposite side of the table and sat in a chair facing a blank wall. A featureless wall was more stimulating than the weasel holding the pen, a pen he should have shoved up his ass.

Barton brought a steaming cup of coffee. "Here you go, sir." He leaned closer and whispered, "Mr. Quinn, as soon as he leaves, I'll fix you anything you want."

"Thanks, but I'm fine with the coffee."

"PFC Barton, finish up with that civilian and get back to your military duties," Bishop said. "When I return from my rounds, I expect to see the missing five jars of mayonnaise, twelve bottles of ketchup and two cases of hamburger patties. It's my duty to insure our taxpayers' money is not wasted. Remember, I write your efficiency reports. You've been nothing but inefficient since we arrived."

On his way out, Bishop stopped at Gabe's table. He drummed his fingers against his thighs and waited.

Gabe took a long, drawn out sip of the coffee before slowly turning his head to face the officer.

"Finish the coffee, then vacate."

Gabe pushed off from the chair's plastic arms and stood. He one-handed the chair and shoved it against the table.

Bishop winced, stumbled back and dropped his hand over the holstered sidearm on his belt.

Gabe glared at the mute officer. "I don't remember pissin' in your corn flakes. What's the problem, General?"

Bishop froze.

Gabe ended the one-sided stare-down with the shocked officer. "Fine, just fine, really fine. Thanks for the coffee. Very generous of you, sir."

Bishop started to speak, but instead, slowly backed up some more until he bumped into a table. He performed a reasonable left face, skirted around tables and chairs until he reached the exit. He flung the door open, stepped through the breach and slammed it behind him.

Gabe drained the cup and readied to leave.

"Refill, sir?" Barton's smiling face hid no secrets. "The General won't be back for hours, maybe never. I think you scared the shit out of him."

"Another cup of the bean is an excellent idea. Care to join me, Private?"

"Sir, I'd love to, but you see what I'm dealing with. Gotta find the missing stuff the boss man knows blew up in the attack. I'm better off than Specialist Gomez, though. He's missing some shit paper and our leader is all over him like it was some lost fuckin' treasure."

"Small minds, big problems." Gabe chuckled. "Private, don't know if you're familiar with 'The Duke', a true American who once said, life's tough enough, even tougher if you're stupid. I think your

253

leader has had a pretty tough life. Wish I could help you, soldier."

"Thanks, but I've got it covered, sir. I'll make a fresh pot and be back with your refill."

Minutes later, Gabe heard the sound of light footsteps approaching. He turned, expecting to see Barton.

"Mister Gabriel Quinn," Hercules said, "I am so overjoyed to see you are well again, sir. I worried about your grievous condition very much. May I join you, Mister Gabriel?"

Gabe gripped the table's edge so hard his sun darkened knuckles whitened. He glared at Hercules.

"Sir, please may I join you and explain? I much regret misrepresenting myself to you, Mister Gabriel, but I had no other choice. Please, you are my friend and I much admire you. I must now tell you the truth."

"Sit."

"Thank you, Mister Gabriel." Hercules sat primly across from him, eyes downcast to the table. He looked like he was ready to pray. "It is true, sir, I am *Shi'ite*, and I am not from the village I told you. My ancestral home is al Amarah."

"Why the lies?" Gabe asked evenly.

Hercules slumped lower in the chair. Finally, he straightened and looked guiltily at him. "Mister Gabriel, I was ordered to lie by the previous commander of the camp. He was concerned about my safety and the safety of my family. He was a kind and generous man, much like you, sir."

"I'm not following you." Gabe had met his share of bullshit artists over the years, and Hercules could be just another in the long, sordid line of frauds, ready to set the hook and reel him in. Yet, Gabe's contempt transformed into curiosity.

"How does lying about your religious sect make you safe?"

"Sir, you see how I dress when we go to a village. I hide behind goggles, a *kufiya* covers my head and face, gloves over my hands. All, sir, to protect my identity. We travel in a *Shi'ite* province. Many, many bad eyes watch us as we work, sir. *Jaish al Mahdi* has eyes everywhere. If the villagers believe me to be *Sunni*, they will simply spit upon the ground and curse me. If they know I am *Shi'ite* they will see me as a traitor."

Gabe spun the empty mug on the table, silently pondering Hercules' explanation and his demeanor. The Iraqi sat straight, eyes fixed on him, no nervous twitches.

"Let's assume I buy what you're selling. I don't understand how it makes you or your family safer. You're always with soldiers when we go outside the wire. Either way, traitor or *Sunni*, you're like us and still a target."

"Yes, Mister Gabriel, you are correct. If they believe me to be *Sunni*, they will hate me, but they would not bother to search for me. They know no one would talk to them, since the *Sunni* have as much hate. If they knew, however, I was *Shi'ite*, they would begin a search to find my village. Mister Gabriel, they would find it. They would have no difficulty locating a Bedouin informant who would speak for a few *dinars*. After they found my home they would do unthinkable things to my wife and children before killing them."

"I've seen what they can do." Gabe looked beyond Hercules, to the dark and bloody bedroom, miles from the camp. He hit the tabletop knocking the coffee mug to the floor.

"They aren't animals. Animals kill to eat. They're fucking savages."

The fury Gabe heaped on Hercules, soon gave way to sagging melancholy. He bent down and picked up the mug, but before setting it on the table, he inspected the empty vessel as if it possessed some magical spell that would end the nightmare of the Afak horror. His mind raced through the events leading up to the slaughter — events that led nowhere — no answers — no resolution — just unrelenting torment. The sight of the brown, delicate man sitting in front of him flicked the internal switch and again unleashed a profound prejudice. Not an innate bias, but earned in trials by fire. Bigotry tempered and honed over years of battling in an environment that begged hatred. If Gabe could not dig deep and dredge up the powerful emotion, he could not kill. His loathing of the enemies' self-aggrandizing view of their place at the top of an iniquitous culture and their manifest sexism, fed the monster that trolled just beneath the surface.

"The girl and her parents — tortured and killed. Tell me, Hercules, you tell me how the enemy knew I questioned — "

Hercules jumped up from his chair. "Mister Gabriel, little girl? Parents? I know not what you are saying, sir."

"Butchered," Gabe shouted, "Damn, butchered like hogs." Pain be damned, he also jumped up from his chair and moved on Hercules.

"Someone told the assassins about my questions, someone who was there." Gabe's eyes focused a fury so intense it blazed through the little man's eyes to the intellect behind. He poked Hercules in the chest again, again, and again. "You, you son of a bitch...you were there."

With each jab, Hercules backed farther away from him until a table blocked his escape. "Sir, I am horrified…horrified by the tragedy. If you mean the child you spoke to at the village, many people saw you. Many *Jaish al Mahdi* and many sympathizers."

Gabe broke off the assault. He glowered at the elfin man with the dazed, panicked expression — the bewildered look of a trapped animal.

PFC Barton ran into the room. "Mr. Quinn, everything all right?"

Gabe frowned at the soldier and said, "Stay out of this."

Hercules rubbed his chest and glanced toward the exit. "Mister Gabriel, I have explained, they have eyes everywhere. Your enemy is the enemy of Iraq, also my enemy. Mister Gabriel, you know I am not trusted with a phone. Your soldiers search me each time I come to the camp and each time I leave. I could not contact anyone outside of these walls even if I wanted. *Allah* as my witness, it was not I who talked."

Gabe studied Hercules' face and body searching for tells. He was confronting either a sociopath, or an innocent man. On an intellectual level, he knew a true sociopath was rare. Law enforcement had ferreted out most. True-crime hack writers and Hollywood pimps had created more for consumption by an irrational, vicarious public. In the real world, a sociopath was about as abundant as a ten-carat pink diamond. His gut told him different — he had unearthed the pink gemstone. But logic won over intuition. Better to keep a potential enemy close and in the light, than cut him loose, only to be stabbed in the dark.

"I'm sorry I accused you, Hercules. It's just this war, this damn brutality, makes me….My friend, join me and have some coffee."

"Thank you, Mister Gabriel, but no." Hercules placed a hand over his heart and continued, "Truly sir, you are my friend and I would like to talk to you about better things, but I hope to speak with Captain Kowalewski. I have not seen him for many days. I am told he never leaves his office."

Soon after Hercules' departed, Gabe downed a third cup of coffee, pocketed a stale cookie sitting on a table and left the dining trailer. When he stepped into the bright sunlight, he saw Hercules run from the operations trailer toward the wooden toilet stalls. *Saddam's revenge must be an equal opportunity bug. No bias between natives and pork-eating crusaders.* He turned from the running man and walked toward the new operations center.

Black shipping plastic, still covering the windows, contrasted with the portable's gleaming, white walls. The building looked out of place in the sullied surroundings. Fresh, new, unscarred by war, trailer trash would have an orgasm. Another few days, its sheen would be lost, replaced by a reddish-tan desert stain. Rocks chunked from passing military vehicles would dent and scratch the sides. In less than a month, the sun would age the metal and paint ten years.

Usually a hubbub of activity, the quiet office surprised him as he stepped inside. The only sounds were static from the radios and white noise created by the air conditioner blasting balmy, sandy air. No light escaped from underneath Captain Ski's closed door. Gabe turned to leave.

"Mr. Quinn, good morning," Sergeant Knowles said as he entered through an interior door. He locked the weapons room behind him, then pointed to a chair. "I'd offer you a cup of coffee, but the pot was another casualty of the attack."

Gabe leaned his weapon against the wall and sat across from the new desk. "Where's everyone?"

"On patrol. You just missed Hercules. I'm surprised he didn't mow you down. When I told him he's on a patrol we added, he flew out of here like he just heard the hajji bazaar slashed prayer mats to half price."

"I saw him, but I think his quick exit was inspired by irritated bowel syndrome."

Knowles turned his chair to face Gabe. "Been a busy week. We've doubled the patrols to get a handle on hajjis' attacks. Not having much success. Actually, no success."

"What attacks?"

"I forgot you've been gold-bricking for a few days. Three convoys passing through hit IEDs, every one of them a damn EFP. Catastrophic kills on two of the trucks. The other, some survivors, but their moms won't recognize them."

"All were EFPs?"

"Roger."

"Lead vehicles?"

"Yes, sir," Knowles said. "How'd you know?"

"Didn't. Their rhino's, how were they set? One meter, two meters, three — "

"Don't know, Gabe. Is that important?"

"Could be if the convoys aren't switching up their tactics. Hajji sees a pattern, he adapts, he exploits, and he kills. How far from the edge of the road were the vehicles when they were hit?"

257

"Don't know."

"What about the frequency bands on their Dukes, Jukeboxes, Warlocks — "

"Gabe, slow down and ask me questions I can answer."

"Sorry, Sergeant, it's a habit. How about the routes and timing of the clearance patrols surrounding each detonation?"

"That, I can help you with. In fact, one patrol went out earlier this morning, another leaves tonight. I'll pull after action reports and a grid map and we'll walk through it."

Knowles pointed to a table cluttered with paper, empty coffee cups and empty weapons magazines. "Clear a spot on the table over there and we'll get at it."

They fleshed out the details about each explosion. Gabe used colored markers to distinguish routes and penned out a timeline for each event. The only interruption was when Barton, the resourceful camp cook, delivered fresh coffee and a stack of 'missing' burgers that leaked 'missing' mayonnaise and ketchup.

Three hours later, his brain overloaded and fatigued, Gabe put down the marker and stroked his mustache. Seconds became minutes. He placed his elbows on the table and rested his head in his palms. More minutes ticked away.

Then he connected the dots. He rapped his finger on the map and blurted, "Son of a bitch! Do you see it, Sergeant? The pattern?"

Knowles leaned in closer and focused on the points Gabe drummed. "All I see are a bunch of colored lines and your scribbles."

Questioning his own findings, Gabe leaned back in his chair. He returned to stable footing and again looked at the map, then grabbed a red marker and drew large circles around checkpoints eighteen-alpha north and nine-bravo south. "It ain't much, but it could be enough. Each attack was at the opposite end of the patrols' route. If a patrol cleared north, hajji hit south. All of the attacks are clustered around these checkpoints."

"All right, that I can see. Could be just coincidence."

"Maybe, but what else we got? The checkpoints have decent ratlines running east and west. The terrain provides good over-watch positions. Afak and Hajil a Bas are nearby. Both villages are under the boot of *Jaish al Mahdi* and probably have weapon caches. Each has direct access to ASR Boston and sit on MSR Tampa, giving them multiple escape routes."

"Agreed. But how does hajji know the direction and times of our patrols?"

Gabe hesitated. He did not know. So he ticked through what he did know. "The information isn't coming from here. The soldiers aren't about to tell hajji and evidently terps can't. Enemy must have spotters calling out once they fix a patrol's direction. Duration of the patrol, turnaround points — they've studied your tactics for a month. They also see patterns, Sergeant."

"If you're right, what do we do about it?"

"Sun Tzu wrote 'all warfare's based on deception.' Unfortunately, another gook, Nguyen Giap, studied history and used Sun Tzu's tactics to bloody our nose in Vietnam. We can read too, Sergeant. Change things up a little and mess with hajji's head. He isn't a linear thinker like us — brain's wired different. If you understand the distinction, you can exploit the weakness. Hajji screws up and becomes predictable, we'll savor a smell sweeter than summer jasmine — dead enemies."

"I'm with you on that one. We need to smell something besides burning shit."

Knowles poured over the map, studying the topographical features, roads and villages. He grabbed one of Gabe's cigarettes and used it as a substitute for a ruler. After he measured the distance between the far-flung checkpoints, he said, "I'd need a whole other platoon to pull it off. We'd need a doable CONOP (concept of operation), that covered both locations simultaneously."

Gabe rubbed his eyes, then stared at the captain's closed door. "We should probably get Ski in on this. Is he in?"

"Yes and no," Knowles said. "While you've been laid up, he's been out to lunch. I've set up an interim shadow command with Sergeant Sandoval to keep things running, but we can't cover for the captain much longer. We let the second lieutenant think he's the one in charge. Keeps him happy and occupied, also keeps him from getting soldiers killed. If Bishop were really in command, someone would frag his ass." Knowles smiled. "Probably me."

"Uh, Sergeant, you'd better get at it before me. What's his problem?"

"Dunno what's buzzing inside his little bird brain." Knowles dropped his smile. "Been getting all kinds of questions about Ski from Brigade. Also several about you."

Gabe stiffened. "What?"

"Viking Warrior Six wants your ass back at Adder as soon as you're good to travel. I've handled it and can probably put him off a day or two, but — "

"I'm ready to get out on patrol again, and a week…a week could be enough. Can you buy me one week?"

"Done. You just experienced a relapse. Goin' on patrol is another matter. Brigade ever gets wind of it…I'll have some serious explaining to do."

"Appreciate your covering for me, but send me out on a patrol. Just as a non-combatant observer. I gotta see if an idea works. I can visualize the broad strokes, just can't finesse the finer brush work."

"Let's hear it."

Gabe thought he had the measure of the man sitting next to him, but also knew he could be wrong. Tactics presented to a professional soldier by an outsider could fall flatter than a runway model's chest. Sometimes it was better to tactfully nudge one to an idea, rather than shove. If the plan were Knowles', he would be inclined to action it.

"Cancel the patrol for tonight. Reschedule for tomorrow night. Late tomorrow night, darker the better. Just before you SP, double the patrol from three vehicles to six. Patrol heads south lighting up the highway with the go-lights. Five or ten clicks out, a vehicle has an issue — flat tire, overheating or even just a routine piss break, doesn't matter. Then — "

"I'm with you." Knowles grinned. "The patrol stops, lights out, dicks around for a few minutes, lights back on, but only half of the vehicles."

"Damn brilliant, Sergeant."

Knowles tapped his finger rapidly on the northern checkpoint. In his excitement, he spilled his coffee on the stack of after action reports. Ignoring the mess, he said, "The lead element pushes south. The rear element goes dark, switches to NODs, flips a bitch and heads north toward checkpoint eighteen-alpha north. It finds suitable defilade off road near a ratline, sets up an OP and waits."

"You're a genius. Simple plan, easily actioned." Gabe wondered why he had questioned the sergeant's ability to see a way to rain down some steel and pain on the enemy. The sergeant's plan was not as good as he envisioned. It was better. Sun Tzu would be proud.

Still grinning, Knowles studied Gabe's face, and then looked down at the grid map. He raised his head. Stone-faced, he said, "You gotta promise me something."

"Name it, Sergeant."

"If the shit hits the fan, you were never there. No hero shit, nothing. You go to ground and disappear. I only have a few more years to make twenty. I wouldn't do well faking it as a civilian."

260

"Sergeant, there's not a single civilian stateside who could hold a candle to you. As to the hero stuff, I'm the biggest coward in Iraq. If things go south, I'll be cowering behind the biggest boulder, near the biggest soldier with the biggest gun, making myself the smallest candy-ass in country."

Knowles chuckled. "Right answer, Gabe."

"Any chance I can see Ski and find out what the problem is?"

"Unless you've got some whiz-bang magic, you'd be wasting your time."

"Just so happens....Do you think you can keep Bishop clear of the TOC for a few hours?"

"No problem. I'll get one of the boys to tell him Brigade called and wanted to know why he hasn't updated the DA forms ID dash ten dash T. Our Boy Scout will go bug-fuck thinkin' he screwed up and come a yellin' at me for the forms. I'll tell him we're out, maybe some in the storage shed."

"I'll need more than a few minutes with Ski. What if he finds them right away?"

"Ain't gonna happen." Knowles handed him a piece of scrap paper. "Write down the form number without dashes."

As instructed, he wrote ID10T. "Sergeant, you're good."

Gabe looked at his watch. "It's five o'clock in Sri Lanka. Back in a few minutes."

Chapter 21
forty-seven

COP 6, July 13, 1545 hours

Gabe returned with a patrol pack hanging from his shoulder by one strap. Seated at his desk, Knowles drew a broad line through the top entry on the duty roster white board, and then wrote 'mission scrubbed.'

Gabe walked to a trashcan and rummaged through it until he found two empty water bottles. He placed them on the table and withdrew the boot dagger from the rucksack. After he removed its scabbard, he started carving the first bottle. He glanced between his hasty knife art and Knowles busily adding names, times and the checkpoints for the next evening's patrol. Handiwork finished, he stuck the makeshift drinking cups in the bag, and then leaned over Knowles still revising the white board. The sergeant had not posted details of the dark patrol's real mission.

"Sergeant, okay to see Ski now?"

"Have at it."

He picked up the bag and walked to the closed door. He knocked lightly — nothing. He knocked harder, but still no sound from the other side. He placed an ear against the door, then turned the knob until the latch barely cleared the strike plate. Easing the door open, he peered through the gap into the dark room. Pushing more, light from the lobby area combined with a faint red glow flickering inside of Ski's office.

"Captain, can I come in?"

He opened the door all the way, showering the room with reflected, fluorescent light. The red safety exit sign fixed above the door went dark. Ski sat in a room that moments before, was as murky as a crypt. His eyes were fixed on a charred picture frame, his hand clenched a Beretta. Magazine inserted — safety off.

"Mind if I flip the lights on, Ski?"

He did not wait for an answer. He turned on the fluorescents, closed the door and eased toward the captain.

"What're you looking at, Captain?"

Gabe set the bag on the floor, slipped around the desk stopping

262

beside Ski. He looked at the blackened photograph, then placed his hand on the officer's shoulder and lightly squeezed. "Beautiful family, son. I have a couple of granddaughters, I reckon about the same age as your girl. Almost as pretty as your little angel."

Ski turned slowly and looked up at Gabe. A thin smile emerged.

Gabe let go of his shoulder and covered Ski's hand and the 9 mm with his. "Your hand must be tired. Why don't you let me help you with the weapon? Only us friends in here today, son."

Gabe sucked in a deep breath then raised his hand several inches above Ski's.

The captain rolled the gun over and loosened his grip. Gabe gently lifted it out of his upturned palm, thumbed the safety and pushed the magazine release. Then he stuffed the loaded magazine in his cargo pocket and racked the Beretta's slide, catching the ejected round as it flew out. He stuck the gun in the small of his back then let out a long sigh.

"Mind if I sit for a spell and chat, Captain?"

Ski didn't answer. Gabe stepped over his rucksack and pushed a chair near the desk.

"I'll take that as a yes. You a drinking man, Captain?"

He pulled the bottle of Glenfiddich from the bag, broke the seal and with a heavy hand, plunked it on the captain's desk.

Engrossed in the portrait, Ski did not flinch.

"You can help me out anytime here, Ski. Conversation usually means two people talking. If it's just me jawin', hell, I'll get bored, pick up my marbles and go home."

Gabe used two fingers to pluck the cups from the rucksack. He held them up to the light, chose the cleaner one and filled it halfway with Scotch. Still seeing no reaction from the officer, he placed the drink in front of Ski then inspected the second cup. He worked up a good bit of saliva and spit into it. Having not thought through the entire process, he looked around the room, until he saw a package of baby wipes on the edge of a file cabinet. He snatched one and wiped the inside of the plastic tumbler. Satisfied he had neutralized the previous owner's germs he filled it to the brim and downed the liquor. He immediately paid a heavy price for his stunted memory span. Gasping for air, he shook his head. Keeping pace with his clattering teeth, his eyes blinked like a strobe light set on the highest speed. Shivers began at the head then shot through the rest of his body. By the time the tremors reached his exposed toes they had morphed into uncontrollable quakes compelling his digits to dance to some podiatric ditty.

"Brrrooooaaaw…wa... whooaa…woof, woof, woof…damn. No. GODDAMN!"

Ski guzzled his drink. The alluring poison produced the exact opposite reaction in him — blasé approaching zilch.

"Good man, Captain, that's the spirit."

Gabe refilled both cups and again emptied his in a single swallow. The elixir raged through the blood stream, yet, amazingly, his anatomy had already built up a tolerance. He was feeling fine.

"Ahoy, Captain. Have another…AAARGH!"

Twenty minutes into the spirits-driven crash derby, Ski had not cracked a smile — he cracked nothing, just slinging the booze back, unfazed like a hardcore alcoholic. Gabe, on the other hand — hammered. His unique physiology permitted the alcohol to by-pass the usual traffic jams at the liver and the other gooey organs. The fluid got in the fast lane on the expressway straight to the brain. No off ramps, no tollbooths, just a clear shot to drunken bliss.

In a moment of coherency lasting about as long as an eyelash is wide, Gabe realized he had forgotten his mission. Plan A was working on him, but doing nothing for the young warrior. It was time for plan B. He wished he had stayed awake during the psych courses and had actually studied for the exams instead of buying them. He did not have a clue what plan B was. He resorted to street psychology.

"Ski, what do you see when you look at that photo?"

The captain looked up from the picture and slowly opened his mouth. His tongue moved, but no words formed. He shook his head, then got lost in the portrait again.

"I'll tell you what I see. I see two beautiful, loving creatures put in your world by some power greater than us. I think you see the dead mother and child in the village. They're not the same, Ski, they are not the same. Your family's safe. They're not here. They're home, a million miles from the madness. Nothing's gonna happen to them, son."

Ski again looked dully at Gabe, then reached for the bottle and poured.

For a moment, Gabe thought he had hit a nerve. He downed another shot and decided to skip plan B and move on to plan C.

"What you have here and now is another family, a family that needs you more than your wife and kid. This family is not safe. It needs a leader, not a brooding zombie. You gotta step up to the plate, Ski. When you signed on to this war, you agreed to carry the water for

264

others back home. Sure, most don't see it that way, but who gives a shit about what they think. What matters is what your brother soldiers think. If they believe they've lost their leader, they're screwed. Carry the water, Ski."

"I'm an engineer, a manager," Ski whispered, "not a combat engineer, not a combat leader, but a civil engineer."

"Holy shit, we have progress with plan C," Gabe blurted. "Wrong, Ski. You are a leader in combat, not a manager. There's a whole world of difference between the two. We have enough tinkering idiots with MBAs to screw things up. In fact, one is floating around our little shithole. Bishop needs a map to find his ass and a manual to show him what it's for."

He leaned forward and patted Ski's hand. "Son, a true leader is an exceptional thing, destined for glory from the very first cooling breath he took into his lungs as a newborn. I've watched you with the men and seen you in combat. Ski, it is within you to walk in the ranks of an elite class of warriors. You can inspire others to forget their abhorrence to killing another human and accomplish America's mission in Iraq."

Ski looked up at him and showed a glimmer of comprehension. Then it was gone. He drained his drink and returned to his girls.

"Ah shit," Gabe muttered, "don't leave me again, son."

Upset more with his limited people skills than with the captain, he pounded his head on the desk. Plan D had not yet gelled, so he fell back on plan C. He raised his aching forehead and looked at Ski.

"I don't think much of hajjis, but there's an Arab proverb that hits home. 'An army of sheep led by a lion would defeat an army of lions led by a sheep.' You have an army of lions, and Captain, you're the meanest lion in the desert. You lead them — you can't lose. Get your act together and roar! Let's do what it takes to send all of the jihadists to *Allah's* waiting room, then get you and the boys home to family."

Nada, zip — his Vince Lombardi locker room pep talk was going nowhere. He decided it was time to shift gears and move on to plan D. He poured another round for the officer and himself. The booze sluiced through Gabe's brain prompting his neural receptors to scour the nooks and crannies for motivational gems from his rapidly depleting bag of tricks.

"The way to get through war is simple," Gabe said. "The day you stepped off the plane in Iraq is the day you died. Accept it. Embrace it. If you're already dead, you can get past the paralysis — fear of dying, fear of killing, fear of making a mistake. First crack of gunfire,

265

I still shit my pants, but if you can master the secret, your time here will pass a lot easier. If at the end of your tour you've survived, accept that, too. Go home, love your family and then train to come back again as a more deadly weapon."

Gabe felt like he was talking to the wall — time to pull out the big gun and bump it up to the next level.

"Throw that picture away. Think of your family as being dead. Forget about them. You must get numb, dead inside, incapable of feelings for those not in the fight. What good is a wife or kid in this place? Just reminders of the person you'll never be again. Captain, once you've seen that elephant, it's gone, buddy — no going back. Family...useless excess baggage you leave on the tarmac for some other schmuck to claim. Otherwise, thoughts of family will get you killed, sure as my shit stinks. You start thinking you got a reason to live, you get cautious. Caution has its place in combat, but caution based on the battle, not problems back in the world. That kind of worry gets your warrior family dead. You owe them more."

Ski glared at him through squinted eyes. Sounds of gnashing teeth crept through his quivering lips. He sucked the contents from the cup and slammed it against the table. Almost as soon as the emotion broke free, it ended. His snarl retreated, replaced by a blank, flaccid expression. He had escaped to his happy place somewhere inside the charred print.

"I was you once," Gabe pressed on, "at that age when I was going to end the world's suffering, believed people were inherently humane, that kind of crap. Just like you, the dead hajjis in Afak bothered me. You get past it, or you'll be lost. Ski, you ain't in the Peace Corps. You're in the killing business."

Eyes closed, Ski twisted uncomfortably in his chair and covered his ears. Gabe reached over and jerked Ski's hands away from his head.

"Listen to me when I'm fucking talking!"

Ski snapped his head toward Gabe, then turned away just as fast and disappeared back into the photo.

Gabe thumped his chest and said, "Don't think with a compassionate heart. It's just a pump poets have elevated to some ridiculous plateau. Use your brain and cultivate a steely cold, cynic's logic. Wrap yourself in a new reality — you can't save the world. You are the tip of the spear, a spear that needs sharpening. Feeling every one's pain dulls the point. Leave that shit to the politicians, preachers and bleeding heart liberals."

"Back in the Reagan years," Gabe continued, "I went to Africa. I felt the people's suffering. It was rampant, even worse than here. Beggars lined street corners, competed for key places in the markets, come to your home at all hours, step in front of your vehicle. They had all kind of deformities — missing limbs, leprosy, you name it. If a kid didn't have a deformity, the Muslim *marabouts* would create one, sort of a public service to *Allah.* In their minds, justified. After all, *zakat,* one of the five pillars of Islam, means helping the needy. They did hideous, awful things to those kids. If it was a war veteran missing arms or legs, *xin loi,* mother-fucker. Sorry about that, but get your ass on the street and beg alms for *Allah.* For the first few weeks, I was going broke saving the world. Then I turned. Hell, they were just Africans. You know what an African life is worth, Ski?"

The captain ignored him.

"About a dime," Gabe said. "When I took a break from the Angola gig, I went to an open bar on a busy street in Kinshasa. All the European expatriates, mission rats and mercenaries from the world over unofficially claimed it as their sanity checkpoint. All of us expats and mercs, sittin' around tables, gettin' wasted on cheap beer loaded with formaldehyde…we were a magnet for every beggar within miles. The cripples used homemade crutches if they had legs. The ones who didn't would strap their stumps to a scrap of plywood, use wood blocks in their hands as feet and scoot around. We'd throw brown money into the traffic and all these urchins would scramble for it, darting between the speeding taxis, motor scooters, trucks….Of course, it evolved into wagering. You know, 'I'll bet you a thousand Z notes the kid gets splattered.' They were fast little *kaffres,* so I always bet they'd make it. Sometimes I lost, but usually I came out ahead. When a car or truck turned them into omelets, there was a new round of betting — how long for him to bleed out, how many times he'd be hit by other cars…that kind of thing."

"My point is, you must view hajjis like I did Africans — not human. You gotta believe me. It's easier on the psyche. Think of your brain as a sponge that can only soak up so much of people's suffering until it's ready to pop. Every once in awhile you must wring it dry so it's ready for the next heartbreak. If you believe hajjis are nothing more than animals, leaves more room for your soldiers' and your needs."

Ski sighed, and for a moment, looked dully at Gabe.

"All right, Ski. You win, I lose. Stay there wherever there is, but I'm not gonna waste the beginning of a good buzz. If I get enough of this booze in my system maybe I'll join you in hell."

Binge is a word, but not the correct one. Closer to an orgy, a love fest between fluids — cerebrospinal and distilled spirits. For the next thirty minutes, Gabe only had three physical motions in his repertoire — pour, bottoms up, pour again. He was approaching a peculiar neighborhood, somewhere between the ozone and the twilight zone, conducive to unfathomable gibberish. Thirty-one minutes into the brain cell gangbang, the game changer appeared. Not due to a deliberate design, or even kismet. It was magic.

"I gotta a fuckin' great joke." Still holding his drink, Gabe raised his legs, slid out of the chair and landed on his butt. He wobbled to a half standing position, teetered left, up, down, then right. Without having spilled one drop throughout the entire acrobatic exhibition, he fell back into the chair.

"That's what ya call a perfect, two-point parashit landing. Right cheek, left cheek. They ever teach ya that one in jump school?"

Ski glanced at him.

"All righty then. Me guess not. Tha joke, it's a frickin', fuckin' doozy. Garrran-damn-fuckinteed! I sorry. I forgot we ain't on speakin' fuckin' terms, are we, buddy? What you think you are, my frickin 'wife? Okey dokey, be my wife and you just sit there and you be all gloomy and shiiiit. I don't fuckin', I don't fuckin'…I mean, I reeeally don't give, don't give, DAMN. I don't glive a flyin' fluck."

Ski looked back to his family, but after several seconds, stole a peek at Gabe.

"There is a crooozz boat. Excoozze me, a crooozz ship. A ship's bigger than a piss ant lil' boat. It's a sailin' in tha Caarrabeein Sea. All these pissingerz, they all sittin' in tha theater. That's right, tha boat, I mean ship, has a theater. It's a big fuckin' boat…damnit, ship. Tha pissingerz bein' entertained by a magician. These croooz boats, well, they don't hire classy acts. They get tha lousy ones 'cause you kind of trapped in tha middle of tha fuckin' ocean, I mean sea, and you got no choice. When you ain't gotta choice, they pretty damn good. You followin' this, Ski?"

He turned his chair and faced Gabe.

"I think I saw you move your lips. Good. Anyhooo, this magic guy is a makin' shit disappear. I mean into thin air. He's a magician, Ski. They do that shit. Did I tell you he's a Jew?"

The captain shook his head.

"Well he is. He's a Heeeebrooo. There's this talkin' animal in tha audience…a talkin' dog. Shit, dogs can't talk. It's some other

268

type of critter. It's a fuckin' bird. Birds can talk, Ski. Yeah, so it's a bird. It's a macow. I mean, macaw. That's a parrot, Ski. That's what it is. It's a parrot. Tha parrots are inda-inda-indagenious ta Deetroit, Minnyeasoda. Or maybe it was Illanoiz. Yep, that's what it was. It was New Jersey. It's a blue parrot and he's gotta red head. Blue parrot with a red fuckin' head, and he's a genius from Deetroit, New Jersey. BRAAAK, BRAAAK! A noisy frickin' parrot, too."

Gabe leaned nearer to Ski and raised a wavering forefinger to within an inch of his face. "Now you gotta stay with me on this one, Captain, 'cause this joke has a reeeally great punch line."

Ski's eyes widened and his head nodded, similar to a child hearing a nursery rhyme for the first time.

"Did I tell you tha blue parrot with tha red fuckin' head is a Baptist?"

Ski covered his mouth and shook his head.

"Well he is. It's ornery, a reeeally mean, nasty parrot — blue parrot with a red fuckin' head. Every time this magic guy does something that wows tha crooozers, tha bird shouts out somethin' like, "it's up your sleeve," or "it's behind tha curtain," or "behind tha mirror," or "you hid it up your ass, dumbass." Damn, I forgot to tell you there's this clown in tha audience wearin' those big, funny lookin' orange shoooes and a big red nose — looks like a red tennis ball stuck on his face. I think he's a Mormon. Yep, well he is, he's a Mormon. A Mormon's almost a Christian, Ski."

Gabe patted the captain's knee and asked, "You still with me?"
Ski nodded.

"I mean every damn trick, tha parrot heckles tha magic man and gives up tha secret magic shit. Magic guy, well, he's pissed, but he finishes tha magic show. Oh yeah, there's this big tittied gal sittin' by tha clown. I mean biiig, big, big jugs that'd knock you out cold if they hit you upside tha head. She's a...I forgot what she is. Buddhist, I think. Yeah that's what she is, Ski. She's a frickin' Buddha belly worshipper. Did I tell you she's also a Democrat?"

On a roll, Gabe did not wait for Ski's response. "Well she is. Yep, she's a Republican. Later in tha night, tha boat, I mean ship, tha ship hits an iceberg. Wait, can't be a frickin' iceberg in tha Carrrabbein Sea. Musta been a boatload of Cuban refugees. Yeah, it was. It was Cuban dope smugglers."

Gabe squeezed his nostrils tight between his thumb and forefinger and held his breath. With cheeks ballooned, eyes closed, he pointed his arm and middle finger straight up and twisted his body, slowly

269

undulating in a sliding descent from chair to floor.

"BLUB, Blub, blub, bluuuub, blu, blu, bluuu…aah…bloooooob. Tha ship sinks, cause they hit tha iceberg."

"Boat load of Cuban refugees," Ski whispered.

"Naw, I said it was a damn iceberg, Ski. Ain't no Cuban refugees anywhere near Iceland. Everybody knows that. They can't handle cold and they is used to palm trees. No fuckin' coconuts in tha fuckin' North Pole."

Gabe crawled back into the chair. "Morning comes and there's only two survivors in tha lifeboat. Just tha two of 'em in tha lifeboat. That's smaller than a ship, Ski. Now it ain't turned into Medooozaz raft and all that cannibalism shit yet, but — you see where this is goin', Ski?"

With a mystified expression on his face, the captain slowly shook his head.

"I'll get you there, Cap'n…don't you worry 'bout that. Tha survivors are tha parrot with tha red fuckin' head, tha magic dude, tha clown and tha big boobed gal."

Speaking a bit louder than before, Ski said, "That's four survivors, not two."

"Huh?" Gabe looked at Ski and frowned. "Whooose frickin' joke is this? Quit fuckin' interruptin' me. You gonna make me mezzup tha punch line. You wanna tell a frickin' joke, wait till it's your damn turn. Okey dokey?"

"Sorry."

"All righty then, damnit. Well, anyways, they float around for days. Days starin' at each other, no talkin', just starin', sort of like you and me is doin'. A gorilla and a tiger are chasin' tha clown with tha pink football ball stuck to his face. There was a goraffe, tooo. He's tryin' to get away. Not tha goraffe, but tha clown with tha purple shooooose and tha yellow basketball ball stuck to his face. Yessiree, he's a skippin', a dancin' and a prancin' around like a frickin' fairy, he was, all over tha lifeboat. Finally, tha blue parrot with tha red fuckin' head loooks at tha Baptist magic guy — okay, Ski. Here it comes. You ready?"

Ski bobbed his head so fast payment to treat the imminent neck injuries would put a chiropractor's entire brood of kids through an actual medical school.

"Okay then. Tha blue parrot with tha red frickin' head says to tha magic guy — did I tell you tha magic man's Catholic? Well he is. Yep, he's one of those frickin' Friday fish eatin' religious dooodz.

Where was I? Oh yeah, tha blue parrot with tha red frickin' head says — tee, hee, hee...ah shit, you ready for this, Ski?"

The captain, with his mouth wide open, looked intently at Gabe and nodded.

"Okey dokey. Tha blue parrot with tha red frickin' head, he's a goin' bird frickin' crazy, flappin' his wings, squawkin' and shit. Well, he says, BRAAAK, BRAAAK, BRAAAK, you wrong, you stupid Irish Mick. BRAAK, BRAAK! It's number forty-seven."

Forty years earlier, during his period of teenage supremacy, Purple Haze, White Flash, Mary Jane, mescaline and other chemical and organic miscreants, ripped through the same circuitry, that in recent years, rum had corroded. Tonight Gabe's noggin was flooded with whisky. Inside his intoxicated belfry, slushy logic convinced him he had nailed it and bested the best of the funny men. The only thing that eclipsed his perfect comedic timing, modulated voice and mastery of the characters' nuances, was the build-up to a flawlessly delivered punch line, executed like a pro. If he wanted a change in career, there would be no need for stops at seedy basement venues, or gigs at off-the-beaten-path comedy clubs. None of that for Gabe. It would be straight to the Vegas strip headlining with two nightly shows, and during ratings weeks, guest appearances on the *Tonight Show* for his good friend, the host.

Gabe's body shook from uncontrolled, earsplitting laughter, occasionally broken by deep, nasally, pig-like snorts. Fighting back hard, he began a slow recovery from his self-amusement. His laughs became chuckles, eventually trailing off to intermittent snickers.

"Oooooh, shiiiit. Didn't I tell you it was a good, fuckin' doozy of a joke, Ski?"

Ski shook his head and stared at Gabe as if he was the goofy kid who shows up at the neighborhood sandlot for a game of baseball wearing football pads and helmet, carrying a first aid kit and holding his mother's hand. Soon, the hint of a smile formed — a twinkle of white teeth surfaced. Muted chuckles escaped through his lips, then a subdued laugh. The tempered laughs turned into runaways. He crossed his arms on his belly and doubled over in a whole-hearted, body bending seizure that shook the desk.

Lazarus' rising from the dead set Gabe off on another boisterous laughing spree.

Ski contained his fit and tried to talk above Gabe's reinvigorated mirth. "That's the stupidest, hell I don't know what it was, but it was the dumbest whatever I've ever heard. It wasn't a joke. It was two, three, four, maybe twenty who knows what, thrown together. And if there was a punch line hidden somewhere in there, you blew the shit out of it. Gabe, you've got to be the worst comic...you belong on that fucking croooz ship with the fuckin' redheaded parrot."

Laugh tears slid down Gabe's cheeks as he beamed at his rediscovered friend. He smiled inwardly   *always a plan E.* He struggled to a standing position and grabbed the nearly depleted bottle of Scotch from the desktop. He raised his hand and snapped a salute. "Welcome home, son."

The inward smile traveled from his thoughts to his face. Gabe blinked several times before closing his eyes. With a final, giddy laugh, he performed a left face — straight down to the floor. Following a resounding thud, the only other sounds came from the Glenfiddich as it tumbled wildly on its journey toward the closed door. After the Scotch decelerated from its protracted, wobbly spin, it came to rest in a pose that resembled its spent owner.

Gabe giggled like a little girl. Then he let out a moan. "Ooooooa...ooooa...who moved tha floor?"

Ski got out of his chair and stepped over him. He picked up the bottle and placed it in Gabe's bag, then opened the door. "Sergeant Knowles, go find Dark Meat and help Mr. Quinn back to his quarters."

"Yes sir, Captain. Good to have you back, Ski."

*****

Jefferson propped Gabe on the bed and steadied his rocking motion with both arms. "Mr. Quinn, time to call it a night."

"Roger fucking that," Gabe said. "I love you man. I loooove you, I really love you, Dark Meat. I love Ski, tooo. And I love Bussard, and I love Knowles, and, and, and, oh yeah, and I love Barton, and, and, Gonzalez. I don't love Bishop though. Nope, not LLMF Bishop." Gabe choked up. "Damnit, I loved White Meat. I reeeally miss White Meat. We're gonna kill tha bastards who kilt White Meat."

"Roger that, sir." Jefferson actually believed the drunken white man. He trusted few Caucasians. Gabe was among those few.

"I can't be callin' you Dark Meat anymore. There's no more White Meat. You can't have dark meat if there ain't no white meat, Dark Meat."

"You can call me Dark Meat. It's fine, sir."

"No man. Seeeriuslee, what's your real name, Dark Meat?"

"PFC Jefferson, sir."

"I fuckin' know that," Gabe said. "What's your reeeal...I mean your real name. Tha one your momma give you?"

"Thomas Hemings Jefferson, sir."

"Whoa shit!" Gabe's head bobbed as he waved his hands conducting an invisible orchestra. He hummed an abysmal rendition of *Hail to the Chief.*

"Hmm...HMM...huh...da, da, DA, TADA, da, da, da, tada... .I'm in tha frickin' presence of a foundin' father. Mister Thomas something Jefferson, don't you call me sir. I'll be callin' you sir, or Mister Prezzident."

"Dark Meat's really okay, sir."

"Okay, Dark Meat, sir." Gabe rubbed his hands between his thighs. "I think I pissed my pants, Mister Prezzident."

Jefferson looked down at Gabe's stained shirt and pants. "No, sir, you didn't. You're bleeding again. You must have popped a few stitches on your stomach. Let's get you out of those clothes and I'll put on a fresh bandage."

Gabe tried to loosen the top Velcro fastener on his uniform blouse, but gave up after several attempts. He dropped his hands to the mattress and stared up at Jefferson through glassy, roadmap eyes.

Jefferson placed a hand on Gabe's shoulder to keep him from falling over and used his free one to remove his shirt. He was used to caring for the helpless. He had cared for his younger siblings when he was permitted to live at home. They were also white. As the children grew older, they learned to despise and shun him because he was a living reminder of the family's dark secret. By some fluke of genetics, he was black. Just like his brothers and sisters, his DNA reached back through the centuries to his distant ancestor, a Negro slave concubine from Monticello. His family could not forgive him for genetics gone awry. The shady branch of the family tree had been exposed to the light of day for all of their white friends to see.

The rejection became reciprocal. Thomas Hemings Jefferson had a loathing distrust for all whites. Until he met White Meat. Jeremiah Jefferson's plight was worse than his tangled lot in life, but more important, Jeremiah did not see him as black or white. He only saw a brother. Then he came to know Ski, Bussard, Knowles, and now, Gabe Quinn. He had found a family to replace the one that abandoned him.

Jefferson applied a fresh dressing to Gabe's stomach and removed the rest of his clothes. He managed to get his limp body under the sheet. Looking down at his beaten friend, already asleep and snoring,

273

he smiled at him as a mother hovering above her child would.

"Good night, Mr. Quinn. I've always got your six, brother."

July 14, 1730 hours

Gabe saw a plume of smoke rising from behind the dining trailer. Even with his head throbbing from a hangover purchased on credit from his brain cells' negative net worth, he was positive he had not heard an explosion.

The smell carried on the breeze was from burning meat. Not human, but bovine. As he rounded the corner of the laundry shack he saw Barton standing over a grill flipping mouth-watering steaks.

"Mr. Quinn, you're just in time," Barton said. "How do you want your steak, sir?"

"What's the occasion, Barton? Is the war over?"

"Negative, sir. Captain Ski ordered it up. He said bravo-sierra to burgers and hot dogs, his men deserve the best."

"Medium rare."

Gabe passed Barton and entered the trailer. He was hit by a sight he had not witnessed since his first day at the outpost — the soldiers he remembered — every one of them laughing, high-fiving, back slapping…alive again.

Knowles, surrounded by a squad of men chewing heartily on the meat, looked up from his plate when he saw him. The sergeant leaned over to the man seated beside him and whispered. The soldier picked up his plate and moved to an adjacent table.

Knowles stood and motioned Gabe to the vacated chair.

"Thanks, Gabe."

"You're welcome, Sergeant, but thanks for what?"

"For last night. Ski's back like never before and ready to go out and get some tonight." Knowles clasped Gabe's hand with both of his. "Thanks again, friend." He cleared the table clutter from the area in front of Gabe's place at the feast and then sat.

"I'm all about that," Gabe said. "Payback in spades."

"Patrol brief next to the motor pool tent at 2100 hours, SP at 2120. Dirty Bird will set you up with a NOD and a firefly." Knowles grinned. "We'll own the night."

Chapter 22
Perfidy rewarded

COP 6, July 14, 1821 hours

Gabe left the dining trailer carrying two canned drinks. Before his sandals touched the gravel, he again smelled the pleasant aroma of charcoal fueled flames kissing prime beef. Still at his post, the cook dutifully guarded the grill; spatula in one hand, a water spray bottle in the other.

"Barton, how about a couple of steaks for Dirty Bird?"

"No problem, sir." The private flipped the meat a final time then placed it inside a foam food tray along with a healthy pile of grilled onions and peppers. "If he wants more, let me know, sir."

Gabe stuffed the sodas inside a pocket, took the steaks from Barton, and then walked the short distance to the operations trailer. He pushed the door open and poked his head around its edge. "Dirty Bird, I've brought some great chow. You in there?"

"In the weapons room gettin' you set up, Mr. Quinn."

Gabe stepped inside just as Bussard locked the arms room door. The soldier turned around holding a night observation device and a clear Ziploc bag and placed both on the only space available on the desk. "Sir, the NOD's accountable so I'll need you to sign a property card. Do you need a Rhino for your helmet?"

"Have one mounted already," Gabe said. "I take it that's a firefly in the bag?"

"Affirmative, sir. I've thrown in an extra battery. Have you ever used one of these infrared strobes?"

"Nope." Gabe balanced the tray and sodas on the weapons rack and moved next to Bussard.

"All you do is connect the leads to the 9-volt then put it in a pocket or strap it to your helmet cat's eye. Hajji won't see it blinking, neither will any one else unless they've gone over to night vision. It helps us track friendlies, and if we call in close air support, maybe we won't get shot by our own wingnuts."

Gabe plucked his reading glasses from a shirt pocket. After several back and forths he found the exact range to make out the squiggly characters on the NOD. "You have a pen handy?"

275

Bussard fumbled through stacked papers, envelopes and empty shipping boxes until he found a ballpoint. He turned to hand it to Gabe, but instead stopped and looked back at the clutter on the desk. He rummaged through several envelopes and loose sheets of paper before he singled out a thick, legal size manila envelope, and another smaller white envelope, franked with a stamp in lieu of metered postage.

"Mr. Quinn, these are for you. Must of come in today."

Gabe took the pen, scribbled his mark on the property card and handed it to Bussard. Then he studied the larger envelope; Law Offices, Finstead and Whorley, P.C., Family Law and Divorce, Myrtle Beach, South Carolina. He frowned when he read the return address on the smaller envelope: Nicole Quinn, The Plantation, Pawleys Island, South Carolina.

"Typed."

"What'd you say, Mr. Quinn?"

"Friendly fire. Thanks for the gadgets, Bussard."

Gabe gathered up his new toys and weapon. On his way out, he dropped both envelopes in the trash can labeled *Sensitive Material-Burn Only*. Then he headed toward his now, only home.

He looked around the trailer, empty except for bunk beds and sundry tools of war scattered around the floor. He placed the rifle on the mattress then groped under the bed for his patrol pack. He unzipped it, reached inside and took out his boot dagger, socks, flashlight, a Ziploc bag protecting a partial roll of white paper currency that in the desert was more valuable than the green form, and laid the items next to his weapon.

Alone at the bottom of the rucksack was the bottle. He considered his new friend, then glanced at his watch — *two hours until the patrol brief*. A thirty-plus year marriage dead, having joined the other 'lost causes' in his byzantine passage through life, he decided not to waste more time on a crisis that was out of his control.

"Fuck it. Deal with it if I make it back."

He moved the survival essentials to the foot of the bed, pulled the bottle out and chugged the remaining Scotch.

"Mr. Quinn, time for the briefing."

Gabe bolted upright. "Be there in five, Dark Meat."

He forced exaggerated yawns to clear the whisky from his head, then lit a cigarette. In a single drag, he sucked a third of it deep into his lungs. Akin to an intumescent Black Snake sold at *Mighty Explodin'*

Mike's Discount Fireworks, the nearly inch long ash continued to mature, hanging on for life from the end of the Marlboro clenched between his discolored smoker's teeth. He bent over to put on his boots that were no longer desert tan, but a mottled black-brown-rust blend of brushed cow hide, grease, dried Iraqi blood and a fair amount of his own. The slinking grey cinder wobbled briefly from the end of the cigarette before it broke free, bouncing off his boot in multiple directions when it hit.

He ignored the mess and focused on the footwear. Smoke rising from the Marlboro irritated his eyes, so with one eye closed, he pried a gap between his leg and boot leather, slid the sheathed dagger in the opening, blade down and handle pressed firmly against his right calf. He reached across the mattress and grabbed the toilet paper and flashlight. The tissue found a home in a thigh cargo pocket and the mini-maglite's refuge was in the left ankle pocket.

He looked at his body armor. First aid kit, combat tourniquet and fire retardant gloves were secured by Velcro straps, shoulder epaulet closures, and snaps. He lightened the load by removing the collar device, throat, groin, deltoid and auxillary protectors — weight saved — five-point-three pounds. Hefting the remaining forty-seven pounds of body armor, SAPI plates, ammo and other necessary doo-dads, he confirmed there were two loaded magazines in each of the three mag pouches, jammed his arms through the heavy vest's openings, snapped the closures and adjusted the fit. Then he slipped on the shoulder holster with twin magazine pouches, cinched down the straps, pulled out and charged the Beretta, checked the safety and returned the handgun to the holster.

He jumped up and down several times, testing for loose equipment that could be lost when he was on the run, crazy scared out of his mind. Then he jumped a few more times, listening for any telltale metallic sounding clinks, clacks or clanks, that could give away his position and make him dead. There were many tells, but he was confident his panicked screams and shouts during a firefight would give away his position before the negligible sounds did. He loosened the snaps and Velcro straps to be more comfortable for the long ride.

He locked the night observation device into the Rhino mount, affixed its 'do not lose me or it'll cost you a fortune' safety lanyard to one of the helmet's webbing rings, and hung the combo from a carabiner attached above the name tape on his armor. A final insurance look inside the bag satisfied him that he was ready for a meet and greet with the enemy, so he picked up his assault rifle, turned off the lights and left the trailer.

Stepping into the night, he was met by a jarring racket from over-taxed generators and air conditioners. After a final drag, he field stripped the cigarette and stuffed the filter in the bottom of the same pocket that protected the toilet paper. Head clear, he set out for the southwest corner of the camp.

He negotiated the dark twists and turns between trailers and blast walls as if he were on autopilot. Cornering the final portable, he saw the artificial aurora of the flood light silhouette two squads crowded around Captain Ski and Sergeant Knowles. He had missed the first five minutes but could guess where the officer was in the briefing.

The enlisted soldiers' demeanor was an easy read — aware and attentive, but not keyed up. Just another routine patrol, one of scores before and countless more to come — a night drive in the desert searching for IEDs they never found and enemies they never saw. The only man who appeared to show more than a casual, professional interest in the briefing was Hercules.

"...and being the astute warriors you are," Ski said, "I'm sure you've noticed we've doubled the size of the patrol."

Soldiers' flat expressions changed.

"Now I'll tell you why," Ski continued. "We will travel south, go-lights blaring, staggered formation, keeping it slow and easy. I don't want to miss an IED and give the enemy a kill tonight. Twenty clicks out my vehicle will overheat."

Several soldiers traded confused looks.

"The patrol will halt, all lights off. Sergeant Knowles' squad will switch to night vision and check for hajjis in the vicinity. If we're clear, my squad will go back on lights and continue beyond checkpoint nine-bravo south. Those of you in Sergeant Knowles' squad will stay dark, turn around and head to checkpoint eighteen-alpha north. Once there, you will establish an OP and set out snipers."

As the news sunk in, some soldiers scratched their heads, others laughed, but all were alert. Muted chatter became louder and distinct. Hercules' voice was not among them. Silent, his expression had gone beyond alert to red alert. He fidgeted in place, shifting from one leg to the other. With a dazed expression, he glanced from Knowles to the captain, then back to the sergeant. He unclenched his fist to press the watch stem, activating its light. The luminous dial cast a green glow across his face. His fascination with time was broken when his name was spoken.

"Hercules," Ski said, "you'll be riding south with me." He turned back to the soldiers and said, "That's all I have. Sergeant Knowles will cover radio frequencies and specific assignments."

"Captain Kowalewski," Hercules said, "please, sir, I must use the toilet facility."

"Damn, Hercules, your timing is terrible. All right, but be quick about it."

Hercules ran to the last stall on the right, flung the door open and scurried inside. As soon as the door slammed behind him, a muted green light escaped through the cracks in the john; the same light Gabe had seen weeks before.

Gabe learned on day one at the outpost the last stall was unofficially designated for Iraqi use only. When dealing with the nasty business they hovered above the cutout in an odd, standing, semi-squat — almost as if they were poised to bolt from whatever discharged. Sometimes they actually hit the target beneath the round hole. The improvised toilet seat became a plywood petri dish growing questionable cultures. Coupled with the other 'east-meets-west' anomaly — how they cleaned their asses — all soldiers, and even Dawud, resolved that the last stall on the right would be Hercules' private domain.

"Captain Ski," Knowles said, "since any contact will probably be made by my squad, don't you think I should take the terp?"

"Good point, Sergeant." Ski looked at Gabe. "The sergeant tells me you were instrumental in developing this CONOP."

"Captain, my contibution was so minor — "

"I don't wanna hear it," Ski interrupted. "In addition to the sergeant's word, a parrot with a red frickin' head confirmed your input, so you're riding with Knowles. You've earned the privilege of being in on the kill if we're successful."

"We'll kill somethin' tonight," Knowles said. "I jus' know it, Cap'n. There's only two reasons my pecker gets hard. My woman ain't here, so it's gotta be the other one." He faced the soldiers. "Listen up, men, the MEDEVAC frequency is...."

For the next five minutes the sergeant covered the intricacies of the patrol that could tilt the odds in their favor. As soon as Knowles finished his portion of the patrol brief, Hercules rejoined the trio.

"I am so sorry for the delay I have caused, Captain Kowalewski. I am ready now, sir."

"Not an issue, Hercules. Change in the manifest. You're going in harm's way with the other squad. You will ride with Sergeant Knowles in the lead vehicle."

"B-but-but sir, that is not possible. I am your interpreter. I must be with you, sir. I am always with the commander and never in the lead vehicle, Captain Kowalewski, sir."

Ski ignored him. "Let's get this show on the road, Sergeant."

"Please, sir," Hercules said, "I must use the toilet again."

"Hercules, you need to — "

Knowles held up a hand, signaling the captain to shut up and allow a hardened, lifer NCO to do his job. The sergeant lit into Hercules.

"Well, knock me over with a feather," Knowles said. "Cap'n, what we have here is a bonafide, code red situation. Yes, sir. Only in Mohammad's special, frickin' Mesopotamian desert is it even thinkable — nowhere else in the whole wide, rest of the normal fuckin' world. Only here. Sir, I bet you didn't know we got us a real special hajji here, one with special needs and a special golden asshole."

Knowles crowded Hercules, bumping his chest against the Iraqi's chin. He stooped lower, going eyeball to eyeball with the interpreter. "You're in my patrol so you'll shove a cork up your a-hole and shit in the desert like everyone else. Now get your stinkin' hajji brown ass in gear and strap same in the rear seat of my Humvee. You *comprendez* my fucking French, terp?"

Hercules' color, the grey pallor of death, his expression hysterical, the look of one in close, knife-distance combat — a contest where only one walks away.

Knowles grinned broadly, then faced the soldiers and bowed his head. "All right, killers, let us pray. Thank you Trijicon, Incorporated, for your revered wisdom and acceptance of divine guidance that helped you to invent the ACOG — a gunsight that exceeds perfection and helps us to send lead downrange straight and true every time we lightly, and with regulated breathing, squeeze the trigger. Sights you so wisely inscribed with blessed scripture from the Good Book that make our rifle the Jesus-rifle, a weapon so powerful it is loathed and feared by every raghead in this godless, Muslim, infested wasteland. And we mustn't forget to thank you, Christ, for givin' us those enemies. So, thank you, Jesus. And Lord, bless us tonight with numerous worthy, putrid, low-life, motherfucking targets so we can do your glorious work and make loads of hajji widows. Amen."

Some soldiers crossed themselves, some said, "amen." All twenty shouted "HOOAH," charged their weapons and hustled toward the armored chariots of death.

An hour south of the outpost, the lead Humvee slowed to a stop.

"Widow-maker six," Ski transmitted on patrol net, "quick stop. Tighten up, lights out. Widow-maker two and our angel, rally on me."

Knowles turned in his seat and tapped Gabe's leg. "That's you and me, buddy."

Bussard angled the truck off the road as it rolled to a stop. Gabe stepped out, switched the night vision goggles to infrared mode and activated his strobe. He took a moment to allow his vision to adjust to the green spectrum of the goggles — somewhere between night's bleak authenticity and the illusory, invented thermal world. He reached back inside the truck for his rifle and then met Knowles at the front of the truck. Together they walked past two Humvees that separated them from the captain. Ski, his firefly pulsing, stood at the rear of his truck.

"Sergeant," Ski said, "who do you have manning the outpost commo?"

"PFC Barton, sir."

"Was he briefed about this mission?"

"Yes, sir."

"We are at the demarcation line. I'll continue south, but soon we'll be out of radio range of each other and we'll need to relay messages through Barton. Another thing, no coalition convoys north or south until just before sunrise, so the only vehicles on the road should be Iraqi police or enemies. We'll sit tight here until we're sure no hajjis are watching, then charlie-mike. Questions?"

"None, sir."

"Stay safe, gentlemen. See you back at the camp."

Fifteen minutes later, the captain told his squad to move out. As planned, the three lead trucks pulled out, lights turning the night into day. Knowles waited another ten minutes, then, cloaked in darkness, reversed direction, staggered the trucks across both north bound lanes and at less than twenty mph, advanced on checkpoint eighteen-alpha north.

For the next two hours, the only sounds inside the truck were the drone of the diesel engine and occasional radio static. Gabe scanned his sector hoping to see nothing out of place on or beside the road. Everything looked out of place through night vision goggles. He raised them to give his eyes a break. The only illumination came from the ECM status lights and the Blue Force Tracker. Although his view was partially blocked, he caught an occasional green flash near Hercules. *He must need to go bad.*

Knowles tapped the zoom control on the tracker then looked

over the dash. "Dark Meat, we're two clicks out from the checkpoint. We'll pass through, then I want you to shout out when you see a good spot to set up on the east side."

Less than a kilometer beyond the overpass designated CP eighteen-alpha north, Dark Meat said, "Got some dunes horseshoed around a *wadi* at your two o'clock, three hundred out. Sand looks hard packed, should support our trucks."

"Roger." Knowles switched to the patrol frequency. "Follow me in. After we stop, three, right flank, four, left flank. Don't rev your engines comin' in then shut 'em down. TCs on me when you're in position."

"Widow-maker four, Roger."

Dead air, static, then...

"Widow-maker three, Roger."

Bussard slowed the truck to a crawl, eased the right, then the left front tire over the concrete curb. When the rear tires crossed the hump, the stiff suspension bottomed out. Gabe bounced, landing hard against the seat. The two-pound, eight-thousand dollar *Star Wars* wizardry suspended from his helmet smacked him on the bridge of his nose and cheekbone. As they continued down the steep, rutted embankment, he collected more scrapes on his face from the NOD and fresh bruises on his ribs from everything else inside the truck.

Bussard slowed to test the compactness of the sand.

Knowles tapped him and said, "It's good. Go to the opening fifty meters out and wheel it around so we face the hardball."

Bussard maneuvered the four plus tons of metal over the sand and around boulders, found the sweet spot, then shut down the diesel. Knowles and Gabe got out and waited for the other truck commanders.

Minutes later, widow-makers three and four were in flanking positions. Gabe saw two blinking lights slowly converging on him from either side. Sandoval and Rentvers stopped when they were within spitting distance. The four men huddled, Knowles at the center acting as the quarterback.

"I want snipers flanking each of your trucks," he whispered, "no more than fifteen meters out. They see something, I want to know. Set up overlapping forward fields of fire with the crew served weapons, but don't forget our exposed asses. Noise and light discipline are in effect until we move out. Radio chatter — minimal. No fuck-ups. Got it?"

They nodded, reoriented themselves to their vehicles, and with rifles held at the combat ready, walked back to their teams.

Knowles moved close enough for his lips to brush against Gabe's ear and said, "It's going to be a long night. Pull up a chair and have a seat."

Gabe picked a path to the rear of the truck and sat cross-legged, resting his back against the tire.

Knowles squatted beside him. Staying in whisper mode, he asked, "We gonna win this war?"

Gabe thought about the question for a long time before responding. "You really want to open that can of worms?"

"Either that, or I jerk off for a few hours." Knowles dropped to the sand, taking on a Yoga sitting pose.

"Short answer — maybe."

"I never figured you for a politician."

"Politician." Gabe fought an urge to light a cigarette. It had been hours. "I've been accused of many things, but never that. Golly, gee-whiz, shee-bang, Sergeant. Which party do you have me plugged in? Republican, Democrat, or some tree huggin' peace party?"

"Doan mean nothin' by it, Gabe. You know what I meant. Really, what're your thoughts?"

"Whoever set up these rules you play by sure wants us to lose, or at best, a draw. Two years ago, small camp outside of Mosul, about every other night they hit us with IDF. Nothing heavy like the one-twenty mortar that killed White Meat. Just sixties, eighty-ones and eighty-twos. Still killers, though. Weeks of that crap, the commander finally decided to send out presence patrols. One night, we watched four enemies set up a tube and lob five or six rounds on our camp. Too far away for us to shoot them, but the dumb asses got in their pickup truck and rolled right up on our position. We lit them up."

"You kill 'em all?"

"Wish we had," Gabe said. "Two survived. We took them back to camp, treated their wounds and tried to interrogate them. Now understand, we had eyes on those cocksuckers the whole time, from shoot to scoot, and found the mortar tube they dumped when they tried to escape. They said they weren't tryin' to kill Americans 'cause they loved Americans. Must have been some other Arabs. We bad Americans were mistaken. They were innocent, only trying to drive to a cousin's wedding, when we trigger happy Yankees killed their Muslim brothers. All of us wrote up statements that pretty much said the same thing. Next day, the Army gators show up to take over the interrogation. Less than hour into it they tell us we had lied, conspired to cover up a bad shoot. Ordered, yes, they *ordered* us to return those sons of bitches to the point of capture and release 'em. Then they said there'd be an AR 15-6 investigation for us killing non-combatants. We can beat hajji, but how do we win against our own?"

"During the '03 invasion," Knowles said, "things were cleaner. Hit 'em hard, mop 'em up, move on. Then they threw the other bullshit mission on us; find the weapons of mass destruction. From where I was standing, if I'm on the receiving end of a 7.62 mm, it's a WMD."

"Validation, Sergeant," Gabe said, "validating the war for public consumption. What you know and see as a soldier; irrelevant. What our well-informed elected leaders know and see, and how they can spin it to their needs; that's what's relevant. They want it tidy and clean. Nothing clean about war."

"Amen, brother."

Gabe went on, "Seems like our anointed ones judge an enemy in civilian garb by a different set of rules. John Patrick Murtha, a friggin' veteran, couldn't wait to blast the Marines after questions came up about the Haditha action. Even before an investigation, he's all over the talk shows — prosecutor, judge and jury — convicting the Marines for murdering innocent civilians. Pressed about his source for the information that allowed him to pass judgment, the bastard said he just knew. Murtha had his Lieutenant William Calley, his My Lai, and wasn't lettin' go. It was a great way for him to fire up his liberal anti-war, anti-Bush base. Better still, a means to divert attention from the ethics investigation about his doings with the other beltway bandits and scum in Congress and on K Street."

"I remember what he said about those Marines," Knowles said. "It sent chills through Fort Bragg and gave new meaning to all of that 'we support the troops' crap. We're fighting a new type of war, the PC war. Bush can't even call it a crusade without all the pussies raising hell about his cultural insensitivity. Can you imagine the ruckus if we had generals like Patton? How long do you think he would have lasted in this war if he said he would grease the tracks of his tanks with hajji guts? The media would've crucified him."

"In '06," Gabe said, "on my first patrol after joining another team, we stopped at the Nineveh provincial police headquarters. Al Jazeera and throngs of homegrown Iraqi reporters were setting up cameras for some big event. The happening — staged release of forty-two rehabilitated insurgents from Abu Ghraib. Rehabilitated my ass. They used the real Iraqi rule of law to free themselves from American custody — tribal connections, bribes, kidnapping and threats. I'm standing next to the LT, and he gets royally pissed. Less than a month before, some of those same detainees ambushed his team and killed four soldiers."

He looked up and searched the black void. "Damn. The lieutenant told me something else about those prisoners, just can't remember. Ain't important. Anyway, he was going to shoot the bastards, and he would've if the first sergeant hadn't grabbed his weapon."

"I hear you, Gabe. It's the shit sandwich we're served every day."

"I know, but it shouldn't be that way, Sergeant. The geniuses back in the world need to stay out of something they'll never understand. The message they're sending — screw it. Put a nineteen-year-old soldier in the field and thirty minutes later, he knows more about this war than any Congressman learns on some fact-finding junket that never seems to get outside of the Green Zone or the Puzzle Palace. After awhile, a soldier learns to take care of business when he's outside the wire. In war, it's natural. Up north, if we were short on proof and knew it was going be another catch and release, we'd turn hajji over to the *Pesh Merga*. The Kurds knew what to do."

"Whatever it takes," Knowles said. "Don't know why this damn war should — "

"America's guilt," Gabe interrupted, "built a wall to commemorate my generation's war, another war we weren't allowed to win. Wars, walls and lost causes — damn! Even with the barbarians at the gates, they want us to play fair. What happened to our country, Sergeant? What happened to our fathers' and grandfathers' country where winning was everything, a country where Americans didn't shirk from the good fight, a country where duty was the essence of manhood?"

"Gone, brother, gone."

"In our lifetime, we've probably seen the last combat veteran who will ever be president. Look at the man who beat him in '92 — a draft dodging, sexual predator — the new anti-hero who felt the commoner's pain. Made me wanna puke."

"Lost a good bud," Knowles said, "at Mogadishu in '93 because of him."

Although Knowles could not see him, Gabe nodded. "He got to that moment in time and position of power to cause the loss of those soldiers through connections and cunning. Senator Fulbright helped him hide behind some bullshit hollow ROTC commitment to keep his chickenshit ass out of Nam, and then just as soon as he was safe with a high draft number — number 311 — screw ROTC, screw America. The whole time he was a student at Oxford he protested against the war and the U.S. of A. Twenty-some years later, 'Slick

Willie' replaces a genuine hero to become the new commander-in-chief. I have more respect for the jerks that went to jail or to Canada. At least they gave up something. The others like him who gamed the system, stayed home and fucked for peace...I don't know how they can sleep knowing there may be a name on the 'Wall' of some poor guy who took a bullet for them. The *prima donnas* who believed their privileged asses were more precious than those who answered the call to duty. Sergeant, they hide among us in plain sight and now make the rules and rewrite the history books to justify their cowardice."

"You're preaching to the choir." Knowles stood and raised his weapon. "Something's up."

Gabe saw a dark figure running toward them from the right flank. He lowered his NOD and aimed his rifle at the advancing mass. When he saw the infrared strobe blinking, he relaxed his grip and allowed the rifle to fall diagonally across his chest.

Sandoval stopped and leaned close to Knowles. "Just spotted a police vehicle cross the bridge from the Afak side. It got on the MSR and is traveling south, lights on."

They glimpsed the speeding SUV before it disappeared behind a rise.

"How about that," Knowles said, "our tax dollars at work. They actually do some patrols between bribes. Any blue forces showing up on the BFT, Sandoval?"

"Negative. Ski's too far south to show up, and nothing's coming from the north. Only us and the hajji cops."

"Let me know if you see anything else." Knowles walked to the far side of the Humvee and got in. He sat sideways, thrusting his right leg through the door-opening, boot resting on the sand. Then he stared at the Blue Force Tracker's screen.

Gabe stretched his legs and pounded on his cramped thighs. He walked around the truck several times, holding his rifle above his head, arching his neck and back. Stopping at the rear of the truck, he unbuttoned his pants and tried to urinate. After a painful eternity, he managed a dribble that hit the topside of his boots. He attempted to milk some more by giving it a final waggle, gave up and buttoned his pants. Then he walked toward the sergeant's open door.

Knowles looked up from the blue glow of the screen toward Gabe, but before he could speak, an intense orange hue engulfed the truck's interior and the surrounding dunes.

Gabe looked over the hood and saw a second, larger fireball. Fifteen seconds later, he heard the explosions. In that time, the sounds had traveled three miles over highway, desert and through thermal inclines. Much of the double 'boom' had dissipated before reaching him. To someone who had been there before, the sounds and the fireballs were distinct. He had been there.

"Somebody hit an IED."

"Can't be," Knowles said. "We cleared that section of the road comin' up."

"We cleared the northbound lanes, Sergeant. Not south."

Knowles looked at the screen, then Gabe. "It ain't one of ours. Get in." He switched to radio, ordered the snipers back to their vehicles and shouted, "Go."

"Lights on?" Bussard asked.

"Don't matter now," Knowles said. "Light 'em up."

They were airborne for most of the distance to the hardball. Every rut sent the truck and its occupants flying. Weightless one instant, weighing a ton the next, Gabe tossed around the cab like loose change in an out-of-balance dryer.

During the mad dash to the road, Knowles called the outpost. "COP 6, widow-maker two." Static.

"COP 6, widow-maker two." More static.

"Cop 6, widow-maker — "

"Send it," Barton said.

"We heard a possible IED detonation approximately four clicks south of our current location. Rolling there now to investigate. Map grid coordinates will follow."

"Widow-maker two, Roger," Barton radioed. "Be advised widow-maker six has actual mechanical issues and will not be able to assist. Are you requesting a QRF (quick reaction force)?"

"Negative at this time," Knowles answered. "Contact Echo, tell them to have a MEDEVAC on stand-by."

"Roger. I'll relay your SITREP and grid coordinates to widow-maker six." Barton whispered his next transmission. "Also be advised, lima-lima-mike-foxtrot in my vicinity."

"You're coming in broken, say again."

Barton repeated, "lima-lima-mike-foxtrot in my area."

"Tango-mike." Knowles switched from external to intercom and said, "Careful with your transmissions on the net. Bishop's in the TOC."

Once on the highway, the patrol resumed a staggered formation, this time in the southbound lanes, traveling at close to fifty mph. Less than two minutes later, and a mile distant, Gabe saw flames sprouting from the desert. It did not look like a place he wanted to be.

Narrowing the gap to the explosion's aftermath, Knowles said, "Widow-maker three and four, cross the median to the northbound lanes and stop a hundred meters this side of the blast. We'll make the approach to investigate. Keep our flanks and six clear."

Following confirmation of his orders by the other truck commanders, the sergeant turned to Bussard and said, "Dirty Bird, angle right when we're fifty meters out — Holy shit!"

It had been a 2006 GMC Jimmy; however, it looked more like a surrealist's twisted interpretation of one. What Salvador Dali had done to a clock, explosives had done to a car.

Amazingly, it had landed upright, almost as if some giant had plucked it from the road, breathed hellfire into it, pulled, pounded, beat and tore the rolled steel, and then gently set it down in the median, primed for another drive. Flames still licked the rear of the SUV. The tires were reduced to belted metal strands dripping rubber. The windows, paint, seats, plastic — charred, melted or burning. Flesh — much the same damage imposed on the inanimate components, but somehow worse.

"Stop!" Knowles cried out. "Light it up!"

The Humvee shuddered to a stop fifty meters short of the devastation — far enough away to provide some protection should there be a secondary explosion — close enough to feel the heat, close enough to smell the burning flesh, close enough to hear human fat sizzling like bacon in a white-hot frying pan.

Gabe contemplated the fate of the Iraqi police. Did they have enough time for a final thought, a last goodbye to this side. Or had the transition between realities taken less than an attosecond — that dimensionless quantity measured in Planck time. Although they were just Muslims, he still had a spark of humanity buried somewhere deep in that place he thought he had lost. He hoped their passing had been the latter because it was the finest way to pass, even surpassing a fantasy death in the midst of coitus. Neither pretty, nor an aroused contemplative, provocative release, but an unthinking, instantaneous demise; the death he hoped for when it was his time.

Knowles reached around his seat and grabbed a fire extinguisher. He tapped Hercules' leg and said, "Stay put." Then he bailed and ran toward the burning SUV.

Gabe loosened a second extinguisher from its fastener, pushed the three-hundred pound door open with his shoulder then chased after Knowles. By the time he arrived, the sergeant had already depleted the retardant. Gabe aimed a stream at the fuel tank and rear tires until his was empty. He dropped the extinguisher, scooped sand and threw it on flames reaching out from the undercarriage.

Sandoval and Gonzalez ran across the highway carrying more extinguishers. Within minutes, the threat of another explosion dwindled to the point they could relax and assess the scene.

The remains of two police were inside the SUV's cab; one's head was gone, his blackened, skinless hands still clutched the steering wheel. The other was scattered in the rear seat, a macabre jigsaw puzzle that would take a dedicated fanatic to piece together. Head and torso on the floorboard, one arm stuck in the headliner, a leg blown to rear the cargo area and still smoldering. The other arm and leg were missing, probably vaporized by the force of the explosion.

Knowles radioed Bussard to move the Humvee closer. As it neared, the added light made clear the full extent of the devastation.

Dark Meat fixed the searchlight's beam on a spot the near edge of the road. "Sergeant Knowles, I've got blood trails on the embankment."

"No way anyone survived."

"Sergeant, I can see blood, drag marks and at least one set of footprints heading down the embankment. They head off to the west."

Knowles walked to the edge of the highway and looked at the area where Dark Meat was shining the light. "I'll be damned."

"Speedy," Knowles transmitted, "grab the CLS bag and meet me at the truck. Dirty Bird, Rentvers, you're security. Bring a SAW and extra ammo."

Knowles walked to the truck, stopping when he was near Gabe. "I don't know what we got, so just stay here until we recon the area."

"Roger."

The sergeant opened Hercules' door and said, "Let's go. May need you."

Within seconds, Gabe lost sight of them and their muted red lights. Fifteen minutes later, and several hundred meters to the northwest, he again saw light. This time white.

Unlikely that there were any humans nearby since this part of the desert was barren of anything resembling civilization even by *Bedouin* standards, Gabe fired up a long overdue cigarette. He removed the red lens from his flashlight and walked to the edge of the asphalt near the beginning of the blood trail.

Choosing a suitable patch of curb, he sat and pondered the force needed to move two and a half tons of a speeding vehicle from point A to point B. He knew point B was in the median where the car landed.

$$v = \frac{s}{t}$$

or the car's forward velocity at the time of the detonation, could be problematic. However, if he could locate the spot where the blast initiated, he could probably figure out point A within a few meters, deduce the force required to send it flying, and then determine its approximate speed.

He field stripped his cigarette and tossed it on the asphalt. When he did, he saw that a large piece of the curb was missing. He had found point A.

One meter behind the gap was a crater surrounded by blackened sand, pieces of rock and jagged metal remnants from something. He stepped down into the middle of the bowl and used his rifle to approximate its depth and diameter. Just under a meter deep and two meters wide, he calculated the amount of explosives used — at least twenty kilos of weapons grade high explosives.

Most of the explosion's energy was directed forward, but any surviving evidence would be in the back blast. He lay on the rim of the crater and swept the beam across and down the embankment. Although not a powerful light, he saw the back blast covered about fifteen meters to either side and thirty meters to the rear of the crater.

He rolled over the edge, sliding down the steep embankment to the bottom. He moved to the center of the debris field and searched in a spiraling pattern. Five minutes into the hunt, he found it. Usable fingerprints were unlikely; still, he gloved up before touching the damaged cell phone. He pulled the Ziploc bag from his cargo pocket, tossed the toilet paper, and then dropped the phone inside. He had found the initiator.

He saw pieces of wire, remains of a motorcycle battery and metal fragments from the containers that housed the explosives. Since they had little forensic value, he left them for the desert to recycle. He then trudged diagonally up the embankment toward the SUV.

The flames were gone, replaced by black smoke that billowed straight up into the calm night air. He opened the passenger side door and shined the light at what was left of the front seats. When he rolled the head over, he saw a ten-millimeter piece of copper protruding from the skinless skull. After a brief search of the front area, he leaned over the headrest and looked at the rear compartment. Something had survived the explosion. He stepped out of the car and moved quickly to the other side.

A damaged Glock 9 mm was sitting on the floorboard. He picked it up by the handgrip. After he released the magazine, he racked the slide back ejecting the chambered round. Then he counted each round he peeled from the magazine. The handgun could hold seventeen bullets but there were only five in the magazine. Not an unusual practice in Iraq, yet, he had a tough time understanding anyone carrying a less than fully-loaded weapon. Seventeen bullets were seventeen chances to survive. However, he also understood they were another form of currency in Iraq. Police augmented their paltry salaries by selling the ammunition to the very insurgents dedicated to killing them. The money they received for a single bullet could feed a family for a day.

He reloaded the six rounds, slammed the magazine in the well, and stuck the Glock in a thigh pocket. Walking toward the back of the car, he saw a cylinder in the rear compartment. Almost six feet long, it looked familiar. After forcing up what remained of the liftgate, he made out a base plate, bipod and tube — a 120 mm mortar, the same caliber used to attack the outpost ten days earlier. He did not see mortar shells, so instead of running, he stayed put and continued his search.

The next thing that captured his interest was the leg. The sight did not bother him, but the object that had appended itself to the remaining flesh and bone intrigued him. He pulled out his dagger and pried it from the thigh — another cellphone. The Nokia probably survived because it was on the side of the leg opposite the blast. Damaged, but not as bad as the one he found earlier, he placed it inside the pocket with the other phone.

Ready for another cigarette, he left the median and crossed the highway. Along the way to his smoking area, he kicked shards of glass and metal, mere yards from the blast's epicenter. He smiled. Back on the curb, he fired up a Marlboro and relaxed. He now knew A, B and the 'V' factor — the car's speed. Equation balanced — mystery solved.

Four cigarettes later, he saw a white light returning from the desert. He lowered his NOD and was able to make out a single soldier walking fast. When the figure started up the embankment, Gabe raised the goggles and stood.

"We found one alive," Knowles said, "or I should say our terp found him. Hercules wrapped the survivor's arm in some raggedy-ass bandana, but the hajji's tore up bad. About bled out. Ain't gonna make it. Couldn't locate the other survivor."

"Is he talking?" Gabe asked.

"Some before he passed out, but it didn't make much sense.

291

Speedy put on a real tourniquet, started an IV and gave him some other shit, but I give him thirty, maybe forty minutes tops."

"What'd he say?"

"Only thing I got was he's a cop named Dool Fikker, Fucker, or something like that, and they were happily driving along at about sixty en route to Hajil a Bas. Next thing he remembered was waking up on the side of the road."

"They were going sixty?"

"Yeah, fifty or sixty."

"Sergeant, walk with me while I tell you a story. Cigarette?"

"Don't smoke. You can tell me the story after I call this in to the outpost."

"Hold that thought until you hear me out, Sergeant."

Gabe led the sergeant to the crater and pointed out the debris in the back blast. "It was an EFP."

"How'd you know?"

"Check out the head in the Jimmy, and you'll see a piece of copper sticking out," Gabe said. "Best I can figure, about twenty kilos of high explosives." He pointed down the embankment and said, "Found the cell phone initiator over there."

Gabe walked toward the median, but stopped in the middle of the road and kicked some metal fragments he had spotted earlier. "You see that?"

"Sure, but so what? The whole country's a dump site."

"I'll get to it later." Gabe pulled both phones from his pocket. "Found another cell in the trunk along with something else you need to see. Take these, and when we get home, you can run your computer program against their SIM cards."

"Runnin' out of time, Gabe. Get to the point."

"Two minutes, Sergeant, two minutes. There's something in the trunk you need to see."

Gabe stuck a hand in his cargo pocket and started to pull out the Glock, but decided it could wait. He walked to the rear of the SUV and shined his flashlight on the weapon. Knowles spoke before he could.

"Shit! I saw one of those when we cleared Samarra few years back. Looks like a *Hadid* one-twenty."

"Probably the same tube used to kill White Meat, Sergeant."

"Hold on, there. That's quite a leap, Gabe."

"Don't think so. These men wore two uniforms — one as police officers and the other as militia, probably *Jaish al Mahdi*."

292

"What in the hell are you saying?"

"The hajji told you they were driving at fifty or sixty mph. Doesn't really matter which, because they were moving at exactly zero point zero inches per hour when the bomb blew. Remember the debris in the road?"

"Yes."

"If you draw a straight line from the crater through the debris, it stops right here where we're standing. Had the vehicle been moving, it would've blown in a trajectory away from the crater in the direction of travel. It didn't. It's perpendicular to the crater — almost a perfect ninety degrees. Only means one thing. It wasn't moving."

"What are you telling me, Gabe?"

"I'm telling you the cops placed the IED. I'm telling you they screwed up. My guess is they entered an arming code as a speed dial number in the trigger cell phone. The one carrying it must've accidentally pocket-dialed and activated the device. Once a warm body crossed the infrared beam, or someone started the engine, the heat signature set it off. I don't know how they knew where we'd be tonight, but I'm also telling you the bomb was meant for us. And I'm telling you that mortar was used to kill White Meat."

Knowles reached inside the trunk, rolled the mortar tube closer and brushed the black soot away from its barrel. He called out the numbers he could make out — 33-4718. He stepped back and said, "I'll take that cigarette."

Gabe lit one and handed it to Knowles. "Can I talk to the cop?"

"I'll call this into the TOC, and then we'll go see our fucking partner helping us combat the enemies of Iraq."

After Knowles radioed Barton, he and Gabe covered the distance to the survivor in less than ten minutes. Along the trail, Gabe saw footprints, drag marks and blood splotches consistent with a serious wound. He thought the second Iraqi cop likely beat feet when he heard the soldiers approach.

Blue Chem lights ringed the medic and his dying charge. Gonzalez could do nothing more for the unconscious patient other than monitor his plunging vitals.

Hercules hovered nearby muttering an Arabic chant. Bussard and Rentvers laid prone atop a dune ten meters further west, scanning the area with night vision goggles.

"Doc," Gabe said, "has he said anything else?"

"*Nada.* Heeez no *bueno* to *habla.*"

"Anything you can give him to wake him up?"

"No *permisso*. *Mi* a medic, *y mi* can only watch heem die."

"Give him a shot or something, Speedy," Knowles said.

Gonzalez shook his head. Nevertheless, he pulled a syringe and a capsule out of the combat life support bag. He jammed the needle into the patient's good arm, then broke the cap of ammonium carbonate, mixed it with water inside a specimen cup and held the mixture under the Iraqi's nose. Within moments, he stirred. He stared blankly at the medic.

Gabe recognized him. The thick mustache was unmistakable. He was the police officer he saw in Afak before the attack on the outpost. "Stop praying, Hercules. Ask if his name is Ghazi."

"Mister Quinn, his name is Dhul Fiqar, sir."

"Let's try this again. I'll tell you what to ask, you translate exactly what I say, then tell me his answer. Do you understand, Hercules?"

"But, sir — "

Gabe held up a hand and turned to Knowles. "Sergeant, I need some quality time with this hajji."

"Ask him whatever you want, Gabe."

"I need to be alone with him."

"Uh-uh, Gabe."

He lowered his voice so only Knowles could hear. "Sergeant, he'll die soon. When he does, the answers die with him. I can get him to talk, but I don't have a lot of time. He needs to believe that only one person can help or hurt him. Everybody standing around is a distraction. Give me the terp, back off to the vehicles and let me do my thing. We need answers, Sergeant. This man tried to kill us."

Knowles stared at him for a long time before he nodded. "I can't leave you here without security, Gabe."

"There's not another hajji within miles. His fellow insurgent is halfway to Baghdad. I'll be fine."

"Speedy, pack it up," Knowles said. "We're returning to the vehicles."

"*El sargento, no puedo abandonar* a *mi paciente. Él está vivo y mi trabajo es ayudarlo.*"

"You're giving me a fucking headache speaking that Mexican shit. All I caught was no. Big, *grande* fucking mistake. Your job is to follow orders and say, '*Sí, sargento.*' We have a priority medical emergency back at the vehicles."

"*Lo sergeant de emergencia?*"

"English, Speedy, fucking English. Sergeant Sandoval has a life-threatening case of crotch rot so get your ass in gear, give me your

294

radio and move out."

"*Sí, sargento.*"

Knowles handed the medic's radio to Gabe. "It's on the patrol frequency. Any problems, I mean anything, you shout out."

"Thanks."

"Dirty Bird, Rentvers, walk slack."

As if on cue, a wind gust kicked up sand, clouding their departure. Within meters, the desert swallowed them up. Alone now, except for Hercules and the dying cop, Gabe took off his helmet and laid it on the ground. When he propped the muzzle of his rifle on top of it, he saw the bloody bandana. He picked it up and turned it over several times. "This yours?"

"Yes, Mister Quinn."

Gabe dropped the cloth to the ground and focused on the cop. Backlit in blue, the light made his leaking blood appear black. There was a lot of black.

"Ask him again if he is Ghazi."

"Sir, as I explained to you before, the name Ghazi Codar el Ahmar is nonsense. Such a man does not exist. It is only a myth, much like the legend of your Superman."

"A myth — Superman." Gabe lit a cigarette and squatted beside the police officer. "*In teh*, are you Ghazi Codar el Ahmar?"

His eyes darted between Gabe and Hercules, but he said nothing.

Gabe held the glowing tip of the cigarette close to the Iraqi's eye.

"*In teh*, Ghazi? Gabe repeated, "*Deh tif tih him*, do you understand?"

He shook his head.

"*Shiss-mek*, what is your name?"

"Dhul Fiqar," he answered.

"Sir, as I told you, he is not Ghazi. There is no Ghazi."

Gabe raised the cigarette and took a long drag. Then he placed it between the officer's lips. Dhul Fiqar smiled weakly.

"Ask him if he wants to live to see the sun again."

"I do not understand, Mister Quinn."

"Let me show you, then."

Gabe loosened the tourniquet on the dying man's arm causing blood to gush. The cigarette fell from the cop's lips when he screamed. Gabe straddled him, pinning his arms with his legs, and then stuffed the bandana inside his mouth.

"You won't believe what's going to happen next, hajji. You will tell me what I want to know."

"Mister Gabriel Quinn, you must not do this, sir."

"Do you know this man, Hercules? Do you know for a fact he is not Ghazi?"

"Sir, I do not know him, but I know he is not Ghazi."

"Let's have a conversation, a little chat between friends, Dhul Fiqar. If you answer my questions, I'll get the Doc back and he'll fix you up. Nod your head."

Gabe yanked the bandana from his mouth. The Iraqi gasped, but did not scream. Dhul Fiqar looked beyond him to Hercules.

Gabe grabbed him by the head and forced him to nod. "Forget about him. It's just you and me, buddy. Now, where is Ghazi and who is he? *Wen nil*, Ghazi? *Mih noo*, Ghazi?"

Dhul Fiqar shut his eyes and moaned. He shook his head and said, "*Meh dah ef tih him*, I do not understand."

"Bullshit!" Gabe probed the wound with a gloved finger. Dhul Fiqar's screams echoed between the dunes. Gabe stopped. The screams trailed off to moans of resignation.

"Suq ash Shuyukh," Dhul Fiqar whispered. "Ali — "

Hercules dropped to his knees and put a hand across Dhul Fiqar's mouth. "*Sah, hada kafie,* shut up, that is enough."

Gabe knocked Hercules to the ground, then jumped up. He kicked the interpreter's legs and feet repeatedly. "What the hell are you telling him? Whose damn side are you on?"

Hercules scrambled backward on his butt until he was yards from the crazy American. He stood and brushed the dirt from his clothes. "I am on your side, Mister Quinn, but this man is delirious. He does not know what he is saying."

"He won't say shit now thanks to you. He seems to know Superman and where he is. This piece of shit tried to kill us tonight. Let me do the thinking and you do your fucking job and translate."

"Of course, Mister Quinn. What is it you want me to ask him?"

"Why he had a mortar in the police car."

Hercules' expression gave away nothing — no hint of the bombshell that followed.

"Sir, he found the weapon during a routine patrol and was transporting it to the police station for safekeeping until he could give it to the American soldiers."

The words exploded over him like an airburst, fracturing his understanding of events. As the fog cleared, the thunderclap resonated like a message from God — Judas lives. He understood. Many lies had been exposed because a perpetrator volunteered information before

296

their consciousness could assimilate the gravity of the question or their circumstances. In law enforcement, excited utterances carried more weight than measured statements.

Gabe picked up the bandana. Even in the artificial light, he could see markings beneath the blood and dirt. Three dots and a crescent moon — dots he could now connect. He remembered the other detail the Army officer had told him about the insurgents released that day long ago in Mosul. Each had a tattoo, the same tattoo. Three dots and a crescent moon — a sign to all that they were mujahedeen and had killed an infidel. Someone else had a tattoo — someone else had killed Americans. Now he knew why the insurgent did not fire the RPG at them. Now he knew why Hercules stood during the firefight in Afak. He was one of them. He was safe, and because of his close proximity to him, Gabe was safe that day. The realization dredged up emotions he had sworn to keep in check.

"You said you don't know this man. You never looked inside the police car because you were here. Doc said the cop was unconscious when he arrived and only roused after he started pumping him with fluids. Yet, you know why a mortar was in the car."

Hercules and the officer were friends, but not his; they were his enemies. He glanced at his rifle next to the man wearing Nikes. Alone in the desert, except for his link to survival several hundred yards away, he allowed the id to override his ego and drive his next action.

Gabe turned his back on the interpreter and lit another cigarette. On a distant dune, he saw the imaginary jury through blowing sand — White Meat, the dead girls from Afak, Sabirra, and all of the others from his past. They spoke in one voice — guilty.

Gabe stared down at his dying enemy.

Dhul Fiqar panicked at the sight of the lit cigarette.

"It is all right, my friend." Gabe leaned down and placed the cigarette between the Iraqi's lips.

Dhul Fiqar nodded and said, *"Shokran."*

Gabe turned toward Hercules. "Fool me once — "

Hercules looked at Gabe, then at the rifle. "What are you saying, Mister Quinn?"

"I'm saying checkmate. Game over, my friend. Or should I say, my enemy."

Hercules dropped the ruse. It was over. "If true, you could not prove anything, and without proof, nothing would happen to me. You are naïve to think you know the ways of my country. Take me in. Please take me in. The elders, police chiefs; even the president, would pressure you American fools to release me. I would be freed within a day. You are no angel, Quinn, you are a devil."

Hercules spat at Gabe. Then he inched toward the rifle.

When it came to justice, the deck was stacked against the Coalition. The only jury that mattered had rendered its verdict in the desert courtroom. The sentence was clear. He removed the damaged Glock from his pocket and jacked a live round into the chamber.

Hercules froze.

Enjoying the cigarette, the condemned did not see it coming. Gabe placed the muzzle an inch from Dhul Fiqar's head. He held his free hand behind the gun and turned his head. The blocking hand contained most of the blowback, yet some of the blood found its way onto his body armor. He raised the weapon above the body and shot the remaining five rounds into the sand. Then he eased the slide forward, giving the weapon the appearance of being loaded.

The smoke from the burning cigarette lying on Dhul Fiqar's chest mixed with the translucent swirls escaping from the hole in his head. Gabe picked up the cigarette and inhaled deep until all that remained was the filter. He pitched the butt to the ground and pivoted. Then he tossed the Glock to the ground near Hercules' feet.

Hercules glanced at Gabe, the rifle, then at the handgun. He scooped up the Glock, took aim and squeezed the trigger. Click. He pulled the slide back, let it slam forward, and tapped the bottom of the magazine. Again, he pulled the trigger. Click.

Gabe smiled.

Hercules dropped the gun and scrambled toward the rifle.

Gabe's marksmanship was better with a knife than with a firearm. The blade struck the back of Hercules' thigh causing him to cartwheel through the air. He landed solidly on his back driving the dagger deeper into his muscle. Squirming in pain, he reached behind and tried to pull the blade out of his leg. The agony was too much; he left it in place and frantically scratched the dirt struggling to escape from his attacker.

Gabe blocked his path. He bent down and yanked the knife out. Hercules screamed.

"That's gotta hurt."

"Pl-pl-please...Gabriel...do no more. I need help."

Gabe rolled him over with his feet then sat across his thighs. Hercules winced and let loose repeated screams. He covered Hercules' mouth with his left hand and shoved down hard. "Shhhh....shhhh. This will end."

He silenced Hercules with a full-mouth kiss. As he did, he rammed the blade deep into the his stomach then slowly worked the steel up through the flesh and organs until it was blocked by the sternum. Using his free hand, he probed the ribs. After he found the gap above the heart he pushed the blade deep enough to nick the spine. Hercules arched his back once. Then he was dead.

Gabe heard the charging diesels and saw the meandering white lights splintering the blowing sand. Yet none of it pierced his consciousness. He removed the knife from the still chest and spread the skin taunt against Hercules' skull. He meticulously carved the Judas mark on his forehead — ح — a mark he hoped Hercules would carry to his maker for final judgment. Maybe a god could forgive his enemy, but not Gabe.

"Mr. Quinn...what are you — " Winded from a two-hundred-yard dash across the desert, Bussard paused to catch his breath and to absorb what he was witnessing. He aimed the flashlight beam at the man still mutilating the corpse. "He's dead...you got him."

Gabe stopped cutting and stared apathetically at the interruption. "Go away."

Then he resumed carving.

"Stop, Mr. Quinn."

Gabe ignored him.

Bussard tackled him so hard, both were knocked breathless when they hit the ground. Bussard pushed up from the sand.

"Gabe, before the others get here, you need to — "

Bussard held out his hand. "You did good, but it's over. Let me help you up, sir."

Gabe dropped the dagger and grasped the soldier's arm.

Bussard ran his hands over Gabe's blood soaked uniform quickly searching for wounds. "I'll get you some water as soon as the scrgcant's here."

Bussard looked at Hercules. The dead man's torso looked like slaughterhouse renderings. Blood still trickled from the gashes on his face. He shook his head and said, "Jesus Christ, Gabe." He pulled a black-tan *shemagh* from his butt pack and covered Hercules face. Then he looked at the dead cop.

"Sir, careful what you say when they get here. I mean, think real hard before you make a sound. You could be in some trouble, sir."

"It had to be done," Gabe said. "White Meat's dead because of them."

The truck stopped ten meters short of the scene. Knowles' feet hit the ground before the engine's final sputter after the ignition had been switched off. Bathed in the light from the Humvee, the battle's aftermath was clear to him, and soon would be to the rest of the squad. "Dark Meat, tell the others to form a perimeter."

As each truck pulled up, drivers and gunners aimed spotlights on the dead. Gabe shielded his eyes from the blinding lights then turned away.

Knowles walked by Gabe to Hercules. He lifted the *shemagh* from the head.

"I don't think all the men need to see that, Sergeant," Bussard said.

Knowles placed the scarf back across Hercules' face. "Get on the horn and tell Barton what happened. Check that. I don't know what happened yet. Mr. Quinn, what in the hell did you do?"

"I fixed a problem, Sergeant."

"I fucking need more than that."

"All right, I'll break it down for you." Gabe lit a cigarette. "The cop volunteered some information. Ghazi is in Suq ash Shuyukh. First name's, Ali. He was about to give up the rest of his name when Hercules cut him off."

Gabe pointed at the Glock near Hercules' body. "Somebody missed the cop's gun. Hercules didn't. Before I knew what was happening he shot the cop and then turned it on me. I was away from my rifle. No time to get to my Beretta, so I used a knife. We fought — he came in second place. Hercules was the leak. Not anymore. End of story."

"That's it?"

"Yep."

"Seems you left out a few details…like the artwork on Hercules' head. Did he carve himself up, or did he have some help?"

Gabe shrugged. He arched his neck back and exhaled a long stream of smoke. He looked at Knowles, then blew several smoke rings.

Knowles shook his head and said, "Right." Then he walked to the Humvee, grabbed the radio handset and hailed the outpost. "COP 6… widow-maker two."

"Send it," Barton said.

"Four dead. Three hajji cops and Hercules. No need for a MEDEVAC. Two bodies are crispy critters, in pieces from the blast. The other cop had a GSW to the head and other wounds from the explosion. We'll mark the area and let the Iraqi authorities deal with them and Hercules. We've secured an enemy 120 mm mortar for transport. ETA at the COP, about an hour."

"Roger," Barton replied. "Uh, widow-maker two — "

"Give me that, Private," Second Lieutenant Bishop said. "How did Hercules die?"

"Sir, we can discuss the details when I return."

"Negative. Tell me now."

"When Captain Ski's in the loop we'll discuss it."

"Until he is available, I am your commander. Sergeant, you will answer to me. How did Hercules die?"

"Sir, you came in broken."

"Don't try that crap on me," Bishop shouted. "Answer my question or I'll have you up on charges."

Knowles looked at Gabe leaning against the Humvee's hood. "Mr. Quinn...well, sir, he was forced to take him out."

The sergeant waited. Then he waited some more. A minute later Bishop said, "Stay put. I'll get back to you."

Knowles dropped the handset on the console and got out of the truck. Gabe had already slumped against the front tire. The medic and several soldiers were inspecting the bodies. "Get the fuck back on security," he yelled.

As the soldiers walked past the sergeant, one stopped and asked, "What the fuck was that on his head, Sergeant?"

"Forget about it."

Thirty minutes later, the sun broke above the horizon. Gabe missed it. He was asleep.

Bussard, who had been monitoring the radio, stepped out from the truck and shouted, "Sergeant, Bishop's on patrol freq. Needs to talk at you."

Gabe awakened. Wanting coffee and a smoke, he settled on a cigarette.

Knowles took the handset from Bussard and said, "Go for widow-maker two, LT."

"I have conferred with JAG," Bishop said. "An AR 15-6 has been initiated. Major Laddick wants the bodies of Hercules and the cop with the gunshot wound for evidence."

Before he keyed the microphone, Knowles muttered, "fucking fantastic." Then he responded to Bishop. "Sir, you're jumping to conclusions...disregard. Roger, I'm on it."

He handed the radio to Bussard. Then he looked at the other vehicles parked nearby. All had extra fuel, razor wire, traffic cones and assorted packs bulging from webbed straps and zip ties attached to their cargo lids. In addition, one was loaded with the enemy mortar tube.

"Bussard, Dark Meat," he said, "Our truck's the meat wagon. Clear the shit from the deck and split it up between the other trucks, then secure the bodies on the back. Since we no longer have a terp, put the mortar in the empty seat."

Knowles walked to the front of the truck and looked down at Gabe. "You know what a fifteen-six is. Ain't fun. Shit. Forget it. Best we don't talk."

The soldiers used ratchet straps and Bungee cords to secure the dead on the rear deck lid. After they finished the grisly task, the pair stepped away out of earshot from the rest of the squad. Bussard talked, Dark Meat nodded.

Just as Gabe finished relieving himself, he felt a hand on his shoulder. It was large and black.

"We've got your six, brother."

"Load up," Knowles shouted. " Let's get the hell out of here before we're assigned a zip code and hajji sends us mail."

*****

The survivor had hidden for hours in a slight depression. After the sounds of the American trucks faded, he worked the cramps from his legs and arms. Thankful he had been posted as a lookout a hundred meters away from the car when the bomb blew prematurely, he did not relish what was now required of him. It could be worse than the explosion. He made the call on his cell phone.

"Ghazi, it did not go well...no...no...yes, we did, but...I understand...Dhul Fiqar is dead...an American...yes...he executed him...no...Gabriel Quinn...Ghazi, the American also killed your brother...Ghazi...are you there, Ghazi?... I am sorry...no, his death was not quick...yes, Ghazi, many Americans will die tonight."

*****

Fifteen kilometers into the silent procession, Dark Meat stood on the bolster seat and reached behind the turret to the deck lid. Shortly after that, he hunkered down in the harness and tapped Bussard's helmet.

Topping a hill two kilometers later, Bussard stomped hard on the brakes, sped up, back on the brake pedal and then the accelerator.

"What the hell," Knowles shouted.

"Thought I saw something, Sarge," Bussard said. "Guess not."

Looking at the side view mirror, Knowles caught a glimpse of something tumbling across the pavement. The trailing Humvee raced over the brim, ran over it, swerved right, hit something else then fishtailed across the highway before coming to a jittery rest. The third vehicle in line finished the job before slamming into the rear of the stopped truck. Both trucks were pushed forward another twenty meters by the impact.

"Widow-maker two…widow-maker three," Sandoval radioed. "Got a situation."

Bussard slowed the truck, finally stopping in the middle of the highway.

"Guns forward," Knowles ordered, "and eyes open until I figure out what the fucking problem is."

Knowles and Gabe got out.

"Get back in the truck," Knowles said.

The sergeant jogged toward the entangled trucks, but stopped short when he saw Hercules' crushed body near the median. Farther back, two soldiers were lying on the ground pointing at something under the rear of the third vehicle. Knowles walked the rest of the way.

Dhul Fiqar's corpse was in parts. Some of him had wrapped around the Humvee's axle. Other pieces were pinned under the tire.

Knowles smiled.

"Un-fuck these trucks. Speedy, get some body bags."

Knowles looked up at the Humvee's turret. A teenaged soldier was spraying the inside of the truck with vomit.

"After you finish abusing government property, help Speedy bag the road kill."

Chapter 23

In a perfect world, Samsāra and Disney would be relevant; a thousand deaths possible, Mickey Mouse would fly

July 15, 0845 hours

Second Lieutenant Bishop did not wait. This could be the shining moment in his brief, non-stellar military career. Before the patrol had a chance to decompress, unload the vehicles, or even see the man about a dog, he was on them.

"Where are the bodies, Sergeant?"

Knowles took off his helmet and body armor, setting both on the hood of the Humvee, then ran fingers across his high and tight military haircut. He pointed at the black bags still on the rear deck lid.

"Get them out of the sun and place them in the reefer storage."

"With our food, LT?"

"Sergeant, you still seem to have an issue with chain of command. I think — you do. Those bodies are evidence and need to be preserved, so follow my orders."

"Yes, sir."

Busy in the turret breaking down the fifty-caliber, Dark Meat looked down at Knowles when he shouted to him.

"Stop what you're doing and get the LT's evidence off the truck."

"Roger, Sergeant."

Dark Meat hopped over the turret's edge and loosened the ratchets on the web straps. He nudged the first bag over the side, then lifted the second one above his head and tossed it to the rocks near Bishop's feet. It split at the seam. The mess that spilled out was identifiable to the soldiers who had scraped it off the road and from the axle. To an outsider, however, it was unrecognizable as anything that had ever breathed.

Bishop scrambled back, falling on his buttocks. He grimaced when he saw the reddish-grey bits and pieces clinging to his pant leg and boot. Legs spread out awkwardly across the gravel, he raised the infected one and tried to shake off the foreign contagion. He gave up. Pointing at the ripped body bag, he yelped, "What is that?"

"Your evidence," Knowles said. "From the looks of it, I'm guessing the hajji cop. Hercules is in a little better shape, except for his head. Wanna see, LT?"

Bishop fumbled with the flap on the holster then pulled out the loaded handgun.

Knowles muttered "shit." Then he ran for cover behind the truck. "Careful there, LT. No need to do him again. I'm pretty sure he's dead, sir."

Bishop ignored the sergeant and used the Beretta to rub the gunk from his uniform. He started to re-holster but stopped when he saw leftovers smeared on the gun barrel. "Yuck." He dropped it and scooted further back, putting a fair amount of distance between him and the weapon. He pointed at the nearest soldier and said, "Clean my gun."

Feeling reasonably safe since Bishop was now weaponless and somewhat harmless, Knowles gave up his cover and walked around the truck.

"Sergeant Knowles," Bishop said, "take the bodies to the cooler. Strip Quinn of all weapons and restrict him to quarters. Colonel Erickson is flying in this evening and will want answers. Be in the TOC in fifteen minutes to provide me those answers. But first, I must shower and change uniforms."

"Is Mr. Quinn under arrest?"

"Just do as I ordered." Bishop stood, looked glaringly at each grinning soldier, did an about face, then ran to his trailer.

Knowles mulled over the needs of the haggard looking soldiers gathered around the bodies. Although still smiling from the comic relief, they needed food, rest and time to blow off steam. That was not going to happen.

"Private, after you clean our feckless leader's weapon make sure it's empty before returning it. Sandoval, form a detail to re-bag this shit. Belay that. Triple bag 'em before they go in with our food. Dirty Bird, I need you to — where's Quinn?"

Bussard pointed to a t-wall twenty meters away. "Over there, Sergeant."

Gabe was squatting next to his body armor, helmet and M9 shoulder rig. Water bottle in hand, he splashed some on his face, then rubbed the hardened bloodstains until they reconstituted. He doused his hair, flicked the excess from his hands and briskly shook his head. The runny mixture trickled down his green-red freckled uniform, eventually forming a cherry colored pool on the ground. The only perceptible white on him was that surrounding the irises. The impromptu bath gave him the appearance of an anguished sunburned

305

demon. He would be at home in hell.

Gabe looked up when the sergeant stopped at his feet.

"You missed some on your forehead." Knowles pulled toilet tissue from his pocket and said, "Let me help."

"Don't need it. After I go to the shitter, I'll grab a shower."

"Shower's not a good idea right now. Maybe later, Gabe."

The sergeant turned toward the soldiers looking for a volunteer. "Dirty Bird. Secure your weapon and get over here."

Bussard handed his rifle to the medic and jogged over to them. "What's up, Sarge?"

"Hang on a second. Gabe, I'm sorry but I got orders. Need your weapons. Dirty Bird will hold them until Ski gets back and clears up this goat-fuck. Take care of your business, then hang out in your rack. I'll send someone over with coffee and food."

Gabe pointed at his gear clumped beside him. "M4, M9, ammo." He pulled out the boot dagger and pitched it to the top of the pile. "Skip the food. Coffee's fine. I've gotta shit."

Gabe pushed up from the ground. Temporarily confused, he looked around to get his bearings. He caught a whiff of his objective, so he forced his right foot, then the left to move, until the motions became automatic. His slow approach gave him time to think. The events from the hours before had not fully registered on him. Reward-driven dopamine still ripped through his nervous system, clouding logic. He slowed the pace more as he tried to dominate the chemical so he could unravel the one burning mystery remaining. *How in hell did Hercules set us up?*

Just before he smacked into the stall, he looked up from his boots. He tried the door on the left.

"In use," a soldier said.

"Sorry." Gabe looked under the second stall door. He saw a pair of boots, one fretfully tapping.

Having come through the patrol's mayhem, he could handle the surprises left on the toilet seat by Hercules. He stepped to the last stall and flung the door open. The makeshift hinges resisted the abuse. The door slammed back, bounced several times, finally coming to rest an inch from the frame. Unperturbed, he elbowed it open, slid sideways through the gap into the dark, stagnant booth. He dropped his pants and perched on the plywood seat above the cutout. He reached out, pulled the door closed then tried to lock it. The latch was broken. It creaked open again. *Can't get any privacy in this damn shithole.*

The stubborn hinge unhinged him. He exploded, taking his

misplaced rage out on the door, the walls and the gravel beneath his feet. The battle brought on cheers from the soldiers in the adjacent stalls, but did little to quell his fury. It seemed as if the door were Iraq, Hercules, Ghazi and everything else gone wrong in life. He pulled up his pants and readied to kick the door free from its binds. A slice of light stopped him. The invasive sunray not only showered light on his boot, it also was a beacon of enlightenment. The internal storm subsided.

Then he saw flecks of dried blood tarnishing the necklace's luster. The sight of her blood took him from puzzling enlightenment to a darker, baser plane. Gale force winds of wrath walloped his fleeting control. The battle was back on. He pounded his fists against the walls, shredding his knuckles and causing blood to splatter the wood. Each blow, each kick, turned another page in a gallery of snapshots of how he imagined Hercules had drilled the child, rammed her with steel, mauled her and ripped out her tongue. Then he thought about his all-too-merciful execution of the fiend. He wanted to breathe life into the child killer so he could kill him again a thousand times, each time drawn out in a more horrific manner than that suffered by the girl.

"Get some more," one of the soldiers said as he left.

"That must be a bunker buster you're dropping," the other said. "I'll get the LT and you can drop his ass down the hole to keep it company. Good luck, buddy."

Cowed by the departing soldiers, he curbed his murky fantasy and fell back on logic. *Mickey Mouse didn't fall out of the sky.*

He scoured every inch of the wooden outhouse, from ground to head height, only stopping when he could see no more from his vantage point.

He stepped on top of the plywood bench and looked above the door. Although dark inside the wooden cavern, he saw a plastic bag crammed deep into the bare frame. He stretched as far as he could and wiggled the bag, finally freeing it from the recess. When he yanked, his fingers grazed something else. He left the bag in place and probed the wooden grotto until he found an edge he could grasp. With a tenuous finger hold on the object, he pushed off the wall, almost falling through the cutout into the waste below. He regained his balance and looked closer at the article — a notebook, about three and a half by five inches, half an inch thick.

He dropped it to the rocks, then reached back and grabbed the plastic bag. As he brought it closer to his face, a strong odor rocked him back on his heels, again almost causing him to fall knee deep in shit. He laid it on top of the plywood and stepped down, then picked up the pad by its spine. As he did, a piece of paper fell out and floated to the ground. He snatched it up from the rocks and along with the notebook, placed it in the same pocket as the necklace.

He picked up the plastic bag and held it an arm's length from his nose. When he kicked the door open, the burst of morning sun shed light on the bag's contents and the mystery of how Hercules communicated with *Jaish al Mahdi*. Inside the Ziploc was a cell phone. His sense of smell had been precise. The soldiers did not perform cavity searches on Hercules when he entered or left the outpost. Gabe doubted the small man could conceal a phone charger and cord in the same space, but he was sure a thorough search of his room would produce the culprit.

Forensics be damned. He held his breath, extracted the phone and pressed the power button. It sputtered to life with a green glow. Another mystery he did not know had been one, laid to rest. He put nature's business on hold and rushed to the operations center.

"Sergeant — " he stopped talking when he realized Knowles was on the radio.

"Captain Ski, can you make it quicker than that?" Knowles said. "Sir, I've gotta deal with Bishop in five minutes....Roger, understood...tell him nothing...stone-wall... Yes, sir. COP 6 out."

Knowles laid the handset on the bookshelf. "Coffee's on the way to your trailer, Gabe. You need to disappear before our junior leader returns from his shower."

Gabe pulled the necklace, notebook and sheet from his pocket. "Found these hidden in Hercules' private shitter. I gave this necklace to a child in Afak; the one who was tortured. The notebook is in Arabic. Could be nothing, could be something. You may want to get Dawud started on translation. I haven't looked at the paper yet."

He placed the book and necklace on top of a chair, unfolded the sheet and then flattened it on the desk.

"Schematic of the outpost, Sergeant. Shows the TOC, weapon locations by type, even details where you eat, sleep and shit. I don't read hajji, but those scribbles are probably measurements noting distances between every structure in the camp. Good target references for indirect fire."

Then he pulled out the cell phone. "Don't want to tell you how to do your job, but I'd sure appreciate it if you'd run this through the decoder-retriever and cross-reference the results against the SIM cards from the others I gave you."

Gabe tossed the phone to Knowles and turned toward the door. Midway to it, he stopped and looked over his shoulder at the speechless sergeant. "The phone has a camera. Check it. May get lucky and put a face to Ghazi, aka Ali...aka the fucking enemy."

Chapter 24
Omertà code of Sicilian monkeys:
non vedo, non sento, non parlo

TOC, COP 6, July 15, 0915 hours

All, except Knowles, looked up when Second Lieutenant Bishop bounced into the trailer looking like a self-assured action figure exuding superhuman strength. His fresh uniform, starched and pressed with decisive, knife-edge creases running the length of the pants, would cause a seasoned sergeant major to experience an apoplectic fit. Not only was the practice against regulations, using starch defeated the integral flame resistant properties of the material and made the uniform less breathable. He looked smoking hot, and probably was.

"PFC Barton," he said, "there is a box of lobster tails and one case of ribeyes in the freezer. Colonel Erickson may join us for dinner. Prepare a surf and turf meal for him and the other officers. Set up table decorations left over from Independence Day, clean the dining room from floor to ceiling, and have it ready for a white-glove inspection by 1400 hours. No enlisted personnel will enter the dining room after my inspection. There are several damaged cases of MREs outside of the dry goods trailer. Distribute those to the soldiers, but no cherry picking. I do not want to find half-eaten vegetarian omelets or pasta entrees in the garbage."

"Yes, sir."

"PFC Bussard, your uniform is a mess. You — "

Dawud stepped out of Captain Ski's office holding the notebook. He stared at Bishop with one eye while the free spirited one took a jerky circuitous route, only pausing long enough for him to conjure an over-the-top smile, then it was off to the races again.

"Sergeant Knowles," Bishop said. "Why is that man here and why is he in my...I mean the commander's office?"

The sergeant did not look up. He shook his head and said, "working," then returned to the task of uploading a second SIM card in the smart card cell phone file retriever.

"Well, he…he needs to work somewhere else. We need to talk."

Knowles took a deep breath, then slowly exhaled. "No disrespect LT, but we don't need to talk. We're busy trying to fight a war."

"Do you realize who you are talking to? I'm an officer and — "

Knowles finally looked up and locked eyes with the officer. "Sir, you're a damn — " He checked himself before crossing the line. "The captain will be back in a few hours. Take it up with him."

"I will, Sergeant. You better believe I will." With that, he skulked out of the trailer.

Knowles choked back the rising bile and turned toward Dawud. "Come up with anything yet?"

"Actually quite a bit," he said. "A long process since Hercules' syntax is a bit of a divergence from proper Arabic, but I have managed to wade through the morass and mine the essentials."

"Drop the bullshit and get to the money shot."

"Certainly. This is a diary of sorts — chronological, with precise information about each outgoing and returning patrol. Hercules was…what is that expression? Oh yes, *"je voudrais être une petite souris."* For your comparable saying in English, insert a fly on the wall, instead of a French mouse."

"Dawud…"

"Sorry. I do sometimes stray a tad off course. The story begins approximately seven months ago during the tenure of the prior unit assigned to the outpost and appears to end yesterday. I have not performed an exact translation, merely an initial skim. In addition to details of daily activities, names and ranks, he included personal tidbits about each soldier. For example, I did not realize your wife had a biblical name."

"Abigail's a name from the Bible?"

"But of course, Sergeant. Abigail is the anglicized version of the Hebrew name, Abigayil, the wife of King David. You really need to study scripture, sport. Why the prurient nature of its content, sexual depictions, deceit, incest, bloodletting, why it is — "

"Get on with it."

"Agreed, my good chap. The money shot. Hercules maintained a running tabulation of those killed and wounded from each attack by roadside bombs, as well as those on the outpost. There is much more; however, I will need several days to fully unmask the simplistic coding and make sense of it all."

"Hours, Dawud. Not days."

1430 hours

The three patrol vehicles limped into the outpost, one hugging the rear of another by a 'V' shaped tow bar. Ski got out of the lead vehicle and walked toward the operations center. Bishop ambushed him.

"Sergeant Knowles disrespected — "

Ski held up his hand. "Stow it, mister. I'm tired, I'm hungry, I'm dirty, but mostly I'm pissed. On top of all that, I got a colonel flying in who will probably relieve me of my command because some idiot went off half-cocked talking through his ass to another idiot. Do you really want to discuss Sergeant Knowles, a soldier whose ass is actually in the game and not used as a trumpet to stir up shit, or do you want to — " Ski stared at his executive officer and sighed. Anxious to get the facts, he pushed by him and headed for the trailer. Yards into the trek, he abruptly stopped and wheeled around.

"Second Lieutenant *lost like a mother fucker*, where'd you put the bodies?"

Bishop looked like a suckling infant who just had the teat yanked from its mouth. "Sir, I am not lost like a...." The switch flicked. "L-L-M-F."

Bishop recovered from the revelation and attempted to defer blame. Speaking loud enough for all within earshot to hear, he said, "Sir, on orders from a superior officer, Major Laddick, I preserved the evidence. He did not actually tell me how, but I am sure he would approve of my decision to store them in the refrigerated trailer."

"You put that enemy shit in with my food! Good God, man! What were you thinking? Stow it by the shitters where it belongs."

Bishop looked at the soldiers who had gathered to watch the show. He pointed at the ranking NCO and said, "Form a detail and move the bodies near the latrine."

"That was not my order," Ski said. "I tasked *you* to move the bodies and when you're finished with that, pack your gear. I may be out of here tonight, but you'll be on the bird with me." He ignored the shocked expression on Bishop's face, turned and plodded over the gravel toward the trailer that housed soldiers with intelligence.

Once inside, he dropped his armor and helmet on the floor, grabbed a water bottle from the refrigerator and fell into a chair in front of Knowles.

"Welcome back, Captain," Knowles said. "I really do mean welcome back. Rough patrol. Rough night."

"Understatement, Top. Bring me up to speed."

1815 hours

"Captain Ski," Bussard said, "chopper's inbound. Be here in fifteen, sir."

"Roger," he said. "Get a security team on the landing zone."

1832 hours

The Black Hawk set down on the highway in front of the outpost while its wingman flew top-cover in a meandering pattern three hundred feet higher. Colonel Erickson and Command Sergeant Major Hacker quickly jumped down and jogged to the nearest Humvee blocking the south side of the road.

As soon as Erickson and Hacker were safely inside the truck, the chopper pilot increased RPM and lifted off. Both helicopters did a pass over the outpost before turning south for the one-hour return flight to the base camp.

Within five minutes, the colonel and his enforcer stepped inside the operations trailer. Knowles jumped up and said, "Attention!"

"As you were." Erickson placed his M4 in the gun rack, handed *Brynhildn* to Hacker and said, "Take care of her for me."

Ski stood in the interior doorway. He had managed a quick shower and fresh uniform before their arrival, but not any sleep. Thirty-six hours was not a record for him but close. "Colonel Erickson, Sergeant Major Hacker, welcome." He turned toward the office and said, "If you would like, sir, more private in here."

Without a word, Erickson strode by him into the office. Hacker was on his heels a half step behind, the battle-axe held at port arms. The colonel scanned the cramped surroundings, finally settling into the chair behind the commander's desk. He glared at Ski and said, "What the fuck happened?"

"Sir, can I bring in Sergeant Knowles?"

Erickson snapped a nod.

"Sergeant," Ski said, "Join us."

Knowles hesitated at the door before he stepped inside.

Four bodies, three chairs, stifling hot. If someone farted, the effects would be incapacitating. Erickson pointed at the axe and said, "Sergeant Major, leave her, get some chow then inspect the bodies."

"Colonel," Ski said, "I suggest the Sergeant Major reverses the order. Check out the dead, then eat."

Erickson raised an eyebrow. Then he said, "Handle it however you want, Sergeant Major."

313

Hacker placed *Brynhildn* on the desk before he left.

As soon as he was gone, Erickson said, "Close it."

Knowles shut the door, but remained standing as did Ski.

"Get comfy, men," Erickson said. "This may take a while."

Both pushed chairs near the front of the desk and sat.

"Now tell me what happened and why Quinn was out there."

"Sir," Ski said, "before we get into my decision to include Mr. Quinn on the patrol, I would like to cover the intel we collected."

The intelligence, although not the mother lode end-all-be-all, was substantial when considered in the context of insurgent warfare's blurry nature.

Knowles read the salient points from the SIGINT report about the damaged phone Gabe found after the failed IED attack on June 27. He described his analysis of the phones Gabe discovered the previous night and the one he found in the latrine. The four phones were interrelated, as was a fifth of unknown origin. He explained how each SIM card recorded calls between known phones and the unidentified number prior to June 27. On June 28, calls to and from the mysterious number abruptly ceased. Then, a sixth phone showed up, following the same calling pattern as before. Prior to, and after every attack against a convoy passing through the AO, there was phone activity. He believed the two unknowns were burn phones used by the insurgent commander. In addition, several were triggers for the failed IED attacks.

Knowles went on and divulged the enemy commander's code name and occupation that Gabe had extracted from the child during the Afak patrol. He also told the colonel what Gabe was able to wring out of the Iraqi cop before he died — Suq ash Shuyukh, the leader's current base of operations, and Ali, a part of his actual name.

"Colonel Erickson," Knowles said, "Our interpreter is still mining the intel in Hercules' diary, so there may be some more surprises. But I want you to see these."

He spread a stack of photos on the desk taken from Hercules' phone.

"I was able to pull thirty-three pictures from the memory card. Thirty-two are of the outpost — gun emplacements, sleeping quarters, operations center — even a few of the inside. Don't know how he managed that. The last one...well, sir, take a look."

Knowles handed the grainy, out-of-focus snapshot to the colonel. "Two Iraqi police, sir. The cop smiling for the camera I recognize. He's the one from last night — Dhul Fiqar. The other one standing

314

in the shadows blocking his face with his hand…you can see how bad the picture is, but you can make out what looks like a scar on the side of his face. Also, look at his size compared to Dhul Fiqar. He's a big sucker, well over six feet tall. That guy, sir…my gut tells me he's Ghazi."

"Fine brief, Sergeant," Erickson said. Then he turned toward Ski. "Why was Quinn allowed on the — "

"Colonel," Ski interrupted, "Hercules was the conduit to the enemy cell leader. He caused the deaths of at least twenty American soldiers in the last six months alone. He set us up in Afak. Then after Mr. Quinn developed a lead on Ghazi, Hercules butchered a girl and her parents the next morning. I'm sure Hercules was the spotter for the mortar attack on July 4th that killed Jefferson and wounded three others. He tried to set up our patrol last night. He killed the insurgent cop when he started to spill the beans. He attempted to kill Gabe. Mr. Quinn did us a huge favor eliminating an enemy who would've gone undetected for who knows how long. Sure, he took a life, an enemy life, but what he did probably saved lives. I wouldn't follow him into a confessional, but I'd walk by his side anyplace else, sir."

"Granted," Erickson said. "His actions took out a rat." He looked at Knowles, then Ski. "But nobody saw or heard a damn thing when he killed the interpreter, yet I'm expected to take his word as gospel. Is that what you're asking me to do, Captain?"

Three brusque knocks rapped the door. Then a voice boomed, "Permission to speak to Colonel Erickson."

Erickson looked past the captain to the closed door. He sighed, but nodded.

"Enter," Knowles said.

Bussard opened the door and took an unconvincing step forward. Dark Meat nudged him several more feet and moved to his side. Both stood at attention.

Erickson put on his war face and demanded, "What do you want to tell me, paratroopers?"

"All the way, sir," Dark Meat said. "Colonel, we saw the whole thing and it went down exactly as Mr. Quinn told you, sir."

"And what exactly went down, soldier?"

"Sir," Bussard said, "well, sir…you know…what Mr. Quinn told you." He added less convincingly, "We saw it all, Colonel."

"Interesting. I have not spoken to Mr. Quinn yet, but please continue and tell me what you saw."

Bussard turned whiter, even Dark Meat paled some as he

315

swallowed.

Dark Meat elbowed his battle buddy into action.

Bussard blurted, "We saw exactly what Mr. Quinn will tell you, Colonel, sir."

"Thank you for clearing matters up for me. Now I would like to know — " Erickson shook his head and chuckled. "Dismissed."

"Yes, sir!" Both did an about face, almost knocking the sergeant major to the floor as he approached the open doorway. He stepped aside and allowed them to pass by him.

"Colonel," Hacker said, "our ride's twenty minutes out. You want them to loiter at Echo and return later?"

"We're almost done here. How do the bodies look?"

Hacker blanched. "That's a negative, sir. My worst shit looks better."

Erickson shifted in the chair and looked directly at Ski. The captain's expression matched that of a master poker player. Then the colonel turned more in his chair and stared at Knowles. The sergeant looked at the ceiling.

"I see," Erickson said. "All right, then. No evidence, two eyewitnesses who saw everything Mr. Quinn might ever say... means only one thing, Sergeant Major — no crime. Leave the bodies. Sergeant Knowles, tell those two fine troopers who just left to help Mr. Quinn with his gear and weapons. When he's packed, ask him to report here."

"Yes, sir."

"Sergeant Major," Ski said. "I need a moment alone with Colonel Erickson."

After Hacker left, Ski closed the door. "Colonel, I'd appreciate it if you allowed Gabe to stay, sir. The man belongs here, maybe more than we do. He has a way of cutting through hajji bullshit — the men like him — I need him. He's effective, sir."

"The loyalty he commands is obvious. But no can do. He's my concern now. Anything else?"

"Sir, if I'm to be relieved — "

Erickson held up his hand. "You're not being relieved."

"Thank you, sir."

"Anything else?"

"Yes sir, there is. I have lost confidence in my executive officer, Second Lieutenant Bishop, and would like him replaced."

"Is he the one who contacted Major Laddick?"

"Yes, sir."

"Tell him to get packed. He'll join us on the flight."

"Already packed, sir."

Erickson laughed. "Pretty cock-sure of yourself, Captain. I like that in my warriors. So you think you got me figured out?"

Ski said nothing.

Still smiling, Erickson said, "As soon as I finish talking with Mr. Quinn, we'll be out of your hair and you can get back to killing the enemy. When Quinn arrives, send him in alone. That is all, Captain."

"Sir, one last thing...the bodies."

"Hell, son, I thought you understood my way of thinking. Do what you should've done in the first place. Burn the bastards."

*****

Erickson barely recognized him when he walked into the office. He was not the man he had first met at Ft. Bragg. The easy smile was gone as was the confident swagger that came with age. The uniform looked nothing like one. Covered with grit, dried blood and other mysteries, it drooped from his frame in folds. Instead of a fleshy, spirited fifty-something-year-old, he was staring at a wilted, skeletal, old man. His shaggy sandy hair that now reached the middle of his ears had taken on the hue of blood. Even his mustache and two-week old beard were tinged red. When their eyes met, Gabe's did not flicker with any life — they merely hung on as if they were anonymous hitchhikers riding in the back of a pickup truck, bound for nowhere. He could not believe the sliding demolition happened in less than a month.

"Sit down, Gabe."

"I'll stand."

"Water?"

He acknowledged the colonel's question with an almost imperceptible quiver, and said, "No thanks." Then he looked down at the linoleum.

"Gabe...what really happened out there?"

After a long pause, he finally looked up and met the colonel's stare. They stared at each other for a long time. The colonel got up and stepped to the side of the desk.

Gabe moved nearer, crossing the line to unnerving closeness. He stopped a breath away from Erickson's side and leaned over, his mouth next to the colonel's ear. He whispered, "War."

Chapter 25
Turns

Sixty kilometers north of FOB Adder, altitude 850 feet, speed 140 knots, July 15, 2015 hours

Gabe faced to the rear in the seven-foot, nine-inch wide aft cabin. Bishop faced forward. Their knees touched. Although mere inches separated them, conversation inside the Black Hawk was hopeless. The constant noise of whipping wide-chord rotor blades and the high-pitched whine of twin General Electric T700 turbines, mixed with cyclone force winds howling through open gun portals to create aural bedlam. It did not matter; they had nothing to say to each other. Both were lost in thought. Both were heading to an uncertain future.

TOC, COP 6, 2020 hours

Dawud ran inside the operations trailer. He caught his breath then shouted, "Captain Ski! Captain Ski!"

The captain opened his office door. Amazed anything could ruffle his rock steady interpreter, he said, "What's got you so — "

"Captain Ski, I broke the code. I just finished the last pages of Hercules' diary. His final entry was that many infidels will die when rockets fall from the heavens."

"Where?"

"Adder."

"When?"

Dawud looked at the wall clock.

"Now."

Twenty-three kilometers north of FOB Adder, altitude 910 feet, speed 138 knots, 2030 hours

Not exactly rising to the level of megalomania, but close, Colonel Erickson was a control freak who needed to know anything and everything in his world. He could never sit still longer than a minute unless he was asleep. He even did that fast. He had commandeered an extra headset from the flight crew so he could follow every detail of the flight.

Bored, he unlatched the safety harness and tapped Hacker's leg. The sergeant major inched over, giving his boss enough space to stand inside the forward cabin.

Erickson hunched behind the starboard crew chief/gunner and looked into the cockpit. The colonel had flown many times in a UH-60L, even making occasional free-fall jumps from the rotary platform. He could identify many of the standard avionics and some of the upgrades spread in front of the helicopter aircraft commander and the left-seater. This Black Hawk model included several systems used on the earlier K variant — forward-looking infrared, terrain-following radar, color weather map generator. The instruments that most interested him, however, were the artificial horizon and heading indicator. One confirmed they were flying level and the other showed they were on course.

Looking through the glass cockpit he saw the jeweled lights of Nasariyah, and thirteen kilometers to the east of the city, runway beacons gleaming almost as bright. *Adder's a damn shining target.* He looked at his watch. *Be on the ground in less than twenty minutes.* As he turned to take his seat, he glimpsed a flash on the horizon. Then another, and more — many more — all peppering the base camp.

The pilot eased the cyclic forward increasing the air speed beyond the recommended maximum. His escort piloting the heavily armed AH-64D attack helicopter, also pushed the envelope and took the lead. What had been a lumbering, routine pickup flying through tame air space above empty desert, was now a combat mission zipping across the skies in a potential shooting gallery.

Both pilots agreed a Stinger surface to air missile would be more devastating than small arms fire, so they dropped to within three-hundred feet of the ground to give the enemy less time to set up a kill shot. Straight and level was out — it was now zigzags, arbitrary speed changes, yaws, climbing turns and altitude wasting plunges. The added speed and maneuvering sucked JP-8 from the fuel tanks.

Sprinting closer toward home, the aviators saw that the short-lived specks of light had evolved into huge pyres of flames. Near the canals that bled water from the Euphrates, eighteen kilometers east of the base camp, smaller flickers came into focus. The Black Hawk pilot radioed his escort and advised he had the identified the rockets' origin. After several short transmissions, both pilots turned hard to starboard away from the attack, in preparation of a western approach on the runway.

When the Apache pilot acknowledged the altered flight plan, Erickson jumped into the fray and countermanded the order. He rapped the co-pilot's helmet and pointed beyond the Ziggurat at the rocket POO site. "Take me there!"

The left-seater shook his head and tapped his finger on the fuel gauge. "We're almost bingo fuel, Colonel. Get back in your seat and buckle up."

"Bullshit!" Erickson shouted as he pointed at outgoing rockets. "The fight is there! Get on top of 'em and make a run."

"Sit the fuck down, sir," the pilot shouted.

Following some spirited radio chatter with his wingman, the pilot relented. Both choppers turned into the attackers and added more air speed, covering the distance in minutes. As soon as they passed over the Ziggurat, they separated into a combat spread of about five-hundred meters — the Apache high, the Black Hawk following low.

The attack helicopter made a steep approach and unleashed six Hydra 70 mm rockets, adding a long burst from the 30-mm chain gun. At the end of the run, the back-seater shot out infrared counter measure flares while the pilot pitched the aircraft up and rolled off the top in a vintage *Immelmann*. He aligned the Apache for a lateral run across the target, dropped the nose, gained more speed and attacked. The exploding ordnance and flares illuminated the objective for the Black Hawk's approach.

During the Black Hawk's attack run, Erickson spotted the enemy scurrying in all directions trying to escape the deadly light show. Yet many die-hards stayed at their posts and continued to launch 122 mm rockets. Some of the enemies got their wish and were martyred.

Both door gunners added hundreds of 7.62 mm rounds into the firestorm with short bursts from the M240 machine guns.

As the pilot pulled out of the gun run, Erickson said, "Make another pass."

"We're on fumes now," the pilot said, "ready to fall out of the sky like bird shit, sir. Our escort's heading to the barn to refuel, exactly where I'm — "

"Make another damn pass," Erickson shouted, "there's a shitload of 'em in the open."

The pilot hesitated. Then he was back on coms, telling his wingman to return to the fight and provide cover.

Although almost equal to the weight of an Apache, the Black

Hawk was less agile and offered a larger profile to the enemy; both head on and to the side. Neither the UH 60, nor the AH 64 handled like a plane. Winged aircraft naturally want to fly, even if an incompetent pilot is at the controls. A rotary winged aircraft falls like a rock if there is the slightest disturbance in the counterintuitive processes engineers dreamed up to keep it aloft. If the choreographed dance between systems hit a snag, there would be little chance to recover.

The pilot did what was possible. He jinked, grabbed altitude with a variety of maneuvers, including a modified high yo-yo. When he came over the top, he kept the nose down and regained speed lost during the climb. A kilometer from the scrap, he leveled out for the second attack run.

Itching for a fight, the colonel pounded on the back of the pilot's headrest.

"Sir, we're busy trying to fly," the co-pilot said. "Get back in your damn seat!"

Erickson ignored the order, moved to the port side gunner's space and stuck his head through the opening. Frustrated, the gunner turned and looked at him. Erickson could not see his face hidden behind the helmet visor, but he got the message. He backed off, moved aft and looked behind the bulkhead webbing toward the rear compartment. Gabe was swimming in puke — Bishop's and his own.

Erickson muttered, "Damn legs," then made his way back toward the cockpit.

The long attack run gave the enemy time to organize. As soon as the helicopter was within the outside range of an AK 47, tracer rounds arced toward the chopper from the desert. There were so many Erickson thought he could walk across them to the ground and beat the enemy with his fists.

In between each red-hot tracer were five other invisible rounds traveling at Mach 2, producing 1,470 foot-pounds of energy. Unknown by the pilot, some found their target. The rounds that hit the starboard gunner's chicken plate knocked him to the deck.

Hacker pulled the wounded gunner away from the M240 and checked him for holes. Erickson stepped over them toward the silenced weapon. Before he could reach it, Second Lieutenant Bishop was all over the machine gun, laying down grazing fire at 750 rounds per minute, sweeping the enemy ranks from left to right. A 7.62 mm tore through Bishop's cheek leaving a jagged edged hole the size of a quarter. Yet he continued to shoot.

Erickson scooted back around Hacker to the port side, pulled out his handgun and banged away.

Gabe tightened the four-point safety harness, dropped his head between his knees then soiled his pants.

Committed to the attack, the pilot pressed on. The initial volley of two rocket-propelled grenades missed low. The follow-on broadside of three more RPGs streamed toward the helicopter from as many directions. Two missed. The golden BB struck the cross member on the canted tail rotor with a bang, blowing off a section of the tail boom and all of the five-foot long blades. Chunks of the stabilizer, missing tail and blades, struck the main rotor.

Not unlike a human, a helicopter has a nervous system, brain, skeleton, muscles and skin. Neither is meant for flight. In place of nerves, the helicopter has wire. In place of a brain, flight computer management systems. Skeleton, steel and aluminum. Skin, thin rolled metal. Muscles, hydraulics. The primary hydraulic system was gone. Without a tail rotor and a stabilizer, inescapable ugly physics took over.

The brain reacted. Audible alarms blared, visual ones blinked, soldiers shouted — the helicopter shuddered like the wounded, marvelous mechanical animal it was. With the loss of tail rotor authority, the nose pulled right opposite the main rotor's spin direction. As the tail rotor assembly fell off, the nose dropped sharply. The artificial horizon and heading indicator spun like slot machines. Since the pilot was making a shallow run, he had neither the time, nor altitude to save the aircraft. However, he tried.

He turned in the direction of the rotation, reduced the collective and lowered the nose more trying to gain enough airspeed to fly out of the emergency. The initial slow yaw to the right was encouraging, so he tried to follow it with the cyclic. When the backup hydraulics failed — it was over. The pilot was good, very good — but not lucky. Gravity intercepted his valiant 'hail Mary' attempt.

The impact sheared the landing gear. The rolls that followed broke its back. One by one, the main rotor blades flogged the rocks and sand, breaking in deadly sections that flew out searching for something to end their flight.

Weapons, equipment and bodies broke free unleashing a maelstrom of debris swirling inside the cabin. The chopper tumbled and flipped across the earth. Skeletal integrity destroyed, the mainframe split into three sections. The main rotor gearbox, the heaviest component on

322

the aircraft besides the twin turbines, crashed into the cabin.

Finally, it settled on its side. For a minute, all that could be heard were the groans of a dying helicopter. Nearly empty of fuel on impact, volatile fumes sparked.

The explosion engulfed the aircraft.

Some survived.

God turned his back.

GLOSSARY

5/25 check: Tactic of checking 5 and 25 meters from a vehicle for IEDs based on duration of stop

AAR: After action review performed following any operation

ACU: Army combat uniform

AO or AOR: Area of operations/responsibility

AQI: Al Qaeda Iraq

ASR: Alternate supply route

ASV: M1117 armored security vehicle

BCT: Brigade combat team

BFT: Blue force tracker, a GPS that tracked coalition vehicles similarly equipped with transponders and also a keyboard used to send messages. Depending on context, also used to mean big friggin' truck.

BIAP: Baghdad International Airport

Buffalo: Route clearance armored IED wheeled vehicle. Also used are the RG-31 and the Husky

Butter-head: slang aimed at female soldiers/civilians who are acceptable in all physical attributes, everything 'but her head'.

CAB: Combat action badge, presented to non-combat MOS soldiers who are in close combat.

CAC: Common Access Card, identification carried by all military and authorized civilian contractors in theater.

Camelback: Military individual hydration system worn on the exterior of a soldier's IBA.

CEXC: Combined explosive exploitation cell

CIB: Combat infantry badge presented to combat MOS soldiers who engage in close combat.

CIVPOL: Civilian police missions located throughout the world generally administered by the UN.

Click: One thousand meters, one kilometer

CLS Bag: Combat life support bag carried by medics and required in each military vehicle that leaves the wire.

CMO: Civil military operation

CONOP: Concept of operation

COP: Combat outpost

CP: Checkpoint

CPATT: Civilian Police Assistance Training Team

CRC: CONUS redeployment center where soldiers and civilians receive equipment, physicals, etc. prior to deployment to either Iraq or Afghanistan. Centers are located in Texas and Georgia.

DFAC: Dining facility, chow hall, mess hall

DUSTOFF: Unarmed helicopter used to evacuate wounded

ECM: Electronic counter-measures

EFP: Explosively formed projectile

EOD: Explosive ordinance disposal team

FOB: Forward Operating Base

FOBBIT: Derogatory slang for soldiers/civilians who never leave the perimeter of the FOB. Term was adapted from the 'Lord of the Rings' story.

FRAGO: Fragmentary order detailing specifics to units charged with executing their section of OPORD

General Order Number One: Order issued by Commanding General, Coalition Forces Iraq, forbidding the use, possession, or distribution of alcohol, pornographic material, photographs of dead Iraqi soldiers, insurgents or civilians. Additional restrictions include no proselytizing, fraternizing with the locals, or pets.

GATORS: Interrogators

Hawala: Muslim money changer

HE: High explosive

HMMWV: High mobility multi-purpose wheeled vehicle, commonly referred to as, Humvee

IBA: Interceptor body armor, including side SAPI (small arms protector inserts) plates, front and back SAPI plates, groin protector, neck protector, throat protector and shoulder daps.

IDF: Indirect fire, either mortar or rocket

IED: Improvised explosive device

JAG: Judge advocates group or General

JAM: Jaysh al-Madhi, the army of Madhi, the militia aligned with Sadr.

Jersey barrier: Ingenious invention for quickly establishing protection from IDF and small arms fire. The product is heavy gauge steel wire with fabric attached that is set upright and then filled with sand or dirt.

JRTC: Joint readiness training center, Ft. Polk, LA

JUKEBOX: Electronic counter measure

Kevlar: Army combat helmet, or ACH

KIA: Killed in action

Kiowa: Two man armed helicopter, smaller than the Apache

MEDEVAC (color): Green, amber, red, black. Denotes the weather conditions as they relate to MEDEVAC flight status. For example, If

MEDEVAC black you self evacuate, no bird is coming.

METT-TC: Mission, enemy, terrain and weather, troops and support available, time available and civil considerations

MRAP: Mine resistant, ambush protected vehicle

MSR: Main supply route.

N1PR: Non-sensitive internet protocol

NOD: Night observation device

OPORD: Operational order

OPSEC: Operational security

PAO: Public affairs office

PAX: Person or passenger

PM: Preventative maintenance

POG: Person other than a grunt (infantry)

POI: Point of impact

POO: Point of origin, related to the site where a mortar or rocket was launched.

PSYOPS: Psychological warfare operations

Puzzle Palace: Derogatory term for central command located in Saddam Hussein's former palace in Baghdad. Can also be benignly interpreted as a reference to the many halls and rooms within the structure.

QRF: Quick reaction force

REDDI: Roadside Explosive Device Defeat Initiative (fictitious)

RCIED: Radio controlled IED

REMF: Rear echelon mother-fucker

RHINO: Black box attached to an extension boom that can be raised and lowered from a military vehicle. Used to combat IED detonations. The device is similar in appearance to a rhino's horn, hence its name.

ROE: Rules of engagement

ROW: Rules of war

RUF: Rules governing use of force

S-1 through S-9: Most NATO countries use the continental staff system (also known as the general staff system) in structuring their militaries' staff functions **S**, for staff roles within headquarters of organizations commanded by a colonel or below.

S-1 for personnel and administration

S-2 for intelligence and security

S-3 for operations

S-4 for logistics

S-5 for Plans

S-6 for signal or communications
S-7 for Training.
S -8 for Finance and contracts.
S-9 for Civil Affairs
SAF: Small arms fire
SALUTE: Military mnemonic to identify the enemy's size, activity, location, uniform, time and equipment.
SECFOR: Security force mission
SIGINT: Signal, or electronic intelligence
SIPR: Secret internet protocol
SITREP: Situation or status report
SVBIED: Suicide vehicle borne IED (car bomber)
Tango Mike: Thanks much, or thanks man
TC: Truck commander
TCP: Traffic control check point
Terp: Slang for an interpreter. There are three levels based on security clearance; Cat 1, Cat 2 and Cat 3.
TOC: Tactical operations center
T-Wall: Concrete blast wall ranging in height from 6 to 14'.
VBIED: Vehicle borne IED
VIC: Vehicles
WARLOCK: ECM apparatus
WIA: Wounded in action

Weapons

Barrett M82: Semi-automatic, .50 caliber sniper rifle
M2: Browning .50 caliber, crew-served heavy machine gun. Also called 'ma deuce'
M4: Shorter and lighter variant of the M16 assault rifle. Fires a 5.56mm NATO round
M9: Beretta semi-automatic 9mm Parabellum pistol
MK19: 40 mm belt-fed grenade launcher
M203: Single shot, 40mm grenade laucher attached to either a M4 or M16 rifle
M240: Belt-fed, gas operated, 7.62mm medium machine gun
M249: 5.56mm light machine gun, squad automatic weapon (SAW)
PKM: 7.62mm general purpose machine gun designed in the Soviet Union

PROSE PRESS
The origin of the word prose is Latin, prosa oratio, meaning straightforward discourse.

Prose Press is looking for stories with strong plots.
We offer an affordable, quality publishing option with
guaranteed worldwide distribution.

Queries: Email only.
proseNcons@live.com

CPSIA information can be obtained at www.ICGtesting.com
Printed in the USA
LVOW120421180712

290533LV00004B/28/P